POEMS OF W. B. YEATS

A New Selection

D1100597

000014038

POEMS OF
W. B. YEATS

A New Selection

Selected, with an Introduction and Notes, by

A. NORMAN JEFFARES

MACMILLAN

First published 1984 by
Higher and Further Education Division
MACMILLAN PUBLISHERS LTD
London and Basingstoke
Companies and representatives
throughout the world

Typeset by Wessex Typesetters Ltd
Frome, Somerset

Printed in Hong Kong

British Library Cataloguing in Publication Data
Yeats, W. B.
Poems of W. B. Yeats.
I. Title   II. Jeffares, A. Norman
821'.8   PR5097
ISBN 0–333–36213–6
ISBN 0–333–36214–4 Pbk

The maps of Co. Galway and Co. Sligo are redrawn versions of those which
appear in *Place Names in the Writings of W. B. Yeats* (1976) by James McGarry
and are reproduced by courtesy of Colin Smythe Limited.

CONTENTS

POEMS

INTRODUCTION

The fact that poems have been chosen for this selection under eighteen different subject headings may indicate something of the diversity to be found in Yeats's poetry. He was a poet straddling two centuries. He began as a poet influenced by the great Victorians, yet seeking to establish his own individual note, writing lyrics with a delicate, haunting beauty. He developed into a leading – some would say *the* leading – twentieth-century poet, a modernist who influenced many of his contemporaries and continues to influence many poets writing today. Yeats wrote poetry from his teens – probably as early as 1883 – until his death in 1939: he developed and changed his style, and startling it seemed to many of those who had admired his early wistful 'twilight' poetry; he was consistently seeking directer, more urgent utterance yet casting his poetry in a rhetorical mould. It is this quality which poses continuous challenging questions to readers and ensures the continuing vitality of his work, its eminently quotable, indeed its insistently memorable dramatic force.

To match this changing, developing style there was the poet, himself a changing, developing man, who as he gained in confidence, skill and success became the subject of his own poetry. That he made himself a fit subject for his art is a measure of his greatness; he contained variety enough of experience; though idiosyncratic, he was in touch with his age in such a way that he could, by concentrating upon subjects and imagery, by presenting them with masterly technique, imbue them with a continuing relevance for subsequent readers' own experiences and ideas. Certain aspects of his work are part of the poetic tradition, and are incorporated in it because that tradition lasts through its universality. An Indian reader, a Japanese, an American, may find Yeats today as vital as he seemed to readers in his lifetime – and yet different aspects of his poetry may appeal to them. There is a variety in the subject matter of his poetry, published during a period of fifty-four years; there is a certain lasting universality in the work of this poet who is so based in the literary history and even the political history of his own island. And yet, ironically perhaps, Yeats once told his wife that he had spent his whole life saying the same thing in different ways.

What had he to say, then? Can we pluck one basic idea from his poems – or indeed his plays, his autobiographies, his essays, his journalism, his letters or his diaries? Or was his remark one of those deep rhetorical phrases that need to be decompressed, translated, brought into the prosaic light of day? Perhaps we can explain the continuing appeal of Yeats if we trace one of his underlying preoccupations which centres upon the common inescapable fact that all of us must die. *'What then?' sang Plato's ghost. 'What then?'* is the refrain of a late poem in which the poet describes his life: desire for fame, acquisition of technical skill, the sheer hard work that laid the foundations for that fame, gaining sufficient money to live a modest life filled with the pleasure of friendships, and the youthful dreams fulfilled – marriage, children, a house, good company – and then? This is the question we all face sooner or later: what happens when we die? Is this the end of us as sentient beings? Or do we have a further existence? A re-incarnation? Or some ghostly existence? Do mortals become immortal, or does this only occur through art giving them continuance in the minds of succeeding generations?

Yeats did not find satisfactory answers in the religion of his forefathers – his paternal grandfather and great grandfather were country clergymen in Ireland – and though on the one hand he wanted to believe, to have faith, on the other he had a strongly sceptical streak in his mental make-up. While still a schoolboy he abandoned science after a brief flirtation with it; and then, after becoming interested in Indian philosophy as a youth, he joined the Theosophical Society only to be asked to leave it because he wanted proof. He remained interested in spiritualism throughout his life, and in cabbalism and astrology. He studied magic; he immersed himself in occultism; he joined and played a large part in the Hermetic Order of the Golden Dawn, a magical order (his imaginative development was obviously affected by the order's elaborately codified symbolism and rituals); and he himself wanted to form an Irish order of mysteries. All of this activity was inspired by a continuous searching, an exploring of the mysteries of life and death.

Yeats found, in his very wide reading, others who shared his quest. William Blake (1757–1827), Emmanuel Swedenborg (1688–1722) and Jacob Boehme (1575–1624) with their interest in contraries appealed to him particularly. Theories of opposites – reinforced later, no doubt, by his reading John Donne – provided a creative theme in his thought: the tension of the self and the soul at variance. And those long periods he spent as a child in the west of Ireland, where his mother's family lived, provided him with an early awareness of the supernatural, as his *Autobiographies* make clear. That, too, he followed up in his subsequent reading, his discussion, his talk. He read the mystics, the Neo-Platonics, and many of the classic philosophers; he read history and political thought. In middle age he moved from translations of Irish mythological literature and folklore into an admiration of eighteenth-century Irish writers in English whom he had scorned in his youth. This reading, an exploration of occult and mystical writings and traditions as well as history and philosophy, culminated in his writing *A Vision*, which was first published in 1926 and then, in revised form, in 1937. Into this strange book Yeats put his thoughts about history and how civilisations perish with all their beauty and achievement, about human personality and how its nature is determined, how it can – perhaps – escape its predestined fate.

Though *A Vision* provided 'stylistic arrangements of experience', the questions remained (apart from the obviously symbolic elements, Yeats said of the fixed periods, 'if sometimes overwhelmed by miracles as all men must be in the midst of it, I have taken such periods literally, my reason has soon recovered') for Yeats was always a great asker of questions, even if, at times, they revealed a tragic despair over the nature of life:

> Man is in love and loves what vanishes,
> What more is there to say?

What indeed? And 'Why should not old men be mad?' This latter poem poses the questions Yeats found liable to recur despite a lifetime spent in searching for belief, in facing the idea of death bravely. Affirmations and theories superseded each other, only to be overcome by the same innate scepticism, with the old questions still challenging him. The only answer, ultimately, for Yeats was that of ignorance. He does not know what will happen, and at last can see the question itself as eternal:

> When a man grows old his joy
> Grows more deep day after day,
> His empty heart is full at length,
> But he has need of all that strength
> Because of the increasing Night
> That opens her mystery and fright . . .

That is how he put it in 'The Apparitions', and here is how he put it in 'Man and the Echo' where the man is initially Yeats in old age going over his life, asking himself questions till, he says,

> I lie awake night after night
> And never get the answers right

He meditates upon death, and upon the role of the intellect in arranging everything in one clear view: he is, in the Irish phrase, 'making his soul'. But when he addresses Rocky Voice, that echo from the rocks in a cleft in the Sligo mountainside, asking if in the great night of death we shall rejoice, he has to answer his query restrictively; we do not know about death:

> What do we know but that we face
> One another in this place?

To portray Yeats as preoccupied by death and the hereafter does not, however, fully convey the cold passion he sought to create, the tragic joy he found in contemplating and celebrating beauty and love, in creating and capturing his own vision of Irish literature, his blending of past achievements with those of the eighteenth-century writers whose inheritor he came to think himself, whose tradition he made into his own view of what it was to be Anglo-Irish.

One of the benefits of his complex literary ancestry was that he attained a magnificent power of expression: words came into his call as the result of intense labour (testified to by the manuscripts and notebooks which survive, containing overwhelming evidence of his endless writing and rewriting in an obsessive search for the right word in the right place).

Yeats was born into the Victorian age, but grew up with the great advantage of having a father who questioned current attitudes and ideas. He was an idealistic painter and a man of ideas, a conversationalist *par excellence*. He recited poetry to his son and discussed it with him, particularly when they both took the train from Howth to Dublin, there to breakfast in the father's studio in York Street before the son took himself up Harcourt Street to the High School, where he studied only what interested him, as his penultimate publication, 'I became an author' (*The Listener*, 4 August 1938), tells us, recording his respect for his father's views and his own attitude to his schooling:

How did I begin to write? I have nothing to say that may help young writers, except that I hope they will not begin as I did. I spent longer than most schoolboys preparing for the next day's work, and yet learnt nothing, and would always have been at the bottom of my class but for one or two subjects that I hardly had to learn at all. My father would say: 'You cannot fix your mind on anything that does not interest you, and it is to study what does not that you are sent to school.' I did not suffer from the 'poetic temperament' but from some psychological weakness. Greater poets than I have been great scholars. Even today I struggle against a lack of confidence, when among average men, come from that daily humiliation, and because I do not know what they know. I can toil through a little French poetry, but nothing remains of the Greek, Latin and German I tried to learn. I have only one memory of my schooldays that gives me pleasure; though in both my English and Irish schools I was near the bottom of the class, my friends were all at the top, for then, as now, I hated fools. When I would find out if some man can be trusted, I ask if he associates with his betters.

He did not seem likely to be able to pass the notoriously easy entrance examination to Trinity College, Dublin, of which his father, grandfather and great-grandfather had been graduates. But he grew up in a milieu where things of the mind were what mattered most. His father's ideas about the need for poetry to be dramatic had a lasting affect on him, and his father's pre-Raphaelitism was also a highly formative influence, to be succeeded later in England by an admiration for William Morris. John Butler Yeats, though deeply worried about the family's lack of money, discouraged his eldest son from seeking regular employment, encouraging him instead to develop his own talent, and welcoming his decision (arrived at when he was a student at the College of Art in Dublin) to become a poet. His father's friend Edward Dowden, the Professor of English at Trinity College, also encouraged him in his early writing of poetry.

These two men were, in effect, urging him on to write in the English romantic tradition — which coloured much of his early work. But Yeats was to experience an Irish inheritance as well, for John O'Leary (a leader of the Fenian movement arrested in 1865, whose sentence of twenty years penal servitude had been commuted to exile after he had served four years of it) returned to Dublin in 1885, and introduced him to Irish literature. Through the medium of often poor prose translations and the poetry of James Clarence Mangan and Sir Samuel Ferguson, and under the stimulus of Standish O'Grady (whose *History of Ireland — The Heroic Period* (1878) and *Cuculain and his Contemporaries* (1880) imparted heroic stature to the figures of Irish mythology, in particular, those of the Ulster cycle of tales), the young Yeats realised that there was an alternative tradition to the English one for him to explore. At the English school he had attended before he went to the High School in Dublin he had been unsatisfied with a mythology based on victories, such as those of Agincourt and Creçy — legendry ultimately to culminate in imperialistic jingoism. Neither did he like the current imagery of Catholic Ireland, based on a mythology of defeat and on the simplistic rhetorical imagery of a popular patriotism which the writers of *The Nation* had brought into being, from 1830 onwards, to provide a sense of nationhood in an Ireland turning from Irish to the use of English for economic and political purposes. And he did not possess enough classical learning to develop his early adventuring into Arcadian realms; nor had he been attracted by the Arthuriad which, after all, Tennyson had made his own. Like any ambitious young poet he wanted to be different, to make his own mark, to speak in his own voice, to be himself. And now, through the books O'Leary lent him, he saw into an exciting and heroic Ireland of the remote past which he could recreate, re-interpreting it as his imagination chose.

Here was the inspiration for the movement called variously the Irish Renaissance, the Irish literary movement, the Irish literary revival, the Celtic revival. Ireland had her own mythology, her own heroic and bardic age which, perhaps because its early literature had been largely oral, had been largely forgotten after Irish aristocratic civilisation finally collapsed with the Flight of the Earls in 1607. Their leaving Ireland, in recognition that they could no longer successfully oppose — or work with — a politically centralised unified English presence, signalled the virtual end of an Irish culture which had, till then, generously supported the Irish poets who kept its traditions, its genealogies, its literatures alive. The patrons gone, the poets dwindled away. The rediscovery by Yeats and his contemporaries of that literature, however incomplete, with its heroic tales of battles, feasts, quarrels and love affairs, through the medium of translations (Yeats himself never knew Irish) was often accompanied by a freshly kindled, sometimes parallel, sometimes coalescing, sometimes diverging enthusiasm for the learning and use of the Irish language, and Irish sports and games, as evinced in the Gaelic League (founded by Douglas Hyde in 1893) and the Gaelic Athletic Association (founded in 1884). These cultural movements were to exert a powerful influence on the political forces that erupted in the Rising of 1916, and resulted in the establishment of the Irish Free State governing the twenty-six southern counties of Ireland and of Northern Ireland, the six northern counties with a parliament in Belfast but also sending MPs to Westminster.

Yeats had the imagination to see that Ireland had in the literature of the remote past a means of regenerating a mythology that could differ from that of England, and achieve an Irish independence of mind. This seemed to him as necessary a thing to achieve as any political independence and indeed a vital part of such an independence. He had the energy and confidence to try to convert his Irish readers from admiring what he saw as the sentimental patriotism of Tom Moore and Thomas Davis to a new attitude which would be more discriminating, which would recognise the merits of a new literature founded upon greater technical skills and greater artistry: that new literature would complete the incomplete ancient Irish one. Irish culture had, he thought, been harassed by Danish invaders, then Norman, then English, but the material was there, if only it could be given original and accomplished handling.

Yeats himself wanted to blend the pagan past with the Christian traditions; he was also greatly influenced by current European interest in the Celtic past. But while he looked back to a remote mythology he learned his trade from contemporary English poets, and he urged Irish writers to use the finest English writers as their models. Careful composition had to underpin apparent spontaneity: criticism had to be international, the literature itself national. Yeats wrote much prose to shape the kind of national literature he wanted his countrymen and countrywomen to write. Ultimately the example of his poetry was probably more effective. His aim was, as he put it in a letter to *United Ireland*, to 'build up a national tradition, a national literature, which shall be none the less Irish in spirit from being English in language'. He had to explain himself to the less imaginative, for his poetry was rooted in this deep conviction: the subject matter could be based upon the simplicity of country people who believed in supernatural forces (they were unlike the Irish of the cities; they provided an antidote to the complexities of Victorian thought and nature description) and upon the sophistication of a remote aristocratic literary tradition. It did not matter to him whether the bardic histories of Ireland were fictional or not: he was able to create his own view of the 'dim' past, while telling his audience in 'To Ireland in the Coming Times' that he was writing in the more recent tradition of 'Davis, Mangan, Ferguson' – no doubt he put in Davis as a sop to the political nationalists, but drew attention to Mangan and Ferguson for their interpretation of the lyric and epic remnants of a heroic past which had been virtually forgotten or totally unknown. *

---

* His own experience is recorded in the Preface he wrote to Lady Gregory, *Cuchulain of Muirthemme* (1903) p. xvii:

When I was a child I had only to climb the hill behind the house [his grandparents' house,

This desire of Yeats to be seen as part of Ireland's literary tradition stemmed perhaps from his awareness of the great power of bards in an aristocratic Irish society. 'To Ireland in the Coming Times' also reminds us of his occult interests; his rhymes 'more than their rhyming tell' because he is in touch with the elemental creatures, because he treads in measured ways. This poem reminds us, too, of his love and his awareness of the brevity of life, his speculation that there may be 'No place for love and dream at all'. His love and his dream were intermingled, and as he had discovered Irish mythology through O'Leary so, too, he discovered through him the woman he was to mythologise. O'Leary gave Maud Gonne a letter of introduction. She was beautiful, well-to-do, independent, unconventional and a revolutionary Irish nationalist. One of the orphaned daughters of a British colonel, she arrived at John Butler Yeats's house in Bedford Place in London one spring morning in 1889, full of talk of revolutionary politics, and Yeats fell in love with her:

> Tall and noble but with face and bosom
> Delicate in colour as apple blossom

He thought at first that he would not tell her of his love because he was penniless and could not contemplate marriage, though in 1891 he made the first of many proposals of marriage to her. She consistently told him that the world would thank her for not marrying him, and that they should remain friends. The poetry he wrote her was beautiful, mainly melancholic, devoted but defeatist – quintessentially poetry of the Celtic twilight: allusive and adjectival, only permitting images of beauty, harking back to an idealised romantic past. He hoped his devotion would eventually persuade her to marry him. Partially to impress her, he began to play a more public role in Irish life and wrote a patriotic play, *The Countess Cathleen*, for her; he even briefly joined the Irish Republican Brotherhood (IRB); but he sought to persuade her that his work for Irish independence was to create a literary movement which would give Irish people a new sense of their cultural heritage, a new sense of self-respect, a new independence of mind. Despite his belief that this work (which included his setting up Irish Literary societies in Dublin and London, as well as writing articles and reviews setting out his views on the kind of literature that was needed) was every bit as important as the work of the political groups with which she was involved, he himself got drawn into politics in 1897 and 1898, as Chairman of the 1798 Association, formed to commemorate the 1798 Revolution in Ireland. This experience showed him the results of violence when there were riots in Dublin, and he turned away from nationalist politics, resigning from the IRB probably about 1901.

Merville, in Sligo] to see long, blue, ragged hills flowing along the southern horizon. What beauty was lost to me, what depth of emotion is still perhaps lacking in me, because nobody told me, not even the merchant captains who knew everything, that Cruachan of the Enchantments lay behind those long, blue, ragged hills!

What followed was a period of practicality: the very effective bringing into being of earlier dreams of an Irish drama: writing plays, 'theatre business, management of men'. With Lady Gregory's considerable collaborative aid, the Abbey Theatre was created and nurtured. This was also a period of disillusion: Maud Gonne married John MacBride in 1903 only to separate from him in 1905, and Yeats's love poems now told of past devotion and how she had failed to understand or appreciate, but still must be celebrated, 'being what she is'. The nationalists – and Maud herself – disliked the kind of plays being staged in the Abbey. Patriotic puritanism did not want the presentation of less than idealised Irish womanhood on the stage, and there followed the riots against Synge's *The Playboy of the Western World* in 1907, an example of the 'great art' Yeats had helped to bring into being. Yet more disillusionment with the Irish public was to follow over the reaction of Dublin Corporation to Sir Hugh Lane's offer to give his French impressionist paintings to Dublin. Yeats reacted angrily in public poems of a new kind. In 'A Coat' he even attacked those who were writing in his former Celtic twilight manner; as far as he was concerned, they could take the coat 'Covered with embroideries/Out of old mythologies'; there was 'more enterprise in walking naked'.

A sumptuous eight-volume edition of Yeats's *Collected Works* was published by A. H. Bullen in 1908, when Yeats was forty-three. With the publication of this edition it must indeed have seemed as if all things could now tempt him from his craft of verse:

> One time it was a woman's face, or worse –
> The seeming needs of my fool-driven land . . .

His long-lasting love for Maud Gonne had come to nothing; in the words of 'Adam's Curse' he was 'weary-hearted'; the vision of a regenerated literature and a national theatre had been tempered by reality, 'the day's war with every knave and dolt'. Up to this point Yeats had had a successful literary life; he had created a distinguished reputation: but it is likely that he would not now be read and studied with such attention and pleasure had his career ended with the publication of his *Collected Works* in 1908. He would probably be seen as the poet of the Celtic twilight, known for some poems of great beauty but outside the main stream of English literature; he would also have been remembered for his energetic effort in bringing the Irish theatre into being.

However, Yeats did not end his poetic career by withering into truth; instead there was a magnificent second flowering of his talent. This is the work of Yeats the modernist, who responded to Ezra Pound's advice, 'Make it new'. Yeats had pursued idealism as far as he could in his elaborate Celtic twilight poetry with its increasing use of an esoteric, rarefied symbolism removed, indeed an escape from modern life. After the turn of the century he pushed a bare kind of realism as far as it would go: it was negative, recording the past tense of his love for Maud Gonne; stripping poetry of adjectival decoration and beauty; recording that the sap had dried out of his veins; expressing scornful anger at the obscure spite of Irish political attitudes, and despair at the lack of imaginative vision in Ireland, an inability to understand and appreciate the art he and his friends were trying to create for their country. There was no real satisfaction in this negativity for Yeats, for though he had a strongly satiric vein as well as a sceptical one, there was in him a powerful reservoir of imagination, a volcanic force of feeling for life and the glories of human achievement; and he had the skill to match his ideas with words that would define precisely and yet reverberate expansively in readers' minds and memories. The great good fortune is that the early dreaming, tempered by middle-aged realism, could eventuate in a poetry which captured violence, hatred, bitterness, uncertainty, politics, friendship, love, passion, the evanescence of beauty, historical change, destruction and revival, death and tragic joy.

How did this happen? How do we account for the terrible beauty of 'Easter 1916', the devastating horror of 'The Second Coming'? How do we explain the strength and affirmation of 'Among School Children'? Or the dazzlingly effective imagery of the two Byzantine poems as they move from the sensual music of Ireland to the artistic and intellectual balance of an imagined Byzantium where the souls of the dead arrive at the purging fires? Or the subtle symbolic significance of 'Meditations in Time of Civil War'? Or the haunting quality of the two Coole poems with their warm memories and cool assessments, their capture of apparent certainty at the mercy of change? Or yet the power of 'The Circus Animals' Desertion' with its recognition of the sources of the Celtic twilight's old themes, the pull of the players and the painted stage, and its awareness that the heart has been at the centre of it all.

Yeats is supremely a poet of the emotions, though as the years go by the wide-ranging power and curiosity of his intellect are now given more praise. He read to find what he wanted, to support his own ideas, to give himself the authority he was always seeking – and never fully finding. But his modernity, his ability to write public poetry, to speak his mind freely, to capture many of our continuing concerns in masterly language which blends simple and complex vocabulary in a syntax suiting the stanzaic forms he used with such technical skill – all these drew strength from the coming together of circumstances which allowed the disparate elements to coalesce, the diffidences and differences, the doubts and contrarities to be expressed in a diversity that was encompassed within the poet's own personality.

Yeats's marriage in 1917 and the births of his children, which continued the Yeats line in which he had become so interested, his restoration of the ancient tower (the first permanent home he owned, in the west of Ireland), his Nobel Prize for poetry, his Senatorship, his Dublin house in Merrion Square, were all signs of achievement, of fulfilment. His marriage led, with Mrs Yeats's automatic writing, to the creation of A *Vision* (1925). The seven and a half years spent in the writing of that book, and then the subsequent process of revising it for the version published in 1937, gave him not only a kind of scaffolding for much of his poetry (such as 'The Double Vision of Michael Robartes', 'The Second Coming', 'Demon and Beast', 'Sailing to Byzantium', 'Nineteen Hundred and Nineteen', 'Two Songs for a Play', 'Leda and the Swan', 'Byzantium', 'Vacillation', 'The Gyres', 'Lapis Lazuli', 'The Statues', 'News for the Delphic Oracle', and 'Under Ben Bulben') but also the confidence to express his ideas in its terminology. Through the process of creating it ('putting it all in order') he was able to face with considerable courage the issues of his time: revolution, guerrilla warfare, civil war, the aftermath of civil war and the creation of a new state. Revolutionary youth had begotten a constructive conservatism in him; even if that conservatism was to veer towards an admiration for authority he remained individualistic. 'My dear' he wrote flippantly in old age to Dorothy Wellesley, 'I remain as anarchic as a sparrow': a remark to be weighed against such things as his continuing, devoted work for the Abbey Theatre, his notable contribution to the work of the Senate in chairing the Commission that gave Ireland an elegant pre-decimal coinage, his creation of an Irish Academy of Letters, and his serious thoughts and comments about how best to educate young people in a country where law (often regarded in the past as being a British institution) had not been respected. There were profound problems outside Ireland too; civilisation might be hooped together, apparently at peace, but man was 'Ravening, raging and uprooting' his way into desolation. And Yeats himself had to face personal pains and problems: increasing ill health; the encroachment of age's limitations upon an active mind and excitable senses; and the ultimate question pressing nearer upon him:

> Bid imagination run
> Much on the Great Questioner;
> What He can question, what if questioned I
> Can with a fitting confidence reply

Thus Yeats, recovering from serious illness at the age of sixty-three, meditated upon death. He had earlier had moments of intense happiness to record, as in the fourth section of 'Vacillation'; moments of contentment, even bravado when, as in 'A Dialogue of Self and Soul', he was

> content to follow to its source
> Every event in action or in thought;
> Measure the lot; forgive myself the lot!
> When such as I cast out remorse
> So great a sweetness flows into the breast
> We must laugh and we must sing
> We are blest by everything,
> Everything we look upon is blest

And though he had 'always hated work', confidence could be placed in the work done: 'something to perfection brought' and yet that too reminds him – and us – of human limitations. They have underlain the brave attitudes, the masks adopted; they are what the mythologies, poetic and personal, are intended to shield us against, to enable us, however briefly, to be freed from the limitations of time, to apprehend infinity.

PRINCIPLES OF SELECTION

The object of this selection is to provide a book which is manageable in size for new readers, to allow Yeats's art to be considered in its kinds rather than in his volume divisions, to give a cross-section of his poetry, presented in chronological order within these groupings. It is not intended as a substitute for the *Poems: A New Edition* or the *Collected Poems*, and if it leads readers on to subsequent familiarity with all his work then it will have fulfilled its intention.

To categorise the items selected here from the 507 poems of the *Poems: A New Edition* or the 382 poems of the *Collected Poems* is not easy, because Yeats's poems are often complex: Irish mythology, for example, obviously informs the Irish narrative poems; a fine piece of speculation on the future of his children which appears in 'My Descendants', section IV of 'Meditations in Time of Civil War' might well have been placed in the section entitled 'The Poet's Family' but to remove it from its context would spoil the total effect of 'Meditations in Time of Civil War'. This is a sequence that might have been considered for inclusion in several sections – in 'The Thought of *A Vision*', perhaps, or in 'Irish Characters and Places' or 'Anglo-Irish Attitudes' or 'Politics and Polemics' – but it seemed best placed in the section entitled 'Moods and Meditations' because of the range of its ideas: its speculation about the link between greatness and violence and what the generations transmit of both; about the poet's tower, its history and its function; about the changelessness of art and the transmission of artistic skills from generation to generation; about the future of the tower if the poet's own descendants were to lose vitality; about those fighting in the Irish civil war and their attitude to death; about the ignorance and the hatred engendered by civil war; about images of hatred and the nature of the poet's own life. 'The supernatural' too, is a category which could overlap with 'Dreams', 'Irish Mythology' and 'Age and After' or with some of the contents of, say, 'Songs from the Plays'. But poems have been categorised, as far as possible, by their predominant strains, and readers will recognise the interrelationships, the recurrent yet often subtly different imagery, the developing and developed symbolism, that link the verse together.

Readers used to the usual division of Yeats's poems may be surprised at some of these juxtapositions, and the order of separate items within the sections. Yeats, however, did not arrange his poems in different volumes in the chronological order of their composition or separate publication; indeed some were deliberately held over, to be included in later volumes, particularly when they were of a very personal nature, as, for instance, in the case of 'Owen Aherne and his Dancers'.

In this selection the date of composition, when it is firmly established or can be reasonably conjectured, is placed below the title of a poem on the left-hand side, in italics; the date on the right-hand side is the date a poem was first published. The date alone is given if a poem appeared in a journal; if, however, a poem first appeared in a volume of Yeats's work then the initials of that volume are given before the date. Dates at the end of poems are those Yeats gave them when published; they do not necessarily correspond with either the dates supplied by the present edition for the date of their composition or of their first publication. In general the poems in this selection are arranged in order of composition, allowance having been made in some cases for Yeats's habit of rewriting much of what he wrote over differing periods of time. In two cases two versions of poems are given to show how the process of rewriting changed their nature. The copy text used is that of W. B. Yeats *The Poems: A New Edition* (1984); the text of this edition differs in some minor respects from that of *Collected Poems* (1950). Those poems which appear as *Last Poems* in *Collected Poems* are collected – some in a different order – as *New Poems* (1938) and [*Last Poems* (1938–39)] in *Poems: A New Edition*, which also contains 125 poems, collected as *Additional Poems*. These poems were not collected by Yeats, but with the exception of eleven texts (see *NC* xxii) are contained in the *Variorum Edition of the Poems of W. B. Yeats* (1957) and the *Collected Plays* (1950). The *Variorum Edition* contains 'Reprisals' which is not included in *Collected Poems*, or in *Poems: A New Edition*.

Some of Yeats's poems were set in italics during his lifetime, and corresponding italics have been used in this edition, as for example in the case of 'To Ireland in the Coming Times'.

The names of Irish people and places are explained and where necessary their pronunciations indicated in Appendices II and III. Four maps, of Ireland, Co. Sligo, Sligo Town and Co. Galway are contained in Appendix IV and a diagram from *A Vision* illustrating the Phases of the Moon is supplied in Appendix V.

ABBREVIATIONS

ABBREVIATIONS USED IN TEXT

A	W. B. Yeats, *Autobiographies* (1955)
AMYO	W. B. Yeats, *A Man Young and Old* (a series of poems first published in *OB* as *The Young Countryman* and *The Old Countryman*, later in *TT*)
AV(1925)/*AV*(1937)	W. B. Yeats, *A Vision* (1925; 2nd ed. 1937)
AWYO	W. B. Yeats, *A Woman Young and Old* (series of poems in *WS* (1929) and *WS* (1933)
BS	W. B. Yeats, *The Bounty of Sweden* (1925)
CP	W. B. Yeats, *Collected Poems* (1933; 2nd ed. 1950)
DWL	*Letters on Poetry from W. B. Yeats to Dorothy Wellesley* (1940)
E	W. B. Yeats, *Explorations* (1962)
E & I	W. B. Yeats, *Essays and Introductions* (1961)
KGCT	W. B. Yeats, *The King of the Great Clock Tower, Commentaries and Poems* (1934)
L	*The Letters of W. B. Yeats*, ed. Allan Wade (1954)
M	W. B. Yeats, *Mythologies* (1959)
NC	A. Norman Jeffares, *A New Commentary on the Poems of W. B. Yeats* (1984)
PNE	W. B. Yeats, *The Poems, A New Edition* (1984)
SS	W. B. Yeats, *Supernatural Songs* (a series of poems in *KGCT* 1934, and *FMIM 1935*)
TT	W. B. Yeats, *The Tower* (1928)
W & B	W. B. Yeats, *Wheels and Butterflies* (1934)
WMP	W. B. Yeats, *Words for Music Perhaps* (1932)
WR	W. B. Yeats, *The Wind Among the Reeds* (1899)
WS (1929)	W. B. Yeats, *The Winding Stair* (1929)

BOOKS BY W. B. YEATS

APEP 1929	*A Packet for Ezra Pound*
ASTP 1937	*A Speech and Two Poems*
CK 1892	*The Countess Kathleen and Various Legends and Lyrics*
CNH 1902	*Cathleen Ni Hoolihan*
CP 1934	*The Collected Plays of W. B. Yeats*
CW 1908	*The Collected Works in Verse and Prose of William Butler Yeats*
EP & S 1925	*Early Poems and Stories*
FMIM 1935	*A Full Moon in March*
FPFD 1921	*Four Plays for Dancers*
GH 1910	*The Green Helmet and Other Poems* (Cuala Press edition)
GH 1912	*The Green Helmet and Other Poems* (Macmillan edition)
ISW 1903	*In the Seven Woods*

KGCT 1934	*The King of the Great Clock Tower, Commentaries and Poems*
LP & TP	*Last Poems and Two Plays*
MRD 1921	*Michael Robartes and The Dancer*
NP 1938	*New Poems*
Nine Poems 1918	*Nine Poems*
OB 1927	*October Blast*
OTB 1939	*On the Boiler*
PWD 1913	*Poems Written in Discouragement*
RPP 1914	*Responsibilities: Poems and a Play*
SKO 1928	*Sophocles' King Oedipus*
SPF 1922	*Seven Poems and a Fragment*
TKT 1904	*The King's Threshold*
TLAM 1897	*The Tables of the Law* [and *The Adoration of the Magi*]
TPFD 1919	*Two Plays for Dancers*
TWOI 1917	*The Well of Immortality* (early version of *At the Hawk's Well*)
W & B 1934	*Wheels and Butterflies*
WMP 1932	*Words for Music Perhaps*
WO 1889	*The Wanderings of Oisin*
WR 1899	*The Wind Among the Reeds*
WS 1929	*The Winding Stair*
WS 1933	*The Winding Stair and Other Poems*
WSC 1917	*The Wild Swans at Coole, other verses and a Play in Verse*
WSC 1919	*The Wild Swans at Coole*

ACKNOWLEDGEMENT

The quotations from the work of W. B. Yeats are reprinted by kind permission of Mr Michael Butler Yeats. The maps in *Appendix IV* are reproduced by kind permission of Colin Smythe.

SECTION I

THE CRAFT OF POETRY

TO THE ROSE UPON THE ROOD OF TIME

CK 1892

Red Rose, proud Rose, sad Rose of all my days!
Come near me, while I sing the ancient ways:
Cuchulain battling with the bitter tide;
The Druid, grey, wood-nurtured, quiet-eyed,
Who cast round Fergus dreams, and ruin untold;
And thine own sadness, whereof stars, grown old
In dancing silver-sandalled on the sea,
Sing in their high and lonely melody.
Come near, that no more blinded by man's fate,
I find under the boughs of love and hate,
In all poor foolish things that live a day,
Eternal beauty wandering on her way.

Come near, come near, come near — Ah, leave me still
A little space for the rose-breath to fill!
Lest I no more hear common things that crave;
The weak worm hiding down in its small cave,
The field mouse running by me in the grass,
And heavy mortal hopes that toil and pass;
But seek alone to hear the strange things said
By God to the bright hearts of those long dead,
And learn to chaunt a tongue men do not know.
Come near; I would before my time to go,
Sing of old Eire and the ancient ways:
Red Rose, proud Rose, sad Rose of all my days.

TO IRELAND IN THE COMING TIMES

CK 1892

Know, that I would accounted be
True brother of a company
That sang, to sweeten Ireland's wrong,
Ballad and story, rann and song;
Nor be I any less of them,
Because the red-rose-bordered hem

Of her, whose history began
Before God made the angelic clan,
Trails all about the written page.
When Time began to rant and rage
The measure of her flying feet
Made Ireland's heart begin to beat;
And Time bade all his candles flare
To light a measure here and there;
And may the thoughts of Ireland brood
Upon a measured quietude.

Nor may I less be counted one
With Davis, Mangan, Ferguson,
Because, to him who ponders well,
My rhymes more than their rhyming tell
Of things discovered in the deep,
Where only body's laid asleep.
For the elemental creatures go
About my table to and fro,
That hurry from unmeasured mind
To rant and rage in flood and wind;
Yet he who treads in measured ways
May surely barter gaze for gaze.
Man ever journeys on with them
After the red-rose-bordered hem.
Ah, faeries, dancing under the moon,
A Druid land, a Druid tune!

While still I may, I write for you
The love I lived, the dream I knew.
From our birthday, until we die,
Is but the winking of an eye;
And we, our singing and our love,
What measurer Time has lit above,
And all benighted things that go
About my table to and fro,
Are passing on to where may be,
In truth's consuming ecstasy,
No place for love and dream at all;
For God goes by with white footfall.
I cast my heart into my rhymes,
That you, in the dim coming times,
May know how my heart went with them
After the red-rose-bordered hem.

UNDER THE MOON

June 1901

I have no happiness in dreaming of Brycelinde,
Nor Avalon the grass-green hollow, nor Joyous Isle,
Where one found Lancelot crazed and hid him for a while;
Nor Ulad, when Naoise had thrown a sail upon the wind;
Nor lands that seem too dim to be burdens on the heart:
Land-under-Wave, where out of the moon's light and the sun's
Seven old sisters wind the threads of the long-lived ones,
Land-of-the-Tower, where Aengus has thrown the gates apart,
And Wood-of-Wonders, where one kills an ox at dawn,
To find it when night falls laid on a golden bier.
Therein are many queens like Branwen and Guinevere;
And Niamh and Laban and Fand, who could change to an otter or
       fawn,
And the wood-woman, whose lover was changed to a blue-eyed hawk;
And whether I go in my dreams by woodland, or dun, or shore,
Or on the unpeopled waves with kings to pull at the oar,
I hear the harp-string praise them, or hear their mournful talk.

Because of something told under the famished horn
Of the hunter's moon, that hung between the night and the day,
To dream of women whose beauty was folded in dismay,
Even in an old story, is a burden not to be borne.

ADAM'S CURSE

Before 20 November 1902   December 1902

           We sat together at one summer's end,
           That beautiful mild woman, your close friend,
           And you and I, and talked of poetry.
           I said, 'A line will take us hours maybe;
           Yet if it does not seem a moment's thought,
           Our stitching and unstitching has been naught.
           Better go down upon your marrow-bones
           And scrub a kitchen pavement, or break stones

Like an old pauper, in all kinds of weather;
For to articulate sweet sounds together
Is to work harder than all these, and yet
Be thought an idler by the noisy set
Of bankers, schoolmasters, and clergymen
The martyrs call the world.'

                                    And thereupon
That beautiful mild woman for whose sake
There's many a one shall find out all heartache
On finding that her voice is sweet and low
Replied, 'To be born woman is to know —
Although they do not talk of it at school —
That we must labour to be beautiful.'

I said, 'It's certain there is no fine thing
Since Adam's fall but needs much labouring.
There have been lovers who thought love should be
So much compounded of high courtesy
That they would sigh and quote with learned looks
Precedents out of beautiful old books;
Yet now it seems an idle trade enough.'

We sat grown quiet at the name of love;
We saw the last embers of daylight die,
And in the trembling blue-green of the sky
A moon, worn as if it had been a shell
Washed by time's waters as they rose and fell
About the stars and broke in days and years.

I had a thought for no one's but your ears:
That you were beautiful, and that I strove
To love you in the old high way of love;
That it had all seemed happy, and yet we'd grown
As weary-hearted as that hollow moon.

[ACCURSED WHO BRINGS TO LIGHT OF DAY]

CW, VIII 1908

Accursed who brings to light of day
The writings I have cast away!
But blessed he that stirs them not
And lets the kind worm take the lot!

ALL THINGS CAN TEMPT ME

Summer 1908   February 1909

All things can tempt me from this craft of verse:
One time it was a woman's face, or worse –
The seeming needs of my fool-driven land;
Now nothing but comes readier to the hand
Than this accustomed toil. When I was young,
I had not given a penny for a song
Did not the poet sing it with such airs
That one believed he had a sword upstairs;
Yet would be now, could I but have my wish,
Colder and dumber and deafer than a fish.

THE COMING OF WISDOM WITH TIME

21/22 March 1909   December 1910

Though leaves are many, the root is one;
Through all the lying days of my youth
I swayed my leaves and flowers in the sun;
Now I may wither into the truth.

THE FASCINATION OF WHAT'S DIFFICULT

1909 (Prose draft, September 1909)–1910   *GH* 1910

The fascination of what's difficult
Has dried the sap out of my veins, and rent
Spontaneous joy and natural content
Out of my heart. There's something ails our colt
That must, as if it had not holy blood
Nor on Olympus leaped from cloud to cloud,
Shiver under the lash, strain, sweat and jolt
As though it dragged road metal. My curse on plays
That have to be set up in fifty ways,
On the day's war with every knave and dolt,
Theatre business, management of men.
I swear before the dawn comes round again
I'll find the stable and pull out the bolt.

A COAT

1912   May 1914

I made my song a coat
Covered with embroideries
Out of old mythologies
From heel to throat;
But the fools caught it,
Wore it in the world's eyes
As though they'd wrought it.
Song, let them take it,
For there's more enterprise
In walking naked.

THE FISHERMAN

4 June 1914   February 1916

Although I can see him still,
The freckled man who goes
To a grey place on a hill
In grey Connemara clothes

At dawn to cast his flies,
It's long since I began
To call up to the eyes
This wise and simple man.
All day I'd looked in the face
What I had hoped 'twould be
To write for my own race
And the reality;
The living men that I hate,
The dead man that I loved,
The craven man in his seat,
The insolent unreproved,
And no knave brought to book
Who has won a drunken cheer,
The witty man and his joke
Aimed at the commonest ear,
The clever man who cries
The catch-cries of the clown,
The beating down of the wise
And great Art beaten down.

Maybe a twelvemonth since
Suddenly I began,
In scorn of this audience,
Imagining a man,
And his sun-freckled face,
And grey Connemara cloth,
Climbing up to a place
Where stone is dark under froth,
And the down-turn of his wrist
When the flies drop in the stream;
A man who does not exist,
A man who is but a dream;
And cried, 'Before I am old
I shall have written him one
Poem maybe as cold
And passionate as the dawn.'

THE SCHOLARS

1914–April 1915   1915

Bald heads forgetful of their sins,
Old, learned, respectable bald heads
Edit and annotate the lines
That young men, tossing on their beds,
Rhymed out in love's despair
To flatter beauty's ignorant ear.

All shuffle there; all cough in ink;
All wear the carpet with their shoes;
All think what other people think;
All know the man their neighbour knows.
Lord, what would they say
Did their Catullus walk that way?

THE PEOPLE

10 January 1915   February 1916

'What have I earned for all that work,' I said,
'For all that I have done at my own charge?
The daily spite of this unmannerly town,
Where who has served the most is most defamed,
The reputation of his lifetime lost
Between the night and morning. I might have lived,
And you know well how great the longing has been,
Where every day my footfall should have lit
In the green shadow of Ferrara wall;
Or climbed among the images of the past –
The unperturbed and courtly images –
Evening and morning, the steep street of Urbino
To where the duchess and her people talked
The stately midnight through until they stood
In their great window looking at the dawn;
I might have had no friend that could not mix
Courtesy and passion into one like those
That saw the wicks grow yellow in the dawn;
I might have used the one substantial right
My trade allows: chosen my company,

And chosen what scenery had pleased me best.'
Thereon my phoenix answered in reproof,
'The drunkards, pilferers of public funds,
All the dishonest crowd I had driven away,
When my luck changed and they dared meet my face,
Crawled from obscurity, and set upon me
Those I had served and some that I had fed;
Yet never have I, now nor any time,
Complained of the people.'

                            All I could reply
Was: 'You, that have not lived in thought but deed,
Can have the purity of a natural force,
But I, whose virtues are the definitions
Of the analytic mind, can neither close
The eye of the mind nor keep my tongue from speech.'
And yet, because my heart leaped at her words,
I was abashed, and now they come to mind
After nine years, I sink my head abashed.

MAD AS THE MIST AND SNOW

12 February 1929   *WMP* 1932

            Bolt and bar the shutter,
            For the foul winds blow:
            Our minds are at their best this night,
            And I seem to know
            That everything outside us is
            Mad as the mist and snow.

            Horace there by Homer stands,
            Plato stands below,
            And here is Tully's open page.
            How many years ago
            Were you and I unlettered lads
            Mad as the mist and snow?

            You ask what makes me sigh, old friend,
            What makes me shudder so?
            I shudder and I sigh to think
            That even Cicero
            And many-minded Homer were
            Mad as the mist and snow.

THE NINETEENTH CENTURY AND AFTER

January–2 March 1929   *WMP* 1932

> Though the great song return no more
> There's keen delight in what we have:
> The rattle of pebbles on the shore
> Under the receding wave.

COOLE AND BALLYLEE, 1931

February 1931   *WMP* 1932

> Under my window-ledge the waters race,
> Otters below and moor-hens on the top,
> Run for a mile undimmed in Heaven's face
> Then darkening through 'dark' Raftery's 'cellar' drop,
> Run underground, rise in a rocky place
> In Coole demesne, and there to finish up
> Spread to a lake and drop into a hole.
> What's water but the generated soul?

> Upon the border of that lake's a wood
> Now all dry sticks under a wintry sun,
> And in a copse of beeches there I stood,
> For Nature's pulled her tragic buskin on
> And all the rant's a mirror of my mood:
> At sudden thunder of the mounting swan
> I turned about and looked where branches break
> The glittering reaches of the flooded lake.

> Another emblem there! That stormy white
> But seems a concentration of the sky;
> And, like the soul, it sails into the sight
> And in the morning's gone, no man knows why;
> And is so lovely that it sets to right
> What knowledge or its lack had set awry,
> So arrogantly pure, a child might think
> It can be murdered with a spot of ink.

Sound of a stick upon the floor, a sound
From somebody that toils from chair to chair;
Beloved books that famous hands have bound,
Old marble heads, old pictures everywhere;
Great rooms where travelled men and children found
Content or joy; a last inheritor
Where none has reigned that lacked a name and fame
Or out of folly into folly came.

A spot whereon the founders lived and died
Seemed once more dear than life; ancestral trees
Or gardens rich in memory glorified
Marriages, alliances and families,
And every bride's ambition satisfied.
Where fashion or mere fantasy decrees
Man shifts about – all that great glory spent –
Like some poor Arab tribesman and his tent.

We were the last romantics – chose for theme
Traditional sanctity and loveliness;
Whatever's written in what poets name
The book of the people; whatever most can bless
The mind of man or elevate a rhyme;
But all is changed, that high horse riderless,
Though mounted in that saddle Homer rode
Where the swan drifts upon a darkening flood.

THE CHOICE

(?) February 1931   *WMP* 1932

[as the sixth stanza of
'Coole and Ballylee 1931']

The intellect of man is forced to choose
Perfection of the life, or of the work,
And if it take the second must refuse
A heavenly mansion, raging in the dark.
When all that story's finished, what's the news?
In luck or out the toil has left its mark:
That old perplexity an empty purse,
Or the day's vanity, the night's remorse.

THREE MOVEMENTS

26 January 1932 (prose version 20 January 1932)   *WMP* 1932

Shakespearean fish swam the sea, far away from land;
Romantic fish swam in nets coming to the hand;
What are all those fish that lie gasping on the strand?

THE SPUR

7 October 1936   March 1938

You think it horrible that lust and rage
Should dance attendance upon my old age;
They were not such a plague when I was young;
What else have I to spur me into song?

THOSE IMAGES

On or before 10 August 1937   March 1938

What if I bade you leave
The cavern of the mind?
There's better exercise
In the sunlight and wind.

I never bade you go
To Moscow or to Rome,
Renounce that drudgery,
Call the Muses home.

Seek those images
That constitute the wild,
The lion and the virgin,
The harlot and the child.

Find in middle air
An eagle on the wing,
Recognise the five
That make the Muses sing.

THE CIRCUS ANIMALS' DESERTION

(?) Between November 1937 and September 1938   January 1939

I

I sought a theme and sought for it in vain,
I sought it daily for six weeks or so.
Maybe at last being but a broken man
I must be satisfied with my heart, although
Winter and summer till old age began
My circus animals were all on show,
Those stilted boys, that burnished chariot,
Lion and woman and the Lord knows what.

II

What can I but enumerate old themes,
First that sea-rider Oisin led by the nose
Through three enchanted islands, allegorical dreams,
Vain gaiety, vain battle, vain repose,
Themes of the embittered heart, or so it seems,
That might adorn old songs or courtly shows;
But what cared I that set him on to ride,
I, starved for the bosom of his fairy bride.

And then a counter-truth filled out its play,
'The Countess Cathleen' was the name I gave it,
She, pity-crazed, had given her soul away
But masterful Heaven had intervened to save it.

I thought my dear must her own soul destroy
So did fanaticism and hate enslave it,
And this brought forth a dream and soon enough
This dream itself had all my thought and love.

And when the Fool and Blind Man stole the bread
Cuchulain fought the ungovernable sea;
Heart mysteries there, and yet when all is said
It was the dream itself enchanted me:
Character isolated by a deed
To engross the present and dominate memory.
Players and painted stage took all my love
And not those things that they were emblems of.

III

Those masterful images because complete
Grew in pure mind but out of what began?
A mound of refuse or the sweepings of a street,
Old kettles, old bottles, and a broken can,
Old iron, old bones, old rags, that raving slut
Who keeps the till. Now that my ladder's gone
I must lie down where all the ladders start
In the foul rag and bone shop of the heart.

SECTION 2
DREAMS

IN THE FIRELIGHT

March 1891

Come and dream of kings and kingdoms,
    Cooking chestnuts on the bars –
Round us the white roads are endless,
    Mournful under mournful stars.

Whisper lest we too may sadden,
    Round us herds of shadows steal –
Care not if beyond the shadows
    Flieth Fortune's furious wheel.

Kingdoms rising, kingdoms falling,
    Bowing nations, plumèd wars –
Weigh them in an hour of dreaming,
    Cooking chestnuts on the bars.

THE CAP AND BELLS

1893
                                       March 1894

The jester walked in the garden:
The garden had fallen still;
He bade his soul rise upward
And stand on her window-sill.

It rose in a straight blue garment,
When owls began to call:
It had grown wise-tongued by thinking
Of a quiet and light footfall;

But the young queen would not listen;
She rose in her pale night-gown;
She drew in the heavy casement
And pushed the latches down.

He bade his heart go to her,
When the owls called out no more;
In a red and quivering garment
It sang to her through the door.

It had grown sweet-tongued by dreaming
Of a flutter of flower-like hair;
But she took up her fan from the table
And waved it off on the air.

'I have cap and bells,' he pondered,
'I will send them to her and die';
And when the morning whitened
He left them where she went by.

She laid them upon her bosom,
Under a cloud of her hair,
And her red lips sang them a love-song
Till stars grew out of the air.

She opened her door and her window,
And the heart and the soul came through,
To her right hand came the red one,
To her left hand came the blue.

They set up a noise like crickets,
A chattering wise and sweet,
And her hair was a folded flower
And the quiet of love in her feet.

HIS DREAM

July 1908   July 1908

I swayed upon the gaudy stern
The butt-end of a steering-oar,
And saw wherever I could turn
A crowd upon a shore.

And though I would have hushed the crowd,
There was no mother's son but said,
'What is the figure in a shroud
Upon a gaudy bed?'

And after running at the brim
Cried out upon that thing beneath
— It had such dignity of limb —
By the sweet name of Death.

Though I'd my finger on my lip,
What could I but take up the song?
And running crowd and gaudy ship
Cried out the whole night long,

Crying amid the glittering sea,
Naming it with ecstatic breath,
Because it had such dignity,
By the sweet name of Death.

TOWARDS BREAK OF DAY

(?) January 1919   November 1920

Was it the double of my dream
The woman that by me lay
Dreamed, or did we halve a dream
Under the first cold gleam of day?

I thought: 'There is a waterfall
Upon Ben Bulben side
That all my childhood counted dear;
Were I to travel far and wide
I could not find a thing so dear.'
My memories had magnified
So many times childish delight.

I would have touched it like a child
But knew my finger could but have touched
Cold stone and water. I grew wild
Even accusing Heaven because
It had set down among its laws:
Nothing that we love over-much
Is ponderable to our touch.

I dreamed towards break of day,
The cold blown spray in my nostril.
But she that beside me lay
Had watched in bitterer sleep
The marvellous stag of Arthur,
That lofty white stag, leap
From mountain steep to steep.

CRAZY JANE GROWN OLD LOOKS AT THE DANCERS

6 March 1929   November 1930

I found that ivory image there
Dancing with her chosen youth,
But when he wound her coal-black hair
As though to strangle her, no scream
Or bodily movement did I dare,
Eyes under eyelids did so gleam:
Love is like the lion's tooth.

When she, and though some said she played
I said that she had danced heart's truth,
Drew a knife to strike him dead,
I could but leave him to his fate;
For, no matter what is said,
They had all that had their hate:
Love is like the lion's tooth.

Did he die or did she die?
Seemed to die or died they both?
God be with the times when I
Cared not a thraneen for what chanced
So that I had the limbs to try
Such a dance as there was danced —
Love is like the lion's tooth.

SECTION 3

IRISH MYTHOLOGY REVIVED

THE MADNESS OF KING GOLL

1884   September 1887

I sat on cushioned otter-skin:
My word was law from Ith to Emain,
And shook at Invar Amargin
The hearts of the world-troubling seamen,
And drove tumult and war away
From girl and boy and man and beast;
The fields grew fatter day by day,
The wild fowl of the air increased;
And every ancient Ollave said,
While he bent down his fading head,
'He drives away the Northern cold.'
They will not hush, the leaves a-flutter round me, the beech leaves old.

I sat and mused and drank sweet wine;
A herdsman came from inland valleys,
Crying, the pirates drove his swine
To fill their dark-beaked hollow galleys.
I called my battle-breaking men
And my loud brazen battle-cars
From rolling vale and rivery glen;
And under the blinking of the stars
Fell on the pirates by the deep,
And hurled them in the gulph of sleep:
These hands won many a torque of gold.
They will not hush, the leaves a-flutter round me, the beech leaves old.

But slowly, as I shouting slew
And trampled in the bubbling mire,
In my most secret spirit grew
A whirling and a wandering fire:
I stood: keen stars above me shone,
Around me shone keen eyes of men:
I laughed aloud and hurried on
By rocky shore and rushy fen;
I laughed because birds fluttered by,

And starlight gleamed, and clouds flew high,
And rushes waved and waters rolled.
They will not hush, the leaves a-flutter round me, the beech leaves old.

And now I wander in the woods
When summer gluts the golden bees.
Or in autumnal solitudes
Arise the leopard-coloured trees;
Or when along the wintry strands
The cormorants shiver on their rocks;
I wander on, and wave my hands,
And sing, and shake my heavy locks.
The grey wolf knows me; by one ear
I lead along the woodland deer;
The hares run by me growing bold.
They will not hush, the leaves a-flutter round me, the beech leaves old.

I came upon a little town
That slumbered in the harvest moon,
And passed a-tiptoe up and down,
Murmuring, to a fitful tune,
How I have followed, night and day,
A tramping of tremendous feet,
And saw where this old tympan lay
Deserted on a doorway seat,
And bore it to the woods with me;
Of some inhuman misery
Our married voices wildly trolled.
They will not hush, the leaves a-flutter round me, the beech leaves old.

I sang how, when day's toil is done,
Orchil shakes out her long dark hair
That hides away the dying sun
And sheds faint odours through the air:
When my hand passed from wire to wire
It quenched, with sound like falling dew,
The whirling and the wandering fire;
But lift a mournful ulalu,
For the kind wires are torn and still,
And I must wander wood and hill
Through summer's heat and winter's cold.
They will not hush, the leaves a-flutter round me, the beech leaves old.

FERGUS AND THE DRUID

May 1892

Fergus. This whole day have I followed in the rocks,
  And you have changed and flowed from shape to shape,
  First as a raven on whose ancient wings
  Scarcely a feather lingered, then you seemed
  A weasel moving on from stone to stone,
  And now at last you wear a human shape,
  A thin grey man half lost in gathering night.

Druid. What would you, king of the proud Red Branch kings?

Fergus. This would I say, most wise of living souls:
  Young subtle Conchubar sat close by me
  When I gave judgment, and his words were wise,
  And what to me was burden without end,
  To him seemed easy, so I laid the crown
  Upon his head to cast away my sorrow.

Druid. What would you, king of the proud Red Branch kings?

Fergus. A king and proud! and that is my despair.
  I feast amid my people on the hill,
  And pace the woods, and drive my chariot-wheels
  In the white border of the murmuring sea;
  And still I feel the crown upon my head.

Druid. What would you, Fergus?

Fergus.   Be no more a king
  But learn the dreaming wisdom that is yours.

Druid. Look on my thin grey hair and hollow cheeks
  And on these hands that may not lift the sword,
  This body trembling like a wind-blown reed.
  No woman's loved me, no man sought my help.

Fergus. A king is but a foolish labourer
  Who wastes his blood to be another's dream.

Druid. Take, if you must, this little bag of dreams;
Unloose the cord, and they will wrap you round.

Fergus. I see my life go drifting like a river
From change to change; I have been many things –
A green drop in the surge, a gleam of light
Upon a sword, a fir-tree on a hill,
An old slave grinding at a heavy quern,
A king sitting upon a chair of gold –
And all these things were wonderful and great;
But now I have grown nothing, knowing all.
Ah! Druid, Druid, how great webs of sorrow
Lay hidden in the small slate-coloured thing!

CUCHULAIN'S FIGHT WITH THE SEA

June 1982

A man came slowly from the setting sun,
To Emer, raddling raiment in her dun,
And said, 'I am that swineherd whom you bid
Go watch the road between the wood and tide,
But now I have no need to watch it more.'

Then Emer cast the web upon the floor,
And raising arms all raddled with the dye,
Parted her lips with a loud sudden cry.

That swineherd stared upon her face and said,
'No man alive, no man among the dead,
Has won the gold his cars of battle bring.'

'But if your master comes home triumphing
Why must you blench and shake from foot to crown?'

Thereon he shook the more and cast him down
Upon the web-heaped floor, and cried his word:
'With him is one sweet-throated like a bird.'

'You dare me to my face,' and thereupon
She smote with raddled fist, and where her son
Herded the cattle came with stumbling feet,
And cried with angry voice, 'It is not meet
To idle life away, a common herd.'

'I have long waited, mother, for that word:
But wherefore now?'
                              'There is a man to die;
You have the heaviest arm under the sky.'

'Whether under its daylight or its stars
My father stands amid his battle-cars.'

'But you have grown to be the taller man.'

'Yet somewhere under starlight or the sun
My father stands.'
                              'Aged, worn out with wars
On foot, on horseback or in battle-cars.'

'I only ask what way my journey lies,
For He who made you bitter made you wise.'

'The Red Branch camp in a great company
Between wood's rim and the horses of the sea.
Go there, and light a camp-fire at wood's rim;
But tell your name and lineage to him
Whose blade compels, and wait till they have found
Some feasting man that the same oath has bound.'

Among those feasting men Cuchulain dwelt,
And his young sweetheart close beside him knelt,
Stared on the mournful wonder of his eyes,
Even as Spring upon the ancient skies,
And pondered on the glory of his days;
And all around the harp-string told his praise,
And Conchubar, the Red Branch king of kings,
With his own fingers touched the brazen strings.

At last Cuchulain spake, 'Some man has made
His evening fire amid the leafy shade.
I have often heard him singing to and fro,
I have often heard the sweet sound of his bow.
Seek out what man he is.'

                    One went and came.
'He bade me let all know he gives his name
At the sword-point, and waits till we have found
Some feasting man that the same oath has bound.'

Cuchulain cried, 'I am the only man
Of all this host so bound from childhood on.'

After short fighting in the leafy shade,
He spake to the young man, 'Is there no maid
Who loves you, no white arms to wrap you round,
Or do you long for the dim sleepy ground
That you have come and dared me to my face?'

'The dooms of men are in God's hidden place'.

'Your head a while seemed like a woman's head
That I loved once.'
                Again the fighting sped,
But now the war-rage in Cuchulain woke,
And through that new blade's guard the old blade broke,
And pierced him.
               'Speak before your breath is done.'

'Cuchulain I, mighty Cuchulain's son.'

'I put you from your pain. I can no more.'

While day its burden on to evening bore,
With head bowed on his knees Cuchulain stayed;
Then Conchubar sent that sweet-throated maid,
And she, to win him, his grey hair caressed;
In vain her arms, in vain her soft white breast.
Then Conchubar, the subtlest of all men,

Ranking his Druids round him ten by ten,
Spake thus: 'Cuchulain will dwell there and brood
For three days more in dreadful quietude,
And then arise, and raving slay us all.
Chaunt in his ear delusions magical,
That he may fight the horses of the sea.'
The Druids took them to their mystery,
And chaunted for three days.
                        Cuchulain stirred,
Stared on the horses of the sea, and heard
The cars of battle and his own name cried;
And fought with the invulnerable tide.

THE ROSE OF BATTLE

CK 1892

Roses of all Roses, Rose of all the World!
The tall thought-woven sails, that flap unfurled
Above the tide of hours, trouble the air,
And God's bell buoyed to be the water's care;
While hushed from fear, or loud with hope, a band
With blown, spray-dabbled hair gather at hand.
Turn if you may from battles never done,
I call, as they go by me one by one,
Danger no refuge holds, and war no peace,
For him who hears love sing and never cease,
Beside her clean-swept hearth, her quiet shade:
But gather all for whom no love hath made
A woven silence, or but came to cast
A song into the air, and singing passed
To smile on the pale dawn; and gather you
Who have sought more than is in rain or dew,
Or in the sun and moon, or on the earth,
Or sighs amid the wandering, starry mirth,

Or comes in laughter from the sea's sad lips,
And wage God's battles in the long grey ships.
The sad, the lonely, the insatiable,
To these Old Night shall all her mystery tell;
God's bell has claimed them by the little cry
Of their sad hearts, that may not live nor die.

Rose of all Roses, Rose of all the World!
You, too, have come where the dim tides are hurled
Upon the wharves of sorrow, and heard ring
The bell that calls us on; the sweet far thing.
Beauty grown sad with its eternity
Made you of us, and of the dim grey sea.
Our long ships loose thought-woven sails and wait,
For God has bid them share an equal fate;
And when at last, defeated in His wars,
They have gone down under the same white stars,
We shall no longer hear the little cry
Of our sad hearts, that may not live nor die.

WHO GOES WITH FERGUS?

CK 1892

Who will go drive with Fergus now,
And pierce the deep wood's woven shade,
And dance upon the level shore?
Young man, lift up your russet brow,
And lift your tender eyelids, maid,
And brood on hopes and fear no more.

And no more turn aside and brood
Upon love's bitter mystery;
For Fergus rules the brazen cars,
And rules the shadows of the wood,
And the white breast of the dim sea
And all dishevelled wandering stars.

INTO THE TWILIGHT

31 June 1893   July 1893

Out-worn heart, in a time out-worn,
Come clear of the nets of wrong and right;
Laugh, heart, again in the grey twilight,
Sigh, heart, again in the dew of the morn.

Your mother Eire is always young,
Dew ever shining and twilight grey;
Though hope fall from you and love decay,
Burning in fires of a slanderous tongue.

Come, heart, where hill is heaped upon hill:
For there the mystical brotherhood
Of sun and moon and hollow and wood
And river and stream work out their will;

And God stands winding His lonely horn,
And time and the world are ever in flight;
And love is less kind than the grey twilight,
And hope is less dear than the dew of the morn.

THE VALLEY OF THE BLACK PIG

April 1896

The dews drop slowly and dreams gather: unknown spears
Suddenly hurtle before my dream-awakened eyes,
And then the clash of fallen horsemen and the cries
Of unknown perishing armies beat about my ears.
We who still labour by the cromlech on the shore,
The grey cairn on the hill, when day sinks drowned in dew,
Being weary of the world's empires, bow down to you,
Master of the still stars and of the flaming door.

THE SECRET ROSE

September 1896

Far-off, most secret, and inviolate Rose,
Enfold me in my hour of hours; where those
Who sought thee in the Holy Sepulchre,
Or in the wine-vat, dwell beyond the stir
And tumult of defeated dreams; and deep
Among pale eyelids, heavy with the sleep
Men have named beauty. Thy great leaves enfold
The ancient beards, the helms of ruby and gold
Of the crowned Magi; and the king whose eyes
Saw the Pierced Hands and Rood of elder rise
In Druid vapour and make the torches dim;
Till vain frenzy awoke and he died; and him
Who met Fand walking among flaming dew
By a grey shore where the wind never blew,
And lost the world and Emer for a kiss;
And him who drove the gods out of their liss,
And till a hundred morns had flowered red
Feasted, and wept the barrows of his dead;
And the proud dreaming king who flung the crown
And sorrow away, and calling bard and clown
Dwelt among wine-stained wanderers in deep woods;
And him who sold tillage, and house, and goods,
And sought through lands and islands numberless years,
Until he found, with laughter and with tears,
A woman of so shining loveliness
That men threshed corn at midnight by a tress,
A little stolen tress. I, too, await
The hour of thy great wind of love and hate.
When shall the stars be blown about the sky,
Like the sparks blown out of a smithy, and die?
Surely thine hour has come, thy great wind blows,
Far-off, most secret, and inviolate Rose?

HE MOURNS FOR THE CHANGE THAT HAS COME UPON HIM AND HIS BELOVED, AND LONGS FOR THE END OF THE WORLD

June 1897   June 1897

Do you not hear me calling, white deer with no horns?
I have been changed to a hound with one red ear;
I have been in the Path of Stones and the Wood of Thorns,
For somebody hid hatred and hope and desire and fear
Under my feet that they follow you night and day.
A man with a hazel wand came without sound;
He changed me suddenly; I was looking another way;
And now my calling is but the calling of a hound;
And Time and Birth and Change are hurrying by.
I would that the Boar without bristles had come from the West
And had rooted the sun and moon and stars out of the sky
And lay in the darkness, grunting, and turning to his rest.

THE WITHERING OF THE BOUGHS

August 1900

I cried when the moon was murmuring to the birds:
'Let peewit call and curlew cry where they will,
I long for your merry and tender and pitiful words,
For the roads are unending, and there is no place to my mind.'
The honey-pale moon lay low on the sleepy hill,
And I fell asleep upon lonely Echtge of streams.
No boughs have withered because of the wintry wind;
The boughs have withered because I have told them my dreams.

I know of the leafy paths that the witches take
Who come with their crowns of pearl and their spindles of wool,
And their secret smile, out of the depths of the lake;
I know where a dim moon drifts, where the Danaan kind
Wind and unwind dancing when the light grows cool
On the island lawns, their feet where the pale foam gleams.
No boughs have withered because of the wintry wind;
The boughs have withered because I have told them my dreams.

I know of the sleepy country, where swans fly round
Coupled with golden chains, and sing as they fly.
A king and a queen are wandering there, and the sound
Has made then so happy and hopeless, so deaf and so blind
With wisdom, they wander till all the years have gone by;
I know, and the curlew and peewit on Echtge of streams.
No boughs have withered because of the wintry wind;
The boughs have withered because I have told them my dreams.

THE HARP OF AENGUS

(?) Late 1899   May 1900

Edain came out of Midhir's hill, and lay
Beside young Aengus in his tower of glass,
Where time is drowned in odour-laden winds
And Druid moons, and murmuring of boughs,
And sleepy boughs, and boughs where apples made
Of opal and ruby and pale chrysolite
Awake unsleeping fires; and wove seven strings,
Sweet with all music, out of his long hair,
Because her hands had been made wild by love.
When Midhir's wife had changed her to a fly,
He made a harp with Druid apple-wood
That she among her winds might know he wept;
And from that hour he has watched over none
But faithful lovers.

THE GREY ROCK

Before 1913   April 1913

Poets with whom I learned my trade,
Companions of the Cheshire Cheese,
Here's an old story I've re-made,
Imagining 'twould better please
Your ears than stories now in fashion,
Though you may think I waste my breath
Pretending that there can be passion
That has more life in it than death,
And though at bottling of your wine
Old wholesome Goban had no say;
The moral's yours because it's mine.

When cups went round at close of day –
Is not that how good stories run? –
The gods were sitting at the board
In their great house at Slievenamon.
They sang a drowsy song, or snored,
For all were full of wine and meat.
The smoky torches made a glare
On metal Goban'd hammered at,
On old deep silver rolling there
Or on some still unemptied cup
That he, when frenzy stirred his thews,
Had hammered out on mountain top
To hold the sacred stuff he brews
That only gods may buy of him.

Now from that juice that made them wise
All those had lifted up the dim
Imaginations of their eyes,
For one that was like woman made
Before their sleepy eyelids ran
And trembling with her passion said,
'Come out and dig for a dead man,
Who's burrowing somewhere in the ground,
And mock him to his face and then

Hollo him on with horse and hound,
For he is the worst of all dead men.'

We should be dazed and terror-struck,
If we but saw in dreams that room,
Those wine-drenched eyes, and curse our luck
That emptied all our days to come.
I knew a woman none could please,
Because she dreamed when but a child
Of men and women made like these;
And after, when her blood ran wild,
Had ravelled her own story out,
And said, 'In two or in three years
I needs must marry some poor lout,'
And having said it, burst in tears.

Since, tavern comrades, you have died,
Maybe your images have stood,
Mere bone and muscle thrown aside,
Before that roomful or as good.
You had to face your ends when young —
'Twas wine or women, or some curse —
But never made a poorer song
That you might have a heavier purse,
Nor gave a loud service to a cause
That you might have a troop of friends.
You kept the Muses' sterner laws,
And unrepenting faced your ends,
And therefore earned the right — and yet
Dowson and Johnson most I praise —
To troop with those the world's forgot,
And copy their proud steady gaze.

'The Danish troop was driven out
Between the dawn and dusk,' she said;
'Although the event was long in doubt,
Although the King of Ireland's dead
And half the kings, before sundown
All was accomplished.

'When this day
Murrough, the King of Ireland's son,
Foot after foot was giving way,
He and his best troops back to back
Had perished there, but the Danes ran,
Stricken with panic from the attack,
The shouting of an unseen man;
And being thankful Murrough found,
Led by a footsole dipped in blood
That had made prints upon the ground,
Where by old thorn-trees that man stood;
And though when he gazed here and there,
He had but gazed on thorn-trees, spoke,
"Who is the friend that seems but air
And yet could give so fine a stroke?"
Thereon a young man met his eye,
Who said, "Because she held me in
Her love, and would not have me die,
Rock-nurtured Aoife took a pin,
And pushing it into my shirt,
Promised that for a pin's sake,
No man should see to do me hurt;
But there it's gone; I will not take
The fortune that had been my shame
Seeing, King's son, what wounds you have."
'Twas roundly spoke, but when night came
He had betrayed me to his grave,
For he and the King's son were dead.
I'd promised him two hundred years,
And when for all I'd done or said –
And these immortal eyes shed tears –
He claimed his country's need was most,
I'd saved his life, yet for the sake
Of a new friend he has turned a ghost.
What does he care if my heart break?
I call for spade and horse and hound

That we may harry him.' Thereon
She cast herself upon the ground
And rent her clothes and made her moan:
'Why are they faithless when their might
Is from the holy shades that rove
The grey rock and the windy light?
Why should the faithfullest heart most love
The bitter sweetness of false faces?
Why must the lasting love what passes,
Why are the gods by men betrayed?'

But thereon every god stood up
With a slow smile and without sound,
And stretching forth his arm and cup
To where she moaned upon the ground,
Suddenly drenched her to the skin;
And she with Goban's wine adrip,
No more remembering what had been,
Stared at the gods with laughing lip.

I have kept my faith, though faith was tried,
To that rock-born, rock-wandering foot,
And the world's altered since you died,
And I am in no good repute
With the loud host before the sea,
That think sword-strokes were better meant
Than lover's music — let that be,
So that the wandering foot's content.

SECTION 4

FRIENDS AND FRIENDSHIP

FRIENDS

January 1911   *GH* 1912

Now must I these three praise —
Three women that have wrought
What joy is in my days:
One because no thought,
Nor those unpassing cares,
No, not in these fifteen
Many-times-troubled years,
Could ever come between
Mind and delighted mind;
And one because her hand
Had strength that could unbind
What none can understand,
What none can have and thrive,
Youth's dreamy load, till she
So changed me that I live
Labouring in ecstasy.
And what of her that took
All till my youth was gone
With scarce a pitying look?
How could I praise that one?
When day begins to break
I count my good and bad,
Being wakeful for her sake,
Remembering what she had,
What eagle look still shows,
While up from my heart's root
So great a sweetness flows
I shake from head to foot.

TO A CHILD DANCING IN THE WIND

December 1912   December 1912

Dance there upon the shore;
What need have you to care
For wind or water's roar?
And tumble out your hair
That the salt drops have wet;
Being young you have not known
The fool's triumph, nor yet
Love lost as soon as won,
Nor the best labourer dead
And all the sheaves to bind.
What need have you to dread
The monstrous crying of wind?

THE NEW FACES

December 1912   *SPF* 1922

If you, that have grown old, were the first dead,
Neither catalpa tree nor scented lime
Should hear my living feet, nor would I tread
Where we wrought that shall break the teeth of Time.
Let the new faces play what tricks they will
In the old rooms; night can outbalance day,
Our shadows rove the garden gravel still,
The living seem more shadowy than they.

TWO YEARS LATER

3 December 1912/1913   May 1914

Has no one said those daring
Kind eyes should be more learn'd?
Or warned you how despairing
The moths are when they are burned?
I could have warned you; but you are young,
So we speak a different tongue.

O you will take whatever's offered
And dream that all the world's a friend,
Suffer as your mother suffered,
Be as broken in the end.
But I am old and you are young,
And I speak a barbarous tongue.

UPON A DYING LADY

The seven poems of 'Upon a Dying Lady' were written   August 1917
between 8 January 1912 and 11 February 1913

I.   *Her Courtesy*

With the old kindness, the old distinguished grace,
She lies, her lovely piteous head amid dull red hair
Propped upon pillows, rouge on the pallor of her face.
She would not have us sad because she is lying there,
And when she meets our gaze her eyes are laughter-lit,
Her speech a wicked tale that we may vie with her,
Matching our broken-hearted wit against her wit,
Thinking of saints and of Petronius Arbiter.

TO A FRIEND WHOSE WORK HAS COME TO NOTHING

16 September 1913   *PWD* 1913

Now all the truth is out,
Be secret and take defeat
From any brazen throat,
For how can you compete,
Being honour bred, with one
Who, were it proved he lies,
Were neither shamed in his own
Nor in his neighbours' eyes?
Bred to a harder thing
Than Triumph, turn away
And like a laughing string
Whereon mad fingers play
Amid a place of stone,
Be secret and exult,
Because of all things known
That is most difficult.

TO A YOUNG GIRL

(?) 1913 or May 1915   October 1918

My dear, my dear, I know
More than another
What makes your heart beat so;
Not even your own mother
Can know it as I know,
Who broke my heart for her
When the wild thought,
That she denies
And has forgot,
Set all her blood astir
And glittered in her eyes.

IN MEMORY OF MAJOR ROBERT GREGORY

14 June 1918   August 1918

I

Now that we're almost settled in our house
I'll name the friends that cannot sup with us
Beside a fire of turf in th' ancient tower,
And having talked to some late hour
Climb up the narrow winding stair to bed:
Discoverers of forgotten truth
Or mere companions of my youth,
All, all are in my thoughts to-night being dead.

II

Always we'd have the new friend meet the old
And we are hurt if either friend seem cold,
And there is salt to lengthen out the smart
In the affections of our heart,
And quarrels are blown up upon that head;
But not a friend that I would bring
This night can set us quarrelling,
For all that come into my mind are dead.

III

Lionel Johnson comes the first to mind,
That loved his learning better than mankind,
Though courteous to the worst; much falling he
Brooded upon sanctity
Till all his Greek and Latin learning seemed
A long blast upon the horn that brought
A little nearer to his thought
A measureless consummation that he dreamed.

IV

And that enquiring man John Synge comes next,
That dying chose the living world for text
And never could have rested in the tomb
But that, long travelling, he had come
Towards nightfall upon certain set apart
In a most desolate stony place,
Towards nightfall upon a race
Passionate and simple like his heart.

V

And then I think of old George Pollexfen,
In muscular youth well known to Mayo men
For horsemanship at meets or at racecourses,
That could have shown how pure-bred horses
And solid men, for all their passion, live
But as the outrageous stars incline
By opposition, square and trine;
Having grown sluggish and contemplative.

VI

They were my close companions many a year,
A portion of my mind and life, as it were,
And now their breathless faces seem to look
Out of some old picture-book;
I am accustomed to their lack of breath,
But not that my dear friend's dear son,
Our Sidney and our perfect man,
Could share in that discourtesy of death.

VII

For all things the delighted eye now sees
Were loved by him; the old storm-broken trees
That cast their shadows upon road and bridge;
The tower set on the stream's edge;
The ford where drinking cattle make a stir
Nightly, and startled by that sound
The water-hen must change her ground;
He might have been your heartiest welcomer.

VIII

When with the Galway foxhounds he would ride
From Castle Taylor to the Roxborough side
Or Esserkelly plain, few kept his pace;
At Moonen he had leaped a place
So perilous that half the astonished meet
Had shut their eyes; and where was it
He rode a race without a bit?
And yet his mind outran the horses' feet.

IX

We dreamed that a great painter had been born
To cold Clare rock and Galway rock and thorn,
To that stern colour and that delicate line
That are our secret discipline
Wherein the gazing heart doubles her might.
Soldier, scholar, horseman, he,
And yet he had the intensity
To have published all to be a world's delight.

X

What other could so well have counselled us
In all lovely intricacies of a house
As he that practised or that understood
All work in metal or in wood,
In moulded plaster or in carven stone?
Soldier, scholar, horseman, he,
And all he did done perfectly
As though he had but that one trade alone.

XI

Some burn damp faggots, others may consume
The entire combustible world in one small room
As though dried straw, and if we turn about
The bare chimney is gone black out
Because the work had finished in that flare.
Soldier, scholar, horseman, he,
As 'twere all life's epitome.
What made us dream that he could comb grey hair?

XII

I had thought, seeing how bitter is that wind
That shakes the shutter, to have brought to mind
All those that manhood tried, or childhood loved
Or boyish intellect approved,
With some appropriate commentary on each;
Until imagination brought
A fitter welcome; but a thought
Of that late death took all my heart for speech.

TO A YOUNG BEAUTY

(? Autumn) 1918   *Nine Poems* 1918

Dear fellow-artist, why so free
With every sort of company,
With every Jack and Jill?
Choose your companions from the best;
Who draws a bucket with the rest
Soon topples down the hill.

You may, that mirror for a school,
Be passionate, not bountiful
As common beauties may,
Who were not born to keep in trim
With old Ezekiel's cherubim
But those of Beauvarlet.

I know what wages beauty gives,
How hard a life her servant lives,
Yet praise the winters gone:
There is not a fool can call me friend,
And I may dine at journey's end
With Landor and with Donne.

MICHAEL ROBARTES AND THE DANCER

1919   November 1920

He.   Opinion is not worth a rush;
In this altar-piece the knight,
Who grips his long spear so to push
That dragon through the fading light,
Loved the lady; and it's plain
The half-dead dragon was her thought,
That every morning rose again
And dug its claws and shrieked and fought.
Could the impossible come to pass
She would have time to turn her eyes,
Her lover thought, upon the glass
And on the instant would grow wise.

She.   You mean they argued.

He.   Put it so;
But bear in mind your lover's wage
Is what your looking-glass can show,
And that he will turn green with rage
At all that is not pictured there.

She.   May I not put myself to college?

He..   Go pluck Athena by the hair;
For what mere book can grant a knowledge
With an impassioned gravity
Appropriate to that beating breast,
That vigorous thigh, that dreaming eye?
And may the devil take the rest.

She.   And must no beautiful woman be
Learned like a man?

He.   Paul Veronese
And all his sacred company
Imagined bodies all their days
By the lagoon you love so much,
For proud, soft, ceremonious proof
That all must come to sight and touch;
While Michael Angelo's Sistine roof,
His 'Morning' and his 'Night' disclose
How sinew that has been pulled tight,
Or it may be loosened in repose,
Can rule by supernatural right
Yet be but sinew.

She.   I have heard said
There is great danger in the body.

He.   Did God in portioning wine and bread
Give man His thought or His mere body?

She.   My wretched dragon is perplexed.

He.   I have principles to prove me right.
It follows from this Latin text
That blest souls are not composite,
And that all beautiful women may
Live in uncomposite blessedness,
And lead us to the like — if they
Will banish every thought, unless
The lineaments that please their view
When the long looking-glass is full,
Even from the foot-sole think it too.

She.   They say such different things at school.

ALL SOULS' NIGHT
Epilogue to 'A Vision'

November 1920   March 1921

Midnight has come and the great Christ Church bell
And many a lesser bell sound through the room;
And it is All Souls' Night.
And two long glasses brimmed with muscatel
Bubble upon the table. A ghost may come;
For it is a ghost's right,
His element is so fine
Being sharpened by his death,
To drink from the wine-breath
While our gross palates drink from the whole wine.

I need some mind that, if the cannon sound
From every quarter of the world, can stay
Wound in mind's pondering,
As mummies in the mummy-cloth are wound;
Because I have a marvellous thing to say,
A certain marvellous thing
None but the living mock,
Though not for sober ear;
It may be all that hear
Should laugh and weep an hour upon the clock.

Horton's the first I call. He loved strange thought
And knew that sweet extremity of pride
That's called platonic love,
And that to such a pitch of passion wrought
Nothing could bring him, when his lady died,
Anodyne for his love.
Words were but wasted breath;
One dear hope had he:
The inclemency
Of that or the next winter would be death.

Two thoughts were so mixed up I could not tell
Whether of her or God he thought the most,
But think that his mind's eye,
When upward turned, on one sole image fell;
And that a slight companionable ghost,
Wild with divinity,
Had so lit up the whole
Immense miraculous house
The Bible promised us,
It seemed a gold-fish swimming in a bowl.

On Florence Emery I call the next,
Who finding the first wrinkles on a face
Admired and beautiful,
And by foreknowledge of the future vexed;
Diminished beauty, multiplied commonplace;
Preferred to teach a school
Away from neighbour or friend,
Among dark skins, and there
Permit foul years to wear
Hidden from eyesight to the unnoticed end.

Before that end much had she ravelled out
From a discourse in figurative speech
By some learned Indian
On the soul's journey. How it is whirled about
Wherever the orbit of the moon can reach,
Until it plunge into the sun;
And there, free and yet fast,
Being both Chance and Choice,
Forget its broken toys
And sink into its own delight at last.

I call MacGregor Mathers from his grave,
For in my first hard spring-time we were friends,
Although of late estranged.
I thought him half a lunatic, half knave,
And told him so, but friendship never ends;

And what if mind seem changed,
And it seem changed with the mind,
When thoughts rise up unbid
On generous things that he did
And I grow half contented to be blind!

He had much industry at setting out,
Much boisterous courage, before loneliness
Had driven him crazed;
For meditations upon unknown thought
Make human intercourse grow less and less;
They are neither paid nor praised.
But he'd object to the host,
The glass because my glass:
A ghost-lover he was
And may have grown more arrogant being a ghost.

But names are nothing. What matter who it be,
So that his elements have grown so fine
The fume of muscatel
Can give his sharpened palate ecstasy
No living man can drink from the whole wine.
I have mummy truths to tell
Whereat the living mock,
Though not for sober ear,
For maybe all that hear
Should laugh and weep an hour upon the clock.

Such thought — such thought have I that hold it tight
Till meditation master all its parts,
Nothing can stay my glance
Until that glance run in the world's despite
To where the damned have howled away their hearts,
And where the blessed dance;
Such thought, that in it bound
I need no other thing,
Wound in mind's wandering
As mummies in the mummy-cloth are wound.

Oxford, Autumn 1920

IN MEMORY OF EVA GORE-BOOTH AND CON MARKIEVICZ

Between 21 September and November 1927   *WS* 1929

The light of evening, Lissadell,
Great windows open to the south,
Two girls in silk kimonos, both
Beautiful, one a gazelle.
But a raving autumn shears
Blossom from the summer's wreath;
The older is condemned to death,
Pardoned, drags out lonely years
Conspiring among the ignorant.
I know not what the younger dreams —
Some vague Utopia — and she seems,
When withered old and skeleton-gaunt,
An image of such politics.
Many a time I think to seek
One or the other out and speak
Of that old Georgian mansion, mix
Pictures of the mind, recall
That table and the talk of youth,
Two girls in silk kimonos, both
Beautiful, one a gazelle.

Dear shadows, now you know it all,
All the folly of a fight
With a common wrong or right.
The innocent and the beautiful
Have no enemy but time;
Arise and bid me strike a match
And strike another till time catch;
Should the conflagration climb,
Run till all the sages know.
We the great gazebo built,
They convicted us of guilt;
Bid me strike a match and blow.

October 1927

COOLE PARK, 1929

Completed 7 September 1928 1931

I meditate upon a swallow's flight,
Upon an aged woman and her house,
A sycamore and lime tree lost in night
Although that western cloud is luminous,
Great works constructed there in nature's spite
For scholars and for poets after us,
Thoughts long knitted into a single thought,
A dance-like glory that those walls begot.

There Hyde before he had beaten into prose
That noble blade the Muses buckled on,
There one that ruffled in a manly pose
For all his timid heart, there that slow man,
That meditative man, John Synge, and those
Impetuous men, Shawe-Taylor and Hugh Lane,
Found pride established in humility,
A scene well set and excellent company.

They came like swallows and like swallows went,
And yet a woman's powerful character
Could keep a swallow to its first intent;
And half a dozen in formation there,
That seemed to whirl upon a compass-point,
Found certainty upon the dreaming air,
The intellectual sweetness of those lines
That cut through time or cross it withershins.

Here, traveller, scholar, poet, take your stand
When all those rooms and passages are gone,
When nettles wave upon a shapeless mound
And saplings root among the broken stone,
And dedicate – eyes bent upon the ground,
Back turned upon the brightness of the sun
And all the sensuality of the shade –
A moment's memory to that laurelled head.

FOR ANNE GREGORY

September 1930   *WMP* 1932

'Never shall a young man,
Thrown into despair
By those great honey-coloured
Ramparts at your ear,
Love you for yourself alone
And not your yellow hair.'

'But I can get a hair-dye
And set such colour there,
Brown, or black, or carrot,
That young men in despair
May love me for myself alone
And not my yellow hair.'

'I heard an old religious man
But yesternight declare
That he had found a text to prove
That only God, my dear,
Could love you for yourself alone
And not your yellow hair.'

THE RESULTS OF THOUGHT

18–28 August 1931   *WMP* 1932

Acquaintance; companion;
One dear brilliant woman;
The best-endowed, the elect,
All by their youth undone,
All, all, by that inhuman
Bitter glory wrecked.

But I have straightened out
Ruin, wreck and wrack;
I toiled long years and at length
Came to so deep a thought
I can summon back
All their wholesome strength.

What images are these
That turn dull-eyed away,
Or shift Time's filthy load,
Straighten aged knees,
Hesitate or stay?
What heads shake or nod?

August 1931

BEAUTIFUL LOFTY THINGS

(?) 1937   *NP* 1938

Beautiful lofty things; O'Leary's noble head;
My father upon the Abbey stage, before him a raging crowd.
'This Land of Saints,' and then as the applause died out,
'Of plaster Saints;' his beautiful mischievous head thrown back.
Standish O'Grady supporting himself between the tables
Speaking to a drunken audience high nonsensical words;
Augusta Gregory seated at her great ormolu table
Her eightieth winter approaching; 'Yesterday he threatened my life,
I told him that nightly from six to seven I sat at this table
The blinds drawn up;' Maud Gonne at Howth station waiting a train
Pallas Athena in that straight back and arrogant head:
All the Olympians; a thing never known again.

THE MUNICIPAL GALLERY RE-VISITED

August–early September 1937   *ASTP* 1937

I

Around me the images of thirty years;
An ambush; pilgrims at the water-side;
Casement upon trial, half hidden by the bars,
Guarded; Griffith staring in hysterical pride;
Kevin O'Higgins' countenance that wears
A gentle questioning look that cannot hide
A soul incapable of remorse or rest;
A revolutionary soldier kneeling to be blessed.

II

An Abbot or Archbishop with an upraised hand
Blessing the Tricolour. 'This is not' I say
'The dead Ireland of my youth, but an Ireland
The poets have imagined, terrible and gay.'
Before a woman's portrait suddenly I stand;
Beautiful and gentle in her Venetian way.
I met her all but fifty years ago
For twenty minutes in some studio.

III

Heart smitten with emotion I sink down
My heart recovering with covered eyes;
Wherever I had looked I had looked upon
My permanent or impermanent images;
Augusta Gregory's son; her sister's son,
Hugh Lane, 'onlie begetter' of all these;
Hazel Lavery living and dying, that tale
As though some ballad singer had sung it all.

IV

Mancini's portrait of Augusta Gregory,
'Greatest since Rembrandt,' according to John Synge;
A great ebullient portrait certainly;
But where is the brush that could show anything
Of all that pride and that humility,
And I am in despair that time may bring
Approved patterns of women or of men
But not that selfsame excellence again.

V

My mediaeval knees lack health until they bend,
But in that woman, in that household where
Honour had lived so long, all lacking found.
Childless I thought 'my children may find here
Deep-rooted things,' but never foresaw its end,
And now that end has come I have not wept;
No fox can foul the lair the badger swept.

VI

(An image out of Spenser and the common tongue)
John Synge, I and Augusta Gregory, thought
All that we did, all that we said or sang
Must come from contact with the soil, from that
Contact everything Antaeus-like grew strong.
We three alone in modern times had brought
Everything down to that sole test again, .
Dream of the noble and the beggarman.

VII

And here's John Synge himself, that rooted man
'Forgetting human words,' a grave deep face.
You that would judge me do not judge alone
This book or that, come to this hallowed place
Where my friends' portraits hang and look thereon;
Ireland's history in their lineaments trace;
Think where man's glory most begins and ends
And say my glory was I had such friends.

SECTION 5

IRISH CHARACTERS AND PLACES

THE BALLAD OF MOLL MAGEE

(?) 1887   WO 1889

Come round me, little childer;
There, don't fling stones at me
Because I mutter as I go;
But pity Moll Magee.

My man was a poor fisher
With shore lines in the say;
My work was saltin' herrings
The whole of the long day.

And sometimes from the saltin' shed
I scarce could drag my feet,
Under the blessed moonlight,
Along the pebbly street.

I'd always been but weakly,
And my baby was just born;
A neighbour minded her by day,
I minded her till morn.

I lay upon my baby;
Ye little childer dear,
I looked on my cold baby
When the morn grew frosty and clear.

A weary woman sleeps so hard!
My man grew red and pale,
And gave me money, and bade me go
To my own place, Kinsale.

He drove me out and shut the door,
And gave his curse to me;
I went away in silence,
No neighbour could I see.

The windows and the doors were shut,
One star shone faint and green,
The little straws were turnin' round
Across the bare boreen.

I went away in silence:
Beyond old Martin's byre
I saw a kindly neighbour
Blowin' her mornin' fire.

She drew from me my story —
My money's all used up,
And still, with pityin', scornin' eye,
She gives me bite and sup.

She says my man will surely come,
And fetch me home agin;
But always, as I'm movin' round,
Without doors or within,

Pilin' the wood or pilin' the turf,
Or goin' to the well,
I'm thinkin' of my baby
And keenin' to mysel'.

And sometimes I am sure she knows
When, openin' wide His door,
God lights the stars, His candles,
And looks upon the poor.

So now, ye little childer,
Ye won't fling stones at me;
But gather with your shinin' looks
And pity Moll Magee.

THE LAMENTATION OF THE OLD PENSIONER

1890

November 1890

I had a chair at every hearth,
When no one turned to see
With 'Look at that old fellow there;
And who may he be?'
And therefore do I wander on,
And the fret is on me.

The road-side trees keep murmuring —
Ah, wherefore murmur ye
As in the old days long gone by,
Green oak and poplar tree!
The well-known faces are all gone,
And the fret is on me.

THE LAMENTATION OF THE OLD PENSIONER

1890

revised version, *EP & S* 1925

Although I shelter from the rain
Under a broken tree,
My chair was nearest to the fire
In every company
That talked of love or politics,
Ere Time transfigured me.

Though lads are making pikes again
For some conspiracy,
And crazy rascals rage their fill
At human tyranny;
My contemplations are of Time
That has transfigured me.

There's not a woman turns her face
Upon a broken tree,
And yet the beauties that I loved
Are in my memory;
I spit into the face of Time
That has transfigured me.

THE LAKE ISLE OF INNISFREE

1890   December 1890

I will arise and go now, and go to Innisfree,
And a small cabin build there, of clay and wattles made:
Nine bean-rows will I have there, a hive for the honey-bee,
And live alone in the bee-loud glade.

And I shall have some peace there, for peace comes dropping slow,
Dropping from the veils of the morning to where the cricket sings;
There midnight's all a glimmer, and noon a purple glow,
And evening full of the linnet's wings.

I will arise and go now, for always night and day
I hear lake water lapping with low sounds by the shore;
While I stand on the roadway, or on the pavements grey,
I hear it in the deep heart's core.

THE FIDDLER OF DOONEY

December 1892

When I play on my fiddle in Dooney,
Folk dance like a wave of the sea;
My cousin is priest in Kilvarnet,
My brother in Mocharabuiee.

I passed my brother and cousin:
They read in their books of prayer;
I read in my book of songs
I bought at the Sligo fair.

When we come at the end of time
To Peter sitting in state,
He will smile on the three old spirits,
But call me first through the gate;

For the good are always the merry,
Save by an evil chance,
And the merry love the fiddle,
And the merry love to dance:

And when the folk there spy me,
They will all come up to me,
With 'Here is the fiddler of Dooney!'
And dance like a wave of the sea.

RED HANRAHAN'S SONG ABOUT IRELAND

August 1894

The old brown thorn-trees break in two high over Cummen Strand,
Under a bitter black wind that blows from the left hand;
Our courage breaks like an old tree in a black wind and dies,
But we have hidden in our hearts the flame out of the eyes
Of Cathleen, the daughter of Houlihan.

The wind has bundled up the clouds high over Knocknarea,
And thrown the thunder on the stones for all that Maeve can say.
Angers that are like noisy clouds have set our hearts abeat;
But we have all bent low and kissed the quiet feet
Of Cathleen, the daughter of Houlihan.

The yellow pool has overflowed high up on Clooth-na-Bare,
For the wet winds are blowing out of the clinging air;
Like heavy flooded waters our bodies and our blood;
But purer than a tall candle before the Holy Rood
Is Cathleen, the daughter of Houlihan.

THE WILD SWANS AT COOLE

1916   June 1917

The trees are in their autumn beauty,
The woodland paths are dry,
Under the October twilight the water
Mirrors a still sky;
Upon the brimming water among the stones
Are nine-and-fifty swans.

The nineteenth autumn has come upon me
Since I first made my count;
I saw, before I had well finished,
All suddenly mount
And scatter wheeling in great broken rings
Upon their clamorous wings.

I have looked upon those brilliant creatures,
And now my heart is sore.
All's changed since I, hearing at twilight,
The first time on this shore,
The bell-beat of their wings above my head,
Trod with a lighted tread.

Unwearied still, lover by lover,
They paddle in the cold
Companionable streams or climb the air;
Their hearts have not grown old;
Passions or conquest, wander where they will,
Attend upon them still.

But now they drift on the still water,
Mysterious, beautiful;
Among what rushes will they build,
By what lake's edge or pool
Delight men's eyes when I awake some day
To find they have flown away?

THE PILGRIM

October 1937

I fasted for some forty days on bread and buttermilk
For passing round the bottle with girls in rags or silk,
In country shawl or Paris cloak, had put my wits astray,
And what's the good of women for all that they can say
Is fol de rol de rolly O.

Round Lough Derg's holy island I went upon the stones,
I prayed at all the Stations upon my marrow bones,
And there I found an old man and though I prayed all day
And that old man beside me, nothing would he say
But fol de rol de rolly O.

All know that all the dead in the world about that place are stuck
And that should mother seek her son she'd have but little luck
Because the fires of Purgatory have ate their shapes away;
I swear to God I questioned them and all they had to say
Was fol de rol de rolly O.

A great black ragged bird appeared when I was in the boat;
Some twenty feet from tip to tip had it stretched rightly out,
With flopping and with flapping it made a great display
But I never stopped to question, what could the boatman say
But fol de rol de rolly O.

Now I am in the public house and lean upon the wall,
So come in rags or come in silk, in cloak or country shawl,
And come with learned lovers or with what men you may
For I can put the whole lot down, and all I have to say
Is fol de rol de rolly O.

SECTION 6
THE POET'S FAMILY

INTRODUCTORY RHYMES

1912 (? December 1913) – 1914   RPP 1914

Pardon, old fathers, if you still remain
Somewhere in ear-shot for the story's end,
Old Dublin merchant 'free of the ten and four'
Or trading out of Galway into Spain;
Old country scholar, Robert Emmet's friend,
A hundred-year-old memory to the poor;
Merchant and scholar who have left me blood
That has not passed through any huckster's loin,
Soldiers that gave, whatever die was cast:
A Butler or an Armstrong that withstood
Beside the brackish waters of the Boyne
James and his Irish when the Dutchman crossed;
Old merchant skipper that leaped overboard
After a ragged hat in Biscay Bay;
You most of all, silent and fierce old man,
Because the daily spectacle that stirred
My fancy, and set my boyish lips to say,
'Only the wasteful virtues earn the sun';
Pardon that for a barren passion's sake,
Although I have come close on forty-nine,
I have no child, I have nothing but a book,
Nothing but that to prove your blood and mine.

January 1914

TO BE CARVED ON A STONE AT THOOR BALLYLEE

(?) Between May and July 1918   MRD 1921

I, the poet William Yeats,
With old mill boards and sea-green slates,
And smithy work from the Gort forge,
Restored this tower for my wife George;
And may these characters remain
When all is ruin once again.

A PRAYER FOR MY DAUGHTER

Between February and June 1919   November 1919

Once more the storm is howling, and half hid
Under this cradle-hood and coverlid
My child sleeps on. There is no obstacle
But Gregory's wood and one bare hill
Whereby the haystack- and roof-levelling wind,
Bred on the Atlantic, can be stayed;
And for an hour I have walked and prayed
Because of the great gloom that is in my mind.

I have walked and prayed for this young child an hour
And heard the sea-wind scream upon the tower,
And under the arches of the bridge, and scream
In the elms above the flooded stream;
Imagining in excited reverie
That the future years had come,
Dancing to a frenzied drum,
Out of the murderous innocence of the sea.

May she be granted beauty and yet not
Beauty to make a stranger's eye distraught,
Or hers before a looking-glass, for such,
Being made beautiful overmuch,
Consider beauty a sufficient end,
Loss natural kindness and maybe
The heart-revealing intimacy
That chooses right, and never find a friend.

Helen being chosen found life flat and dull
And later had much trouble from a fool,
While that great Queen, that rose out of the spray,
Being fatherless could have her way
Yet chose a bandy-leggèd smith for man.
It's certain that fine women eat
A crazy salad with their meat
Whereby the Horn of Plenty is undone.

In courtesy I'd have her chiefly learned;
Hearts are not had as a gift but hearts are earned
By those that are not entirely beautiful;
Yet many, that have played the fool
For beauty's very self, has charm made wise,
And many a poor man that has roved,
Loved and thought himself beloved,
From a glad kindness cannot take his eyes.

May she become a flourishing hidden tree
That all her thoughts may like the linnet be,
And have no business but dispensing round
Their magnanimities of sound,
Nor but in merriment begin a chase,
Nor but in merriment a quarrel.
O may she live like some green laurel
Rooted in one dear perpetual place.

My mind, because the minds that I have loved,
The sort of beauty that I have approved,
Prosper but little, has dried up of late,
Yet knows that to be choked with hate
May well be of all evil chances chief.
If there's no hatred in a mind
Assault and battery of the wind
Can never tear the linnet from the leaf.

An intellectual hatred is the worst,
So let her think opinions are accursed.
Have I not seen the loveliest woman born
Out of the mouth of Plenty's horn,
Because of her opinionated mind
Barter that horn and every good
By quiet natures understood
For an old bellows full of angry wind?

Considering that, all hatred driven hence,
The soul recovers radical innocence
And learns at last that it is self-delighting,
Self-appeasing, self-affrighting,

And that its own sweet will is Heaven's will;
She can, though every face should scowl
And every windy quarter howl
Or every bellows burst, be happy still.

And may her bridegroom bring her to a house
Where all's accustomed, ceremonious;
For arrogance and hatred are the wares
Peddled in the thoroughfares.
How but in custom and in ceremony
Are innocence and beauty born?
Ceremony's a name for the rich horn,
And custom for the spreading laurel tree.

June 1919

UNDER SATURN

November 1919   November 1920

Do not because this day I have grown saturnine
Imagine that lost love, inseparable from my thought
Because I have no other youth, can make me pine;
For how should I forget the wisdom that you brought,
The comfort that you made? Although my wits have gone
On a fantastic ride, my horse's flanks are spurred
By childish memories of an old cross Pollexfen,
And of a Middleton, whose name you never heard,
And of a red-haired Yeats whose looks, although he died
Before my time, seem like a vivid memory.
You heard that labouring man who had served my people. He said
Upon the open road, near to the Sligo quay –
No, no, not said, but cried it out – 'You have come again,
And surely after twenty years it was time to come.'
I am thinking of a child's vow sworn in vain
Never to leave that valley his fathers called their home.

November 1919

FATHER AND CHILD

During 1926 and 1927 WS 1929

She hears me strike the board and say
That she is under ban
Of all good men and women,
Being mentioned with a man
That has the worst of all bad names;
And thereupon replies
That his hair is beautiful,
Cold as the March wind his eyes.

ARE YOU CONTENT?

April 1938

I call on those that call me son,
Grandson, or great-grandson,
On uncles, aunts, great-uncles or great-aunts
To judge what I have done.
Have I, that put it into words,
Spoilt what old loins have sent?
Eyes spiritualised by death can judge,
I cannot, but I am not content.

He that in Sligo at Drumcliff
Set up the old stone Cross,
That red-headed rector in County Down
A good man on a horse,
Sandymount Corbets, that notable man
Old William Pollexfen,
The smuggler Middleton, Butlers far back,
Half legendary men.

Infirm and aged I might stay
In some good company,
I who have always hated work,
Smiling at the sea,
Or demonstrate in my own life
What Robert Browning meant
By an old hunter talking with Gods;
But I am not content.

SECTION 7

MOODS AND MEDITATIONS

THE COLD HEAVEN

GH 1912

Suddenly I saw the cold and rook-delighting heaven
That seemed as though ice burned and was but the more ice,
And thereupon imagination and heart were driven
So wild that every casual thought of that and this
Vanished, and left but memories, that should be out of season
With the hot blood of youth, of love crossed long ago;
And I took all the blame out of all sense and reason,
Until I cried and trembled and rocked to and fro,
Riddled with light. Ah! when the ghost begins to quicken,
Confusion of the death-bed over, is it sent
Out naked on the roads, as the books say, and stricken
By the injustice of the skies for punishment?

THE DAWN

20 June 1914   February 1916

I would be ignorant as the dawn
That has looked down
On that old queen measuring a town
With the pin of a brooch,
Or on the withered men that saw
From their pedantic Babylon
The careless planets in their courses,
The stars fade out where the moon comes,
And took their tablets and did sums;
I would be ignorant as the dawn
That merely stood, rocking the glittering coach
Above the cloudy shoulders of the horses;
I would be – for no knowledge is worth a straw –
Ignorant and wanton as the dawn.

A MEDITATION IN TIME OF WAR

9 November 1914   November 1920

For one throb of the artery,
While on that old grey stone I sat
Under the old wind-broken tree,
I knew that One is animate,
Mankind inanimate phantasy.

DEMON AND BEAST

23 November 1918   November 1920

For certain minutes at the least
That crafty demon and that loud beast
That plague me day and night
Ran out of my sight;
Though I had long perned in the gyre,
Between my hatred and desire,
I saw my freedom won
And all laugh in the sun.

The glittering eyes in a death's head
Of old Luke Wadding's portrait said
Welcome, and the Ormondes all
Nodded upon the wall,
And even Strafford smiled as though
It made him happier to know
I understood his plan.
Now that the loud beast ran
There was no portrait in the Gallery
But beckoned to sweet company,
For all men's thoughts grew clear
Being dear as mine are clear.

But soon a tear-drop started up,
For aimless joy had made me stop
Beside the little lake
To watch a white gull take
A bit of bread thrown up into the air;
Now gyring down and perning there
He splashed where an absurd
Portly green-pated bird
Shook off the water from his back;
Being no more demoniac
A stupid happy creature
Could rouse my whole nature.

Yet I am certain as can be
That every natural victory
Belongs to beast or demon,
That never yet had freeman
Right mastery of natural things,
And that mere growing old, that brings
Chilled blood, this sweetness brought;
Yet have no dearer thought
Than that I may find out a way
To make it linger half a day.

O what a sweetness strayed
Through barren Thebaid,
Or by the Mareotic sea
When the exultant Anthony
And twice a thousand more
Starved upon the shore
And withered to a bag of bones!
What had the Caesars but their thrones?

THE WHEEL

13 September 1921   *SPF 1922*

Through winter-time we call on spring,
And through the spring on summer call,
And when abounding hedges ring
Declare that winter's best of all;
And after that there's nothing good
Because the spring-time has not come —
Nor know that what disturbs our blood
Is but its longing for the tomb.

MEDITATIONS IN TIME OF CIVIL WAR

I *1921;* II–VII *1922*   January 1923

I. *Ancestral Houses*

Surely among a rich man's flowering lawns,
Amid the rustle of his planted hills,
Life overflows without ambitious pains;
And rains down life until the basin spills,
And mounts more dizzy high the more it rains
As though to choose whatever shape it wills
And never stoop to a mechanical
Or servile shape, at others' beck and call.

Mere dreams, mere dreams! Yet Homer had not sung
Had he not found it certain beyond dreams
That out of life's own self-delight had sprung
The abounding glittering jet; though now it seems
As if some marvellous empty sea-shell flung
Out of the obscure dark of the rich streams,
And not a fountain, were the symbol which
Shadows the inherited glory of the rich.

Some violent bitter man, some powerful man
Called architect and artist in, that they,
Bitter and violent men, might rear in stone
The sweetness that all longed for night and day,
The gentleness none there had ever known;
But when the master's buried mice can play,
And maybe the great-grandson of that house,
For all its bronze and marble, 's but a mouse.

O what if gardens where the peacock strays
With delicate feet upon old terraces,
Or else all Juno from an urn displays
Before the indifferent garden deities;
O what if levelled lawns and gravelled ways
Where slippered Contemplation finds his ease
And Childhood a delight for every sense,
But take our greatness with our violence?

What if the glory of escutcheoned doors,
And buildings that a haughtier age designed,
The pacing to and fro on polished floors
Amid great chambers and long galleries, lined
With famous portraits of our ancestors;
What if those things the greatest of mankind
Consider most to magnify, or to bless,
But take our greatness with our bitterness?

II. *My House*

An ancient bridge, and a more ancient tower,
A farmhouse that is sheltered by its wall,
An acre of stony ground,
Where the symbolic rose can break in flower,
Old ragged elms, old thorns innumerable,
The sound of the rain or sound
Of every wind that blows;
The stilted water-hen
Crossing stream again
Scared by the splashing of a dozen cows;
A winding stair, a chamber arched with stone,
A grey stone fireplace with an open hearth,

A candle and written page.
Il Penseroso's Platonist toiled on
In some like chamber, shadowing forth
How the daemonic rage
Imagined everything.
Benighted travellers
From markets and from fairs
Have seen his midnight candle glimmering.

Two men have founded here. A man-at-arms
Gathered a score of horse and spent his days
In this tumultuous spot,
Where through long wars and sudden night alarms
His dwindling score and he seemed castaways
Forgetting and forgot;
And I, that after me
My bodily heirs may find,
To exalt a lonely mind,
Befitting emblems of adversity.

III. *My Table*

Two heavy trestles, and a board
Where Sato's gift, a changeless sword,
By pen and paper lies,
That it may moralise
My days out of their aimlessness.
A bit of an embroidered dress
Covers its wooden sheath.
Chaucer had not drawn breath
When it was forged. In Sato's house,
Curved like new moon, moon-luminous
It lay five hundred years.
Yet if no change appears
No moon; only an aching heart
Conceives a changeless work of art.
Our learned men have urged
That when and where 'twas forged
A marvellous accomplishment,
In painting or in pottery, went

From father unto son
And through the centuries ran
And seemed unchanging like the sword.
Soul's beauty being most adored,
Men and their business took
The soul's unchanging look;
For the most rich inheritor,
Knowing that none could pass Heaven's door
That loved inferior art,
Had such an aching heart
That he, although a country's talk
For silken clothes and stately walk,
Had waking wits; it seemed
Juno's peacock screamed.

IV. *My Descendants*

Having inherited a vigorous mind
From my old fathers, I must nourish dreams
And leave a woman and a man behind
As vigorous of mind, and yet it seems
Life scarce can cast a fragrance on the wind,
Scarce spread a glory to the morning beams,
But the torn petals strew the garden plot;
And there's but common greenness after that.

And what if my descendants lose the flower
Through natural declension of the soul,
Through too much business with the passing hour,
Through too much play, or marriage with a fool?
May this laborious stair and this stark tower
Become a roofless ruin that the owl
May build in the cracked masonry and cry
Her desolation to the desolate sky.

The Primum Mobile that fashioned us
Has made the very owls in circles move;
And I, that count myself most prosperous,
Seeing that love and friendship are enough,
For an old neighbour's friendship chose the house
And decked and altered it for a girl's love,
And know whatever flourish and decline
These stones remain their monument and mine.

v. *The Road at My Door*

An affable Irregular,
A heavily-built Falstaffian man,
Comes cracking jokes of civil war
As though to die by gunshot were
The finest play under the sun.

A brown Lieutenant and his men,
Half dressed in national uniform,
Stand at my door, and I complain
Of the foul weather, hail and rain,
A pear tree broken by the storm.

I count those feathered balls of soot
The moor-hen guides upon the stream,
To silence the envy in my thought;
And turn towards my chamber, caught
In the cold snows of a dream.

vi. *The Stare's Nest by My Window*

The bees build in the crevices
Of loosening masonry, and there
The mother birds bring grubs and flies.
My wall is loosening; honey-bees,
Come build in the empty house of the stare.

We are closed in, and the key is turned
On our uncertainty; somewhere
A man is killed, or a house burned,
Yet no clear fact to be discerned:
Come build in the empty house of the stare.

A barricade of stone or of wood;
Some fourteen days of civil war;
Last night they trundled down the road
That dead young soldier in his blood:
Come build in the empty house of the stare.

We had fed the heart on fantasies,
The heart's grown brutal from the fare;
More substance in our enmities
Than in our love; O honey-bees,
Come build in the empty house of the stare.

VII. *I see Phantoms of Hatred and of the Heart's Fullness and of the Coming Emptiness*

I climb to the tower-top and lean upon broken stone,
A mist that is like blown snow is sweeping over all,
Valley, river, and elms, under the light of a moon
That seems unlike itself, that seems unchangeable,
A glittering sword out of the east. A puff of wind
And those white glimmering fragments of the mist sweep by.
Frenzies bewilder, reveries perturb the mind;
Monstrous familiar images swim to the mind's eye.

'Vengeance upon the murderers', the cry goes up,
'Vengeance for Jacques Molay.' In cloud-pale rags, or in lace,
The rage-driven, rage-tormented, and rage-hungry troop,
Trooper belabouring trooper, biting at arm or at face,
Plunges towards nothing, arms and fingers spreading wide
For the embrace of nothing; and I, my wits astray
Because of all that senseless tumult, all but cried
For vengeance on the murderers of Jacques Molay.

Their legs long, delicate and slender, aquamarine their eyes,
Magical unicorns bear ladies on their backs.
The ladies close their musing eyes. No prophecies,
Remembered out of Babylonian almanacs,
Have closed the ladies' eyes, their minds are but a pool
Where even longing drowns under its own excess;
Nothing but stillness can remain when hearts are full
Of their own sweetness, bodies of their loveliness.

The cloud-pale unicorns, the eyes of aquamarine,
The quivering half-closed eyelids, the rags of cloud or of lace,
Or eyes that rage has brightened, arms it has made lean,
Give place to an indifferent multitude, give place
To brazen hawks. Nor self-delighting reverie,
Nor hate of what's to come, nor pity for what's gone,
Nothing but grip of claw, and the eye's complacency,
The innumerable clanging wings that have put out the moon.

I turn away and shut the door, and on the stair
Wonder how many times I could have proved my worth
In something that all others understand or share;
But O! ambitious heart, had such a proof drawn forth
A company of friends, a conscience set at ease,
It had but made us pine the more. The abstract joy,
The half-read wisdom of daemonic images,
Suffice the ageing man as once the growing boy.

    1923

AMONG SCHOOL CHILDREN

14 June 1926   August 1927

I

I walk through the long schoolroom questioning;
A kind old nun in a white hood replies;
The children learn to cipher and to sing,
To study reading-books and history,
To cut and sew, be neat in everything
In the best modern way – the children's eyes
In momentary wonder stare upon
A sixty-year-old smiling public man.

II

I dream of a Ledaean body, bent
Above a sinking fire, a tale that she
Told of a harsh reproof, or trivial event
That changed some childish day to tragedy —
Told, and it seemed that our two natures blent
Into a sphere from youthful sympathy,
Or else, to alter Plato's parable,
Into the yolk and white of the one shell.

III

And thinking of that fit of grief or rage
I look upon one child or t'other there
And wonder if she stood so at that age —
For even daughters of the swan can share
Something of every paddler's heritage —
And had that colour upon cheek or hair,
And thereupon my heart is driven wild:
She stands before me as a living child.

IV

Her present image floats into the mind —
Did Quattrocento finger fashion it
Hollow of cheek as though it drank the wind
And took a mess of shadows for its meat?
And I though never of Ledaean kind
Had pretty plumage once — enough of that,
Better to smile on all that smile, and show
There is a comfortable kind of old scarecrow.

V

What youthful mother, a shape upon her lap
Honey of generation had betrayed,
And that must sleep, shriek, struggle to escape
As recollection or the drug decide,
Would think her son, did she but see that shape
With sixty or more winters on its head,
A compensation for the pang of his birth,
Or the uncertainty of his setting forth?

VI

Plato thought nature but a spume that plays
Upon a ghostly paradigm of things;
Solider Aristotle played the taws
Upon the bottom of a king of kings;
World-famous golden-thighed Pythagoras
Fingered upon a fiddle-stick or strings
What a star sang and careless Muses heard:
Old clothes upon old sticks to scare a bird.

VII

Both nuns and mothers worship images,
But those the candles light are not as those
That animate a mother's reveries,
But keep a marble or a bronze repose.
And yet they too break hearts – O Presences
That passion, piety or affection knows,
And that all heavenly glory symbolise –
O self-born mockers of man's enterprise;

VIII

Labour is blossoming or dancing where
The body is not bruised to pleasure soul,
Nor beauty born out of its own despair,
Nor blear-eyed wisdom out of midnight oil.
O chestnut tree, great rooted blossomer,
Are you the leaf, the blossom or the bole?
O body swayed to music, O brightening glance,
How can we know the dancer from the dance?

A DIALOGUE OF SELF AND SOUL

Between July and September 1927   *WS* 1929

I

My Soul. I summon to the winding ancient stair;
            Set all your mind upon the steep ascent,
            Upon the broken, crumbling battlement,
            Upon the breathless starlit air,
            Upon the star that marks the hidden pole;
            Fix every wandering thought upon
            That quarter where all thought is done:
            Who can distinguish darkness from the soul?

My Self. The consecrated blade upon my knees
            Is Sato's ancient blade, still as it was,
            Still razor-keen, still like a looking-glass
            Unspotted by the centuries;
            That flowering, silken, old embroidery, torn
            From some court-lady's dress and round
            The wooden scabbard bound and wound,
            Can, tattered, still protect, faded adorn.

My Soul. Why should the imagination of a man
            Long past his prime remember things that are
            Emblematical of love and war?
            Think of ancestral night that can,
            If but imagination scorn the earth
            And intellect its wandering
            To this and that and t'other thing,
            Deliver from the crime of death and birth.

My Self. Montashigi, third of his family, fashioned it
            Five hundred years ago, about it lie
            Flowers from I know not what embroidery —
            Heart's purple — and all these I set
            For emblems of the day against the tower
            Emblematical of the night,
            And claim as by a soldier's right
            A charter to commit the crime once more.

My Soul.   Such fullness in that quarter overflows
And falls into the basin of the mind
That man is stricken deaf and dumb and blind,
For intellect no longer knows
Is from the *Ought*, or *Knower* from the *Known* —
That is to say, ascends to Heaven;
Only the dead can be forgiven;
But when I think of that my tongue's a stone.

My Self.   A living man is blind and drinks his drop.
What matter if the ditches are impure?
What matter if I live it all once more?
Endure that toil of growing up;
The ignominy of boyhood; the distress
Of boyhood changing into man;
The unfinished man and his pain
Brought face to face with his own clumsiness;

The finished man among his enemies? —
How in the name of Heaven can he escape
That defiling and disfigured shape
The mirror of malicious eyes
Casts upon his eyes until at last
He thinks that shape must be his shape?
And what's the good of an escape
If honour find him in the wintry blast?

I am content to live it all again
And yet again, if it be life to pitch
Into the frog-spawn of a blind man's ditch,
A blind man battering blind men;
Or into that most fecund ditch of all,
The folly that man does
Or must suffer, if he woos
A proud woman not kindred of his soul.

I am content to follow to its source
Every event in action or in thought;
Measure the lot; forgive myself the lot!
When such as I cast out remorse
So great a sweetness flows into the breast
We must laugh and we must sing,
We are blest by everything,
Everything we look upon is blest.

VACILLATION

1931 and 1932 (I, *December 1931;*
IV *November 1931;* VI *between January
and 5 March 1932;* VII *on 3 and 4
January 1932; and* VIII *on 3 January 1932)*   *WMP* 1932

I

Between extremities
Man runs his course;
A brand, or flaming breath,
Comes to destroy
All those antinomies
Of day and night;
The body calls it death,
The heart remorse.
But if these be right
What is joy?

II

A tree there is that from its topmost bough
Is half all glittering flame and half all green
Abounding foliage moistened with the dew;
And half is half and yet is all the scene;
And half and half consume what they renew,
And he that Attis' image hangs between
That staring fury and the blind lush leaf
May know not what he knows, but knows not grief.

III

Get all the gold and silver that you can,
Satisfy ambition, or animate
The trivial days and ram them with the sun,
And yet upon these maxims meditate:
All women dote upon an idle man
Although their children need a rich estate;
No man has ever lived that had enough
Of children's gratitude or woman's love.

No longer in Lethean foliage caught
Begin the preparation for your death
And from the fortieth winter by that thought
Test every work of intellect or faith
And everything that your own hands have wrought,
And call those works extravagance of breath
That are not suited for such men as come
Proud, open-eyed and laughing to the tomb.

IV

My fiftieth year had come and gone,
I sat, a solitary man,
In a crowded London shop,
An open book and empty cup
On the marble table-top.

While on the shop and street I gazed
My body of a sudden blazed;
And twenty minutes more or less
It seemed, so great my happiness,
That I was blessèd and could bless.

V

Although the summer sunlight gild
Cloudy leafage of the sky,
Or wintry moonlight sink the field
In storm-scattered intricacy,
I cannot look thereon,
Responsibility so weighs me down.

Things said or done long years ago,
Or things I did not do or say
But thought that I might say or do,
Weigh me down, and not a day
But something is recalled,
My conscience or my vanity appalled.

VI

A rivery field spread out below,
An odour of the new-mown hay
In his nostrils, the great lord of Chou
Cried, casting off the mountain snow,
'Let all things pass away'.

Wheels by milk-white asses drawn
Where Babylon or Nineveh
Rose; some conqueror drew rein
And cried to battle-weary men,
'Let all things pass away.'

From man's blood-sodden heart are sprung
Those branches of the night and day
Where the gaudy moon is hung.
What's the meaning of all song?
'Let all things pass away.'

VII

The Soul.   Seek out reality, leave things that seem.

The Heart.   What, be a singer born and lack a theme?

The Soul.   Isaiah's coal, what more can man desire?

The Heart.   Struck dumb in the simplicity of fire!

The Soul.   Look on that fire, salvation walks within.

The Heart.   What theme had Homer but original sin?

VIII

Must we part, Von Hügel, though much alike, for we
Accept the miracles of the saints and honour sanctity?
The body of Saint Teresa lies undecayed in tomb,
Bathed in miraculous oil, sweet odours from it come,
Healing from its lettered slab. Those self-same hands perchance
Eternalised the body of a modern saint that once
Had scooped out Pharaoh's mummy. I – though heart might find relief
Did I become a Christian man and choose for my belief
What seems most welcome in the tomb – play a predestined part.
Homer is my example and his unchristened heart.
The lion and the honeycomb, what has Scripture said?
So get you gone, Von Hügel, though with blessings on your head.

1932

CRAZY JANE ON GOD

18 July 1931   *WPM* 1932

That lover of a night
Came when he would,
Went in the dawning light
Whether I would or no;
Men come, men go:
All things remain in God.

Banners choke the sky;
Men-at-arms tread;
Armoured horses neigh
Where the great battle was
In the narrow pass:
All things remain in God.

Before their eyes a house
That from childhood stood
Uninhabited, ruinous,
Suddenly lit up
From door to top:
All things remain in God.

I had wild Jack for a lover;
Though like a road
That men pass over
My body makes no moan
But sings on:
All things remain in God.

OLD TOM AGAIN

October 1931   *WMP* 1932

Things out of perfection sail
And all their swelling canvas wear,
Nor shall the self-begotten fail
Though fantastic men suppose
Building-yard and stormy shore,
Winding-sheet and swaddling-clothes.

STREAM AND SUN AT GLENDALOUGH

23 June 1932   *WMP* 1932

Through intricate motions ran
Stream and gliding sun
And all my heart seemed gay:
Some stupid thing that I had done
Made my attention stray.

Repentance keeps my heart impure;
But what am I that dare
Fancy that I can
Better conduct myself or have more
Sense than a common man?

What motion of the sun or stream
Or eyelid shot the gleam
That pierced my body through?
What made me live like these that seem
Self-born, born anew?

June 1932

[THE BRAVEST FROM THE GODS BUT ASK]

W & B 1934

The bravest from the gods but ask:
A house, a sword, a ship, a mask.

A BRONZE HEAD

(?) 1937–1938   March 1939

Here at right of entrance this bronze head,
Human, super-human, a bird's round eye,
Everything else withered and mummy-dead.
What great tomb-haunter sweeps the distant sky;
(Something may linger there though all else die;)
And finds there nothing to make its terror less
Hysterica-passio of its own emptiness?

No dark tomb-haunter once; her form all full
As though with magnanimity of light
Yet a most gentle woman's; who can tell
Which of her forms has shown her substance right
Or may be substance can be composite,
Profound McTaggart thought so, and in a breath
A mouthful hold the extreme of life and death.

But even at the starting post, all sleek and new,
I saw the wildness in her and I thought
A vision of terror that it must live through
Had shattered her soul. Propinquity had brought
Imagination to that pitch where it casts out
All that is not itself, I had grown wild
And wandered murmuring everywhere 'my child, my child.'

Or else I thought her supernatural;
As though a sterner eye looked through her eye
On this foul world in its decline and fall,
On gangling stocks grown great, great stocks run dry,
Ancestral pearls all pitched into a sty,
Heroic reverie mocked by clown and knave
And wondered what was left for massacre to save.

SECTION 8

IRISH NARRATIVE POEMS

THE WANDERINGS OF OISIN

First version completed Autumn 1887   *WO* 1889

BOOK I

S. Patrick. You who are bent, and bald, and blind,
    With a heavy heart and a wandering mind,
    Have known three centuries, poets sing,
    Of dalliance with a demon thing.

Oisin. Sad to remember, sick with years,
    The swift innumerable spears,
    The horsemen with their floating hair,
    And bowls of barley, honey, and wine,
    Those merry couples dancing in tune,
    And the white body that lay by mine;
    But the tale, though words be lighter than air,
    Must live to be old like the wandering moon.

    Caoilte, and Conan, and Finn were there,
    When we followed a deer with our baying hounds,
    With Bran, Sceolan, and Lomair,
    And passing the Firbolgs' burial-mounds,
    Came to the cairn-heaped grassy hill
    Where passionate Maeve is stony-still;
    And found on the dove-grey edge of the sea
    A pearl-pale, high-born lady, who rode
    On a horse with bridle of findrinny;
    And like a sunset were her lips,
    A stormy sunset on doomed ships;
    A citron colour gloomed in her hair,
    But down to her feet white vesture flowed,
    And with the glimmering crimson glowed
    Of many a figured embroidery;
    And it was bound with a pearl-pale shell
    That wavered like the summer streams,
    As her soft bosom rose and fell.

S. Patrick. You are still wrecked among heathen dreams.

Oisin. 'Why do you wind no horn?' she said.
  'And every hero drop his head?
  The hornless deer is not more sad
  That many a peaceful moment had,
  More sleek than any granary mouse,
  In his own leafy forest house
  Among the waving fields of fern:
  The hunting of heroes should be glad.'

  'O pleasant woman,' answered Finn,
  'We think on Oscar's pencilled urn,
  And on the heroes lying slain
  On Gabhra's raven-covered plain;
  But where are your noble kith and kin,
  And from what country do you ride?'

  'My father and my mother are
  Aengus and Edain, my own name
  Niamh, and my country far
  Beyond the tumbling of this tide.'

  'What dream came with you that you came
  Through bitter tide on foam-wet feet?
  Did your companion wander away
  From where the birds of Aengus wing?'

  Thereon did she look haughty and sweet:
  'I have not yet, war-weary king,
  Been spoken of with any man;
  Yet now I choose, for these four feet
  Ran through the foam and ran to this
  That I might have your son to kiss.'

  'Were there no better than my son
  That you through all that foam should run?'

  'I loved no man, though kings besought,
  Until the Danaan poets brought
  Rhyme that rhymed upon Oisin's name,
  And now I am dizzy with the thought
  Of all that wisdom and the fame

Of battles broken by his hands,
Of stories builded by his words
That are like coloured Asian birds
At evening in their rainless lands.'

O Patrick, by your brazen bell,
There was no limb of mine but fell
Into a desperate gulph of love!
'You only will I wed,' I cried,
'And I will make a thousand songs,
And set your name all names above,
And captives bound with leathern thongs
Shall kneel and praise you, one by one,
At evening in my western dun.'

'O Oisin, mount by me and ride
To shores by the wash of the tremulous tide,
Where men have heaped no burial-mounds,
And the days pass by like a wayward tune,
Where broken faith has never been known,
And the blushes of first love never have flown;
And there I will give you a hundred hounds;
No mightier creatures bay at the moon;
And a hundred robes of murmuring silk,
And a hundred calves and a hundred sheep
Whose long wool whiter than sea-froth flows,
And a hundred spears and a hundred bows,
And oil and wine and honey and milk,
And always never-anxious sleep;
While a hundred youths, mighty of limb,
But knowing nor tumult nor hate nor strife,
And a hundred ladies, merry as birds,
Who when they dance to a fitful measure
Have a speed like the speed of the salmon herds,
Shall follow your horn and obey your whim,
And you shall know the Danaan leisure;
And Niamh be with you for a wife.'
Then she sighed gently, 'It grows late.
Music and love and sleep await,
Where I would be when the white moon climbs,
The red sun falls and the world grows dim.'

And then I mounted and she bound me
With her triumphing arms around me,
And whispering to herself enwound me;
But when the horse had felt my weight,
He shook himself and neighed three times:
Caoilte, Conan, and Finn came near,
And wept, and raised their lamenting hands,
And bid me stay, with many a tear;
But we rode out from the human lands.

In what far kingdom do you go,
Ah, Fenians, with the shield and bow?
Or are you phantoms white as snow,
Whose lips had life's most prosperous glow?
O you, with whom in sloping valleys,
Or down the dewy forest alleys,
I chased at morn the flying deer,
With whom I hurled the hurrying spear,
And heard the foemen's bucklers rattle,
And broke the heaving ranks of battle!
And Bran, Sceolan, and Lomair,
Where are you with your long rough hair?
You go not where the red deer feeds,
Nor tear the foemen from their steeds.

S. Patrick. Boast not, nor mourn with drooping head
    Companions long acurst and dead,
    And hounds for centuries dust and air.

Oisin. We galloped over the glossy sea:
    I know not if days passed or hours,
    And Niamh sang continually
    Danaan songs, and their dewy showers
    Of pensive laughter, unhuman sound,
    Lulled weariness, and softly round
    My human sorrow her white arms wound.
    We galloped; now a hornless deer
    Passed by us, chased by a phantom hound
    All pearly white, save one red ear;

And now a lady rode like the wind
With an apple of gold in her tossing hand;
And a beautiful young man followed behind
With quenchless gaze and fluttering hair.

'Were those two born in the Danaan land,
Or have they breathed the mortal air?'

'Vex them no longer,' Niamh said,
And sighing bowed her gentle head,
And sighing laid the pearly tip
Of one long finger on my lip.

But now the moon like a white rose shone
In the pale west, and the sun's rim sank,
And clouds arrayed their rank on rank
About his fading crimson ball:
The floor of Almhuin's hosting hall
Was not more level than the sea,
As, full of loving fantasy,
And with low murmurs, we rode on,
Where many a trumpet-twisted shell
That in immortal silence sleeps
Dreaming of her own melting hues,
Her golds, her ambers, and her blues,
Pierced with soft light the shallowing deeps.
But now a wandering land breeze came
And a far sound of feathery quires;
It seemed to blow from the dying flame,
They seemed to sing in the smouldering fires.
The horse towards the music raced,
Neighing along the lifeless waste;
Like sooty fingers, many a tree
Rose ever out of the warm sea;
And they were trembling ceaselessly,
As though they all were beating time,
Upon the centre of the sun,
To that low laughing woodland rhyme.
And, now our wandering hours were done,
We cantered to the shore, and knew

The reason of the trembling trees:
Round every branch the song-birds flew,
Or clung thereon like swarming bees;
While round the shore a million stood
Like drops of frozen rainbow light,
And pondered in a soft vain mood
Upon their shadows in the tide,
And told the purple deeps their pride,
And murmured snatches of delight;
And on the shores were many boats
With bending sterns and bending bows,
And carven figures on their prows
Of bitterns, and fish-eating stoats,
And swans with their exultant throats:
And where the wood and waters meet
We tied the horse in a leafy clump,
And Niamh blew three merry notes
Out of a little silver trump;
And then an answering whispering flew
Over the bare and woody land,
A whisper of impetuous feet,
And even nearer, nearer grew;
And from the woods rushed out a band
Of men and ladies, hand in hand,
And singing, singing all together;
Their brows were white as fragrant milk,
Their cloaks made out of yellow silk,
And trimmed with many a crimson feather;
And when they saw the cloak I wore
Was dim with mire of a mortal shore,
They fingered it and gazed on me
And laughed like murmurs of the sea;
But Niamh with a swift distress
Bid them away and hold their peace;
And when they heard her voice they ran
And knelt there, every girl and man,
And kissed, as they would never cease,
Her pearl-pale hand and the hem of her dress.
She bade them bring us to the hall

Where Aengus dreams, from sun to sun,
A Druid dream of the end of days
When the stars are to wane and the world be done.

They led us by long and shadowy ways
Where drops of dew in myriads fall,
And tangled creepers every hour
Blossom in some new crimson flower,
And once a sudden laughter sprang
From all their lips, and once they sang
Together, while the dark woods rang,
And made in all their distant parts,
With boom of bees in honey-marts,
A rumour of delighted hearts.
And once a lady by my side
Gave me a harp, and bid me sing,
And touch the laughing silver string;
But when I sang of human joy
A sorrow wrapped each merry face,
And, Patrick! by your beard, they wept,
Until one came, a tearful boy;
'A sadder creature never stept
Than this strange human bard,' he cried;
And caught the silver harp away,
And, weeping over the white strings, hurled
It down in a leaf-hid, hollow place
That kept dim waters from the sky;
And each one said, with a long, long sigh,
'O saddest harp in all the world,
Sleep there till the moon and the stars die!'

And now, still sad, we came to where
A beautiful young man dreamed within
A house of wattles, clay, and skin;
One hand upheld his beardless chin,
And one a sceptre flashing out
Wild flames of red and gold and blue,
Like to a merry wandering rout

Of dancers leaping in the air;
And men and ladies knelt them there
And showed their eyes with teardrops dim,
And with low murmurs prayed to him,
And kissed the sceptre with red lips,
And touched it with their finger-tips.

He held that flashing sceptre up.
'Joy drowns the twilight in the dew,
And fills with stars night's purple cup,
And wakes the sluggard seeds of corn,
And stirs the young kid's budding horn,
And makes the infant ferns unwrap,
And for the peewit paints his cap,
And rolls along the unwieldy sun,
And makes the little planets run:
And if joy were not on the earth,
There were an end of change and birth,
And Earth and Heaven and Hell would die,
And in some gloomy barrow lie
Folded like a frozen fly;
Then mock at Death and Time with glances
And wavering arms and wandering dances.

'Men's hearts of old were drops of flame
That from the saffron morning came,
Or drops of silver joy that fell
Out of the moon's pale twisted shell;
But now hearts cry that hearts are slaves,
And toss and turn in narrow caves;
But here there is nor law nor rule,
Nor have hands held a weary tool;
And here there is nor Change nor Death,
But only kind and merry breath,
For joy is God and God is joy.'
With one long glance for girl and boy
And the pale blossom of the moon,
He fell into a Druid swoon.

And in a wild and sudden dance
We mocked at Time and Fate and Chance
And swept out of the wattled hall
And came to where the dewdrops fall
Among the foamdrops of the sea,
And there we hushed the revelry;
And, gathering on our brows a frown,
Bent all our swaying bodies down,
And to the waves that glimmer by
That sloping green De Danaan sod
Sang, 'God is joy and joy is God,
And things that have grown sad are wicked,
And things that fear the dawn of the morrow
Or the grey wandering osprey Sorrow.'

We danced to where in the winding thicket
The damask roses, bloom on bloom,
Like crimson meteors hang in the gloom,
And bending over them softly said,
Bending over them in the dance,
With a swift and friendly glance
From dewy eyes: 'Upon the dead
Fall the leaves of other roses,
On the dead dim earth encloses:
But never, never on our graves,
Heaped beside the glimmering waves,
Shall fall the leaves of damask roses.
For neither Death nor Change comes near us,
And all listless hours fear us,
And we fear no dawning morrow,
Nor the grey wandering osprey Sorrow.'

The dance wound through the windless woods;
The ever-summered solitudes;
Until the tossing arms grew still
Upon the woody central hill;
And, gathered in a panting band,
We flung on high each waving hand,
And sang unto the starry broods.

In our raised eyes there flashed a glow
Of milky brightness to and fro
As thus our song arose: 'You stars,
Across your wandering ruby cars
Shake the loose reins: you slaves of God,
He rules you with an iron rod,
He holds you with an iron bond,
Each one woven to the other,
Each one woven to his brother
Like bubbles in a frozen pond;
But we in a lonely land abide
Unchainable as the dim tide,
With hearts that know nor law nor rule,
And hands that hold no wearisome tool,
Folded in love that fears no morrow,
Nor the grey wandering osprey Sorrow.'

O Patrick! for a hundred years
I chased upon that woody shore
The deer, the badger, and the boar.
O Patrick! for a hundred years
At evening on the glimmering sands,
Beside the piled-up hunting spears,
These now outworn and withered hands
Wrestled among the island bands.
O Patrick! for a hundred years
We went a-fishing in long boats
With bending sterns and bending bows,
And carven figures on their prows
Of bitterns and fish-eating stoats.
O Patrick! for a hundred years
The gentle Niamh was my wife;
But now two things devour my life;
The things that most of all I hate;
Fasting and prayers.

S. Patrick.   Tell on.

Oisin.   Yes, yes,
For these were ancient Oisin's fate
Loosed long ago from Heaven's gate,
For his last days to lie in wait.

When one day by the tide I stood,
I found in that forgetfulness
Of dreamy foam a staff of wood
From some dead warrior's broken lance:
I turned it in my hands; the stains
Of war were on it, and I wept,
Remembering how the Fenians stept
Along the blood-bedabbled plains,
Equal to good or grievous chance:
Thereon young Niamh softly came
And caught my hands, but spake no word
Save only many times my name,
In murmurs, like a frightened bird.
We passed by woods, and lawns of clover,
And found the horse and bridled him,
For we knew well the old was over.
I heard one say, 'His eyes grow dim
With all the ancient sorrow of men';
And wrapped in dreams rode out again
With hoofs of the pale findrinny
Over the glimmering purple sea.
Under the golden evening light,
The Immortals moved among the fountains
By rivers and the woods' old night;
Some danced like shadows on the mountains,
Some wandered ever hand in hand;
Or sat in dreams on the pale strand,
Each forehead like an obscure star
Bent down above each hookèd knee,
And sang, and with a dreamy gaze
Watched where the sun in a saffron blaze
Was slumbering half in the sea-ways;
And, as they sang, the painted birds
Kept time with their bright wings and feet;
Like drops of honey came their words,
But fainter than a young lamb's bleat.

'An old man stirs the fire to a blaze,
In the house of a child, of a friend, of a brother.
He has over-lingered his welcome; the days,
Grown desolate, whisper and sigh to each other;
He hears the storm in the chimney above,
And bends to the fire and shakes with the cold,
While his heart still dreams of battle and love,
And the cry of the hounds on the hills of old.

'But we are apart in the grassy places,
Where care cannot trouble the least of our days,
Or the softness of youth be gone from our faces,
Or love's first tenderness die in our gaze.
The hare grows old as she plays in the sun
And gazes around her with eyes of brightness;
Before the swift things that she dreamed of were done
She limps along in an aged whiteness;
A storm of birds in the Asian trees
Like tulips in the air a-winging,
And the gentle waves of the summer seas,
That raise their heads and wander singing,
Must murmur at last, "Unjust, unjust";
And "My speed is a weariness," falters the mouse,
And the kingfisher turns to a ball of dust,
And the roof falls in of his tunnelled house.
But the love-dew dims our eyes till the day
When God shall come from the sea with a sigh
And bid the stars drop down from the sky,
And the moon like a pale rose wither away.'

BOOK III

Fled foam underneath us, and round us, a wandering and milky smoke,
High as the saddle-girth, covering away from our glances the tide;
And those that fled, and that followed, from the foam-pale distance broke;
The immortal desire of Immortals we saw in their faces, and sighed.

I mused on the chase with the Fenians, and Bran, Sceolan, Lomair,
And never a song sang Niamh, and over my finger-tips
Came now the sliding of tears and sweeping of mist-cold hair,
And now the warmth of sighs, and after the quiver of lips.

Were we days long or hours long in riding, when, rolled in a grisly peace,
An isle lay level before us, with dripping hazel and oak?
And we stood on a sea's edge we saw not; for whiter than new-washed fleece
Fled foam underneath us, and round us, a wandering and milky smoke.

And we rode on the plains of the sea's edge; the sea's edge barren and grey,
Grey sand on the green of the grasses and over the dripping trees,
Dripping and doubling landward, as though they would hasten away,
Like an army of old men longing for rest from the moan of the seas.

But the trees grew taller and closer, immense in their wrinkling bark;
Dropping; a murmurous dropping; old silence and that one sound;
For no live creatures lived there, no weasels moved in the dark:
Long sighs arose in our spirits, beneath us bubbled the ground.

And the ears of the horse went sinking away in the hollow night,
For, as drift from a sailor slow drowning the gleams of the world and the sun,
Ceased on our hands and our faces, on hazel and oak leaf, the light,
And the stars were blotted above us, and the whole of the world was one.

Till the horse gave a whinny; for, cumbrous with stems of the hazel and oak,
A valley flowed down from his hoofs, and there in the long grass lay,
Under the starlight and shadow, a monstrous slumbering folk,
Their naked and gleaming bodies poured out and heaped in the way.

And by them were arrow and war-axe, arrow and shield and blade;
And dew-blanched horns, in whose hollow a child of three years old
Could sleep on a couch of rushes, and all inwrought and inlaid,
And more comely than man can make them with bronze and silver and gold.

And each of the huge white creatures was huger than fourscore men;
The tops of their ears were feathered, their hands were the claws of birds,
And, shaking the plumes of the grasses and the leaves of the mural glen,
The breathing came from those bodies, long warless, grown whiter than curds.

The wood was so spacious above them, that He who has stars for His flocks
Could fondle the leaves with His fingers, nor go from His dew-cumbered skies;
So long were they sleeping, the owls had builded their nests in their locks,
Filling the fibrous dimness with long generations of eyes.

And over the limbs and the valley the slow owls wandered and came,
Now in a place of star-fire, and now in a shadow-place wide;
And the chief of the huge white creatures, his knees in the soft star-flame,
Lay loose in a place of shadow: we drew the reins by his side.

Golden the nails of his bird-claws, flung loosely along the dim ground;
In one was a branch soft-shining with bells more many than sighs
In midst of an old man's bosom; owls ruffling and pacing around
Sidled their bodies against him, filling the shade with their eyes.

And my gaze was thronged with the sleepers; no, not since the world began,
In realms where the handsome were many, nor in glamours by demons flung,
Have faces alive with such beauty been known to the salt eye of man,
Yet weary with passions that faded when the sevenfold seas were young.

And I gazed on the bell-branch, sleep's forebear, far sung by the Sennachies.
I saw how those slumberers, grown weary, there camping in grasses deep,
Of wars with the wide world and pacing the shores of the wandering seas,
Laid hands on the bell-branch and swayed it, and fed of unhuman sleep.

Snatching the horn of Niamh, I blew a long lingering note.
Came sound from those monstrous sleepers, a sound like the stirring of flies.
He, shaking the fold of his lips, and heaving the pillar of his throat,
Watched me with mournful wonder out of the wells of his eyes.

I cried, 'Come out of the shadow, king of the nails of gold!
And tell of your goodly household and the goodly works of your hands,
That we may muse in the starlight and talk of the battles of old;
Your questioner, Oisin, is worthy, he comes from the Fenian lands.'

Half open his eyes were, and held me, dull with the smoke of their dreams;
His lips moved slowly in answer, no answer out of them came;
Then he swayed in his fingers the bell-branch, slow dropping a sound in faint
     streams
Softer than snow-flakes in April and piercing the marrow like flame.

Wrapt in the wave of that music, with weariness more than of earth,
The moil of my centuries filled me; and gone like a sea-covered stone
Were the memories of the whole of my sorrow and the memories of the whole of
     my mirth,
And a softness came from the starlight and filled me full to the bone.

In the roots of the grasses, the sorrels, I laid my body as low;
And the pearl-pale Niamh lay by me, her brow on the midst of my breast;
And the horse was gone in the distance, and years after years 'gan flow;
Square leaves of the ivy moved over us, binding us down to our rest.

And man of the many white croziers, a century there I forgot
How the fetlocks drip blood in the battle, when the fallen on fallen lie rolled;
How the falconer follows the falcon in the weeds of the heron's plot,
And the name of the demon whose hammer made Conchubar's sword-blade of
     old.

And, man of the many white croziers, a century there I forgot
That the spear-shaft is made out of ashwood, the shield out of osier and hide;
How the hammers spring on the anvil, on the spear-head's burning spot;
How the slow, blue-eyed oxen of Finn low sadly at evening tide.

But in dreams, mild man of the croziers, driving the dust with their throngs,
Moved round me, of seamen or landsmen, all who are winter tales;
Came by me the kings of the Red Branch, with roaring of laughter and songs,
Or moved as they moved once, love-making or piercing the tempest with sails.

Came Blanid, Mac Nessa, tall Fergus who feastward of old time slunk,
Cook Barach, the traitor; and warward, the spittle on his beard never dry,
Dark Balor, as old as a forest, car-borne, his mighty head sunk
Helpless, men lifting the lids of his weary and death-making eye.

And by me, in soft red raiment, the Fenians moved in loud streams,
And Grania, walking and smiling, sewed with her needle of bone.
So lived I and lived not, so wrought I and wrought not, with creatures of
     dreams,
In a long iron sleep, as a fish in the water goes dumb as a stone.

At times our slumber was lightened. When the sun was on silver or gold;
When brushed with the wings of the owls, in the dimness they love going by;
When a glow-worm was green on a grass-leaf, lured from his lair in the mould;
Half wakening, we lifted our eyelids, and gazed on the grass with a sigh.

So watched I when, man of the croziers, at the heel of a century fell,
Weak, in the midst of the meadow, from his miles in the midst of the air,
A starling like them that forgathered 'neath a moon waking white as a shell
When the Fenians made foray at morning with Bran, Sceolan, Lomair.

I awoke: the strange horse without summons out of the distance ran,
Thrusting his nose to my shoulder; he knew in his bosom deep
That once more moved in my bosom the ancient sadness of man,
And that I would leave the Immortals, their dimness, their dews dropping
    sleep.

O, had you seen beautiful Niamh grow white as the waters are white,
Lord of the croziers, you even had lifted your hands and wept:
But, the bird in my fingers, I mounted, remembering alone that delight
Of twilight and slumber were gone, and that hoofs impatiently stept.

I cried, 'O Niamh! O white one! if only a twelve-houred day,
I must gaze on the beard of Finn, and move where the old men and young
In the Fenians' dwellings of wattle lean on the chess-boards and play,
Ah, sweet to me now were even bald Conan's slanderous tongue!

'Like me were some galley forsaken far off in Meridian isle,
Remembering its long-oared companions, sails turning to threadbare rags;
No more to crawl on the seas with long oars mile after mile,
But to be amid shooting of flies and flowering of rushes and flags.'

Their motionless eyeballs of spirits grown mild with mysterious thought,
Watched her those seamless faces from the valley's glimmering girth;
As she murmured, 'O wandering Oisin, the strength of the bell-branch is
    naught,
For there moves alive in your fingers the fluttering sadness of earth.

'Then go through the lands in the saddle and see what the mortals do,
And softly come to your Niamh over the tops of the tide;
But weep for your Niamh, O Oisin, weep; for if only your shoe
Brush lightly as haymouse earth's pebbles, you will come no more to my side.

'O flaming lion of the world, O when will you turn to your rest?'
I saw from a distant saddle; from the earth she made her moan:
'I would die like a small withered leaf in the autumn, for breast unto breast
We shall mingle no more, nor our gazes empty their sweetness lone

'In the isles of the farthest seas where only the spirits come.
Were the winds less soft than the breath of a pigeon who sleeps on her nest,
Nor lost in the star-fires and odours the sound of the sea's vague drum?
O flaming lion of the world, O when will you turn to your rest?'

The wailing grew distant; I rode by the woods of the wrinkling bark,
Where ever is murmurous dropping, old silence and that one sound;
For no live creatures live there, no weasels move in the dark;
In a reverie forgetful of all things, over the bubbling ground.

And I rode by the plains of the sea's edge, where all is barren and grey,
Grey sand on the green of the grasses and over the dripping trees,
Dripping and doubling landward, as though they would hasten away,
Like an army of old men longing for rest from the moan of the seas.

And the winds made the sands of the sea's edge turning and turning go,
As my mind made the names of the Fenians. Far from the hazel and oak,
I rode away on the surges, where, high as the saddle-bow,
Fled foam underneath me, and round me, a wandering and milky smoke.

Long fled the foam-flakes around me, the winds fled out of the vast,
Snatching the bird in secret; nor knew I, embosomed apart,
When they froze the cloth on my body like armour riveted fast,
For Remembrance, lifting her leanness, keened in the gates of my heart.

Till, fattening the winds of the morning, an odour of new-mown hay
Came, and my forehead fell low, and my tears like berries fell down;
Later a sound came, half lost in the sound of a shore far away,
From the great grass-barnacle calling, and later the shore-weeds brown.

If I were as I once was, the strong hoofs crushing the sand and the shells,
Coming out of the sea as the dawn comes, a chaunt of love on my lips,
Not coughing, my head on my knees, and praying, and wroth with the bells,
I would leave no saint's head on his body from Rachlin to Bera of ships.

Making way from the kindling surges, I rode on a bridle-path
Much wondering to see upon all hands, of wattles and woodwork made,
Your bell-mounted churches, and guardless the sacred cairn and the rath,
And a small and a feeble populace stooping with mattock and spade,

Or weeding or ploughing with faces a-shining with much-toil wet;
While in this place and that place, with bodies unglorious, their chieftains
    stood,
Awaiting in patience the straw-death, croziered one, caught in your net:
Went the laughter of scorn from my mouth like the roaring of wind in a wood.

And because I went by them so huge and so speedy with eyes so bright,
Came after the hard gaze of youth, or an old man lifted his head:
And I rode and I rode, and I cried out, 'The Fenians hunt wolves in the night,
So sleep thee by daytime.' A voice cried, 'The Fenians a long time are dead.'

A whitebeard stood hushed on the pathway, the flesh of his face as dried grass,
And in folds round his eyes and his mouth, he sad as a child without milk;
And the dreams of the islands were gone, and I knew how men sorrow and pass,
And their hound, and their horse, and their love, and their eyes that glimmer
    like silk.

And wrapping my face in my hair, I murmured, 'In old age they ceased';
And my tears were larger than berries, and I murmured, 'Where white clouds lie
    spread
On Crevroe or broad Knockfefin, with many of old they feast
On the floors of the gods.' He cried, 'No, the gods a long time are dead.'

And lonely and longing for Niamh, I shivered and turned me about,
The heart in me longing to leap like a grasshopper into her heart;
I turned and rode to the westward, and followed the sea's old shout
Till I saw where Maeve lies sleeping till starlight and midnight part.

And there at the foot of the mountain, two carried a sack full of sand,
They bore it with staggering and sweating, but fell with their burden at length.
Leaning down from the gem-studded saddle, I flung it five yards with my hand,
With a sob for men waxing so weakly, a sob for the Fenians' old strength.

The rest you have heard of, O croziered man; how, when divided the girth,
I fell on the path, and the horse went away like a summer fly;
And my years three hundred fell on me, and I rose, and walked on the earth,
A creeping old man, full of sleep, with the spittle on his beard never dry.

How the men of the sand-sack showed me a church with its belfry in air;
Sorry place, where for swing of the war-axe in my dim eyes the crozier gleams;
What place have Caoilte and Conan, and Bran, Sceolan, Lomair?
Speak, you too are old with your memories, an old man surrounded with
    dreams.

S. Patrick. Where the flesh of the footsole clingeth on the burning stones is their
    place;
    Where the demons whip them with wires on the burning stones of wide
      Hell,
    Watching the blessèd ones move far off, and the smile on God's face,
    Between them a gateway of brass, and the howl of the angels who fell.

Oisin. Put the staff in my hands; for I go to the Fenians, O cleric, to chaunt
    The war-songs that roused them of old; they will rise, making clouds with
      their breath,
    Innumerable, singing, exultant; the clay underneath them shall pant,
    And demons be broken in pieces, and trampled beneath them in death.

    And demons afraid in their darkness; deep horror of eyes and of wings,
    Afraid, their ears on the earth laid, shall listen and rise up and weep;
    Hearing the shaking of shields and the quiver of stretched bowstrings,
    Hearing Hell loud with a murmur, as shouting and mocking we sweep.

    We will tear out the flaming stones, and batter the gateway of brass
    And enter, and none sayeth 'No' when there enters the strongly armed
      guest;
    Make clean as a broom cleans, and march on as oxen move over young
      grass;
    Then feast, making converse of wars, and of old wounds, and turn to our
      rest.

S. Patrick. On the flaming stones, without refuge, the limbs of the Fenians are
    tost;
    None war on the masters of Hell, who could break up the world in their
      rage;
    But kneel and wear out the flags and pray for your soul that is lost
    Through the demon love of its youth and its godless and passionate age.

Oisin. Ah me! to be shaken with coughing and broken with old age and pain,
    Without laughter, a show unto children, alone with remembrance and
      fear;
    All emptied of purple hours as a beggar's cloak in the rain,
    As a hay-cock out on the flood, or wolf sucked under a weir.

It were sad to gaze on the blessèd and no man I loved of old there;
I throw down the chain of small stones! when life in my body has ceased,
I will go to Caoilte, and Conan, and Bran, Sceolan, Lomair,
And dwell in the house of the Fenians, be they in flames or at feast.

THE OLD AGE OF QUEEN MAEVE

April 1903

A certain poet in outlandish clothes
Gathered a crowd in some Byzantine lane,
Talked of his country and its people, sang
To some stringed instrument none there had seen,
A wall behind his back, over his head
A latticed window. His glance went up at times
As though one listened there, and his voice sank
Or let its meaning mix into the strings.

Maeve the great queen was pacing to and fro,
Between the walls covered with beaten bronze,
In her high house at Cruachan[1]; the long hearth,
Flickering with ash and hazel, but half showed
Where the tired horse-boys lay upon the rushes,
Or on the benches underneath the walls,
In comfortable sleep; all living slept
But that great queen, who more than half the night
Had paced from door to fire and fire to door.
Though now in her old age, in her young age
She had been beautiful in that old way
That's all but gone; for the proud heart is gone,

---

[1] Pronounced in modern Gaelic as if spelt 'Crockan'.

And the fool heart of the counting-house fears all
But soft beauty and indolent desire.
She could have called over the rim of the world
Whatever woman's lover had hit her fancy,
And yet had been great-bodied and great-limbed,
Fashioned to be the mother of strong children;
And she'd had lucky eyes and a high heart,
And wisdom that caught fire like the dried flax,
At need, and made her beautiful and fierce,
Sudden and laughing.
                              O unquiet heart,
Why do you praise another, praising her,
As if there were no tale but your own tale
Worth knitting to a measure of sweet sound?
Have I not bid you tell of that great queen
Who has been buried some two thousand years?

When night was at its deepest, a wild goose
Cried from the porter's lodge, and with long clamour
Shook the ale-horns and shields upon their hooks;
But the horse-boys slept on, as though some power
Had filled the house with Druid heaviness;
And wondering who of the many-changing Sidhe
Had come as in the old times to counsel her,
Maeve walked, yet with slow footfall, being old,
To that small chamber by the outer gate.
The porter slept, although he sat upright
With still and stony limbs and open eyes.
Maeve waited, and when that ear-piercing noise
Broke from his parted lips and broke again,
She laid a hand on either of his shoulders,
And shook him wide awake, and bid him say
Who of the wandering many-changing ones
Had troubled his sleep. But all he had to say
Was that, the air being heavy and the dogs
More still than they had been for a good month,
He had fallen asleep, and, though he had dreamed nothing,
He could remember when he had had fine dreams.
It was before the time of the great war
Over the White-Horned Bull and the Brown Bull.
She turned away; he turned again to sleep

That no god troubled now, and, wondering
What matters were afoot among the Sidhe,
Maeve walked through that great hall, and with a sigh
Lifted the curtain of her sleeping-room,
Remembering that she too had seemed divine
To many thousand eyes, and to her own
One that the generations had long waited
That work too difficult for mortal hands
Might be accomplished. Bunching the curtain up
She saw her husband Ailell sleeping there,
And thought of days when he'd had a straight body,
And of that famous Fergus, Nessa's husband,
Who had been the lover of her middle life.

Suddenly Ailell spoke out of his sleep,
And not with his own voice or a man's voice,
But with the burning, live, unshaken voice
Of those that, it may be, can never age.
He said, 'High Queen of Cruachan and Magh Ai,
A king of the Great Plain would speak with you.'
And with glad voice Maeve answered him, 'What king
Of the far-wandering shadows has come to me,
As in the old days when they would come and go
About my threshold to counsel and to help?'
That parted lips replied, 'I seek your help,
For I am Aengus, and I am crossed in love.'
'How may a mortal whose life gutters out
Help them that wander with hand clasping hand,
Their haughty images that cannot wither,
For all their beauty's like a hollow dream,
Mirrored in streams that neither hail nor rain
Nor the cold North has troubled?'
                              He replied,
'I am from those rivers and I bid you call
The children of the Maines out of sleep,
And set them digging under Bual's hill.
We shadows, while they uproot his earthy house,
Will overthrow his shadows and carry off
Caer, his blue-eyed daughter that I love.
I helped your fathers when they built these walls,

And I would have your help in my great need,
Queen of high Cruachan.'
                    'I obey your will
With speedy feet and a most thankful heart:
For you have been, O Aengus of the birds,
Our giver of good counsel and good luck.'
And with a groan, as if the mortal breath
Could but awaken sadly upon lips
That happier breath had moved, her husband turned
Face downward, tossing in a troubled sleep;
But Maeve, and not with a slow feeble foot,
Came to the threshold of the painted house
Where her grandchildren slept, and cried aloud,
Until the pillared dark began to stir
With shouting and the clang of unhooked arms.
She told them of the many-changing ones;
And all that night, and all through the next day
To middle night, they dug into the hill.
At middle night great cats with silver claws,
Bodies of shadow and blind eyes like pearls,
Came out of the hole, and red-eared hounds
With long white bodies came out of the air
Suddenly, and ran at them and harried them.

The Maines' children dropped their spades, and stood
With quaking joints and terror-stricken faces,
Till Maeve called out, 'These are but common men.
The Maines' children have not dropped their spades
Because Earth, crazy for its broken power,
Casts up a show and the winds answer it
With holy shadows.' Her high heart was glad,
And when the uproar ran along the grass
She followed with a light footfall in the midst,
Till it died out where an old thorn-tree stood.

Friend of these many years, you too had stood
With equal courage in that whirling rout;
For you, although you've not her wandering heart,
Have all that greatness, and not hers alone,
For there is no high story about queens
In any ancient book but tells of you;
And when I've heard how they grew old and died,
Or fell into unhappiness, I've said,
'She will grow old and die, and she has wept!'
And when I'd write it out anew, the words,
Half crazy with the thought, She too has wept!
Outrun the measure.
                         I'd tell of that great queen
Who stood amid a silence by the thorn
Until two lovers came out of the air
With bodies made out of soft fire. The one,
About whose face birds wagged their fiery wings,
Said, 'Aengus and his sweetheart give their thanks
To Maeve and to Maeve's household, owing all
In owing them the bride-bed that gives peace.'
Then Maeve: 'O Aengus, Master of all lovers,
A thousand years ago you held high talk
With the first kings of many-pillared Cruachan.
O when will you grow weary?'
                         They had vanished;
But out of the dark air over her head there came
A murmur of soft words and meeting lips.

THE TWO KINGS

October 1912   October 1913

King Eochaid came at sundown to a wood
Westward of Tara. Hurrying to his queen
He had outridden his war-wasted men
That with empounded cattle trod the mire,
And where beech trees had mixed a pale green light
With the ground-ivy's blue, he saw a stag

Whiter than curds, its eyes the tint of the sea.
Because it stood upon his path and seemed
More hands in height than any stag in the world
He sat with tightened rein and loosened mouth
Upon his trembling horse, then drove the spur;
But the stag stooped and ran at him, and passed,
Rending the horse's flank. King Eochaid reeled,
Then drew his sword to hold its levelled point
Against the stag. When horn and steel were met
The horn resounded as though it had been silver,
A sweet, miraculous, terrifying sound.
Horn locked in sword, they tugged and struggled there
As though a stag and unicorn were met
Among the African Mountains of the Moon,
Until at last the double horns, drawn backward,
Butted below the single and so pierced
The entrails of the horse. Dropping his sword
King Eochaid seized the horns in his strong hands
And stared into the sea-green eye, and so
Hither and thither to and fro they trod
Till all the place was beaten into mire.
The strong thigh and the agile thigh were met,
The hands that gathered up the might of the world,
And hoof and horn that had sucked in their speed
Amid the elaborate wilderness of the air.
Through bush they plunged and over ivied root,
And where the stone struck fire, while in the leaves
A squirrel whinnied and a bird screamed out;
But when at last he forced those sinewy flanks
Against a beech-bole, he threw down the beast
And knelt above it with drawn knife. On the instant
It vanished like a shadow, and a cry
So mournful that it seemed the cry of one
Who had lost some unimaginable treasure
Wandered between the blue and the green leaf
And climbed into the air, crumbling away,
Till all had seemed a shadow or a vision
But for the trodden mire, the pool of blood,
The disembowelled horse.

King Eochaid ran
Toward peopled Tara, nor stood to draw his breath
Until he came before the painted wall,
The posts of polished yew, circled with bronze,
Of the great door; but though the hanging lamps
Showed their faint light through the unshuttered windows,
Nor door, nor mouth, nor slipper made a noise,
Nor on the ancient beaten paths, that wound
From well-side or from plough-land, was there noise;
Nor had there been the noise of living thing
Before him or behind, but that far off
On the horizon edge bellowed the herds.
Knowing that silence brings no good to kings,
And mocks returning victory, he passed
Between the pillars with a beating heart
And saw where in the midst of the great hall
Pale-faced, alone upon a bench, Edain
Sat upright with a sword before her feet.
Her hands on either side had gripped the bench,
Her eyes were cold and steady, her lips tight.
Some passion had made her stone. Hearing a foot
She started and then knew whose foot it was;
But when he thought to take her in his arms
She motioned him afar, and rose and spoke:
'I have sent among the fields or to the woods
The fighting-men and servants of this house,
For I would have your judgment upon one
Who is self-accused. If she be innocent
She would not look in any known man's face
Till judgment has been given, and if guilty,
Would never look again on known man's face.'
And at these words he paled, as she had paled,
Knowing that he should find upon her lips
The meaning of that monstrous day.
                              Then she:
'You brought me where your brother Ardan sat
Always in his one seat, and bid me care him
Through that strange illness that had fixed him there,
And should he die to heap his burial-mound
And carve his name in Ogham.' Eochaid said,

'He lives?' 'He lives and is a healthy man.'
'While I have him and you it matters little
What man you have lost, what evil you have found.'
'I bid them make his bed under this roof
And carried him his food with my own hands,
And so the weeks passed by. But when I said,
"What is this trouble?" he would answer nothing,
Though always at my words his trouble grew;
And I but asked the more, till he cried out,
Weary of many questions: "There are things
That make the heart akin to the dumb stone."
Then I replied, "Although you hide a secret,
Hopeless and dear, or terrible to think on,
Speak it, that I may send through the wide world
For medicine." Thereon he cried aloud,
"Day after day you question me, and I,
Because there is such a storm amid my thoughts
I shall be carried in the gust, command,
Forbid, beseech and waste my breath." Then I:
"Although the thing that you have hid were evil,
The speaking of it could be no great wrong,
And evil must it be, if done 'twere worse
Than mound and stone that keep all virtue in,
And loosen on us dreams that waste our life,
Shadows and shows that can but turn the brain."
But finding him still silent I stooped down
And whispering that none but he should hear,
Said, "If a woman has put this on you,
My men, whether it please her or displease,
And though they have to cross the Loughlan waters
And take her in the middle of armed men,
Shall make her look upon her handiwork,
That she may quench the rick she has fired; and though
She may have worn silk clothes, or worn a crown,
She'll not be proud, knowing within her heart
That our sufficient portion of the world
Is that we give, although it be brief giving,
Happiness to children and to men."

Then he, driven by his thought beyond his thought,
And speaking what he would not though he would,
Sighed, "You, even you yourself, could work the cure!"
And at those words I rose and I went out
And for nine days he had food from other hands,
And for nine days my mind went whirling round
The one disastrous zodiac, muttering
That the immedicable mound's beyond
Our questioning, beyond our pity even.
But when nine days had gone I stood again
Before his chair and bending down my head
I bade him go when all his household slept
To an old empty woodman's house that's hidden
Westward of Tara, among the hazel-trees —
For hope would give his limbs the power — and await
A friend that could, he had told her, work his cure
And would be no harsh friend.

                  When night had deepened,
I groped my way from beech to hazel wood,
Found that old house, a sputtering torch within,
And stretched out sleeping on a pile of skins
Ardan, and though I called to him and tried
To shake him out of sleep, I could not rouse him.
I waited till the night was on the turn,
Then fearing that some labourer, on his way
To plough or pasture-land, might see me there,
Went out.

        Among the ivy-covered rocks,
As on the blue light of a sword, a man
Who had unnatural majesty, and eyes
Like the eyes of some great kite scouring the woods,
Stood on my path. Trembling from head to foot
I gazed at him like grouse upon a kite;
But with a voice that had unnatural music,
"A weary wooing and a long," he said,
"Speaking of love through other lips and looking
Under the eyelids of another, for it was my craft
That put a passion in the sleeper there,
And when I had got my will and drawn you here,

Where I may speak to you alone, my craft
Sucked up the passion out of him again
And left mere sleep. He'll wake when the sun wakes,
Push out his vigorous limbs and rub his eyes,
And wonder what has ailed him these twelve months."
I cowered back upon the wall in terror,
But that sweet-sounding voice ran on: "Woman,
I was your husband when you rode the air,
Danced in the whirling foam and in the dust,
In days you have not kept in memory,
Being betrayed into a cradle, and I come
That I may claim you as my wife again."
I was no longer terrified – his voice
Had half awakened some old memory –
Yet answered him, "I am King Eochaid's wife
And with him have found every happiness
Women can find." With a most masterful voice,
That made the body seem as it were a string
Under a bow, he cried, "What happiness
Can lovers have that know their happiness
Must end at the dumb stone? But where we build
Our sudden palaces in the still air
Pleasure itself can bring no weariness,
Nor can time waste the cheek, nor is there foot
That has grown weary of the wandering dance,
Nor an unlaughing mouth, but mine that mourns,
Among those mouths that sing their sweethearts' praise,
Your empty bed." "How should I love," I answered,
"Were it not that when the dawn has lit my bed
And shown my husband sleeping there, I have sighed,
'Your strength and nobleness will pass away.'
Or how should love be worth its pains were it not
That when he has fallen asleep within my arms,
Being wearied out, I love in man the child?
What can they know of love that do not know
She builds her nest upon a narrow ledge
Above a windy precipice?" Then he:
"Seeing that when you come to the deathbed
You must return, whether you would or no,
This human life blotted from memory,

Why must I live some thirty, forty years,
Alone with all this useless happiness?"
Thereon he seized me in his arms, but I
Thrust him away with both my hands and cried,
"Never will I believe there is any change
Can blot out of my memory this life
Sweetened by death, but if I could believe,
That were a double hunger in my lips
For what is doubly brief."
                              And now the shape
My hands were pressed to vanished suddenly.
I staggered, but a beech tree stayed my fall,
And clinging to it I could hear the cocks
Crow upon Tara.'
                    King Eochaid bowed his head
And thanked her for her kindness to his brother,
For that she promised, and for that refused.
Thereon the bellowing of the empounded herds
Rose round the walls, and through the bronze-ringed door
Jostled and shouted those war-wasted men,
And in the midst King Eochaid's brother stood,
And bade all welcome, being ignorant.

SECTION 9

ANGLO-IRISH ATTITUDES

AN IRISH AIRMAN FORESEES HIS DEATH

1918   *WSC* 1919

I know that I shall meet my fate
Somewhere among the clouds above;
Those that I fight I do not hate,
Those that I guard I do not love;
My country is Kiltartan Cross,
My countrymen Kiltartan's poor,
No likely end could bring them loss
Or leave them happier than before.
Nor law, nor duty bade me fight,
Nor public men, nor cheering crowds,
A lonely impulse of delight
Drove to this tumult in the clouds;
I balanced all, brought all to mind,
The years to come seemed waste of breath,
A waste of breath the years behind
In balance with this life, this death.

NINETEEN HUNDRED AND NINETEEN

1919   September 1921

I

Many ingenious lovely things are gone
That seemed sheer miracle to the multitude,
Protected from the circle of the moon
That pitches common things about. There stood
Amid the ornamental bronze and stone
An ancient image made of olive wood –
And gone are Phidias' famous ivories
And all the golden grasshoppers and bees.

We too had many pretty toys when young;
A law indifferent to blame or praise,
To bribe or threat; habits that made old wrong
Melt down, as it were wax in the sun's rays;
Public opinion ripening for so long
We thought it would outlive all future days.
O what fine thought we had because we thought
That the worst rogues and rascals had died out.

All teeth were drawn, all ancient tricks unlearned,
And a great army but a showy thing;
What matter that no cannon had been turned
Into a ploughshare? Parliament and king
Thought that unless a little powder burned
The trumpeters might burst with trumpeting
And yet it lack all glory; and perchance
The guardsmen's drowsy chargers would not prance.

Now days are dragon-ridden, the nightmare
Rides upon sleep; a drunken soldiery
Can leave the mother, murdered at her door,
To crawl in her own blood, and go scot-free;
The night can sweat with terror as before
We pieced our thoughts into philosophy,
And planned to bring the world under a rule,
Who are but weasels fighting in a hole.

He who can read the signs nor sink unmanned
Into the half-deceit of some intoxicant
From shallow wits; who knows no work can stand,
Whether health, wealth or peace of mind were spent
On master-work of intellect or hand,
No honour leave its mighty monument,
Has but one comfort left: all triumph would
But break upon his ghostly solitude.

But is there any comfort to be found?
Man is in love and loves what vanishes,
What more is there to say? That country round
None dared admit, if such a thought were his,
Incendiary or bigot could be found
To burn that stump on the Acropolis,
Or break in bits the famous ivories
Or traffic in the grasshoppers or bees.

II

When Loie Fuller's Chinese dancers enwound
A shining web, a floating ribbon of cloth,
It seemed that a dragon of air
Had fallen among dancers, had whirled them round
Or hurried them off on its own furious path;
So the Platonic Year
Whirls out new right and wrong,
Whirls in the old instead;
All men are dancers and their tread
Goes to the barbarous clangour of a gong.

III

Some moralist or mythological poet
Compares the solitary soul to a swan;
I am satisfied with that,
Satisfied if a troubled mirror show it,
Before that brief gleam of its life be gone,
An image of its state;
The wings half spread for flight,
The breast thrust out in pride
Whether to play, or to ride
Those winds that clamour of approaching night.

A man in his own secret meditation
Is lost amid the labyrinth that he has made
In art or politics;
Some Platonist affirms that in the station
Where we should cast off body and trade
The ancient habit sticks,

And that if our works could
But vanish with our breath
That were a lucky death,
For triumph can but mar our solitude.

The swan has leaped into the desolate heaven:
That image can bring wildness, bring a rage
To end all things, to end
What my laborious life imagined, even
The half-imagined, the half-written page;
O but we dreamed to mend
Whatever mischief seemed
To afflict mankind, but now
That winds of winter blow
Learn that we were crack-pated when we dreamed.

IV

We, who seven years ago
Talked of honour and of truth,
Shriek with pleasure if we show
The weasel's twist, the weasel's tooth.

V

Come let us mock at the great
That had such burdens on the mind
And toiled so hard and late
To leave some monument behind,
Nor thought of the levelling wind.

Come let us mock at the wise;
With all those calendars whereon
They fixed old aching eyes,
They never saw how seasons run,
And now but gape at the sun.

Come let us mock at the good
That fancied goodness might be gay,
And sick of solitude
Might proclaim a holiday:
Wind shrieked — and where are they?

Mock mockers after that
That would not lift a hand maybe
To help good, wise or great
To bar that foul storm out, for we
Traffic in mockery.

VI

Violence upon the roads: violence of horses;
Some few have handsome riders, are garlanded
On delicate sensitive ear or tossing mane,
But wearied running round and round in their courses
All break and vanish, and evil gathers head:
Herodias' daughters have returned again,
A sudden blast of dusty wind and after
Thunder of feet, tumult of images,
Their purpose in the labyrinth of the wind;
And should some crazy hand dare touch a daughter
All turn with amorous cries, or angry cries,
According to the wind, for all are blind.
But now wind drops, dust settles; thereupon
There lurches past, his great eyes without thought
Under the shadow of stupid straw-pale locks,
That insolent fiend Robert Artisson
To whom the love-lorn Lady Kyteler brought
Bronzed peacock feathers, red combs of her cocks.

THE TOWER

Probably 1925; MS of Section III dated 7 October 1925;   June 1927
the final date appended to whole poem in Collected
Poems is 1926.

I

What shall I do with this absurdity —
O heart, O troubled heart — this caricature,
Decrepit age that has been tied to me
As to a dog's tail?
              Never had I more
Excited, passionate, fantastical
Imagination, nor an ear and eye
That more expected the impossible —
No, not in boyhood when with rod and fly,
Or the humbler worm, I climbed Ben Bulben's back
And had the livelong summer day to spend.
It seems that I must bid the Muse go pack,
Choose Plato and Plotinus for a friend
Until imagination, ear and eye,
Can be content with argument and deal
In abstract things; or be derided by
A sort of battered kettle at the heel.

II

I pace upon the battlements and stare
On the foundations of a house, or where
Tree, like a sooty finger, starts from the earth;
And send imagination forth
Under the day's declining beam, and call
Images and memories
From ruin or from ancient trees,
For I would ask a question of them all.

Beyond that ridge lived Mrs. French, and once
When every silver candlestick or sconce
Lit up the dark mahogany and the wine,
A serving-man, that could divine
That most respected lady's every wish,
Ran and with the garden shears
Clipped an insolent farmer's ears
And brought them in a little covered dish.

Some few remembered still when I was young
A peasant girl commended by a song,
Who'd lived somewhere upon that rocky place,
And praised the colour of her face,
And had the greater joy in praising her,
Remembering that, if walked she there,
Farmers jostled at the fair
So great a glory did the song confer.

And certain men, being maddened by those rhymes,
Or else by toasting her a score of times,
Rose from the table and declared it right
To test their fancy by their sight;
But they mistook the brightness of the moon
For the prosaic light of day –
Music had driven their wits astray –
And one was drowned in the great bog of Cloone.

Strange, but the man who made the song was blind;
Yet, now I have considered it, I find
That nothing strange; the tragedy began
With Homer that was a blind man,
And Helen has all living hearts betrayed.
O may the moon and sunlight seem
One inextricable beam,
For if I triumph I must make men mad.

And I myself created Hanrahan
And drove him drunk or sober through the dawn
From somewhere in the neighbouring cottages.
Caught by an old man's juggleries
He stumbled, tumbled, fumbled to and fro
And had but broken knees for hire
And horrible splendour of desire;
I thought it all out twenty years ago:

Good fellows shuffled cards in an old bawn;
And when that ancient ruffian's turn was on
He so bewitched the cards under his thumb
That all but the one card became
A pack of hounds and not a pack of cards,
And that he changed into a hare.
Hanrahan rose in frenzy there
And followed up those baying creatures towards —

O towards I have forgotten what — enough!
I must recall a man that neither love
Nor music nor an enemy's clipped ear
Could, he was so harried, cheer;
A figure that has grown so fabulous
There's not a neighbour left to say
When he finished his dog's day:
An ancient bankrupt master of this house.

Before that ruin came, for centuries,
Rough men-at-arms, cross-gartered to the knees
Or shod in iron, climbed the narrow stairs,
And certain men-at-arms there were
Whose images, in the Great Memory stored,
Come with loud cry and panting breast
To break upon a sleeper's rest
While their great wooden dice beat on the board.

As I would question all, come all who can;
Come old, necessitous, half-mounted man;
And bring beauty's blind rambling celebrant;
The red man the juggler sent
Through God-forsaken meadows; Mrs. French,
Gifted with so fine an ear;
The man drowned in a bog's mire,
When mocking muses chose the country wench.

Did all old men and women, rich and poor,
Who trod upon these rocks or passed this door,
Whether in public or in secret rage
As I do now against old age?
But I have found an answer in those eyes
That are impatient to be gone;
Go therefore; but leave Hanrahan,
For I need all his mighty memories.

Old lecher with a love on every wind,
Bring up out of that deep considering mind
All that you have discovered in the grave,
For it is certain that you have
Reckoned up every unforeknown, unseeing
Plunge, lured by a softening eye,
Or by a touch or a sigh,
Into the labyrinth of another's being;

Does the imagination dwell the most
Upon a woman won or woman lost?
If on the lost, admit you turned aside
From a great labyrinth out of pride,
Cowardice, some silly over-subtle thought
Or anything called conscience once;
And that if memory recur, the sun's
Under eclipse and the day blotted out.

III

It is time that I wrote my will;
I choose upstanding men
That climb the streams until
The fountain leap, and at dawn
Drop their cast at the side
Of dripping stone; I declare
They shall inherit my pride,
The pride of people that were
Bound neither to Cause nor to State,
Neither to slaves that were spat on,
Nor to the tyrants that spat,
The people of Burke and of Grattan
That gave, though free to refuse —
Pride, like that of the morn,
When the headlong light is loose,
Or that of the fabulous horn,
Or that of the sudden shower
When all streams are dry,
Or that of the hour
When the swan must fix his eye
Upon a fading gleam,
Float out upon a long
Last reach of glittering stream
And there sing his last song.
And I declare my faith:
I mock Plotinus' thought
And cry in Plato's teeth,
Death and life were not
Till man made up the whole,
Made lock, stock and barrel
Out of his bitter soul,

Aye, sun and moon and star, all,
And further add to that
That, being dead, we rise,
Dream and so create
Translunar Paradise.
I have prepared my peace
With learned Italian things
And the proud stones of Greece,
Poet's imaginings
And memories of love,
Memories of the words of women,
All those things whereof
Man makes a superhuman
Mirror-resembling dream.

As at the loophole there
The daws chatter and scream,
And drop twigs layer upon layer.
When they have mounted up,
The mother bird will rest
On their hollow top,
And so warm her wild nest.

I leave both faith and pride
To young upstanding men
Climbing the mountain side,
That under bursting dawn
They may drop a fly;
Being of that metal made
Till it was broken by
This sedentary trade.

Now shall I make my soul,
Compelling it to study
In a learned school
Till the wreck of body,
Slow decay of blood,
Testy delirium
Or dull decrepitude,
Or what worse evil come –
The death of friends, or death
Of every brilliant eye
That made a catch in the breath –
Seem but the clouds of the sky
When the horizon fades;
Or a bird's sleepy cry
Among the deepening shades.

1926

BLOOD AND THE MOON

August 1927   *WS* 1929

I

Blessed be this place,
More blessed still this tower;
A bloody, arrogant power
Rose out of the race
Uttering, mastering it,
Rose like these walls from these
Storm-beaten cottages –
In mockery I have set
A powerful emblem up,
And sing it rhyme upon rhyme
In mockery of a time
Half dead at the top.

II

Alexandria's was a beacon tower, and Babylon's
An image of the moving heavens, a log-book of the sun's journey and the
    moon's;
And Shelley had his towers, thought's crowned powers he called them once.

I declare this tower is my symbol; I declare
This winding, gyring, spiring treadmill of a stair is my ancestral stair;
That Goldsmith and the Dean, Berkeley and Burke have travelled there.

Swift beating on his breast in sibylline frenzy blind
Because the heart in his blood-sodden breast had dragged him down into
    mankind,
Goldsmith deliberately sipping at the honey-pot of his mind,

And haughtier-headed Burke that proved the State a tree,
That this unconquerable labyrinth of the birds, century after century,
Cast but dead leaves to mathematical equality;

And God-appointed Berkeley that proved all things a dream,
That this pragmatical, preposterous pig of a world, its farrow that so solid seem,
Must vanish on the instant if the mind but change its theme;

Saeve Indignatio and the labourer's hire,
The strength that gives our blood and state magnanimity of its own desire;
Everything that is not God consumed with intellectual fire.

III

    The purity of the unclouded moon
    Has flung its arrowy shaft upon the floor.
    Seven centuries have passed and it is pure;
    The blood of innocence has left no stain.
    There, on blood-saturated ground, have stood
    Soldier, assassin, executioner,
    Whether for daily pittance or in blind fear
    Or out of abstract hatred, and shed blood,
    But could not cast a single jet thereon.
    Odour of blood on the ancestral stair!
    And we that have shed none must gather there
    And clamour in dunken frenzy for the moon.

IV

Upon the dusty, glittering windows cling,
And seem to cling upon the moonlit skies,
Tortoiseshell butterflies, peacock butterflies.
A couple of night-moths are on the wing.
Is every modern nation like the tower,
Half dead at the top? No matter what I said,
For wisdom is the property of the dead,
A something incompatible with life; and power,
Like everything that has the stain of blood,
A property of the living; but no stain
Can come upon the visage of the moon
When it has looked in glory from a cloud.

THE SEVEN SAGES

30 January 1931   *WMP* 1932

The First. My great-grandfather spoke to Edmund Burke
     In Grattan's house.

The Second.   My great-grandfather shared
     A pot-house bench with Oliver Goldsmith once.

The Third. My great-grandfather's father talked of music,
     Drank tar-water with the Bishop of Cloyne.

The Fourth. But mine saw Stella once.

The Fifth.   Whence came our thought?

The Sixth. From four great minds that hated Whiggery.

The Fifth. Burke was a Whig.

The Sixth. Whether they knew or not,
    Goldsmith and Burke, Swift and the Bishop of Cloyne
    All hated Whiggery; but what is Whiggery?
    A levelling, rancorous, rational sort of mind
    That never looked out of the eye of a saint
    Or out of drunkard's eye.

The Seventh. All's Whiggery now,
                But we old men are massed against the world.

The First. American colonies, Ireland, France and India
    Harried, and Burke's great melody against it.

The Second. Oliver Goldsmith sang what he had seen,
    Roads full of beggars, cattle in the fields,
    But never saw the trefoil stained with blood,
    The avenging leaf those fields raised up against it.

The Fourth. The tomb of Swift wears it away.

The Third.   A voice
    Soft as the rustle of a reed from Cloyne
    That gathers volume; now a thunder-clap.

The Sixth. What schooling had these four?

The Seventh.   They walked the roads
    Mimicking what they heard, as children mimic;
    They understood that wisdom comes of beggary.

REMORSE FOR INTEMPERATE SPEECH

28 August 1931   *WMP* 1932

I ranted to the knave and fool,
But outgrew that school,
Would transform the part,
Fit audience found but cannot rule
My fanatic[1] heart.

I sought my betters: though in each
Fine manners, liberal speech,
Turn hatred into sport,
Nothing said or done can reach
My fanatic heart.

Out of Ireland have we come.
Great hatred, little room,
Maimed us at the start.
I carry from my mother's womb
A fanatic heart.

28 August 1931

PARNELL'S FUNERAL

1932–April 1933   April–June 1932 (lines 16–23)
whole poem October 1934

I

Under the Great Comedian's tomb the crowd.
A bundle of tempestuous cloud is blown
About the sky; where that is clear of cloud
Brightness remains; a brighter star shoots down;
What shudders run through all that animal blood?
What is this sacrifice? Can someone there
Recall the Cretan barb that pierced a star?

---

[1] I pronounce 'fanatic' in what is, I suppose, the older and more Irish way, so that the last line of each stanza contains but two beats.

Rich foliage that the starlight glittered through,
A frenzied crowd, and where the branches sprang
A beautiful seated boy; a sacred bow;
A woman, and an arrow on a string;
A pierced boy, image of a star laid low.
That woman, the Great Mother imaging,
Cut out his heart. Some master of design
Stamped boy and tree upon Sicilian coin.

An age is the reversal of an age:
When strangers murdered Emmet, Fitzgerald, Tone,
We lived like men that watch a painted stage.
What matter for the scene, the scene once gone:
It had not touched our lives. But popular rage,
Hysterica passio dragged this quarry down.
None shared our guilt; not did we play a part
Upon a painted stage when we devoured his heart.

Come, fix upon me that accusing eye.
I thirst for accusation. All that was sung,
All that was said in Ireland is a lie
Bred out of the contagion of the throng,
Saving the rhyme rats hear before they die.
Leave nothing but the nothings that belong
To this bare soul, let all men judge that can
Whether it be an animal or a man.

II

The rest I pass, one sentence I unsay.
Had de Valéra eaten Parnell's heart
No loose-lipped demagogue had won the day,
No civil rancour torn the land apart.

Had Cosgrave eaten Parnell's heart, the land's
Imagination had been satisfied,
Or lacking that, government in such hands,
O'Higgins its sole statesman had not died.

Had even O'Duffy — but I name no more —
Their school a crowd, his master solitude;
Through Jonathan Swift's dark grove he passed, and there
Plucked bitter wisdom that enriched his blood.

THE CURSE OF CROMWELL

Between November 1936 and 8 January 1937   August 1937

You ask what I have found and far and wide I go,
Nothing but Cromwell's house and Cromwell's murderous crew,
The lovers and the dancers are beaten into the clay,
And the tall men and the swordsmen and the horsemen where are they?
And there is an old beggar wandering in his pride
His fathers served their fathers before Christ was crucified.

> *O what of that, O what of that*
> *What is there left to say?*

All neighbourly content and easy talk are gone,
But there's no good complaining, for money's rant is on,
He that's mounting up must on his neighbour mount
And we and all the Muses are things of no account.
They have schooling of their own but I pass their schooling by,
What can they know that we know that know the time to die?

> *O what of that, O what of that*
> *What is there left to say?*

But there's another knowledge that my heart destroys
As the fox in the old fable destroyed the Spartan boy's
Because it proves that things both can and cannot be;
That the swordsmen and the ladies can still keep company;
Can pay the poet for a verse and hear the fiddle sound,
That I am still their servant though all are underground.

> *O what of that, O what of that*
> *What is there left to say?*

I came on a great house in the middle of the night
Its open lighted doorway and its windows all alight,
And all my friends were there and made me welcome too;
But I woke in an old ruin that the winds howled through;
And when I pay attention I must out and walk
Among the dogs and horses that understand my talk.

> *O what of that, O what of that*
> *What is there left to say?*

SECTION 10
LOVE AND SEX

EPHEMERA

1884   *WO* 1889

'Your eyes that once were never weary of mine
Are bowed in sorrow under pendulous lids,
Because our love is waning.'
                              And then she:
'Although our love is waning, let us stand
By the lone border of the lake once more,
Together in that hour of gentleness
When the poor tired child, Passion, falls asleep:
How far away the stars seem, and how far
Is our first kiss, and ah, how old my heart!'

Pensive they paced along the faded leaves,
While slowly he whose hand held hers replied:
'Passion has often worn our wandering hearts.'

The woods were round them, and the yellow leaves
Fell like faint meteors in the gloom, and once
A rabbit old and lame limped down the path;
Autumn was over him: and now they stood
On the lone border of the lake once more:
Turning, he saw that she had thrust dead leaves
Gathered in silence, dewy as her eyes,
In bosom and hair.
                          'Ah, do not mourn,' he said,
'That we are tired, for other loves await us;
Hate on and love through unrepining hours.
Before us lies eternity; our souls
Are love, and a continual farewell.'

THE FALLING OF THE LEAVES

WO 1889

Autumn is over the long leaves that love us,
And over the mice in the barley sheaves;
Yellow the leaves of the rowan above us,
And yellow the wet wild-strawberry leaves.

The hour of the waning of love has beset us,
And weary and worn are our sad souls now;
Let us part, ere the season of passion forget us,
With a kiss and a tear on thy dropping brow.

THE PITY OF LOVE

CK 1892

A pity beyond all telling
Is hid in the heart of love:
The folk who are buying and selling,
The clouds on their journey above,
The cold wet winds ever blowing,
And the shadowy hazel grove
Where mouse-grey waters are flowing,
Threaten the head that I love.

THE SORROW OF LOVE

1891

CK 1892

The quarrel of the sparrows in the eaves
The full round moon and the star-laden sky,
And the loud song of the ever-singing leaves
Had hid away earth's old and weary cry.

And then you came with those red mournful lips,
And with you came the whole of the world's tears,
And all the sorrows of her labouring ships
And all burden of her myriad years.

And now the sparrows warring in the eaves,
The crumbling moon, the white stars in the sky,
And the loud chanting of the unquiet leaves,
Are shaken with earth's old and weary cry.

THE SORROW OF LOVE

1891   Revised version, *EP & S* 1925

The brawling of a sparrow in the eaves,
The brilliant moon and all the milky sky,
And all that famous harmony of leaves,
Had blotted out man's image and his cry.

A girl arose that had red mournful lips
And seemed the greatness of the world in tears,
Doomed like Odysseus and the labouring ships
And proud as Priam murdered with his peers;

Arose, and on the instant clamorous eaves,
A climbing moon upon an empty sky,
And all that lamentation of the leaves,
Could but compose man's image and his cry.

THE WHITE BIRDS

May 1892

I would that we were, my beloved, white birds on the foam of the sea!
We tire of the flame of the meteor, before it can fade and flee;
And the flame of the blue star of twilight, hung low on the rim of the sky,
Has awaked in our hearts, my beloved, a sadness that may not die.

A weariness comes from those dreamers, dew-dabbled, the lily and rose;
Ah, dream not of them, my beloved, the flame of the meteor that goes,
Or the flame of the blue star that lingers hung low in the fall of the dew:
For I would we were changed to white birds on the wandering foam: I and you!

I am haunted by numberless islands, and many a Danaan shore,
Where Time would surely forget us, and Sorrow come near us no more;
Soon far from the rose and the lily and fret of the flames would we be,
Were we only white birds, my beloved, buoyed out on the foam of the sea!

THE LOVER TELLS OF THE ROSE IN HIS HEART

November 1892

All things uncomely and broken, all things worn out and old,
The cry of a child by the roadway, the creak of a lumbering cart,
The heavy steps of the ploughman, splashing the wintry mould,
Are wronging your image that blossoms a rose in the deeps of my heart.

The wrong of unshapely things is a wrong too great to be told;
I hunger to build them anew and sit on a green knoll apart,
With the earth and the sky and the water, re-made, like a casket of gold
For my dreams of your image that blossoms a rose in the deeps of my heart.

THE SONG OF WANDERING AENGUS

31 January (?) 1893   August 1897

I went out to the hazel wood,
Because a fire was in my head,
And cut and peeled a hazel wand,
And hooked a berry to a thread;
And when white moths were on the wing,
And moth-like stars were flickering out,
I dropped the berry in a stream
And caught a little silver trout.

When I had laid it on the floor
I went to blow the fire aflame,
But something rustled on the floor,
And some one called me by my name:
It had become a glimmering girl
With apple blossom in her hair
Who called me by my name and ran
And faded through the brightening air.

Though I am old with wandering
Through hollow lands and hilly lands,
I will find out where she has gone,
And kiss her lips and take her hands;
And walk among long dappled grass,
And pluck till time and times are done
The silver apples of the moon,
The golden apples of the sun.

HE BIDS HIS BELOVED BE AT PEACE

24 September 1895   January 1896

I hear the Shadowy Horses, their long manes a-shake,
Their hoofs heavy with tumult, their eyes glimmering white;
The North unfolds above them clinging, creeping night,
The East her hidden joy before the morning break,
The West weeps in pale dew and sighs passing away,
The South is pouring down roses of crimson fire:
O vanity of Sleep, Hope, Dream, endless Desire,
The Horses of Disaster plunge in the heavy clay:
Beloved, let your eyes half close, and your heart beat
Over my heart, and your hair fall over my breast,
Drowning love's lonely hour in deep twilight of rest,
And hiding their tossing manes and their tumultuous feet.

HE GIVES HIS BELOVED CERTAIN RHYMES

1895　　　　　　　　　　　　　　　　　　　　　January 1896

Fasten your hair with a golden pin,
And bind up every wandering tress;
I bade my heart build these poor rhymes:
It worked at them, day out, day in,
Building a sorrowful loveliness
Out of the battles of old times.

You need but lift a pearl-pale hand,
And bind up your long hair and sigh;
And all men's hearts must burn and beat;
And candle-like foam on the dim sand,
And stars climbing the dew-dropping sky,
Live but to light your passing feet.

THE TRAVAIL OF PASSION

January 1896

When the flaming lute-thronged angelic door is wide;
When an immortal passion breathes in mortal clay;
Our hearts endure the scourge, the plaited thorns, the way
Crowded with bitter faces, the wounds in palm and side,
The vinegar-heavy sponge, the flowers by Kedron stream;
We will bend down and loosen our hair over you,
That it may drop faint perfume, and be heavy with dew,
Lillies of death-pale hope, roses of passionate dream.

HE REMEMBERS FORGOTTEN BEAUTY

July 1896

When my arms wrap you round I press
My heart upon the loveliness
That has long faded from the world;
The jewelled crowns that kings have hurled
In shadowy pools, when armies fled;
The love-tales wrought with silken thread
By dreaming ladies upon cloth
That has made fat the murderous moth;
The roses that of old time were
Woven by ladies in their hair,
The dew-cold lilies ladies bore
Through many a sacred corridor
Where such grey clouds of incense rose
That only God's eyes did not close:
For that pale breast and lingering hand
Come from a more dream-heavy land,
A more dream-heavy hour than this;
And when you sigh from kiss to kiss
I hear white Beauty sighing, too,
For hours when all must fade like dew,
But flame on flame, and deep on deep,
Throne over throne where in half sleep,
Their swords upon their iron knees,
Brood her high lonely mysteries.

HE REPROVES THE CURLEW

November 1896

O curlew, cry no more in the air,
Or only to the water in the West;
Because your crying brings to my mind
Passion-dimmed eyes and long heavy hair
That was shaken out over my breast:
There is enough evil in the crying of wind.

HE HEARS THE CRY OF THE SEDGE

May 1898

I wander by the edge
Of this desolate lake
Where wind cries in the sedge:
Until the axle break
That keeps the stars in their round,
And hands hurl in the deep
The banners of East and West,
And the girdle of light is unbound,
Your breast will not lie by the breast
Of your beloved in sleep.

HE THINKS OF HIS PAST GREATNESS WHEN A PART OF THE CONSTELLATIONS OF HEAVEN

October 1898

I have drunk ale from the Country of the Young
And weep because I know all things now:
I have been a hazel-tree, and they hung
The Pilot Star and the Crooked Plough
Among my leaves in times out of mind:
I became a rush that horses tread:
I became a man, a hater of the wind,
Knowing one, out of all things, alone, that his head
May not lie on the breast nor his lips on the hair
Of the woman that he loves, until he dies.
O beast of the wilderness, bird of the air,
Must I endure your amorous cries?

HE WISHES FOR THE CLOTHS OF HEAVEN

WR 1899

Had I the heavens' embroidered cloths,
Enwrought with golden and silver light,
The blue and the dim and the dark cloths
Of night and light and the half-light,
I would spread the cloths under your feet:
But I, being poor, have only my dreams;
I have spread my dreams under your feet;
Tread softly because you tread on my dreams.

THE ARROW

1901   *ISW* 1903

I thought of your beauty, and this arrow,
Made out of a wild thought, is in my marrow.
There's no man may look upon her, no man,
As when newly grown to be a woman,
Tall and noble but with face and bosom
Delicate in colour as apple blossom.
This beauty's kinder, yet for a reason
I could weep that the old is out of season.

O DO NOT LOVE TOO LONG

Before 23 February 1905   October 1905

Sweetheart, do not love too long:
I loved long and long,
And grew to be out of fashion
Like an old song.

All through the years of our youth
Neither could have known
Their own thought from the other's,
We were so much at one.

But O, in a minute she changed –
O do not love too long,
Or you will grow out of fashion
Like an old song.

NEVER GIVE ALL THE HEART

December 1905

Never give all the heart, for love
Will hardly seem worth thinking of
To passionate women if it seem
Certain, and they never dream
That it fades out from kiss to kiss;
For everything that's lovely is
But a brief, dreamy, kind delight.
O never give the heart outright,
For they, for all smooth lips can say,
Have given their hearts up to the play.
And who could play it well enough
If deaf and dumb and blind with love?
He that made this knows all the cost,
For he gave all his heart and lost.

WORDS

22 January 1908   *GH* 1910

I had this thought a while ago,
'My darling cannot understand
What I have done, or what would do
In this blind bitter land'.

And I grew weary of the sun
Until my thoughts cleared up again,
Remembering that the best I have done
Was done to make it plain;

That every year I have cried, 'At length
My darling understands it all,
Because I have come into my strength,
And words obey my call';

That had she done so who can say
What would have shaken from the sieve?
I might have thrown poor words away
And been content to live.

RECONCILIATION

September 1908   *GH* 1910

Some may have blamed you that you took away
The verses that could move them on the day
When, the ears being deafened, the sight of the eyes blind
With lightning, you went from me, and I could find
Nothing to make a song about but kings,
Helmets, and swords, and half-forgotten things
That were like memories of you — but now
We'll out, for the world lives as long ago;
And while we're in our laughing, weeping fit,
Hurl helmets, crowns, and swords into the pit.
But, dear, cling close to me; since you were gone,
My barren thoughts have chilled me to the bone.

NO SECOND TROY

December 1908   *GH* 1910

Why should I blame her that she filled my days
With misery, or that she would of late
Have taught to ignorant men most violent ways,
Or hurled the little streets upon the great,
Had they but courage equal to desire?
What could have made her peaceful with a mind
That nobleness made simple as a fire,
With beauty like a tightened bow, a kind
That is not natural in an age like this,
Being high and solitary and most stern?
Why, what could she have done, being what she is?
Was there another Troy for her to burn?

AGAINST UNWORTHY PRAISE

11 May 1910   *GH* 1910

O heart, be at peace, because
Nor knave nor dolt can break
What's not for their applause,
Being for a woman's sake.
Enough if the work has seemed,
So did she your strength renew,
A dream that a lion had dreamed
Till the wilderness cried aloud,
A secret between you two,
Between the proud and the proud.

What, still you would have their praise!
But here's a haughtier text,
The labyrinth of her days
That her own strangeness perplexed;
And how what her dreaming gave
Earned slander, ingratitude,
From self-same dolt and knave;
Aye, and worse wrong than these.
Yet she, singing upon her road,
Half lion, half child, is at peace.

FALLEN MAJESTY

1912   December 1912

Although crowds gathered once if she but showed her face,
And even old men's eyes grew dim, this hand alone,
Like some last courtier at a gypsy camping-place
Babbling of fallen majesty, records what's gone.

The lineaments, a heart that laughter has made sweet,
These, these remain, but I record what's gone. A crowd
Will gather, and not know it walks the very street
Whereon a thing once walked that seemed a burning cloud.

WHEN HELEN LIVED

Between 20–29 September 1913   May 1914

We have cried in our despair
That men desert,
For some trivial affair
Or noisy, insolent sport,
Beauty that we have won
From bitterest hours;
Yet we, had we walked within
Those topless towers
Where Helen walked with her boy,
Had given but as the rest
Of the men and women of Troy,
A word and a jest.

HER PRAISE

27 January 1915   February 1916

She is foremost of those that I would hear praised.
I have gone about the house, gone up and down
As a man does who has published a new book,
Or a young girl dressed out in her new gown,
And though I have turned the talk by hook or crook
Until her praise should be the uppermost theme,
A woman spoke of some new tale she had read,
A man confusedly in a half dream
As though some other name ran in his head.
She is foremost of those that I would hear praised.
I will talk no more of books or the long war
But walk by the dry thorn until I have found
Some beggar sheltering from the wind, and there
Manage the talk until her name come round.
If there be rags enough he will know her name
And be well pleased remembering it, for in the old days,
Though she had young men's praise and old men's blame,
Among the poor both old and young gave her praise.

PRESENCES

November 1915   June 1917

This night has been so strange that it seemed
As if the hair stood up on my head.
From going-down of the sun I have dreamed
That women laughing, or timid or wild,
In rustle of lace or silken stuff,
Climbed up my creaking stair. They had read
All I had rhymed of that monstrous thing
Returned and yet unrequited love.
They stood in the door and stood between
My great wooden lectern and the fire
Till I could hear their hearts beating:
One is a harlot, and one a child
That never looked upon man with desire,
And one, it may be, a queen.

OWEN AHERNE AND HIS DANCERS

I *24 October 1917;* II *27 October 1917*   June 1924

I

A strange thing surely that my Heart, when love had come unsought
Upon the Norman upland or in that poplar shade,
Should find no burden but itself and yet should be worn out.
It could not bear that burden and therefore it went mad.

The south wind brought it longing, and the east wind despair,
The west wind made it pitiful, and the north wind afraid.
It feared to give its love a hurt with all the tempest there;
It feared the hurt that she could give and therefore it went mad.

I can exchange opinion with any neighbouring mind,
I have as healthy flesh and blood as any rhymer's had,
But O! my Heart could bear no more when the upland caught the
        wind;
I ran, I ran, from my love's side because my Heart went mad.

II

The Heart behind its rib laughed out. 'You have called me mad,' it
      said.
'Because I made you turn away and run from that young child;
How could she mate with fifty years that was so wildly bred?
Let the cage bird and the cage bird mate and the wild bird mate in
      the wild.'

'You but imagine lies all day, O murderer,' I replied.
'And all those lies have but one end, poor wretches to betray;
I did not find in any cage the woman at my side.
O but her heart would break to learn my thoughts are far away.'

'Speak all your mind,' my Heart sang out, 'speak all your mind; who
      cares,
Now that your tongue cannot persuade the child till she mistake
Her childish gratitude for love and match your fifty years?
O let her choose a young man now and all for his wild sake.'

SOLOMON AND THE WITCH

1918   MRD dated 1920, published 1921

And thus declared that Arab lady:
'Last night, where under the wild moon
On grassy mattress I had laid me,
Within my arms great Solomon,
I suddenly cried out in a strange tongue
Not his, not mine.'
                        Who understood
Whatever has been said, sighed, sung,
Howled, miau-d, barked, brayed, belled, yelled, cried, crowed,
Thereon replied: 'A cockerel
Crew from a blossoming apple bough
Three hundred years before the Fall,
And never crew again till now,
And would not now but that he thought,
Chance being at one with Choice at last,

All that the brigand apple brought
And this foul world were dead at last.
He that crowed out eternity
Thought to have crowed it in again.
For though love has a spider's eye
To find out some appropriate pain —
Aye, though all passion's in the glance —
For every nerve, and tests a lover
With cruelties of Choice and Chance;
And when at last that murder's over
Maybe the bride-bed brings despair,
For each an imagined image brings
And finds a real image there;
Yet the world ends when these two things,
Though several, are a single light,
When oil and wick are burned in one;
Therefore a blessed moon last night
Gave Sheba to her Solomon.'

'Yet the world stays.'
                              'If that be so,
Your cockerel found us in the wrong
Although he thought it worth a crow.
Maybe an image is too strong
Or maybe is not strong enough.'

'The night has fallen; not a sound
In the forbidden sacred grove
Unless a petal hit the ground,
Nor any human sight within it
But the crushed grass where we have lain;
And the moon is wilder every minute.
O! Solomon! let us try again.'

A LAST CONFESSION

June, July 23 and 24, August 1926   WS 1929

What lively lad most pleasured me
Of all that with me lay?
I answer that I gave my soul
And loved in misery,
But had great pleasure with a lad
That I loved bodily.

Flinging from his arms I laughed
To think his passion such
He fancied that I gave a soul
Did but our bodies touch,
And laughed upon his breast to think
Beast gave beast as much.

I gave what other women gave
That stepped out of their clothes,
But when this soul, its body off,
Naked to naked goes,
He it has found shall find therein
What none other knows,

And give his own and take his own
And rule in his own right;
And though it loved in misery
Close and cling so tight,
There's not a bird of day that dare
Extinguish that delight.

PARTING

August 1926
                                                       WS 1929

He. Dear, I must be gone
    While night shuts the eyes
    Of the household spies;
    That song announces dawn.

She. No, night's bird and love's
    Bids all true lovers rest,
    While his loud song reproves
    The murderous stealth of day.

He. Daylight already flies
    From mountain crest to crest.

She. That light is from the moon

He. That bird . . .

She.   Let him sing on,
    I offer to love's play
    My dark declivities.

FIRST LOVE

(1926 and 1927)   May 1927

    Though nurtured like the sailing moon
    In beauty's murderous brood,
    She walked awhile and blushed awhile
    And on my pathway stood
    Until I thought her body bore
    A heart of flesh and blood.

    But since I laid a hand thereon
    And found a heart of stone
    I have attempted many things
    And not a thing is done,
    For every hand is lunatic
    That travels on the moon.

She smiled and that transfigured me
And left me but a lout,
Maundering here, and maundering there,
Emptier of thought
Than the heavenly circuit of its stars
When the moon sails out.

THE MERMAID

1926 and 1927   May 1927

A mermaid found a swimming lad,
Picked him for her own,
Pressed her body to his body,
Laughed; and plunging down
Forgot in cruel happiness
That even lovers drown.

CONSOLATION

(?) June 1927   *WS* 1929

O but there is wisdom
In what the sages said;
But stretch that body for a while
And lay down that head
Till I have told the sages
Where man is comforted.

How could passion run so deep
Had I never thought
That the crime of being born
Blackens all our lot?
But where the crime's committed
The crime can be forgot.

CRAZY JANE AND THE BISHOP

2 March 1929   November 1930

Bring me to the blasted oak
That I, midnight upon the stroke,
(All find safety in the tomb.)
May call down curses on his head
Because of my dear Jack that's dead.
Coxcomb was the least he said:
The solid man and the coxcomb.

Nor was he Bishop when his ban
Banished Jack the Journeyman,
(All find safety in the tomb.)
Nor so much as parish priest,
Yet he, an old book in his fist,
Cried that we lived like beast and beast:
The solid man and the coxcomb.

The Bishop has a skin, God knows,
Wrinkled like the foot of a goose,
(All find safety in the tomb.)
Nor can he hide in holy black,
But a birch-tree stood my Jack:
The solid man and the coxcomb.

Jack had my virginity,
And bids me to the oak, for he
(All find safety in the tomb.)
Wanders out into the night
And there is shelter under it,
But should that other come, I spit:
The solid man and the coxcomb.

GIRL'S SONG

29 March 1929   October 1930

I went out alone
To sing a song or two,
My fancy on a man,
And you know who.

Another came in sight
That on a stick relied
To hold himself upright:
I sat and cried.

And that was all my song —
When everything is told,
Saw I an old man young
Or young man old?

LULLABY

1931

Beloved, may your sleep be sound
That have found it where you fed.
What were all the world's alarms
To mighty Paris when he found
Sleep upon a golden bed
That first dawn in Helen's arms?

Sleep, beloved, such a sleep
As did that wild Tristram know
When, the potion's work being done,
Roe could run or doe could leap
Under oak and beechen bough,
Roe could leap or doe could run;

Such a sleep and sound as fell
Upon Eurotas' grassy bank
When the holy bird, that there
Accomplished his predestined will,
For the limbs of Leda sank
But not from her protecting care.

AFTER LONG SILENCE

November 1929   *WMP* 1932

Speech after long silence; it is right,
All other lovers being estranged or dead,
Unfriendly lamplight hid under its shade,
The curtains drawn upon unfriendly night,
That we descant and yet again descant
Upon the supreme theme of Art and Song:
Bodily decrepitude is wisdom; young
We loved each other and were ignorant.

HER TRIUMPH

29 November 1929   *WS* 1929

I did the dragon's will until you came
Because I had fancied love a casual
Improvisation, or a settled game
That followed if I let the kerchief fall·
Those deeds were best that gave the minute wings
And heavenly music if they gave it wit;
And then you stood among the dragon-rings.
I mocked, being crazy, but you mastered it
And broke the chain and set my ankles free,
Saint George or else a pagan Perseus;
And now we stare astonished at the sea,
And a miraculous strange bird shrieks at us.

CRAZY JANE TALKS WITH THE BISHOP

November 1931   *WS* 1933

I met the Bishop on the road
And much said he and I.
'Those breasts are flat and fallen now
Those veins must soon be dry;
Live in a heavenly mansion,
Not in some foul sty.'

'Fair and foul are near of kin,
And fair needs foul,' I cried.
'My friends are gone, but that's a truth
Nor grave nor bed denied,
Learned in bodily lowliness
And in the heart's pride.

'A woman can be proud and stiff
When on love intent;
But Love has pitched his mansion in
The place of excrement;
For nothing can be sole or whole
That has not been rent.'

RIBH AT THE TOMB OF BAILE AND AILLINN

Completed by 24 July 1934   December 1934

Because you have found me in the pitch-dark night
With open book you ask me what I do.
Mark and digest my tale, carry it afar
To those that never saw this tonsured head
Nor heard this voice that ninety years have cracked.
Of Baile and Aillinn you need not speak,
All know their tale, all know what leaf and twig,
What juncture of the apple and the yew,
Surmount their bones; but speak what none have heard.

The miracle that gave them such a death
Transfigured to pure substance what had once
Been bone and sinew; when such bodies join
There is no touching here, nor touching there,
Nor straining joy, but whole is joined to whole;
For the intercourse of angels is a light
Where for its moment both seem lost, consumed.

Here in the pitch-dark atmosphere above
The trembling of the apple and the yew,
Here on the anniversary of their death,
The anniversary of their first embrace,
Those lovers, purified by tragedy,
Hurry into each other's arms; these eyes,
By water, herb and solitary prayer
Made aquiline, are open to that light.
Though somewhat broken by the leaves, that light
Lies in a circle on the grass; therein
I turn the pages of my holy book.

THE WILD OLD WICKED MAN

(?) Spring 1937   April 1938

'Because I am mad about women
I am mad about the hills,'
Said that wild old wicked man
Who travels where God wills,
'Not to die on the straw at home,
Those hands to close these eyes,
That is all I ask, my dear,
From the old man in the skies.'
          Day-break and a candle end.

'Kind are all your words, my dear,
Do not the rest withhold,
Who can know the year, my dear,
When an old man's blood grows cold.
I have what no young man can have
Because he loves too much.
Words I have that can pierce the heart,
But what can he do but touch?'
                    Day-break and a candle end.

Then said she to that wild old man
His stout stick under his hand,
'Love to give or to withhold
Is not at my command.
I gave it all to an older man
That old man in the skies.
Hands that are busy with His beads
Can never close those eyes.'
                    Day-break and a candle end.

'Go your ways, O go your ways
I choose another mark,
Girls down on the seashore
Who understand the dark;
Bawdy talk for the fishermen
A dance for the fisher lads;
When dark hangs upon the water
They turn down their beds.'
                    Day-break and a candle end.

'A young man in the dark am I
But a wild old man in the light
That can make a cat laugh, or
Can touch by mother wit
Things hid in their marrow bones
From time long passed away,
Hid from all those warty lads
That by their bodies lay.'
                    Day-break and a candle end.

'All men live in suffering
I know as few can know,
Whether they take the upper road
Or stay content on the low,
Rower bent in his row-boat
Or weaver bent at his loom,
Horsemen erect upon horseback
Or child hid in the womb.'
                    Day-break and a candle end.

'That some stream of lightning
From the old man in the skies
Can burn out that suffering
No right taught man denies.
But a coarse old man am I,
I choose the second-best,
I forget it all awhile
Upon a woman's breast.'
                    Day-break and a candle end.

SECTION 11

THE SUPERNATURAL

THE STOLEN CHILD

Where dips the rocky highland
Of Sleuth Wood in the lake,
There lies a leafy island
Where flapping herons wake
The drowsy water-rats;
There we've hid our faery vats,
Full of berries
And of reddest stolen cherries.
Come away, O human child!
To the waters and the wild
With a faery, hand in hand,
For the world's more full of weeping than you can understand.

Where the wave of moonlight glosses
The dim grey sands with light,
Far off by furthest Rosses
We foot it all the night,
Waving olden dances,
Mingling hands and mingling glances
Till the moon has taken flight;
To and fro we leap
And chase the frothy bubbles,
While the world is full of troubles
And is anxious in its sleep.
Come away, O human child!
To the waters and the wild
With a faery, hand in hand,
For the world's more full of weeping than you can understand.

Where the wandering water gushes
From the hills above Glen-Car,
In pools among the rushes
That scarce could bathe a star,
We seek for slumbering trout
And whispering in their ears
Give them unquiet dreams;
Leaning softly out
From ferns that drop their tears
Over the young streams.
Come away, O human child!
To the waters and the wild
With a faery, hand in hand,
For the world's more full of weeping than you can understand.

Away with us he's going,
The solemn-eyed:
He'll hear no more the lowing
Of the calves on the warm hillside
Or the kettle on the hob
Sing peace into his breast,
Or see the brown mice bob
Round and round the oatmeal-chest.
For he comes, the human child,
To the waters and the wild
With a faery, hand in hand,
From a world more full of weeping than he can understand.

THE MAN WHO DREAMED OF FAERYLAND

February 1891

He stood among a crowd at Drumahair;
His heart hung all upon a silken dress,
And he had known at last some tenderness,
Before earth took him to her stony care;
But when a man poured fish into a pile,
It seemed they raised their little silver heads,
And sang what gold morning or evening sheds
Upon a woven world-forgotten isle
Where people love beside the ravelled seas;
That Time can never mar a lover's vows
Under that woven changeless roof of boughs:
The singing shook him out of his new ease.

He wandered by the sands of Lissadell;
His mind ran all on money cares and fears,
And he had known at last some prudent years
Before they heaped his grave under the hill;
But while he passed before a plashy place,
A lug-worm with its grey and muddy mouth
Sang that somewhere to north or west or south
There dwelt a gay, exulting, gentle race
Under the golden or the silver skies;
That if a dancer stayed his hungry foot
It seemed the sun and moon were in the fruit:
And at that singing he was no more wise.

He mused beside the well of Scanavin,
He mused upon his mockers: without fail
His sudden vengeance were a country tale,
When earthy night had drunk his body in;
But one small knot-grass growing by the pool
Sang where – unnecessary cruel voice –
Old silence bids its chosen race rejoice,
Whatever ravelled waters rise and fall
Or stormy silver fret the gold of day,
And midnight there enfold them like a fleece
And lover there by lover be at peace.
The tale drove his fine angry mood away.

He slept under the hill of Lugnagall;
And might have known at last unhaunted sleep
Under that cold and vapour-turbaned steep,
Now that the earth had taken man and all:
Did not the worms that spired about his bones
Proclaim with that unwearied, reedy cry
That God has laid His fingers on the sky,
That from those fingers glittering summer runs
Upon the dancer by the dreamless wave.
Why should those lovers that no lovers miss
Dream, until God burn Nature with a kiss?
The man has found no comfort in the grave.

THE DANAAN QUICKEN TREE

May 1893

Beloved, hear my bitter tale! —
    Now making busy with the oar,
Now flinging loose the slanting sail,
    I hurried from the woody shore,
And plucked small fruits on Innisfree.
(Ah, mournful Danaan quicken tree!)

A murmuring faery multitude,
    When flying to the heart of light
From playing hurley in the wood
    With creatures of our heavy night,
A berry threw for me — or thee.
(Ah, mournful Danaan quicken tree!)

And thereon grew a tender root,
    And thereon grew a tender stem,
And thereon grew the ruddy fruit
    That are a poison to all men
And meat to the Aslauga Shee.
(Ah, mournful Danaan quicken tree!)

If when the battle is half won,
   I fling away my sword, blood dim,
Or leave some service all undone,
   Beloved, blame the Danaan whim,
And blame the snare they set for me.
(Ah, mournful Danaan quicken tree!)

Cast out all hope, cast out all fear,
   And taste with me the faeries' meat.
For while I blamed them I could hear
   Dark Joan call the berries sweet,
Where Niamh heads the revelry.
(Ah, mournful Danaan quicken tree!)

THE HOST OF THE AIR

1 October 1893   November 1893

O'Driscoll drove with a song
The wild duck and the drake
From the tall and the tufted reeds
Of the drear Hart Lake.

And he saw how the reeds grew dark
At the coming of night-tide,
And dreamed of the long dim hair
Of Bridget his bride.

He heard while he sang and dreamed
A piper piping away,
And never was piping so sad,
And never was piping so gay.

And he saw young men and young girls
Who danced on a level place,
And Bridget his bride among them,
With a sad and a gay face.

The dancers crowded about him
And many a sweet thing said,
And a young man brought him red wine
And a young girl white bread.

But Bridget drew him by the sleeve
Away from the merry bands,
To old men playing at cards
With a twinkling of ancient hands.

The bread and the wine had a doom,
For these were the host of the air;
He sat and played in a dream
Of her long dim hair.

He played with the merry old men
And thought not of evil chance,
Until one bore Bridget his bride
Away from the merry dance.

He bore her away in his arms,
The handsomest young man there,
And his neck and his breast and his arms
Were drowned in her long dim hair.

O'Driscoll scattered the cards
And out of his dream awoke:
Old men and young men and young girls
Were gone like a drifting smoke;

But he heard high up in the air
A piper piping away,
And never was piping so sad,
And never was piping so gay.

TO SOME I HAVE TALKED WITH BY THE FIRE

May 1895

While I wrought out these fitful Danaan rhymes,
My heart would brim with dreams about the times
When we bent down above the fading coals
And talked of the dark folk who live in souls
Of passionate men, like bats in the dead trees;
And of the wayward twilight companies
Who sigh with mingled sorrow and content,
Because their blossoming dreams have never bent
Under the fruit of evil and of good:
And of the embattled flaming multitude
Who rise, wing above wing, flame above flame,
And, like a storm, cry the Ineffable Name,
And with the clashing of their sword-blades make
A rapturous music, till the morning break
And the white hush end all but the loud beat
Of their long wings, the flash of their white feet.

[OUT OF SIGHT IS OUT OF MIND]

September 1895

Out of sight is out of mind:
Long have man and woman-kind,
Heavy of will and light of mood,
Taken away our wheaten food,
Taken away our Altar stone;
Hail and rain and thunder alone,
And red hearts we turn to grey,
Are true till Time gutter away.

THE UNAPPEASABLE HOST

April 1896

The Danaan children laugh, in cradles of wrought gold,
And clap their hands together, and half close their eyes,
For they will ride the North when the ger-eagle flies,
With heavy whitening wings, and a heart fallen cold:
I kiss my wailing child and press it to my breast,
And hear the narrow graves calling my child and me.
Desolate winds that cry over the wandering sea;
Desolate winds that hover in the flaming West;
Desolate winds that beat the doors of Heaven, and beat
The doors of Hell and blow there many a whimpering ghost;
O heart the winds have shaken, the unappeasable host
Is comelier than candles at Mother Mary's feet.

THE MOUNTAIN TOMB

August 1912   December 1912

Pour wine and dance if manhood still have pride,
Bring roses if the rose be yet in bloom;
The cataract smokes upon the mountain side,
Our Father Rosicross is in his tomb.

Pull down the blinds, bring fiddle and clarionet
That there be no foot silent in the room
Nor mouth from kissing, nor from wine unwet;
Our Father Rosicross is in his tomb.

In vain, in vain; the cataract still cries;
The everlasting taper lights the gloom;
All wisdom shut into his onyx eyes,
Our father Rosicross sleeps in his tomb.

OIL AND BLOOD

(?) December 1927; revised 1928 and 1929   *WS* 1929

In tombs of gold and lapis lazuli
Bodies of holy men and women exude
Miraculous oil, odour of violet.

But under heavy loads of trampled clay
Lie bodies of the vampires full of blood;
Their shrouds are bloody and their lips are wet.

CUCHULAIN COMFORTED

13 January 1939

A man that had six mortal wounds, a man
Violent and famous, strode among the dead;
Eyes stared out of the branches and were gone.

Then certain Shrouds that muttered head to head
Came and were gone. He leant upon a tree
As though to meditate on wounds and blood.

A Shroud that seemed to have authority
Among those bird-like things came, and let fall
A bundle of linen. Shrouds by two and three

Came creeping up because the man was still.
And thereupon that linen-carrier said
'Your life can grow much sweeter if you will

'Obey our ancient rule and make a shroud;
Mainly because of what we only know
The rattle of those arms makes us afraid.

'We thread the needles' eyes, and all we do
All must together do'. That done, the man
Took up the nearest and began to sew.

'Now must we sing and sing the best we can
But first you must be told our character:
Convicted cowards all by kindred slain

'Or driven from home and left to die in fear.'
They sang, but had nor human tunes nor words,
Though all was done in common as before;

They had changed their throats and had the throats of birds.

SECTION 12
FROM THE PLAYS

[I AM COME TO CRY WITH YOU, WOMAN]

CNH 1902

I am come to cry with you, woman,
My hair is unwound and unbound;
I remember him ploughing his field,
Turning up the red side of the ground,
And building his barn on the hill
With the good mortared stone;
O! we'd have pulled down the gallows
Had it happened in Enniscrone!

[THE FOUR RIVERS THAT RUN THERE]

TKT 1904

The four rivers than run there,
Through well-mown level ground,
Have come out of a blessed well
That is all bound and wound
By the great roots of an apple
And all the fowls of the air
Have gathered in the wide branches
And keep singing there.

[NOTHING THAT HE HAS DONE]

February 1910

Nothing that he has done;
His mind that is fire,
His body that is sun,
Have set my head higher
Than all the world's wives.
Himself on the wind
Is the gift that he gives,
Therefore women-kind,
When their eyes have met mine,
Grow cold and grow hot,
Troubled as with wine
By a secret thought,
Preyed upon, fed upon
By jealousy and desire,
For I am moon to that sun,
I am steel to that fire.

THE MASK

Between August 1910–May 1911   GH 1910

'Put off that mask of burning gold
With emerald eyes.'
'O no, my dear, you make so bold
To find if hearts be wild and wise,
And yet not cold.'

'I would but find what's there to find,
Love or deceit.'
'It was the mask engaged your mind,
And after set your heart to beat,
Not what's behind.'

'But lest you are my enemy,
I must enquire.'
'O no, my dear, let all that be;
What matter, so there is but fire
In you, in me?'

A SONG FROM 'THE PLAYER QUEEN'

May 1914

My mother dandled me and sang,
'How young it is, how young!'
And made a golden cradle
That on a willow swung.

'He went away,' my mother sang,
'When I was brought to bed,'
And all the while her needle pulled
The gold and silver thread.

She pulled the thread and bit the thread
And made a golden gown,
And wept because she had dreamt that I
Was born to wear a crown.

'When she was got,' my mother sang,
'I heard a sea-mew cry,
And saw a flake of the yellow foam
That dropped upon my thigh.'

How therefore could she help but braid
The gold into my hair,
And dream that I should carry
The golden top of care?

[I CALL TO THE EYE OF THE MIND]

TWOI 1917

I call to the eye of the mind
A well long choked up and dry
And boughs long stripped by the wind,
And I call to the mind's eye
Pallor of an ivory face,
Its lofty dissolute air,
A man climbing up to a place
The salt sea wind has swept bare.

What were his life soon done!
Would he lose by that or win?
A mother that saw her son
Doubled over a speckled shin,
Cross-grained with ninety years,
Would cry, 'How little worth
Were all my hopes and fears
And the hard pain of his birth!'

[HE HAS LOST WHAT MAY NOT BE FOUND]

TWOI 1917

He has lost what may not be found
Till men heap his burial-mound
And all the history ends.
He might have lived at his ease,
An old dog's head on his knees,
Among his children and friends.

[AT THE GREY ROUND OF THE HILL]

TPFD 1919

I

At the grey round of the hill
Music of a lost kingdom
Runs, runs and is suddenly still.
The winds out of Clare-Galway
Carry it: suddenly it is still.

I have heard in the night air
A wandering airy music;
And moidered in that snare
A man is lost of a sudden,
In that sweet wandering snare.

What finger first began
Music of a lost kingdom?
They dream that laughed in the sun.
Dry bones that dream are bitter,
They dream and darken our sun.

Those crazy fingers play
A wandering airy music;
Our luck is withered away,
And wheat in the wheat-ear withered,
And the wind blows it away.

II

My heart ran wild when it heard
The curlew cry before dawn
And the eddying cat-headed bird;
But now the night is gone.
I have heard from far below
The strong March birds a-crow.
Stretch neck and clap the wing,
Red cocks, and crow!

[A WOMAN'S BEAUTY IS LIKE A WHITE FRAIL BIRD]

TPFD 1919

A woman's beauty is like a white
Frail bird, like a white sea-bird alone
At daybreak after stormy night
Between two furrows upon the ploughed land:
A sudden storm, and it was thrown
Between dark furrows upon the ploughed land.
How many centuries spent
The sedentary soul
In toils of measurement
Beyond eagle or mole,
Beyond hearing or seeing,
Or Archimedes' guess,
To raise into being
That loveliness?

A strange, unserviceable thing,
A fragile, exquisite, pale shell,
That the vast troubled waters bring
To the loud sands before day has broken.
The storm arose and suddenly fell
Amid the dark before day had broken.
What death? what discipline?
What bonds no man could unbind,
Being imagined within
The labyrinth of the mind,
What pursuing or fleeing,
What wounds, what bloody press,
Dragged into being
This loveliness?

[0, BUT THE MOCKERS' CRY]

FPFD 1921

O, but the mockers' cry
Makes my heart afraid,
As though a flute of bone
Taken from a heron's thigh,
A heron crazed by the moon,
Were cleverly, softly played.

[LONELY THE SEA-BIRD LIES AT HER REST]

FPFD 1921

First Musician.   Lonely the sea-bird lies at her rest,
   Blown like a dawn-blenched parcel of spray
   Upon the wind, or follows her prey
   Under a great wave's hollowing crest.

Second Musician.   God has not appeared to the birds.

Third Musician.   The ger-eagle has chosen his part
   In blue deep of the upper air
   Where one-eyed day can meet his stare;
   He is content with his savage heart.

Second Musician.   God has not appeared to the birds.

First Musician.   But where have last year's cygnets gone?
   The lake is empty; why do they fling
   White wing out beside white wing?
   What can a swan need but a swan?

Second Musician.   God has not appeared to the birds.

[O, BUT I SAW A SOLEMN SIGHT]

November 1934

First Attendant.   O, but I saw a solemn sight;
   Said the rambling, shambling travelling-man;
   Castle Dargan's ruin all lit,
   Lovely ladies dancing in it.

Second Attendant.   What though they danced! Those days are gone,
   Said the wicked, crooked, hawthorn tree;
   Lovely lady or gallant man
   Are blown cold dust or a bit of bone.

First Attendant.   O, what is life but a mouthful of air?
   Said the rambling, shambling travelling-man;
   Yet all the lovely things that were
   Live, for I saw them dancing there.

Second Attendant.   Nobody knows what may befall,
   Said the wicked, crooked, hawthorn tree.
   I have stood so long by a gap in the wall
   Maybe I shall not die at all.

[I SING A SONG OF JACK AND JILL]

March 1935

I sing a song of Jack and Jill.
Jill had murdered Jack;
The moon shone brightly;
Ran up the hill, and round the hill,
Round the hill and back.
A full moon in March.

Jack had a hollow heart, for Jill
Had hung his heart on high;
The moon shone brightly;
Had hung his heart beyond the hill.
A twinkle in the sky.
A full moon in March.

SECTION 13

IDIOSYNCRASIES AND GROTESQUERIES

RUNNING TO PARADISE

20 September 1913   May 1914

As I came over Windy Gap
They threw a halfpenny into my cap,
For I am running to Paradise;
And all that I need do is to wish
And somebody puts his hand in the dish
To throw me a bit of salted fish:
And there the king is but as the beggar.

My brother Mourteen is worn out
With skelping his big brawling lout,
And I am running to Paradise;
A poor life, do what he can,
And though he keep a dog and a gun,
A serving-maid and a serving-man:
And there the king is but as the beggar.

Poor men have grown to be rich men,
And rich men grown to be poor again,
And I am running to Paradise;
And many a darling wit's grown dull
That tossed a bare heel when at school,
Now it has filled an old sock full:
And there the king is but as the beggar.

The wind is old and still at play
While I must hurry upon my way,
For I am running to Paradise;
Yet never have I lit on a friend
To take my fancy like the wind
That nobody can buy or bind:
And there the king is but as the beggar.

THE PEACOCK

May 1914

What's riches to him
That has made a great peacock
With the pride of his eye?
The wind-beaten, stone-grey,
And desolate Three Rock
Would nourish his whim.
Live he or die
Amid wet rocks and heather,
His ghost will be gay
Adding feather to feather
For the pride of his eye.

THE CAT AND THE MOON

1917   *Nine Poems* 1918

The cat went here and there
And the moon spun round like a top,
And the nearest kin of the moon,
The creeping cat, looked up.
Black Minnaloushe stared at the moon,
For, wander and wail as he would,
The pure cold light in the sky
Troubled his animal blood.
Minnaloushe runs in the grass
Lifting his delicate feet.
Do you dance, Minnaloushe, do you dance?
When two close kindred meet,
What better than call a dance?
Maybe the moon may learn,
Tired of that courtly fashion,
A new dance turn.

Minnaloushe creeps through the grass
From moonlit place to place,
The sacred moon overhead
Has taken a new phase.
Does Minnaloushe know that his pupils
Will pass from change to change,
And that from round to crescent,
From crescent to round they range?
Minnaloushe creeps through the grass
Alone, important and wise,
And lifts to the changing moon
His changing eyes.

UNDER THE ROUND TOWER

March 1918   October 1918

'Although I'd lie lapped up in linen
A deal I'd sweat and little earn
If I should live as live the neighbours,'
Cried the beggar, Billy Byrne;
'Stretch bones till the daylight come
On great-grandfather's battered tomb.'

Upon a grey old battered tombstone
In Glendalough beside the stream,
Where the O'Byrnes and Byrnes are buried,
He stretched his bones and fell in a dream
Of sun and moon that a good hour
Bellowed and pranced in the round tower;

Of golden king and silver lady,
Bellowing up and bellowing round,
Till toes mastered a sweet measure,
Mouth mastered a sweet sound,
Prancing round and prancing up
Until they pranced upon the top.

That golden king and that wild lady
Sang till stars began to fade,
Hands gripped in hands, toes close together,
Hair spread on the wind they made;
That lady and that golden king
Could like a brace of blackbirds sing.

'It's certain that my luck is broken,'
That rambling jailbird Billy said;
'Before nightfall I'll pick a pocket
And snug it in a feather-bed.
I cannot find the peace of home
On great-grandfather's battered tomb.'

ANOTHER SONG OF A FOOL

WSC 1919

This great purple butterfly,
In the prison of my hands,
Has a learning in his eye
Not a poor fool understands.

Once he lived a schoolmaster
With a stark, denying look;
A string of scholars went in fear
Of his great birch and his great book.

Like the clangour of a bell,
Sweet and harsh, harsh and sweet,
That is how he learnt so well
To take the roses for his meat.

CRAZY JANE REPROVED

27 March 1929   November 1930

I care not what the sailors say:
All those dreadful thunder-stones,
All that storm that blots the day
Can but show that Heaven yawns;
Great Europa played the fool
That changed a lover for a bull.
Fol de rol, fol de rol.

To round that shell's elaborate whorl,
Adorning every secret track
With the delicate mother-of-pearl,
Made the joints of Heaven crack:
So never hang your heart upon
A roaring, ranting journeyman.
Fol de rol, fol de rol.

A STATESMAN'S HOLIDAY

Completed April 1938   OTB 1939

I lived among great houses,
Riches drove out rank,
Base drove out the better blood,
And mind and body shrank.
No Oscar ruled the table,
But I'd a troop of friends
That knowing better talk had gone
Talked of odds and ends.
Some knew what ailed the world
But never said a thing,
So I have picked a better trade
And night and morning sing:
Tall dames go walking in grass green Avalon.

Am I a great Lord Chancellor
That slept upon the Sack?
Commanding officer that tore
The khaki from his back?
Or am I de Valéra,
Or the King of Greece,
Or the man that made the motors?
Ach, call me what you please!
Here's a Montenegrin lute
And its old sole string
Makes me sweet music
And I delight to sing:
Tall dames go walking in grass green Avalon.

With boys and girls about him,
With any sort of clothes,
With a hat out of fashion,
With old patched shoes,
With a ragged bandit cloak,
With an eye like a hawk,
With a stiff straight back,
With a strutting turkey walk,
With a bag full of pennies,
With a monkey on a chain,
With a great cock's feather,
With an old foul tune.
Tall dames go walking in grass green Avalon.

HIGH TALK

29 July–August 1938   December 1938

Processions that lack high stilts have nothing that catches the eye.
What if my great-granddad had a pair that were twenty foot high,
And mine were but fifteen foot, no modern stalks upon higher,
Some rogue of the world stole them to patch up a fence or a fire.

Because piebald ponies, led bears, caged lions, make but poor shows,
Because children demand Daddy-long-legs upon his timber toes,
Because women in the upper stories demand a face at the pane
That patching old heels they may shriek, I take to chisel and plane.

Malachi Stilt-Jack am I, whatever I learned has run wild,
From collar to collar, from stilt to stilt, from father to child.

All metaphor, Malachi, stilts and all. A barnacle goose
Far up in the stretches of night; night splits and the dawn breaks loose;
I, through the terrible novelty of light, stalk on, stalk on;
Those great sea-horses bare their teeth and laugh at the dawn.

[CRAZY JANE ON THE MOUNTAIN]

July 1938   *OTB* 1939

I am tired of cursing the Bishop,
(Said Crazy Jane)
Nine books or nine hats
Would not make him a man.
I have found something worse
To meditate on.
A King had some beautiful cousins,
But where are they gone?
Battered to death in a cellar,
And he stuck to his throne.
Last night I lay on the mountain,
(Said Crazy Jane)
There in a two horsed carriage
That on two wheels ran
Great bladdered Emer sat,
Her violent man
Cuchulain sat at her side;
Thereupon,
Propped upon my two knees,
I kissed a stone;
I lay stretched out in the dirt
And I cried tears down.

SECTION 14

ARCADIAN AND INDIAN POEMS

THE SONG OF THE HAPPY SHEPHERD

1885   October 1885

The woods of Arcady are dead,
And over is their antique joy;
Of old the world on dreaming fed;
Grey Truth is now her painted toy;
Yet still she turns her restless head:
But O, sick children of the world,
Of all the many changing things
In dreary dancing past us whirled,
To the cracked tune that Chronos sings,
Words alone are certain good.
Where are now the warring kings,
Word be-mockers? — By the Rood
Where are now the warring kings?
An idle word is now their glory,
By the stammering schoolboy said,
Reading some entangled story:
The kings of the old time are dead;
The wandering earth herself may be
Only a sudden flaming word,
In clanging space a moment heard,
Troubling the endless reverie.

Then nowise worship dusty deeds,
Nor seek, for this is also sooth,
To hunger fiercely after truth,
Lest all thy toiling only breeds
New dreams, new dreams; there is no truth
Saving in thine own heart. Seek, then,
No learning from the starry men,
Who follow with the optic glass
The whirling ways of stars that pass —
Seek, then, for this is also sooth,
No word of theirs — the cold star-bane
Has cloven and rent their hearts in twain,
And dead is all their human truth.

Go gather by the humming sea
Some twisted, echo-harbouring shell,
And to its lips thy story tell,
And they thy comforters will be,
Rewarding in melodious guile
Thy fretful words a little while,
Till they shall singing fade in ruth
And die a pearly brotherhood;
For words alone are certain good:
Sing, then, for this is also sooth.

I must be gone: there is a grave
Where daffodil and lily wave,
And I would please the hapless faun,
Buried under the sleepy ground,
With mirthful songs before the dawn.
His shouting days with mirth were crowned;
And still I dream he treads the lawn,
Walking ghostly in the dew,
Pierced by my glad singing through,
My songs of old earth's dreamy youth:
But ah! she dreams not now; dream thou!
For fair are poppies on the brow:
Dream, dream, for this is also sooth.

THE SAD SHEPHERD

1885   October 1886

There was a man whom Sorrow named his friend,
And he, of his high comrade Sorrow dreaming,
Went walking with slow steps along the gleaming
And humming sands, where windy surges wend:
And he called loudly to the stars to bend
From their pale thrones and comfort him, but they
Among themselves laugh on and sing alway:
And then the man whom Sorrow named his friend
Cried out, *Dim sea, hear my most piteous story!*

The sea swept on and cried her old cry still,
Rolling along in dreams from hill to hill.
He fled the persecution of her glory
And, in a far-off, gentle valley stopping,
Cried all his story to the dewdrops glistening.
But naught they heard, for they are always listening,
The dewdrops, for the sound of their own dropping.
And then the man whom Sorrow named his friend
Sought once again the shore, and found a shell,
And thought, *I will my heavy story tell*
Till my own words, re-echoing, shall send
Their sadness through a hollow, pearly heart;
And my own tale again for me shall sing,
And my own whispering words be comforting,
And lo! my ancient burden may depart.
Then he sang softly nigh the pearly rim;
But the sad dweller by the sea-ways lone
Changed all he sang to inarticulate moan
Among her wildering whirls, forgetting him

THE INDIAN TO HIS LOVE

1886   December 1886

The island dreams under the dawn
And great boughs drop tranquillity;
The peahens dance on a smooth lawn,
A parrot sways upon a tree,
Raging at his own image in the enamelled sea.

Here we will moor our lonely ship
And wander ever with woven hands,
Murmuring softly lip to lip,
Along the grass, along the sands,
Murmuring how far away are the unquiet lands:

How we alone of mortals are
Hid under quiet boughs, apart,
While our love grows an Indian star,
A meteor of the burning heart,
One with the tide that gleams, the wings that gleam and dart,

The heavy boughs, the burnished dove
That moans and sighs a hundred days:
How when we die our shade will rove,
When eve has hushed the feathered ways,
With vapoury footsole by the water's drowsy blaze.

MOHINI CHATTERJEE

23 January–9 February 1929   *APEP* 1929

I asked if I should pray,
But the Brahmin said,
'Pray for nothing, say
Every night in bed,
"I have been a king,
I have been a slave,
Nor is there anything,
Fool, rascal, knave,
That I have not been,
And yet upon my breast
A myriad heads have lain." '

That he might set at rest
A boy's turbulent days
Mohini Chatterjee
Spoke these, or words like these.
I add in commentary,
'Old lovers yet may have
All that time denied —
Grave is heaped on grave
That they be satisfied —
Over the blackened earth
The old troops parade,
Birth is heaped on birth
That such cannonade
May thunder time away,
Birth-hour and death-hour meet,
Or, as great sages say,
Men dance on deathless feet.'

1928

MERU

(?) Between August 1933 and June 1934   December 1934

Civilisation is hooped together, brought
Under a rule, under the semblance of peace
By manifold illusion; but man's life is thought,
And he, despite his terror, cannot cease
Ravening through century after century,
Ravening, raging, and uprooting that he may come
Into the desolation of reality:
Egypt and Greece good-bye, and good-bye, Rome!
Hermits upon Mount Meru or Everest,
Caverned in night under the drifted snow,
Or where that snow and winter's dreadful blast
Beat down upon their naked bodies, know
That day brings round the night, that before dawn
His glory and his monuments are gone.

SECTION 15
THE THOUGHT OF *A VISION*

THE TWO TREES

CK 1892

Beloved, gaze in thine own heart,
The holy tree is growing there;
From joy the holy branches start,
And all the trembling flowers they bear.
The changing colours of its fruit
Have dowered the stars with merry light;
The surety of its hidden root
Has planted quiet in the night;
The shaking of its leafy head
Has given the waves their melody,
And made my lips and music wed,
Murmuring a wizard song for thee.
There the Loves a circle go,
The flaming circle of our days,
Gyring, spiring to and fro
In those great ignorant leafy ways;
Remembering all that shaken hair
And how the wingèd sandals dart,
Thine eyes grow full of tender care:
Beloved, gaze in thine own heart.

Gaze no more in the bitter glass
The demons, with their subtle guile,
Lift up before us when they pass,
Or only gaze a little while;
For there a fatal image grows
That the stormy night receives,
Roots half hidden under snows,
Broken boughs and blackened leaves.
For all things turn to barrenness
In the dim glass the demons hold,
The glass of outer weariness,
Made when God slept in times of old.

There, through the broken branches, go
The ravens of unresting thought;
Flying, crying, to and fro,
Cruel claw and hungry throat,
Or else they stand and sniff the wind,
And shake their ragged wings; alas!
Thy tender eyes grow all unkind:
Gaze no more in the bitter glass

THE MAGI

20 September 1913   May 1914

Now as at all times I can see in the mind's eye,
In their stiff, painted clothes, the pale unsatisfied ones
Appear and disappear in the blue depth of the sky
With all their ancient faces like rain-beaten stones,
And all their helms of silver hovering side by side,
And all their eyes still fixed, hoping to find once more,
Being by Calvary's turbulence unsatisfied,
The uncontrollable mystery on the bestial floor

EGO DOMINUS TUUS

5 October 1915   October 1917

Hic.   On the grey sand beside the shallow stream
        Under your old wind-beaten tower, where still
        A lamp burns on beside the open book
        That Michael Robartes left, you walk in the moon
        And though you have passed the best of life still trace,
        Enthralled by the unconquerable delusion,
        Magical shapes.

Ille.   By the help of an image
        I call to my own opposite, summon all
        That I have handled least, least looked upon.

Hic.   And I would find myself and not an image.

Ille.   That is our modern hope and by its light
        We have lit upon the gentle, sensitive mind
        And lost the old nonchalance of the hand;
        Whether we have chosen chisel, pen or brush,
        We are but critics, or but half create,
        Timid, entangled, empty and abashed,
        Lacking the countenance of our friends.

Hic.   And yet
      The chief imagination of Christendom,
      Dante Alighieri, so utterly found himself
      That he has made that hollow face of his
      More plain to the mind's eye than any face
      But that of Christ.

Ille.   And did he find himself
      Or was the hunger that had made it hollow
      A hunger for the apple on the bough
      Most out of reach? and is that spectral image
      The man that Lapo and that Guido knew?
      I think he fashioned from his opposite
      An image that might have been a stony face
      Staring upon a Bedouin's horse-hair roof
      From doored and windowed cliff, or half upturned
      Among the coarse grass and the camel-dung.
      He set his chisel to the hardest stone.
      Being mocked by Guido for his lecherous life,
      Derided and deriding, driven out
      To climb that stair and eat that bitter bread,
      He found the unpersuadable justice, he found
      The most exalted lady loved by a man.

Hic.   Yet surely there are men who have made their art
      Out of no tragic war, lovers of life,
      Impulsive men that look for happiness
      And sing when they have found it.

Ille.   No, not sing,
For those that love the world serve it in action,
Grow rich, popular and full of influence,
And should they paint or write, still it is action:
The struggle of the fly in marmalade.
The rhetorician would deceive his neighbours,
The sentimentalist himself; while art
Is but a vision of reality.
What portion in the world can the artist have
Who has awakened from the common dream
But dissipation and despair?

Hic.   And yet
No one denies to Keats love of the world;
Remember his deliberate happiness.

Ille.   His art is happy, but who knows his mind?
I see a schoolboy when I think of him,
With face and nose pressed to a sweet-shop window,
For certainly he sank into his grave
His senses and his heart unsatisfied,
And made – being poor, ailing and ignorant,
Shut out from all the luxury of the world,
The coarse-bred son of a livery-stable keeper –
Luxuriant song.

Hic.   Why should you leave the lamp
Burning alone beside an open book,
And trace these characters upon the sands?
A style is found by sedentary toil
And by the imitation of great masters.

Ille.   Because I seek an image, not a book.
Those men that in their writings are most wise
Own nothing but their blind, stupefied hearts.
I call to the mysterious one who yet
Shall walk the wet sands by the edge of the stream
And look most like me, being indeed my double,
And prove of all imaginable things
The most unlike, being my anti-self,
And standing by these characters disclose
All that I seek; and whisper it as though
He were afraid the birds, who cry aloud
Their momentary cries before it is dawn,
Would carry it away to blasphemous men.

THE PHASES OF THE MOON

1918   *WSC* 1919

An old man cocked his ear upon a bridge;
He and his friend, their faces to the South,
Had trod the uneven road. Their boots were soiled,
Their Connemara cloth worn out of shape;
They had kept a steady pace as though their beds,
Despite a dwindling and late risen moon,
Were distant still. An old man cocked his ear.

Aherne   What made that sound?

Robartes   A rat or water-hen
   Splashed, or an otter slid into the stream.
   We are on the bridge; that shadow is the tower,
   And the light proves that he is reading still.
   He has found, after the manner of his kind,

Mere images; chosen this place to live in
Because, it may be, of the candle-light
From the far tower where Milton's Platonist
Sat late, or Shelley's visionary prince:
The lonely light that Samuel Palmer engraved,
An image of mysterious wisdom won by toil;
And now he seeks in book or manuscript
What he shall never find.

Aherne   Why should not you
Who know it all ring at his door, and speak
Just truth enough to show that his whole life
Will scarcely find for him a broken crust
Of all those truths that are your daily bread;
And when you have spoken take the roads again?

Robartes   He wrote of me in that extravagant style
He had learned from Pater, and to round his tale
Said I was dead; and dead I choose to be.

Aherne   Sing me the changes of the moon once more;
True song, though speech: 'mine author sung it me'.

Robartes   Twenty-and-eight the phases of the moon,
The full and the moon's dark and all the crescents.
Twenty-and-eight, and yet but six-and-twenty
The cradles that a man must needs be rocked in;
For there's no human life at the full or the dark.
From the first crescent to the half, the dream
But summons to adventure, and the man
Is always happy like a bird or a beast;
But while the moon is rounding towards the full
He follows whatever whim's most difficult
Among whims not impossible, and though scarred,
As with the cat-o'-nine-tails of the mind,
His body moulded from within his body
Grows comelier. Eleven pass, and then
Athena takes Achilles by the hair,
Hector is in the dust, Nietzsche is born,
Because the hero's crescent is the twelfth.

And yet, twice born, twice buried, grow he must,
Before the full moon, helpless as a worm.
The thirteenth moon but sets the soul at war
In its own being, and when that war's begun
There is no muscle in the arm; and after,
Under the frenzy of the fourteenth moon,
The soul begins to tremble into stillness,
To die into the labyrinth of itself!

Aherne   Sing out the song; sing to the end, and sing
The strange reward of all that discipline.

Robartes   All thought becomes an image and the soul
Becomes a body: that body and that soul
Too perfect at the full to lie in a cradle,
Too lonely for the traffic of the world:
Body and soul cast out and cast away
Beyond the visible world.

Aherne   All dreams of the soul
End in a beautiful man's or woman's body.

Robartes   Have you not always known it?

Aherne   The song will have it
That those that we have loved got their long fingers
From death, and wounds, or on Sinai's top,
Or from some bloody whip in their own hands.
They ran from cradle to cradle till at last
Their beauty dropped out of the loneliness
Of body and soul.

Robartes   The lover's heart knows that

Aherne   It must be that the terror in their eyes
Is memory or foreknowledge of the hour
When all is fed with light and heaven is bare.

Robartes   When the moon's full those creatures of the full
          Are met on the waste hills by country men
          Who shudder and hurry by: body and soul
          Estranged amid the strangeness of themselves,
          Caught up in contemplation, the mind's eye
          Fixed upon images that once were thought,
          For perfected, completed, and immovable
          Images can break the solitude
          Of lovely, satisfied, indifferent eyes.

          And thereupon with aged, high-pitched voice
          Aherne laughed, thinking of the man within,
          His sleepless candle and laborious pen.

Robartes   And after that the crumbling of the moon:
          The soul remembering its loneliness
          Shudders in many cradles; all is changed.
          It would be the world's servant, and as it serves,
          Choosing whatever task's most difficult
          Among tasks not impossible, it takes
          Upon the body and upon the soul
          The coarseness of the drudge.

Aherne   Before the full
          It sought itself and afterwards the world.

Robartes   Because you are forgotten, half out of life,
          And never wrote a book, your thought is clear.
          Reformer, merchant, statesman, learned man,
          Dutiful husband, honest wife by turn,
          Cradle upon cradle, and all in flight and all
          Deformed, because there is no deformity
          But saves us from a dream.

Aherne   And what of those
          That the last servile crescent has set free?

Robartes   Because all dark, like those that are all light,
     They are cast beyond the verge, and in a cloud,
     Crying to one another like the bats;
     But having no desire they cannot tell
     What's good or bad, or what it is to triumph
     At the perfection of one's own obedience;
     And yet they speak what's blown into the mind
     Deformed beyond deformity, unformed,
     Insipid as the dough before it is baked,
     They change their bodies at a word

Aherne   And then?

Robartes   When all the dough has been so kneaded up
     That it can take what form cook Nature fancies,
     The first thin crescent is wheeled round once more.

Aherne   But the escape; the song's not finished yet.

Robartes   Hunchback and Saint and Fool are the last crescents.
     The burning bow that once could shoot an arrow
     Out of the up and down, the wagon-wheel
     Of beauty's cruelty and wisdom's chatter –
     Out of that raving tide – is drawn betwixt
     Deformity of body and of mind.

Aherne   Were not our beds far off I'd ring the bell,
     Stand under the rough roof-timbers of the hall
     Beside the castle door, where all is stark
     Austerity, a place set out for wisdom
     That he will never find; I'd play a part;
     He would never know me after all these years
     But take me for some drunken country man;
     I'd stand and mutter there until he caught
     "Hunchback and Saint and Fool", and that they came
     Under the three last crescents of the moon,
     And then I'd stagger out. He'd crack his wits
     Day after day, yet never find the meaning.

And then he laughed to think that what seemed hard
Should be so simple — a bat rose from the hazels
And circled round him with its squeaky cry,
The light in the tower window was put out.

THE DOUBLE VISION OF MICHAEL ROBARTES

1919　　　　　　　　　　　　　　　　　　　　　*WSC* 1919

I

On the grey rock of Cashel the mind's eye
Has called up the cold spirits that are born
When the old moon is vanished from the sky
And the new still hides her horn.

Under blank eyes and fingers never still
The particular is pounded till it is man.
When had I my own will?
O not since life began.

Constrained, arraigned, baffled, bent and unbent
By these wire-jointed jaws and limbs of wood,
Themselves obedient,
Knowing not evil and good;

Obedient to some hidden magical breath.
They do not even feel, so abstract are they,
So dead beyond our death,
Triumph that we obey.

II

On the grey rock of Cashel I suddenly saw
A Sphinx with woman breast and lion paw,
A Buddha, hand at rest,
Hand lifted up that blest;

And right between these two a girl at play
That, it may be, had danced her life away,
For now being dead it seemed
That she of dancing dreamed.

Although I saw it all in the mind's eye
There can be nothing solider till I die;
I saw by the moon's light
Now at its fifteenth night.

One lashed her tail; her eyes lit by the moon
Gazed upon all things known, all things unknown
In triumph of intellect
With motionless head erect.

That other's moonlit eyeballs never moved,
Being fixed on all things loved, all things unloved,
Yet little peace he had,
For those that love are sad.

O little did they care who danced between,
And little she by whom her dance was seen
So she had outdanced thought.
Body perfection brought,

For what but eye and ear silence the mind
With the minute particulars of mankind?
Mind moved yet seemed to stop
As 'twere a spinning-top.

In contemplation had those three so wrought
Upon a moment, and so stretched it out
That they, time overthrown,
Were dead yet flesh and bone.

III

I knew that I had seen, had seen at last
That girl my unremembering nights hold fast
Or else my dreams that fly
If I should rub an eye,

And yet in flying fling into my meat
A crazy juice that makes the pulses beat
As though I had been undone
By Homer's Paragon

Who never gave the burning town a thought;
To such a pitch of folly I am brought,
Being caught between the pull
Of the dark moon and the full,

The commonness of thought and images
That have the frenzy of our western seas.
Thereon I made my moan,
And after kissed a stone,

And after that arranged it in a song
Seeing that I, ignorant for so long,
Had been rewarded thus
In Cormac's ruined house.

THE SECOND COMING

January 1919   November 1920

Turning and turning in the widening gyre
The falcon cannot hear the falconer;
Things fall apart; the centre cannot hold;
Mere anarchy is loosed upon the world,
The blood-dimmed tide is loosed, and everywhere
The ceremony of innocence is drowned;
The best lack all conviction, while the worst
Are full of passionate intensity.

Surely some revelation is at hand;
Surely the Second Coming is at hand.
The Second Coming! Hardly are those words out
When a vast image out of *Spiritus Mundi*
Troubles my sight: somewhere in sands of the desert
A shape with lion body and the head of a man,
A gaze blank and pitiless as the sun,
Is moving its slow thighs, while all about it
Reel shadows of the indignant desert birds.
The darkness drops again; but now I know
That twenty centuries of stony sleep
Were vexed to nightmare by a rocking cradle,
And what rough beast, its hour come round at last,
Slouches towards Bethlehem to be born?

LEDA AND THE SWAN

18 September 1923   June 1924

A sudden blow: the great wings beating still
Above the staggering girl, her thighs caressed
By the dark webs, her nape caught in his bill,
He holds her helpless breast upon his breast.

How can those terrified vague fingers push
The feathered glory from her loosening thighs?
And how can body, laid in that white rush,
But feel the strange heart beating where it lies?

A shudder in the loins engenders there
The broken wall, the burning roof and tower
And Agamemnon dead.
                                Being so caught up,
So mastered by the brute blood of the air,
Did she put on his knowledge with his power
Before the indifferent beak could let her drop?

1923

HER VISION IN THE WOOD

August 1926   *WS* 1929

Dry timber under that rich foliage,
At wine-dark midnight in the sacred wood,
Too old for a man's love I stood in rage
Imagining men. Imagining that I could
A greater with a lesser pang assuage
Or but to find if withered vein ran blood,
I tore my body that its wine might cover
Whatever could recall the lip of lover.

And after that I held my fingers up,
Stared at the wine-dark nail, or dark that ran
Down every withered finger from the top;
But the dark changed to red, and torches shone,
And deafening music shook the leaves; a troop
Shouldered a litter with a wounded man,
Or smote upon the string and to the sound
Sang of the beast that gave the fatal wound.

All stately women moving to a song
With loosened hair or foreheads grief-distraught,
It seemed a Quattrocento painter's throng,
A thoughtless image of Mantegna's thought —
Why should they think that are forever young?
Till suddenly in grief's contagion caught,
I stared upon his blood-bedabbled breast
And sang my malediction with the rest.

That thing all blood and mire, that beast-torn wreck,
Half turned and fixed a glazing eye on mine,
And, though love's bitter-sweet had all come back,
Those bodies from a picture or a coin
Nor saw my body fall nor heard it shriek,
Nor knew, drunken with singing as with wine,
That they had brought no fabulous symbol there
But my heart's victim and its torturer.

SAILING TO BYZANTIUM

Autumn (probably September) 1926   OB 1927

I

That is no country for old men. The young
In one another's arms, birds in the trees,
— Those dying generations — at their song,
The salmon-falls, the mackerel-crowded seas,
Fish, flesh, or fowl, commend all summer long
Whatever is begotten, born, and dies.
Caught in that sensual music all neglect
Monuments of unageing intellect.

II

An aged man is but a paltry thing,
A tattered coat upon a stick, unless
Soul clap its hands and sing, and louder sing
For every tatter in its mortal dress,
Nor is there singing school but studying
Monuments of its own magnificence;
And therefore I have sailed the seas and come
To the holy city of Byzantium.

III

O sages standing in God's holy fire
As in the gold mosaic of a wall,
Come from the holy fire, perne in a gyre,
And be the singing-masters of my soul.
Consume my heart away; sick with desire
And fastened to a dying animal
It knows not what it is; and gather me
Into the artifice of eternity.

IV

Once out of nature I shall never take
My bodily form from any natural thing,
But such a form as Grecian goldsmiths make
Of hammered gold and gold enamelling
To keep a drowsy Emperor awake;
Or set upon a golden bough to sing
To lords and ladies of Byzantium
Of what is past, or passing, or to come.

TWO SONGS FROM A PLAY

1926; last stanza of II *(?) 1930–1*   I and first stanza of II June 1927;
                                                whole poem *OB* 1931

I

I saw a staring virgin stand
Where holy Dionysus died,
And tear the heart out of his side,
And lay the heart upon her hand
And bear that beating heart away;
And then did all the Muses sing
Of Magnus Annus at the spring,
As though God's death were but a play.

Another Troy must rise and set,
Another lineage feed the crow,
Another Argo's painted prow
Drive to a flashier bauble yet.
The Roman Empire stood appalled:
It dropped the reins of peace and war
When that fierce virgin and her Star
Out of the fabulous darkness called.

II

In pity for man's darkening thought
He walked that room and issued thence
In Galilean turbulence;
The Babylonian starlight brought
A fabulous, formless darkness in;
Odour of blood when Christ was slain
Made all Platonic tolerance vain
And vain all Doric discipline.

Everything that man esteems
Endures a moment or a day.
Love's pleasure drives his love away,
The painter's brush consumes his dreams;
The herald's cry, the soldier's tread
Exhaust his glory and his might:
Whatever flames upon the night
Man's own resinous heart has fed.

WISDOM

OB 1927

The true faith discovered was
When painted panel, statuary,
Glass-mosaic, window-glass,
Amended what was told awry
By some peasant gospeller;
Swept the sawdust from the floor
Of that working-carpenter.
Miracle had its playtime where
In damask clothed and on a seat
Chryselephantine, cedar-boarded,
His majestic Mother sat
Stitching at a purple hoarded
That He might be nobly breeched
In starry towers of Babylon
Noah's freshet never reached.
King Abundance got Him on
Innocence; and Wisdom He.
That cognomen sounded best
Considering what wild infancy
Drove horror from His mother's breast.

BYZANTIUM

September 1930   *WMP* 1932

The unpurged images of day recede;
The Emperor's drunken soldiery are abed;
Night resonance recedes, night-walkers' song
After great cathedral gong;
A starlit or a moonlit dome disdains
All that man is,
All mere complexities,
The fury and the mire of human veins.

Before me floats an image, man or shade,
Shade more than man, more image than a shade;
For Hades' bobbin bound in mummy-cloth
May unwind the winding path;
A mouth that has no moisture and no breath
Breathless mouths may summon;
I hail the superhuman;
I call it death-in-life and life-in-death.

Miracle, bird or golden handiwork,
More miracle than bird or handiwork,
Planted on the starlit golden bough,
Can like the cocks of Hades crow,
Or, by the moon embittered, scorn aloud
In glory of changeless metal
Common bird or petal
And all complexities of mire or blood.

At midnight on the Emperor's pavement flit
Flames that no faggot feeds, nor steel has lit,
Nor storm disturbs, flames begotten of flame,
Where blood-begotten spirits come
And all complexities of fury leave,
Dying into a dance,
An agony of trance,
As agony of flame that cannot singe a sleeve.

Astraddle on the dolphin's mire and blood,
Spirit after spirit! The smithies break the flood,
The golden smithies of the Emperor!
Marbles of the dancing floor
Break bitter furies of complexity,
Those images that yet
Fresh images beget,
That dolphin-torn, that gong-tormented sea.

1930

THERE

(?) Late 1934/early 1935   FMIM 1935

There all the barrel-hoops are knit,
There all the serpent-tails are bit,
There all the gyres converge in one,
There all the planets drop in the Sun.

RIBH CONSIDERS CHRISTIAN LOVE INSUFFICIENT

(?) 1934   December 1934

Why should I seek for love or study it?
It is of God and passes human wit;
I study hatred with great diligence,
For that's a passion in my own control,
A sort of besom that can clear the soul
Of everything that is not mind or sense.

Why do I hate man, woman or event?
That is a light my jealous soul has sent.
From terror and deception freed it can
Discover impurities, can show at last
How soul may walk when all such things are past,
How soul could walk before such things began.

Then my delivered soul herself shall learn
A darker knowledge and in hatred turn
From every thought of God mankind has had.
Thought is a garment and the soul's a bride
That cannot in that trash and tinsel hide:
Hatred of God may bring the soul to God

At stroke of midnight soul cannot endure
A bodily or mental furniture.
What can she take until her Master give!
Where can she look until He make the show!
What can she know until He bid her know!
How can she live till in her blood He live!

WHAT MAGIC DRUM?

(?) 1934   *FMIM* 1935

He holds him from desire, all but stops his breathing lest
Primordial Motherhood forsake his limbs, the child no longer rest,
Drinking joy as it were milk upon his breast.

Through light-obliterating garden foliage what magic drum?
Down limb and breast or down that glimmering belly move his mouth and
    sinewy tongue.
What from the forest came? What beast has licked its young?

LAPIS LAZULI
(For Harry Clifton)

Completed 25 July 1936   March 1938

I have heard that hysterical women say
They are sick of the palette and fiddle-bow,
Of poets that are always gay,
For everybody knows or else should know
That if nothing drastic is done
Aeroplane and Zeppelin will come out,
Pitch like King Billy bomb-balls in
Until the town lie beaten flat.

All perform their tragic play,
There struts Hamlet, there is Lear,
That's Ophelia, that Cordelia;
Yet they, should the last scene be there,
The great stage curtain about to drop,
If worthy their prominent part in the play,
Do not break up their lines to weep.
They know that Hamlet and Lear are gay;
Gaiety transfiguring all that dread.

All men have aimed at, found and lost;
Black out; Heaven blazing into the head:
Tragedy wrought to its uttermost.
Though Hamlet rambles and Lear rages,
And all the drop scenes drop at once
Upon a hundred thousand stages,
It cannot grow by an inch or an ounce.

On their own feet they came, or on shipboard,
Camel-back, horse-back, ass-back, mule-back,
Old civilisations put to the sword.
Then they and their wisdom went to rack:
No handiwork of Callimachus
Who handled marble as if it were bronze,
Made draperies that seemed to rise
When sea-wind swept the corner, stands;
His long lamp chimney shaped like the stem
Of a slender palm, stood but a day;
All things fall and are built again
And all those that build them again are gay.

Two Chinamen, behind them a third,
Are carved in Lapis Lazuli,
Over them flies a long-legged bird
A symbol of longevity;
The third, doubtless a serving-man,
Carries a musical instrument.

Every discolouration of the stone,
Every accidental crack or dent
Seems a water-course or an avalanche,
Or lofty slope where it still snows
Though doubtless plum or cherry-branch
Sweetens the little half-way house
Those Chinamen climb towards, and I
Delight to imagine them seated there;
There, on the mountain and the sky,
On all the tragic scene they stare.
One asks for mournful melodies;
Accomplished fingers begin to play.
Their eyes mid many wrinkles, their eyes,
Their ancient, glittering eyes, are gay.

THE GYRES

(?) Between July 1936 and January 1937   NP 1938

The gyres! the gyres! Old Rocky Face look forth;
Things thought too long can be no longer thought
For beauty dies of beauty, worth of worth,
And ancient lineaments are blotted out.
Irrational streams of blood are staining earth;
Empedocles has thrown all things about;
Hector is dead and there's a light in Troy;
We that look on but laugh in tragic joy.

What matter though numb nightmare ride on top
And blood and mire the sensitive body stain?
What matter? Heave no sigh, let no tear drop,
A greater, a more gracious time has gone;
For painted forms or boxes of make-up
In ancient tombs I sighed, but not again;
What matter? Out of Cavern comes a voice
And all it knows is that one word 'Rejoice.'

Conduct and work grow coarse, and coarse the soul,
What matter! Those that Rocky Face holds dear,
Lovers of horses and of women, shall
From marble of a broken sepulchre
Or dark betwixt the polecat and the owl,
Or any rich, dark nothing disinter
The workman, noble and saint, and all things run
On that unfashionable gyre again.

THE GREAT DAY

January 1937   March 1938

Hurrah for revolution and more cannon shot;
A beggar upon horseback lashes a beggar upon foot;
Hurrah for revolution and cannon come again,
The beggars have changed places but the lash goes on.

LONG-LEGGGED FLY

Between November 1937 and (?)
11 April 1938   March 1939

That civilisation may not sink
Its great battle lost,
Quiet the dog, tether the pony
To a distant post.
Our master Caesar is in the tent
Where the maps are spread,
His eyes fixed upon nothing,
A hand under his head.

Like a long-legged fly upon the stream
His mind moves upon silence.

That the topless towers be burnt
And men recall that face,
Move most gently if move you must
In this lonely place.
She thinks, part woman, three parts a child,
That nobody looks; her feet
Practise a tinker shuffle
Picked up on the street.

Like a long-legged fly upon the stream
Her mind moves upon silence.

That girls at puberty may find
The first Adam in their thought,
Shut the door of the Pope's chapel,
Keep those children out.
There on that scaffolding reclines
Michael Angelo.
With no more sound than the mice make
His hand moves to and fro.

Like a long-legged fly upon the stream
His mind moves upon silence.

THE STATUES

9 April (?revised up to June) 1938   March 1939

Pythagoras planned it. Why did the people stare?
His numbers though they moved or seemed to move
In marble or in bronze, lacked character.
But boys and girls pale from the imagined love
Of solitary beds knew what they were,
That passion could bring character enough;
And pressed at midnight in some public place
Live lips upon a plummet-measured face.

No; greater than Pythagoras, for the men
That with a mallet or a chisel modelled these
Calculations that look but casual flesh, put down
All Asiatic vague immensities,
And not the banks of oars that swam upon
The many-headed foam at Salamis.
Europe put off that foam when Phidias
Gave women dreams and dreams their looking-glass.

One image crossed the many-headed, sat
Under the tropic shade, grew round and slow,
No Hamlet thin from eating flies, a fat
Dreamer of the Middle-Ages. Empty eye-balls knew
That knowledge increases unreality, that
Mirror on mirror mirrored is all the show.
When gong and conch declare the hour to bless
Grimalkin crawls to Buddha's emptiness.

When Pearse summoned Cuchulain to his side,
What stalked through the Post Office? What intellect,
What calculation, number, measurement, replied?
We Irish, born into that ancient sect
But thrown upon this filthy modern tide
And by its formless, spawning, fury wrecked,
Climb to our proper dark, that we may trace
The lineaments of a plummet-measured face.

NEWS FOR THE DELPHIC ORACLE

(?) 1938   March 1939

I

There all the golden codgers lay,
There the silver dew,
And the great water sighed for love
And the wind sighed too.
Man-picker Niamh leant and sighed
By Oisin on the grass;
There sighed amid his choir of love
Tall Pythagoras.
Plotinus came and looked about,
The salt flakes on his breast,
And having stretched and yawned awhile
Lay sighing like the rest.

II

Straddling each a dolphin's back
And steadied by a fin
Those Innocents re-live their death,
Their wounds open again.
The ecstatic waters laugh because
Their cries are sweet and strange,
Through their ancestral patterns dance,
And the brute dolphins plunge
Until in some cliff-sheltered bay
Where wades the choir of love
Proffering its sacred laurel crowns,
They pitch their burdens off.

III

Slim adolescence that a nymph has stripped,
Peleus on Thetis stares,
Her limbs are delicate as an eyelid,
Love has blinded him with tears;
But Thetis' belly listens.
Down the mountain walls
From where Pan's cavern is
Intolerable music falls.
Foul goat-head, brutal arm appear,
Belly, shoulder, bum,
Flash fishlike; nymphs and satyrs
Copulate in the foam.

THE BLACK TOWER

21 January 1939   *LPTP* 1939

Say that the men of the old black tower
Though they but feed as the goatherd feeds,
Their money spent, their wine gone sour,
Lack nothing that a soldier needs,
That are all oath-bound men;
Those banners come not in.

There in the tomb stand the dead upright,
But winds come up from the shore;
They shake when the winds roar
Old bones upon the mountain shake.

Those banners come to bribe or threaten
Or whisper that a man's a fool
Who when his own right king's forgotten
Cares what king sets up his rule.
If he died long ago
Why do you dread us so?

There in the tomb drops the faint moonlight
But wind comes up from the shore.
They shake when the winds roar
Old bones upon the mountain shake.

The tower's old cook that must climb and clamber
Catching small birds in the dew of the morn
When we hale men lie stretched in slumber
Swears that he hears the great king's horn.
But he's a lying hound;
Stand we on guard oath-bound!

There in the tomb the dark grows blacker,
But wind comes up from the shore.
They shake when the winds roar
Old bones upon the mountain shake.

SECTION 16
ADAPTATIONS AND TRANSLATIONS

DOWN BY THE SALLEY GARDENS

(?) 1888   *WO* 1889

Down by the salley gardens my love and I did meet;
She passed the salley gardens with little snow-white feet.
She bid me take love easy, as the leaves grow on the tree;
But I, being young and foolish, with her would not agree.

In a field by the river my love and I did stand,
And on my leaning shoulder she laid her snow-white hand.
She bid me take life easy, as the grass grows on the weirs;
But I was young and foolish, and now am full of tears.

WHEN YOU ARE OLD

21 October 1891   *CK* 1892

When you are old and grey and full of sleep,
And nodding by the fire, take down this book,
And slowly read, and dream of the soft look
Your eyes had once, and of their shadows deep;

How many loved your moments of glad grace,
And loved your beauty with love false or true,
But one man loved the pilgrim soul in you,
And loved the sorrows of your changing face;

And bending down beside the glowing bars,
Murmur, a little sadly, how Love fled
And paced upon the mountains overhead
And hid his face amid a crowd of stars.

[SEVEN PATERS SEVEN TIMES]

TLAM 1897

Seven paters seven times,
Send Mary by her Son,
Send Bridget by her mantle,
Send God by His strength,
Between us and the faery host,
Between us and the demons of the air.

A THOUGHT FROM PROPERTIUS

Before November 1915   *WSC* 1917

She might, so noble from head
To great shapely knees
The long flowing line,
Have walked to the altar
Through the holy images
At Pallas Athena's side,
Or been fit spoil for a centaur
Drunk with the unmixed wine.

[MAKE WAY FOR OEDIPUS. ALL PEOPLE SAID]

Before September 1926   *SKO* 1928

Make way for Oedipus. All people said,
'That is a fortunate man';
And now what storms are beating on his head!
Call no man fortunate that is not dead.
The dead are free from pain.

FROM 'OEDIPUS AT COLONUS'

Before 13 March 1927 OB 1927

Endure what life God gives and ask no longer span;
Cease to remember the delights of youth, travel-wearied aged man;
Delight becomes death-longing if all longing else be vain.

Even from that delight memory treasures so,
Death, despair, division of families, all entanglements of mankind grow,
As that old wandering beggar and these God-hated children know.

In the long echoing street the laughing dancers throng,
The bride is carried to the bridegroom's chamber through torchlight and
    tumultuous song;
I celebrate the silent kiss that ends short life or long.

Never to have lived is best, ancient writers say;
Never to have drawn the breath of life, never to have looked into the eye of day;
The second best's a gay goodnight and quickly turn away.

[I CALL UPON PERSEPHONE, QUEEN OF THE DEAD]

Before September 1927 CPI 1934

I call upon Persephone, queen of the dead,
And upon Hades, king of night, I call;
Chain all the Furies up that he may tread
The perilous pathway to the Stygian hall
And rest among his mighty peers at last,
For the entanglements of God are past.

Nor may the hundred-headed dog give tongue
Until the daughter of Earth and Tartarus
That even bloodless shades call Death has sung
The travel-broken shade of Oedipus
Through triumph of completed destiny
Into eternal sleep, if such there be.

'I AM OF IRELAND'

August 1929   *WMP* 1932

'I am of Ireland,
And the Holy Land of Ireland,
And time runs on,' cried she.
'Come out of charity,
Come dance with me in Ireland.'

One man, one man alone
In that outlandish gear,
One solitary man
Of all that rambled there
Had turned his stately head.
'That is a long way off,
And time runs on,' he said,
'And the night grows rough.'

'I am of Ireland,
And the Holy Land of Ireland,
And time runs on,' cried she.
'Come out of charity
And dance with me in Ireland.'

'The fiddlers are all thumbs,
Or the fiddle-string accursed,
The drums and the kettledrums
And the trumpets all are burst,
And the trombone,' cried he,
'The trumpet and trombone,'
And cocked a malicious eye,
'But time runs on, runs on.'

'I am of Ireland,
And the Holy Land of Ireland,
And time runs on,' cried she.
'Come out of charity
And dance with me in Ireland.'

SWIFT'S EPITAPH

Summer 1929–September 1930   October–December 1931

Swift has sailed into his rest;
Savage indignation there
Cannot lacerate his breast.
Imitate him if you dare,
World-besotted traveller; he
Served human liberty.

THE DANCER AT CRUACHAN[1] AND CRO-PATRICK

August 1931   *WMP* 1932

I, proclaiming that there is
Among birds or beasts or men,
One that is perfect or at peace,
Danced on Cruachan's windy plain,
Upon Cro-Patrick sang aloud;
All that could run or leap or swim
Whether in wood, water or cloud,
Acclaiming, proclaiming, declaiming Him.

THE DELPHIC ORACLE UPON PLOTINUS

9 August 1931   *WMP* 1932

Behold that great Plotinus swim
Buffeted by such seas;
Bland Rhadamanthus beckons him,
But the Golden Race looks dim,
Salt blood blocks his eyes.

[1] Pronounced in modern Gaelic as if spelt 'Crockan'.

Scattered on the level grass
Or winding through the grove
Plato there and Minos pass,
There stately Pythagoras
And all the choir of Love.

August 19, 1931

IMITATED FROM THE JAPANESE

*Late December 1936; final version
dated October 1937*   *NP* 1938

A most astonishing thing
Seventy years have I lived;

(Hurrah for the flowers of Spring
For Spring is here again.)

Seventy years have I lived
No ragged beggar man,
Seventy years have I lived,
Seventy years man and boy,
And never have I danced for joy.

SECTION 17
AGE AND AFTER

[THE POET, OWEN HANRAHAN, UNDER A BUSH OF MAY]

September 1894

The poet, Owen Hanrahan, under a bush of may
Calls down a curse on his own head because it withers grey;
Then on the speckled eagle cock of Ballygawley Hill
Because it is the oldest thing that knows of cark and ill;
And on the yew that has been green from the times out of mind
By the Steep Place of the Strangers and the Gap of the Wind;
And on the great grey pike that broods in Castle Dargan Lake
Having in his long body a many a hook and ache;
Then curses he old Paddy Bruen of the Well of Bride
Because no hair is on his head and drowsiness inside.
Then Paddy's neighbour, Peter Hart, and Michael Gill, his friend,
Because their wandering histories are never at an end.
And then old Shemus Cullinan, shepherd of the Green Lands
Because he holds two crutches between his crooked hands;
Then calls a curse from the dark North upon old Paddy Doe,
Who plans to lay his withering head upon a breast of snow,
Who plans to wreck a singing voice and break a merry heart;
He bids a curse hang over him till breath and body part,
But he calls down a blessing on the blossom of the may
Because it comes in beauty, and in beauty blows away.

THE THREE HERMITS

5 *March 1913*   September 1913

Three old hermits took the air
By a cold and desolate sea,
First was muttering a prayer,
Second rummaged for a flea;
On a windy stone, the third,
Giddy with his hundredth year,
Sang unnoticed like a bird:
'Though the Door of Death is near
And what waits behind the door,
Three times in a single day
I, though upright on the shore,
Fall asleep when I should pray.'
So the first, but now the second:
'We're but given what we have earned
When all thoughts and deeds are reckoned,
So it's plain to be discerned
That the shades of holy men
Who have failed, being weak of will,
Pass the Door of Birth again,
And are plagued by crowds, until
They've the passion to escape.'
Moaned the other, 'They are thrown
Into some most fearful shape.'
But the second mocked his moan:
'They are not changed to anything,
Having loved God once, but maybe
To a poet or a king
Or a witty lovely lady.'
While he'd rummaged rags and hair,
Caught and cracked his flea, the third,
Giddy with his hundreth year,
Sang unnoticed like a bird.

A SONG

(?) 1915   October 1918

I thought no more was needed
Youth to prolong
Than dumb-bell and foil
To keep the body young.
O who could have foretold
That the heart grows old?

Though I have many words,
What woman's satisfied,
I am no longer faint
Because at her side?
O who could have foretold
That the heart grows old?

I have not lost desire
But the heart that I had;
I thought 'twould burn my body
Laid on the death-bed,
For who could have foretold
That the heart grows old?

MEN IMPROVE WITH THE YEARS

19 July 1916   June 1917

I am worn out with dreams;
A weather-worn, marble triton
Among the streams;
And all day long I look
Upon this lady's beauty
As though I had found in a book
A pictured beauty,
Pleased to have filled the eyes
Or the discerning ears,
Delighted to be but wise,
For men improve with the years;
And yet, and yet,
Is this my dream, or the truth?
O would that we had met
When I had my burning youth!
But I grow old among dreams,
A weather-worn, marble triton
Among the streams.

DEATH

13/17 September 1927   *WS* 1929

Nor dread nor hope attend
A dying animal;
A man awaits his end
Dreading and hoping all;
Many times he died,
Many times rose again.
A great man in his pride
Confronting murderous men
Casts derision upon
Supersession of breath;
He knows death to the bone —
Man has created death.

AT ALGECIRAS – A MEDITATION UPON DEATH

November 1928 (? revised 23 January/4 February 1929)   **APEP** 1929

The heron-billed pale cattle-birds
That feed on some foul parasite
Of the Moroccan flocks and herds
Cross the narrow Straits to light
In the rich midnight of the garden trees
Till the dawn break upon those mingled seas.

Often at evening when a boy
Would I carry to a friend –
Hoping more substantial joy
Did an older mind commend –
Not such as are in Newton's metaphor,
But actual shells of Rosses' level shore.

Greater glory in the sun,
An evening chill upon the air,
Bid imagination run
Much on the Great Questioner;
What He can question, what if questioned I
Can with a fitting confidence reply.

November 1928

A PRAYER FOR OLD AGE

1934   November 1934

God guard me from those thoughts men think
In the mind alone;
He that sings a lasting song
Thinks in a marrow-bone;

From all that makes a wise old man
That can be praised of all;
O what am I that I should not seem
For the song's sake a fool?

I pray — for fashion's word is out
And prayer comes round again —
That I may seem, though I die old,
A foolish, passionate man.

THE FOUR AGES OF MAN

6 August 1934   December 1934

He with body waged a fight,
But body won; it walks upright.

Then he struggled with the heart;
Innocence and peace depart.

Then he struggled with the mind;
His proud heart he left behind.

Now his wars on God begin;
At stroke of midnight God shall win.

[WHY SHOULD NOT OLD MEN BE MAD?]

January 1936   *OTB* 1939

Why should not old men be mad?
Some have known a likely lad
That had a sound fly-fisher's wrist
Turn to a drunken journalist;
A girl that knew all Dante once
Live to bear children to a dunce;
A Helen of social welfare dream,
Climb on a wagonette to scream.
Some think it matter of course that chance
Should starve good men and bad advance,
That if their neighbours figured plain,
As though upon a lighted screen,
No single story would they find
Of an unbroken happy mind,
A finish worthy of the start.
Young men know nothing of this sort,
Observant old men know it well;
And when they know what old books tell
And that no better can be had,
Know why an old man should be mad.

WHAT THEN?

(?) 1936   April 1937

His chosen comrades thought at school
He must grow a famous man;
He thought the same and lived by rule,
All his twenties crammed with toil;
'What then?' sang Plato's ghost, 'what then?'

Everything he wrote was read,
After certain years he won
Sufficient money for his need,
Friends that have been friends indeed;
'What then?' sang Plato's ghost, 'what then?'

All his happier dreams came true –
A small old house, wife, daughter, son,
Grounds where plum and cabbage grew,
Poets and Wits about him drew;
'What then?' sang Plato's ghost, 'what then?'

'The work is done,' grown old he thought,
'According to my boyish plan;
Let the fools rage, I swerved in nought,
Something to perfection brought;'
But louder sang that ghost, 'What then?'

AN ACRE OF GRASS

November 1936   April 1938

Picture and book remain,
An acre of green grass
For air and exercise,
Now strength of body goes;
Midnight an old house
Where nothing stirs but a mouse.

My temptation is quiet.
Here at life's end
Neither loose imagination,
Nor the mill of the mind
Consuming its rag and bone,
Can make the truth known.

Grant me an old man's frenzy.
Myself must I remake
Till I am Timon and Lear
Or that William Blake
Who beat upon the wall
Till truth obeyed his call;

A mind Michael Angelo knew
That can pierce the clouds
Or inspired by frenzy
Shake the dead in their shrouds;
Forgotten else by mankind
An old man's eagle mind.

IN TARA'S HALLS

June 1938   *LPTP* 1939

A man I praise that once in Tara's Halls
Said to the woman on his knees 'Lie still,
My hundredth year is at an end. I think
That something is about to happen, I think
That the adventure of old age begins.
To many women I have said "lie still"
And given everything that a woman needs
A roof, good clothes, passion, love perhaps
But never asked for love, should I ask that
I shall be old indeed.'
                        Thereon the king
Went to the sacred house and stood between
The golden plough and harrow and spoke aloud
That all attendants and the casual crowd might hear:
'God I have loved, but should I ask return
Of God or women the time were come to die.'

He bade, his hundred and first year at end,
Diggers and carpenters make grave and coffin,
Saw that the grave was deep, the coffin sound,
Summoned the generations of his house
Lay in the coffin, stopped his breath and died.

MAN AND THE ECHO

July 1938–October 1938   January 1939

Man.   In a cleft that's christened Alt
          Under broken stone I halt
          At the bottom of a pit
          That broad noon has never lit,
          And shout a secret to the stone.
          All that I have said and done,
          Now that I am old and ill,
          Turns into a question till
          I lie awake night after night
          And never get the answers right.
          Did that play of mine send out
          Certain men the English shot?
          Did words of mine put too great strain
          On that woman's reeling brain?
          Could my spoken words have checked
          That whereby a house lay wrecked?
          And all seems evil until I
          Sleepless would lie down and die.

Echo.   Lie down and die.

Man.   That were to shirk
The spiritual intellect's great work
And shirk it in vain. There is no release
In a bodkin or disease,
Nor can there be a work so great
As that which cleans man's dirty slate.
While man can still his body keep
Wine or love drug him to sleep,
Waking he thanks the Lord that he
Has body and its stupidity,
But body gone he sleeps no more
And till his intellect grows sure
That all's arranged in one clear view
Pursues the thoughts that I pursue,
Then stands in judgment on his soul,
And, all work done, dismisses all
Out of intellect and sight
And sinks at last into the night.

Echo. Into the night.

Man.   O rocky voice
Shall we in that great night rejoice?
What do we know but that we face
One another in this place?
But hush, for I have lost the theme
Its joy or night seem but a dream;
Up there some hawk or owl has struck
Dropping out of sky or rock,
A stricken rabbit is crying out
And its cry distracts my thought.

UNDER BEN BULBEN

Completed 4 September 1938   February 1939

I

Swear by what the Sages spoke
Round the Mareotic Lake
That the Witch of Atlas knew,
Spoke and set the cocks a-crow.

Swear by those horsemen, by those women,
Complexion and form prove superhuman,
That pale, long visaged company
That airs an immortality
Completeness of their passions won;
Now they ride the wintry dawn
Where Ben Bulben sets the scene.

Here's the gist of what they mean.

II

Many times man lives and dies
Between his two eternities
That of race and that of soul
And ancient Ireland knew it all.
Whether man dies in his bed
Or the rifle knocks him dead,
A brief parting from those dear
Is the worst man has to fear.

Though grave-diggers' toil is long,
Sharp their spades, their muscle strong,
They but thrust their buried men
Back in the human mind again.

III

You that Mitchel's prayer have heard
'Send war in our time, O Lord!'
Know that when all words are said
And a man is fighting mad,
Something drops from eyes long blind
He completes his partial mind,
For an instant stands at ease,
Laughs aloud, his heart at peace,
Even the wisest man grows tense
With some sort of violence
Before he can accomplish fate
Know his work or choose his mate.

IV

Poet and sculptor do the work
Nor let the modish painter shirk
What his great forefathers did,
Bring the soul of man to God,
Make him fill the cradles right.

Measurement began our might:
Forms a stark Egyptian thought,
Forms that gentler Phidias wrought.

Michael Angelo left a proof
On the Sistine Chapel roof,
Where but half-awakened Adam
Can disturb globe-trotting Madam
Till her bowels are in heat,
Proof that there's a purpose set
Before the secret working mind:
Profane perfection of mankind.

Quattro-cento put in paint,
On backgrounds for a God or Saint,
Gardens where a soul's at ease;
Where everything that meets the eye
Flowers and grass and cloudless sky
Resemble forms that are, or seem
When sleepers wake and yet still dream,
And when it's vanished still declare,
With only bed and bedstead there,
That Heavens had opened.

                             Gyres run on;
When that greater dream had gone
Calvert and Wilson, Blake and Claude
Prepared a rest for the people of God,
Palmer's phrase, but after that
Confusion fell upon our thought.

V

Irish poets, learn your trade,
Sing whatever is well made,
Scorn the sort now growing up
All out of shape from toe to top,
Their unremembering hearts and heads
Base-born products of base beds.
Sing the peasantry, and then
Hard-riding country gentlemen,
The holiness of monks, and after
Porter-drinkers' randy laughter;
Sing the lords and ladies gay
That were beaten into the clay
Through seven heroic centuries;
Cast your mind on other days
That we in coming days may be
Still the indomitable Irishry.

VI

Under bare Ben Bulben's head
In Drumcliff churchyard Yeats is laid,
An ancestor was rector there
Long years ago; a church stands near,
By the road an ancient Cross.
No marble, no conventional phrase,
On limestone quarried near the spot
By his command these words are cut:

> Cast a cold eye
> On life, on death.
> Horseman, pass by!

SECTION 18

POLITICS AND POLEMICS

AN APPOINTMENT

1907/1908

February 1909

Being out of heart with government
I took a broken root to fling
Where the proud, wayward squirrel went,
Taking delight that he could spring;
And he, with that low whinnying sound
That is like laughter, sprang again
And so to the other tree at a bound.
Nor the tame will, nor timid brain,
Nor heavy knitting of the brow
Bred that fierce tooth and cleanly limb
And threw him up to laugh on the bough;
No government appointed him.

ON THOSE THAT HATED 'THE PLAYBOY OF THE WESTERN WORLD', 1907

5 April 1909

December 1911

Once, when midnight smote the air,
Eunuchs ran through Hell and met
On every crowded street to stare
Upon great Juan riding by:
Even like these to rail and sweat
Staring upon his sinewy thigh.

UPON A HOUSE SHAKEN BY THE LAND AGITATION

Prose draft and text of poem, 7 August 1910   December 1910

How should the world be luckier if this house,
Where passion and precision have been one
Time out of mind, became too ruinous
To breed the lidless eye that loves the sun?
And the sweet laughing eagle thoughts that grow
Where wings have memory of wings, and all
That comes of the best knit to the best? Although
Mean roof-trees were the sturdier for its fall,
How should their luck run high enough to reach
The gifts that govern men, and after these
To gradual Time's last gift, a written speech
Wrought of high laughter, loveliness and ease?

TO A WEALTHY MAN WHO PROMISED A SECOND SUBSCRIPTION TO THE DUBLIN MUNICIPAL GALLERY IF IT WERE PROVED THE PEOPLE WANTED PICTURES

24 December 1912/8 January 1913   January 1913

You gave, but will not give again
Until enough of Paudeen's pence
By Biddy's halfpennies have lain
To be 'some sort of evidence,'
Before you'll put your guineas down,
That things it were a pride to give
Are what the blind and ignorant town
Imagines best to make it thrive.

What cared Duke Ercole, that bid
His mummers to the market-place,
What th' onion-sellers thought or did
So that his Plautus set the pace
For the Italian comedies?
And Guidobaldo, when he made
That grammar school of courtesies
Where wit and beauty learned their trade
Upon Urbino's windy hill,
Had sent no runners to and fro
That he might learn the shepherds' will.
And when they drove out Cosimo,
Indifferent how the rancour ran,
He gave the hours they had set free
To Michelozzo's latest plan
For the San Marco Library,
Whence turbulent Italy should draw
Delight in Art whose end is peace,
In logic and in natural law
By sucking at the dugs of Greece.

Your open hand but shows our loss,
For he knew better how to live.
Let Paudeens play at pitch and toss,
Look up in the sun's eye and give
What the exultant heart calls good
That some new day may breed the best
Because you gave, not what they would,
But the right twigs for an eagle's nest!

December 1912

SEPTEMBER 1913

7 September 1913   September 1913

What need you, being come to sense,
But fumble in a greasy till
And add the halfpence to the pence
And prayer to shivering prayer, until
You have dried the marrow from the bone;
For men were born to pray and save:
Romantic Ireland's dead and gone,
It's with O'Leary in the grave.

Yet they were of a different kind,
The names that stilled your childish play,
They have gone about the world like wind,
But little time had they to pray
For whom the hangman's rope was spun,
And what, God help us, could they save?
Romantic Ireland's dead and gone,
It's with O'Leary in the grave.

Was it for this the wild geese spread
The grey wing upon every tide;
For this that all the blood was shed,
For this Edward Fitzgerald died,
And Robert Emmet and Wolfe Tone,
All that delirium of the brave?
Romantic Ireland's dead and gone,
It's with O'Leary in the grave.

Yet could we turn the years again,
And call those exiles as they were
In all their loneliness and pain,
You'd cry, 'Some woman's yellow hair
Has maddened every mother's son':
They weighed so lightly what they gave.
But let them be, they're dead and gone,
They're with O'Leary in the grave.

TO A SHADE

29 September 1913   *PWD* 1913

If you have revisited the town, thin Shade,
Whether to look upon your monument
(I wonder if the builder has been paid)
Or happier-thoughted when the day is spent
To drink of that salt breath out of the sea
When grey gulls flit about instead of men,
And the gaunt houses put on majesty:
Let these content you and be gone again;
For they are at their old tricks yet.
                      A man
Of your own passionate serving kind who had brought
In his full hands what, had they only known,
Had given their children's children loftier thought,
Sweeter emotion, working in their veins
Like gentle blood, has been driven from the place,
And insult heaped upon him for his pains,
And for his open-handedness, disgrace;
Your enemy, an old foul mouth, had set
The pack upon him.
                Go, unquiet wanderer,
And gather the Glasnevin coverlet
About your head till the dust stops your ear,
The time for you to taste of that salt breath
And listen at the corners has not come;
You had enough of sorrow before death —
Away, away! You are safer in the tomb.

September 29, 1913

EASTER, 1916

25 September 1916   1916 (privately printed); 23 October 1923

I have met them at close of day
Coming with vivid faces
From counter or desk among grey
Eighteenth-century houses.
I have passed with a nod of the head
Or polite meaningless words,
Or have lingered awhile and said
Polite meaningless words,
And thought before I had done
Of a mocking tale or a gibe
To please a companion
Around the fire at the club,
Being certain that they and I
But lived where motley is worn:
All changed, changed utterly:
A terrible beauty is born.

That woman's days were spent
In ignorant good-will,
Her nights in argument
Until her voice grew shrill.
What voice more sweet than hers
When, young and beautiful,
She rode to harriers?
This man had kept a school
And rode our wingèd horse;
This other his helper and friend
Was coming into his force;
He might have won fame in the end,
So sensitive his nature seemed,
So daring and sweet his thought.
This other man I had dreamed
A drunken, vainglorious lout.
He had done most bitter wrong
To some who are near my heart,
Yet I number him in the song;
He, too, has resigned his part
In the casual comedy;

He, too, has been changed in his turn,
Transformed utterly:
A terrible beauty is born.

Hearts with one purpose alone
Through summer and winter seem
Enchanted to a stone
To trouble the living stream.
The horse that comes from the road,
The rider, the birds that range
From cloud to tumbling cloud,
Minute by minute they change;
A shadow of cloud on the stream
Changes minute by minute;
A horse-hoof slides on the brim,
And a horse plashes within it;
The long-legged moor-hens dive,
And hens to moor-cocks call;
Minute by minute they live:
The stone's in the midst of all.

Too long a sacrifice
Can make a stone of the heart.
O when may it suffice?
That is Heaven's part, our part
To murmur name upon name,
As a mother names her child
When sleep at last has come
On limbs that had run wild.
What is it but nightfall?
No, no, not night but death;
Was it needless death after all?
For England may keep faith
For all that is done and said.
We know their dream; enough
To know they dreamed and are dead;
And what if excess of love
Bewildered them till they died?
I write it out in a verse —
MacDonagh and MacBride
And Connolly and Pearse

Now and in time to be,
Wherever green is worn,
Are changed, changed utterly:
A terrible beauty is born.

September 25, 1916

THE ROSE TREE

7 April 1917   November 1920

'O words are lightly spoken,'
Said Pearse to Connolly,
'Maybe a breath of politic words
Has withered our Rose Tree;
Or maybe but a wind that blows
Across the bitter sea.'

'It needs to be but watered,'
James Connolly replied,
'To make the green come out again
And spread on every side,
And shake the blossom from the bud
To be the garden's pride.'

'But where can we draw water,'
Said Pearse to Connolly,
'When all the wells are parched away?
O plain as plain can be
There's nothing but our own red blood
Can make a right Rose Tree.'

THE LEADERS OF THE CROWD

1918   *MRD* 1921

They must to keep their certainty accuse
All that are different of a base intent;
Pull down established honour; hawk for news
Whatever their loose phantasy invent
And murmur it with bated breath, as though
The abounding gutter had been Helicon
Or calumny a song. How can they know
Truth flourishes where the student's lamp has shone,
And there alone, that have no solitude?
So the crowd come they care not what may come.
They have loud music, hope every day renewed
And heartier loves; that lamp is from the tomb.

ON A POLITICAL PRISONER

10–29 January 1919   November 1920

She that but little patience knew,
From childhood on, had now so much
A grey gull lost its fear and flew
Down to her cell and there alit,
And there endured her fingers' touch
And from her fingers ate its bit.

Did she in touching that lone wing
Recall the years before her mind
Became a bitter, an abstract thing,
Her thought some popular enmity:
Blind and leader of the blind
Drinking the foul ditch where they lie?

When long ago I saw her ride
Under Ben Bulben to the meet,
The beauty of her country-side
With all youth's lonely wildness stirred,
She seemed to have grown clean and sweet
Like any rock-bred, sea-borne bird:

Sea-borne, or balanced on the air
When first it sprang out of the nest
Upon some lofty rock to stare
Upon the cloudy canopy,
While under its storm-beaten breast
Cried out the hollows of the sea.

REPRISALS

1921   Autumn 1948

Some nineteen German planes, they say,
You had brought down before you died.
We called it a good death. Today
Can ghost or man be satisfied?
Although your last exciting year
Outweighed all other years, you said,
Though battle joy may be so dear
A memory, even to the dead,
It chases other thought away,
Yet rise from your Italian tomb,
Flit to Kiltartan cross and stay
Till certain second thoughts have come
Upon the cause you served, that we
Imagined such a fine affair:
Half-drunk or whole-mad soldiery
Are murdering your tenants there.
Men that revere your father yet
Are shot at on the open plain.

Where many new-married women sit
And suckle children now? Armed men
May murder them in passing by
Nor law nor parliament take heed.
Then close your ears with dust and lie
Among the other cheated dead.

[SHOULD H. G. WELLS AFFLICT YOU]

April–June 1932

Should H. G. Wells afflict you
Put whitewash in a pail;
Paint: 'Science – opium of the suburbs'
On some waste wall.

CHURCH AND STATE

August 1934   November 1934

Here is fresh matter, poet,
Matter for old age meet;
Might of the Church and the State,
Their mobs put under their feet.
O but heart's wine shall run pure,
Mind's bread grow sweet.

That were a cowardly song,
Wander in dreams no more;
What if the Church and the State
Are the mob that howls at the door!
Wine shall run thick to the end,
Bread taste sour.

August 1934

COME GATHER ROUND ME PARNELLITES

8 September 1936   January 1937

Come gather round me Parnellites
And praise our chosen man,
Stand upright on your legs awhile,
Stand upright while you can,
For soon we lie where he is laid
And he is underground;
Come fill up all those glasses
And pass the bottle round.

And here's a cogent reason
And I have many more,
He fought the might of England
And saved the Irish poor,
Whatever good a farmer's got
He brought it all to pass;
And here's another reason,
That Parnell loved a lass.

And here's a final reason,
He was of such a kind
Every man that sings a song
Keeps Parnell in his mind
For Parnell was a proud man,
No prouder trod the ground,
And a proud man's a lovely man
So pass the bottle round.

The Bishops and the Party
That tragic story made,
A husband that had sold his wife
And after that betrayed;
But stories that live longest
Are sung above the glass,
And Parnell loved his country
And Parnell loved his lass.

THE GHOST OF ROGER CASEMENT

October 1936   *NP* 1938

O what has made that sudden noise?
What on the threshold stands?
It never crossed the sea because
John Bull and the sea are friends;
But this is not the old sea
Nor this the old seashore.
What gave that roar of mockery,
That roar in the sea's roar?

The ghost of Roger Casement
Is beating on the door.

John Bull has stood for Parliament,
A dog must have his day,
The country thinks no end of him
For he knows how to say
At a beanfeast or a banquet,
That all must hang their trust
Upon the British Empire,
Upon the Church of Christ.

The ghost of Roger Casement
Is beating on the door.

John Bull has gone to India
And all must pay him heed
For histories are there to prove
That none of another breed
Has had a like inheritance,
Or sucked such milk as he,
And there's no luck about a house
If it lack honesty.

The ghost of Roger Casement
Is beating on the door.

I poked about a village church
And found his family tomb
And copied out what I could read
In that religious gloom;
Found many a famous man there;
But fame and virtue rot.
Draw round beloved and bitter men,
Draw round and raise a shout;

The ghost of Roger Casement
Is beating on the door.

PARNELL

January 1937   March 1938

Parnell came down the road, he said to a cheering man;
'Ireland shall get her freedom and you still break stone.'

THE O'RAHILLY

January 1937   NP 1938

Sing of the O'Rahilly
Do not deny his right;
Sing a 'the' before his name;
Allow that he, despite
All those learned historians,
Established it for good;
He wrote out that word himself,
He christened himself with blood.
                    How goes the weather?

Sing of the O'Rahilly
That had such little sense,
He told Pearse and Connolly
He'd gone to great expense
Keeping all the Kerry men
Out of that crazy fight;
That he might be there himself
Had travelled half the night.

How goes the weather?

'Am I such a craven that
I should not get the word
But for what some travelling man
Had heard I had not heard?'
Then on Pearse and Connolly
He fixed a bitter look,
'Because I helped to wind the clock
I come to hear it strike.'

How goes the weather?

What remains to sing about
But of the death he met
Stretched under a doorway
Somewhere off Henry Street;
They that found him found upon
The door above his head
'Here died the O'Rahilly
R.I.P.' writ in blood.

How goes the weather?

POLITICS

'In our time the destiny of man presents its meanings in political terms.'
THOMAS MANN.

23 May 1938   January 1939

> How can I, that girl standing there,
> My attention fix
> On Roman or on Russian
> Or on Spanish politics,
> Yet here's a travelled man that knows
> What he talks about,
> And there's a politician
> That has both read and thought,
> And maybe what they say is true
> Of war and war's alarms,
> But O that I were young again
> And held her in my arms.

WILLIAM BUTLER YEATS:
BIOGRAPHICAL SUMMARY

1865   William Butler Yeats, the son of John Butler Yeats and his wife, Susan (*née* Pollexfen), born at 1 George's Ville, Sandymount Avenue, Dublin, 13 June.

1867   John Butler Yeats moves with his family to 23 Fitzroy Road, Regent's Park, London. Robert (*d.* 1873), John Butler (Jack), Elizabeth Corbet (Lolly) were born here. Susan Mary (Lily), the elder daughter, was born at Enniscrone. Frequent visits were made to Sligo to Mrs Yeats's parents, the Pollexfens.

1874   The family moves to 14 Edith Villas, West Kensington.

1876   The family moves to 8 Woodstock Road, Bedford Park.

1877   Yeats goes to the Godolphin School, Hammersmith. Holidays spent in Sligo.

1880   John Butler Yeats's income declines because of Land War and decline in economy.

1881   Family returns to Ireland, is lent Balscadden Cottage, Howth, Dublin. W. B. Yeats goes to the High School, Harcourt Street, Dublin (until 1883).

1882   Family moves to Island View, small house overlooking Howth Harbour. Yeats thinks himself in love with his cousin Laura Armstrong.

1884   W. B. Yeats enters School of Art, Dublin.

1885   Family moves to 10 Ashfield Terrace, off Harold's Cross Road, Dublin. First published poems (and Charles Johnston's article on esoteric Buddhism) appear in *Dublin University Review*. Founder member of Dublin Hermetic Society. Becomes friend of Katharine Tynan and John O'Leary.

1886   First experience of seance. Attacks Anglo-Irish, begins to read Irish poets who wrote in English and translations of Gaelic sagas.

1887   Family moves to 58 Eardley Crescent, Earls Court, London. Mrs Yeats has two strokes. W. B. Yeats visits William Morris at Kelmscott House. Joins London Lodge of Theosophists.

1888   Family installed in 3 Blenheim Road, Bedford Park (J. B. Yeats's home until 1902). Last of Yeats family land sold in accordance with Ashbourne Act (1888). Contributions to American journals. Visits Oxford to work in Bodleian. Joins esoteric section of Theosophists

1889   Mild collapse. Prepares selections for Walter Scott. *The Wanderings of Oisin and Other Poems*. Visits W. E. Henley, meets Oscar Wilde, John Todhunter, York Powell, John Nettleship and Edwin Ellis (with whom he decides to edit Blake's poems). Edits *Fairy and Folk Tales of the Irish Peasantry*. Maud Gonne visits Bedford Park; he falls in love with her; offers to write *The Countess Cathleen* for her.

1890   'The Lake Isle of Innisfree'. Asked to resign from Theosophists. Meets Florence Farr, who was acting in John Todhunter's *A Sicilian Idyll*.

1891   *Representative Irish Tales. John Sherman and Dhoya*. The Rhymers' Club founded in London. Friendship with Johnson and Dowson. Asks Maud Gonne to marry him. She goes to France. He meets her on her return on ship with Parnell's body. Writes poems on Parnell. Founds London-Irish Literary Society with T. W. Rolleston. Founds National Literary Society in Dublin with John O'Leary as President.

1892   *The Countess Kathleen and Various Legends and Lyrics. Irish Fairy Tales*.

1893   *The Celtic Twilight. The Works of William Blake* (ed. Ellis and Yeats, 3 vols).

1894   First visit to Paris; stays with MacGregor Mathers and proposes to Maud Gonne again. Sees

Axel. Meets 'Diana Vernon'. Revises *The Countess Cathleen* in Sligo while staying with George Pollexfen and conducting experiments with symbols. *The Land of Heart's Desire* produced. Visits Gore-Booths at Lissadell.

1895   *Poems.* Not on good terms with Dowden and Mahaffy. Lionel Johnson drinking heavily. Shares rooms in the Temple with Arthur Symons for a few months (between 1895 and 1896, date uncertain).

1896   Takes rooms in Woburn Buildings; affair with 'Diana Vernon' lasts a year. Visits Edward Martyn with Arthur Symons, meets Lady Gregory, visits Aran Islands. Meets Synge in Paris, when there to found order of Celtic Mysteries. Member of IRB; forms idea of uniting Irish political parties.

1897   *The Adoration of the Magi. The Secret Rose.* Disturbed by effects of Jubilee Riots in Dublin. Visits Coole; collects folklore there with Lady Gregory; writing *The Speckled Bird* (posthumously published novel).

1898   Accompanies Maud Gonne on tour of Irish in England and Scotland. Forms idea of creating Irish Theatre with Lady Gregory and Edward Martyn. 'Spiritual marriage' with Maud Gonne.

1899   *The Wind Among the Reeds.* In Paris, again proposes marriage to Maud Gonne. *The Countess Cathleen* and Martyn's *Heather Field* produced in Antient Concert Rooms, Dublin, as programme of Irish Literary Theatre.

1900   Proposes marriage to Maud Gonne in London. Leaves IRB (probably in 1900). Forms new order of Golden Dawn after trouble with Mathers and Aleister Crowley. Helps George Moore to rewrite Martyn's *The Tale of a Town*, which became *The Bending of the Bough.*

1901   Proposes marriage to Maud Gonne again.

1902   Lectures on the psalteries. *Diarmid and Grania* written in collaboration with George Moore. Becomes President of Irish National Dramatic Society. *Cathleen ni Houlihan* performed in Dublin with Maud Gonne in title role.

1903   Maud Gonne marries John MacBride. *The Countess Cathleen, The Pot of Broth* and *The Hour Glass* produced in visit of Irish National Dramatic Company to London. First lecture tour in US, arranged by John Quinn.

1904   Abbey Theatre opens with Yeats as producer-manager. *The King's Threshold* and *On Baile's Strand.*

1905   Limited company replaces National Theatre. Co-director with Lady Gregory and Synge. *Stories of Red Hanrahan.*

1906   *Poems 1895–1905.*

1907   Crisis over Synge's *The Playboy of the Western World.* Visits Italy with Lady Gregory and her son. Works on *The Player Queen.* Father goes to New York.

1908   *Collected Works* (in 8 vols). Stays with Maud Gonne in Paris. Meets Ezra Pound.

1910   Accompanies Abbey players to US. Meets Georgie Hyde-Lees.

1912   Stays with Maud Gonne in Normandy.

1913   Receives Civil List pension of £150 p.a. *Poems Written in Discouragement* (dealing with Lane Gallery controversy). Stays at Stone Cottage, Coleman's Hatch, Sussex, in autumn with Ezra Pound.

1914   Visits US (January). Returns for Ezra Pound's marriage to Mrs Shakespear's daughter. Investigates miracle at Mirebeau with Maud Gonne MacBride and the Hon. Everard Feilding (May). *Responsibilities: poems and a play.* Becomes interested in family history; finishes *Reveries* (first part of *Autobiographies*).

1915   Hugh Lane goes down with *Lusitania.* Refuses knighthood.

1916   With Ezra Pound (winter). First of the *Plays for Dancers* produced in Lady Cunard's house,

London (March). Easter Rising, writes 'Easter 1916'. In Normandy proposes marriage to Maud Gonne. Reads French poets with Iseult Gonne.

1917 Buys Castle at Ballylee. Proposes to Iseult Gonne. Marries Georgie Hyde-Lees on 20 October. *The Wild Swans at Coole.*

1918 They stay at Oxford, then Glendalough, then visit Sligo; stay at Coole (and supervise restoration of tower), later at 73 St Stephen's Green (Maud Gonne's house) until December. *Per Amica Silentia Lunae.*

1919 Anne Butler Yeats born (26 February) in Dublin. Summer at Ballylee. Winter spent in Oxford in Broad Street.

1920 American lecture tour until May. Yeats in Ireland in autumn.

1921 Michael Butler Yeats born (22 August). *Michael Robartes and the Dancer. Four Plays for Dancers.*

1922 Buys Georgian house, 82 Merrion Square, Dublin. J.B. Yeats dies in New York. D.Litt. of Dublin University. Spends summer at Ballylee. *The Trembling of the Veil. Later Poems. The Player Queen.* Becomes Senator of Irish Free State.

1923 Nobel Prize for Poetry. Visits Stockholm in December for award of Nobel Prize.

1924 *Essays. The Cat and the Moon and certain poems.* Year mainly spent in final work on *A Vision.* Reading history and philosophy. High blood pressure. Visits Sicily (November).

1925 Visits Capri, Rome, Milan (February). May at Ballylee. Reading Burke and Berkeley. Speech on divorce in Senate. *A Vision* (dated 1925, published January 1926).

1926 *Estrangement.* Chairman of Coinage Committee in Senate. Visits St Otteran's School in Waterford ('Among School Children').

1927 Ballylee in summer. *October Blast.* Congestion of lungs (October). Algeciras, Seville (lung bleeding). Cannes.

1928 Cannes (till February). *The Tower.* Rapallo (April). Dublin house sold. Ballylee (June). Furnished house at Howth (July). Last Senate Speech (July).

1929 Rapallo (winter). Summer in Ireland, in flat (Fitzwillian Square, Dublin), at Coole and Ballylee, then at Howth. *A Packet for Ezra Pound* (August). *The Winding Stair* (October). Rapallo. Malta fever (December). Ezra Pound and George Antheil at Rapallo.

1930 Portofino (April). Writes 'Byzantium'. Renvyle, Connemara (June). Coole. *Words upon the Window-pane* produced at Abbey Theatre (November). Visits Masefield at Boar's Hill, Oxford, thirtieth anniversary of their first meeting. Spends winter in Dublin, in furnished house on Killiney Hill.

1931 Writes 'The Seven Sages'. D.Litt. at Oxford (May). Writes much verse at Coole in summer. Broadcast BBC Belfast (September). Spends winter at Coole, reading Balzac; Lady Gregory dying.

1932 Works on 'Coole Park and Ballylee, 1931'. Winter and spring at Coole. Lady Gregory dies. Foundation of Irish Academy of Letters (September). Last American tour (October). *Words for Music Perhaps and other poems* (November). Leases Riversdale, Rathfarnham, Co. Dublin.

1933 Interested in O'Duffy's blueshirt movement. *The Winding Stair and other poems* (September), *Collected Poems* (November).

1934 Steinach operation. Rapallo (June). Rome (autumn). *Wheels and Butterflies. Collected Plays. The King of the Great Clock Tower.*

1935 Majorca (winter). Shri Purohit Swami collaborates in translation of *Upanishads. Dramatis Personae. A Full Moon in March* (November).

1936 Seriously ill; heart missing beat (January); nephritis. Returns to Riversdale. Broadcasts on modern poetry, BBC, London (summer). *Oxford Book of Modern Verse (1892–1935).*

1937 Elected member Athenaeum. Broadcasts BBC London (April, July, September). *A Speech and Two Poems* (August). Visits Lady Gerald Wellesley. *A Vision* (October). Mentone (winter). *Essays 1931–1936* (December).

1938   *The Herne's Egg* (January). Visits Sussex, stays with Lady Gerald Wellesley, and with Edith Shackleton Heald. *New Poems* (May). Sussex (June). Last public appearance at Abbey Theatre for performance of *Purgatory* (August). Maud Gonne visits him at Riversdale (late summer). Sussex (September).

1939   Dies 28 January, buried at Roquebrune. *Last Poems and Two Plays* (June). *On the Boiler*.

1948   Body reinterred at Drumcliff Churchyard, Sligo.

NOTES

Section 1: THE CRAFT OF POETRY

P. 3 'To the Rose upon the Rood of Time' *Red Rose*: by 1891 Yeats had begun to use the rose as a complex symbol. He knew how it had been used by Irish poets, not only in love poems but in addresses to Ireland. (In 1891 he cited its use by the Irish poets Aubrey De Vere (1814–1902) and James Clarence Mangan.) Rose, a girl with black hair (*Irish* Roisin Dubh, Dark Rosaleen), personified Ireland. The Rose was also the Rose of Friday, of austerity in Irish religious poems. Yeats used it to symbolise spiritual and eternal beauty. Having become a Member of the Order of the Golden Dawn, an occult society or Rosicrucian order, in 1890, he was influenced by Rosicrucian symbolism, in which a four-leafed rose and cross stand for a mystic marriage, the rose with feminine elements, the cross masculine; the rose is the flower that blooms upon the sacrifice of the cross. Yeats also read deeply in mystic tradition (see *NC*, pp. 21–2) and was involved in plans to found an Irish order of (Celtic) mysteries (see *NC*, p. 23). He quoted the second stanza of this poem in *Autobiographies* (1956), p. 254, saying that he thought for a time he could rhyme of love, calling it *The Rose* because of the Rose's double meaning. . . . 'all these things that "popular poets" write of, but that I must some day – on that day when the gates began to open – become difficult or obscure. With a rhythm that still echoed [William] Morris I prayed to the Red Rose, to Intellectual Beauty'. The Rose also symbolised Maud Gonne, whom Yeats first met in 1889; he fell in love with her, and wrote her many love poems in which he linked her with Ireland *Cuchulain*: *Irish*, Cu Culann, the Hound of Culain, a hero of the Red Branch tales. See notes on 'The Madness of King Goll', p. 319, and the entry for Cuchulain in Glossary, p. 397. In one tale he kills his own son; this is the subject of Yeats's play *On Baile's Strand* (1904). Cuchulain subsequently dies fighting the sea in delusion, thinking he is attacking Conchubar, King of Ulster, who had forbidden him to be a friend of his son, the unknown young man who had been sent by his mother Aoife from Scotland to challenge Cuchulain, who was unaware that he had a son. See Cuchulain's 'Fight with the Sea', p. 30. *Druid*: Druids were priests, magicians and soothsayers *Fergus*: Fergus MacRoy was King of Ulster in the Red Branch tales. He was the lover of Maeve, queen of Connacht; his wife Ness tricked him into handing over his kingdom to his step-son Conchubar. Yeats, following Sir Samuel Ferguson's 'The Abdication of Fergus MacRoy', which departs from the Irish sources, called him King of Ireland and a poet who lived at peace hunting in the woods *Eire*: Irish for Ireland; originally a name of a queen of the Tuatha de Danaan. See notes on 'The Madness of King Goll', p. 319

P. 3 'To Ireland in the Coming Times' The poem defends the obscurity accompanying 'the symbolism of the mystical rose'; explains Yeats's view that his poetry continues the patriotic tradition of the Young Ireland movement and of earlier writers even though its full meanings are not immediately obvious; and is written in part as a love poem to Maud Gonne *rann*: a verse of a poem in Irish *Davis, Mangan, Ferguson*: Thomas Osborne Davis (1814–45) was the leader of the Young Ireland party, founded the influential paper *The Nation* in 1842, and wrote popular poems and influential, patriotic prose. James Clarence Mangan (1803–49) was a romantic Irish poet and essayist, sometimes translating or adapting Irish and German originals. Sir Samuel Ferguson (1810–86) was an Irish lawyer, poet and antiquary who translated Irish legends in a masculine manner *more than their rhyming*: Yeats was trying to infuse new life into Irish mythology, blending Christian and other symbols with it, and drawing upon his knowledge of magic and the occult to give his poetry mystic and universal dimensions rather than merely national

P. 5   'Under the Moon'   *Brycelinde*: in Arthurian legend the forest of Broceliande in Brittany where the wizard Merlin was bewitched by Viviane   *Avalon*: the island to which Arthur was brought to be cured of his wounds; but he was mortally wounded   *Joyous Isle*: where Lancelot lived with Elayne for some years in the Castle of Blyaunt   *Lancelot crazed*: after Elayne's son Galahad was born she came to Arthur's court where Dame Brysen, her friend, practised her arts on Lancelot. Queen Guinevere became so jealous of Elayne that she drove her from the court. Lancelot became mad for several years, until he came to Corbyn, where Elayne and Dame Brysen, recognising him, had him bound and placed by the vessel of the Holy Grail. He then recovered his senses and asked Elayne to request her father, King Pelles, to give them a place to live together, and the King assigned them the Castle of Blyaunt   *Ulad*: Irish for Ulster   *Naoise*: one of the sons of Usna, he ran away with Deirdre (daughter of Fedlimid, Conchubar's harper) whom the king intended to marry. Naoise and Deirdre went to Scotland with his brothers Ainnle and Ardan, but returned later under the safe-conduct of Fergus MacRoy. The sons of Usna were killed treacherously by Conchubar, and Deirdre committed suicide (in the ending to the tale adopted by Yeats, in his play *Deirdre*, 1907)   *Land-under-Wave*: Irish Tir-fa-thon, the enchanted land which sank under the sea   *Seven old sisters*: possibly the planets   *Land-of-the-Tower*: possibly the house of glass in which Aengus, the 'Master of Love', lived (cf. the 'tower of glass' in 'The Harp of Aengus' p. 38)   *Wood-of-Wonders . . . golden bier*: in the folk tale 'Adventures of the Children of the King of Norway', *Irish Texts Society* I (1899), pp. 119–31, the hero Cod kills a golden-horned ox in the Forest of Wonders, then later sees a queen and 'a fair bevy of women' and a golden bier borne by four, and the lady (the queen) says to him 'Son of the King of Norway, there is the ox for thee that thou woundest a little while back, which we have in the bier'   *Branwen*: the daughter of Llyr in the *Mabinogion* (a collection of Welsh tales), which Yeats read in Lady Guest's translation   *Guinevere*: the queen of King Arthur   *Niamh, Laban and Fand*: Niamh was the daughter of Aengus and Edain who took Oisin to the other world for three hundred years. Laban was a sister of Fand, the wife of Manannan MacLir, the god of the sea   *wood-woman . . . blue-eyed hawk*: in 'Adventures of the Children of the King of Norway' she meets Cod before he enters the Forest of Wonders and tells him that the vindictive daughter of the King of Greece has changed her lover into a blue-eyed hawk   *dun*: Irish, a fort, often one situated on a hill   *hunter's moon*: a name for the full moon next after the Harvest moon (the moon, which is full within a fortnight of the autumn equinox (22/23 September) which rises nearly at the same time for several nights at points successively further north on the eastern horizon

P. 5   'Adam's Curse'   *That . . . mild woman*: Maud Gonne's sister Mrs Kathleen Pilcher   *And you and I*: Maud Gonne and Yeats. The story of the poem's inspiration is given in Maud Gonne's autobiography *A Servant of the Queen* (1938):

> I was still in my dark clothes with the veil I always wore when travelling instead of a hat, and we must have made a strange contrast. I saw Willie Yeats looking critically at me and he told Kathleen he liked her dress and that she was looking younger than ever. It was on that occasion Kathleen remarked that it was hard work being beautiful which Willie turned into his poem 'Adam's Curse'.
>
> Next day when he called to take me out to pay my customary visit to the Lia Fail, he said: 'You don't take care of yourself as Kathleen does, so she looks younger than you; your face is worn and thin; but you will always be beautiful, more beautiful than anyone I have known. You can't help that. Oh Maud, why don't you marry me and give up this tragic struggle and

live a peaceful life? I could make such a beautiful life for you among artists and writers who would understand you.'

'Willie, are you not tired of asking that question? How often have I told you to thank the gods that I will not marry you. You would not be happy with me.'

'I am not happy without you.'

'Oh yes, you are, because you make beautiful poetry out of what you call your unhappiness and you are happy in that. Marriage would be such a dull affair. Poets should never marry. The world should thank me for not marrying you. I will tell you one thing, our friendship has meant a great deal to me; it has helped me often when I needed help, needed it perhaps more than you or anybody know, for I never talk or even think of these things.'

'Are you happy or unhappy?' he asked.

'I have been happier and unhappier than most, but I don't think about it. You and I are so different in this. It is a great thing to know one can never suffer again as much as one has suffered; it gives one great calm and great strength and makes one afraid of nothing. I am interested in the work I have undertaken; that is my life and I live, – while so many people only exist. Those are the people to be pitied; those who lead dull, uneventful lives; they might as well be dead in the ground. And now, Willie, let us talk of the Lia Fail. You know I hate talking of myself; I am not going to let you make me.

Adam's fall: he was expelled from the Garden of Eden for disobeying God's command not to eat the fruit of the tree of knowledge. See the Bible, Genesis III   *high courtesy*: Yeats thought that true love was a discipline that required wisdom

P. 7 [Accursed who brings to light of day]   This poem was written for Allan Wade, *A Bibliography of the Writings of William Butler Yeats* (1908) which was included in Yeats *CW*, viii (1908). The Bibliography was published in November 1908, *CW* viii in December of that year

P. 7 'All Things can Tempt Me'   *Tempt me*: Yeats did not write much verse during the period that he was Manager of the Abbey Theatre (1904–10)

P. 7 'The Coming of Wisdom with Time'   This poem was originally entitled 'Youth and Age'

P. 8 'The Fascination of What's Difficult'   The prose draft reads:

Subject: To complain at the fascination of what's difficult. It spoils spontaneity and pleasure, and wastes time. Repeat the line ending difficult three times and rhyme on bolt, exalt, coalt, jolt. One could use the thought that the winged and unbroken coalt must drag a cart of stones out of pride because it is difficult, and end by denouncing drama, accounts, public contests and all that's merely difficult.

our colt: Pegasus, the winged horse of Greek mythology, who sprang from the blood of the Gorgon Medusa and flew to Olympus, the home of the gods. In one legend he lived on Mount Helicon and raised the Fountain of Hippocrene there, after which the Muses regarded him as their favourite

P. 8 'A Coat'   *embroideries*: perhaps the somewhat pre-Raphaelite decoration of the early poems and plays   *old mythologies*: the Irish legends and stories Yeats had read in translations (such as those of John O'Donovan, Eugene O'Curry, Brian O'Looney, James Clarence Mangan, Sir Samuel Ferguson, Standish O'Grady, and Lady Gregory)   *the fools*: probably a reference to the younger poets gathered round Yeats's friend AE (George Russell (1867–1935)), such as 'Seumas O'Sullivan' (James Sullivan Starkey (1879–1958)) who wrote 'Celtic twilight' poetry in imitation of Yeats's earlier manner

P. 8 'The Fisherman'   *The freckled man*: an ideal man   *grey Connemara clothes*: homespun tweed from Connemara (see Glossary), a district in the west of Ireland *All day . . . and the reality*: the contrast is between writing for the ideal audience (the fishermen) and the reality, the actual audience in Ireland *The dead man*: probably Yeats's friend John Millington Synge *The beating down . . . great Art*: probably a reference to the controversy over the Lane Gallery. See notes on 'To a Wealthy Man . . . Pictures', p. 382 *a twelvemonth since*: probably Yeats is reverting to a 'subject for a poem' written in a Manuscript Book between 18–25 May 1913, which forms the substance of the last sixteen lines of the poem. See *NC*, p. 180

P. 10   'The Scholars' *Catullus*: Caius Valerius Catullus (?84–?54BC) a Roman poet known for his love poems to 'Lesbia' (Clodia, the sister of Publius Clodius)

P. 10   'The People' The poem stems from a conversation between Yeats and Maud Gonne *all that work . . . all that I have done*: probably Yeats's early work for the Irish literary movement as well as his work for the establishment of an Irish theatre, which resulted in the creation of the Abbey Theatre in 1904, of which he was a Director all his life, and of which he was Manager from 1904–10 *this unmannerly town*: Dublin *Ferrara wall*: Yeats visited this Italian city in 1907 *Urbino . . . the duchess and her people talked*: for Urbino see note on 'Upon a Wealthy Man . . . Pictures' p. 382. The Duchess is Elizabetta Gonzaga (1471–1526), Duchess of Urbino. These lines probably derived from Castiglione's *The Book of the Courtier* where the manners of the court are described, as well as the night when the duchess and her court talked till dawn (see Opdycke's translation (1902), p. 308) *my phoenix*: Maud Gonne *when my luck changed*: an oblique reference to the breakdown of her marriage to John MacBride in 1905 *set upon me*: probably a reference to her reception when she attended the Abbey Theatre on 20 October 1906; she was hissed because of the split between her and MacBride which had resulted in an official decree of separation, after she had sought a divorce in the French courts *after nine years*: this places the conversation in 1906, shortly after the incident at the Abbey

P. 11   'Mad as the Mist and Snow' This poem was first numbered XVIII in *WMP* in *WS* (1933). Yeats wrote in *On the Boiler* (1938) that when he was ill it seemed that great genius was 'mad as the mist and snow' *Horace*: the Roman poet Quintus Horatius Flaccus (65–8BC), whose patron Maecenas gave him a Sabine farm; he wrote odes, epodes, satires, epistles and the *Ars Poetica Homer*: the Greek epic poet (?born between 1050 and 850BC), regarded as the author of the *Iliad* and the *Odyssey*. Seven cities claimed to be his birthplace; tradition represents him as blind and poor in his old age *Plato*: the Greek philosopher (427–348BC), a pupil and admirer of Socrates after whose death he retired from Athens to Megara and Sicily; he returned to teach in the Academy in 386BC and spent the rest of his life teaching and composing dialogues in some of which Socrates appears *Tully's open page*: Marcus Tullius Cicero (106–43BC) became consul in 63BC. Pardoned by Caesar (he fought on Pompey's side at the Battle of Pharsalia) he attacked Mark Anthony in his Phillipic orations, was prosecuted by the triumvirate and put to death in 43BC. He wrote on rhetoric, political and moral philosophy; his prose style was famous

P. 12   'The Nineteenth Century and After' Yeats had been reading Robert Browning and afterwards read William Morris's *Defence of Guinevere* and some of his prose fragments 'with great wonder'; he wrote to Mrs Shakespear on 2 March 1929 to say that he had come to fear the world's last great poetical period was over

P. 12   'Coole and Ballylee, 1931' *my window-ledge*: at Thoor Ballylee *'dark' Raftery's 'cellar'*: Eoghan O'Rahilly (1670–1726) the Irish poet, 'dark' because he was blind; see notes on 'The Tower' p. 346. The 'cellar' is where the river goes underground in a swallow hole *the generated soul*: water was used as a symbol of generation by the Neoplatonics, and Yeats probably had a passage from *On the Cave of the Nymphs* in mind; this was written by Porphry (233–304) who studied at Athens under Longinus and at Rome under Plotinus, the

Neoplatonic philosopher whose life he wrote and whose works he edited *buskin*: the cothurnus, a high thick-skinned boot worn in Athenian tragedy (opposed to the soccus, or low shoe worn in comedy) *sudden . . . mounting swan*: intended as a symbol of inspiration *murdered with a spot of ink*: an allusion to M. *Triboulat Bombomet* (1887) a novel by the French symbolist writer Comte Auguste de Villiers de l'Isle Adam (1838–89) in which Dr Bonhomet is a hunter of swans *somebody*: Lady Gregory (1852–1932). See notes on 'Friends', p. 324. Her book *Coole* (1931) describes the contents of the house and its surroundings well; see also Yeats *A* pp. 388–91, cited *NC*, pp. 289–90) *a last inheritor*: her only child Robert was killed in 1918; see notes on 'In Memory of Major Robert Gregory', p. 325 *that high horse:* Pegasus. See notes on 'The Fascination of what's difficult', p. 315

P. 13   'The Choice' *a heavenly mansion*: probably an echo of Christ's saying 'In my Father's house are many mansions; if it were not so, I would not have told you; for I go to prepare a place for you.' John XIV. 2

P. 14   'Three Movements' The prose draft of this poem read 'Passion in Shakespeare was a great fish in the sea, but from Goethe to the end of the Romantic movement the fish was in the net. It will soon be dead upon the shore'

P. 14   'The Spur' Yeats included this poem in a letter of 9 December 1936 to Dorothy Wellesley, calling it his 'final apology'. An earlier letter of 4 December 1936 ended 'I have told you that my poetry all comes from rage or lust'. In a letter to Ethel Mannin he prefaced the poem with the remark that 'certain things drive me mad and I lose control of my tongue'. (*L.* p. 872)

P. 14   'Those Images' The poem arose out of the dislike Yeats formed for C. E. M. Joad's (1891–1953) talk on politics when he met him (Joad was a populariser of philosophy, a successful controversialist, and, up to his last book in 1952, a fashionable atheist) on a visit to Lady Dorothy Wellesley's house in Sussex in April 1937. He wrote to her in August 1937 telling her of his own speech about the need to hold the Irish together – thirty millions of them outside Ireland. And yet, he added, 'I am as anarchic as a sparrow' and quoted Blake's remark that kings and parliament seem something other than human life and Victor Hugo's comment that they are not worth 'one blade of grass that God gives for the nest of the linnet' *cavern of the mind*: pure intellect *Moscow . . . Rome*: symbols for the extremes of Marxism and Fascism *those images*: Yeats cited an Indian tale in which 'the greatest of sages was asked who were his masters and he replied "The wind and the harlot, the Virgin and the child, the lion and the eagle" ' (*E & I*, p. 530)

P. 15   'The Circus Animals' Desertion' *Winter and summer*: circuses, unlike the poet, usually worked a half-year season *My circus animals . . . Lord knows what*: the poet's work: the stilted boys may be the larger-than-life heroes of his early poems and plays, the chariot may be Cuchulain's; the lion and woman may refer to Maud Gonne, described in the poem, 'Against Unworthy Praise' as 'half lion, half child' *old themes*: probably the chivalrous poetry written in the 1880s and 1890s, in particular *The Wanderings of Oisin* (1889) *Oisin led by the nose*: see 'The Wanderings of Oisin' which tells how the immortal Niamh, 'his faery bride', fell in love with him and brought him to fairyland with her (NB while preferring the form 'faery' Yeats's spelling was not always consistent and he also used 'fairy') *three enchanted islands, allegorical dreams*: symbolising infinite feeling, infinite battle, and infinite repose, the 'three incompatible things which man is always seeking'. Yeats described the whole poem in 1888 as 'full of symbols' *'The Countess Cathleen'*: the play Yeats wrote for Maud Gonne, published in 1892 *given her soul away*: in the play two agents of the Devil come to Ireland in a time of famine and offer to buy the souls of the starving peasants for gold. The Countess sacrifices her goods to get money to buy food for her people and is about to sell her soul when the poet tries, in vain, to stop her (Maud Gonne had become ill through over-strain in helping in relief work among peasants threatened by famine in Co. Donegal); the Countess symbolises all those who lose their peace of fineness of soul or beauty of spirit in political service, and Maud Gonne seemed to Yeats at the time to have an unduly restless soul   *my dear*: Maud Gonne   *Fool and Blind Man*: characters in Yeats's play *On Baile's Strand* (1903) in which Cuchulain dies fighting the sea. Cf. also 'Cuchulain's Fight with the Sea'   *Heart mysteries there*: possibly a reference to John MacBride's marrying Maud Gonne in 1903   *players . . . stage*: Yeats was deeply involved in the work of the Abbey Theatre as Manager from 1904–10. Cf. 'The Fascination of What's Difficult' and 'All Things can Tempt me'

Section 2: DREAMS

P. 19   'In the Firelight'   *Fortune's furious wheel*: the wheel of Fortune, a late classical goddess, is fabled to turn and is an emblem of mutability

P. 19   'The Cap and Bells'   Yeats's note in *WR* read:

> I dreamed this story exactly as I have written it, and dreamed another long dream after it, trying to make out its meaning, and whether I was to write it in prose or verse. The first dream was more a vision than a dream, for it was beautiful and coherent, and gave me the sense of illumination and exaltation that one gets from visions, while the second dream was confused and meaningless. The poem has always meant a great deal to me, though, as is the way with symbolic poems, it has not always meant quite the same thing. Blake would have said, 'The authors are in eternity,' and I am quite sure they can only be questioned in dreams.

his soul: the jester first sends his soul, then his heart to the lady who rejects them but, after accepting his cap and bells, accepts them too

P. 20   'His Dream'   Yeats's note read:

> A few days ago I dreamed that I was steering a very gay and elaborate ship upon some narrow water with many people upon its banks, and that there was a figure upon a bed in the middle of the ship. The people were pointing to the figure and questioning, and in my dream I sang verses which faded as I awoke, all but this fragmentary thought, 'We call it, it has such dignity of limb, by the sweet name of Death'. I have made my poem out of my dream and the sentiment of my dream, and can almost say, as Blake did, 'The Authors are in *Eternity*.'

P. 21   'Towards Break of Day'   The poem records two dreams experienced by Yeats and his wife on the same night when staying at the Powerscourt Arms Hotel, Enniskerry, Co. Wicklow in January 1919   *a waterfall*: it resembled the one at Glencar, Co. Sligo (it might well have been suggested by the waterfall in the grounds of Powerscourt which the Yeatses had seen on this visit to Enniskerry)   *she that beside me lay*: Mrs Yeats   *the marvellous stag*: in Malory, *Le Morte d'Arthur*, III, v, the stag appears at the marriage feast of Arthur and Guinevere; it is pursued by a white brachet and thirty couple of running hounds. In *The Celtic Twilight* (1902) p. 109, Yeats alluded to the white stag that flits in and out of the tales of Arthur; but he had in mind here, according to Mrs W. B. Yeats, the passage in Malory

P. 22   'Crazy Jane grown old looks at the dancers'   When first published this poem was entitled 'Cracked Mary and the Dancers' (for identity of Crazy Jane see notes on 'Crazy Jane and the Bishop', p. 355); it was first numbered VII in *WMP* in *WS* (1933)   *that ivory image*: the source of this poem is a dream, as Yeats told Mrs Shakespear (see notes on 'Friends', p. 324) in a letter of 2 March 1929:

> Last night I saw in a dream strange ragged excited people singing in a crowd. The most visible were a man and woman who were I think dancing. The man was swinging around his head a weight at the end of a rope or leather thong and I knew that he did not know whether he would strike her dead or not, and both had their eyes fixed on each other, and both sang their love for one another. I suppose it was Blake's old thought 'sexual love is founded on spiritual hate' – I will probably find I have written it in a poem in a few days – though my remembering my dream may prevent that – by making my criticism work upon it. (At least there is evidence to that effect.)

cared not a thraneen: didn't care. A thraneen is Irish for a blade of grass, a straw

Section 3: IRISH MYTHOLOGY REVIVED

P. 27   'The Madness of King Goll'   This poem was frequently rewritten; it is about a third-century Irish King whom Yeats described in a note as hiding himself in a valley near Cork 'where it is said all the madmen in Ireland would gather were they free'. He gives as his source Eugene O'Curry, *Lectures on the Manuscript Materials of Ancient History* (1878), who makes Gall (Yeats's Goll) a son of the King of Ulster, who lost his reason after fighting bravely in battle and fled in a state of madness to Glen-na-Gealt, the Glen of the Lunatics. O'Curry derived the tale from a fifteenth-century version in which Gall died in battle; the element of withdrawal in frenzy comes from a king called Mad Sweeney (who left the Battle of Moira in 637) to whom many poems are attributed, thirty-one of them gathered in *Sweeney's Frenzy*   *1th to Emain*: *Irish* Magh Itha, a plain near Raphoe, Co. Donegal; *Irish* Emain Macha, the Twins of Macha, near modern Armagh, the capital of Ulster in the period of the Red Branch tales. They were probably orally transmitted in the early Christian period, transcribed by monks in the seventh or eighth centuries, and incorporated in late manuscripts of between the eleventh and fifteenth centuries   *Invar Amargin*: Amergin's estuary, the mouth of the Avoca River, Co. Wicklow. Amergin was the mythical poet of the Milesian invaders in the *Book of Invasions*, where he was a son of Mil and a druid   The Milesians were thought to have come to Ireland from Spain about the time of Alexander the Great. Mil's three sons Heber, Heremon and Ir conquered the Tuatha de Danaan, the tribes of the goddess Dana, traditionally divine Masters of Magic. In the Red Branch tales Amergin was the druid of King Conchubar of Ulster   *the world-troubling seamen*: possibly the Milesians, but more likely the Fomorians, the powers of night, death and cold with whom the Tuatha de Danaan, the powers of light, life and warmth, battled   *Ollave*: an Irish scholar/poet of the highest grade in the order of filidh; poets were the keepers of the learning and lore of Ireland and thus knew law, history, philosophy, music, language, druidism and poetry; they were trained (for twelve years) in composition and recitation, both of prose and verse   *Northern cold*: the Fomorians came from the north; they were unshapely and had 'now the heads of goats and bulls, and now but one leg, and one arm that came out of the middle of their breasts'; they were evil gods or demons and included

giants and leprechauns   *pirates*: the Fomorians became pirates in the *Book of Invasions*
tympan: a kettle drum   *Orchil*: a Formorian sorceress, probably derived from Standish
O'Grady, *The Coming of Cuchulain: A Romance of the Heroic Age* (1894), pp. 62n and 109n. Yeats
said in *Poems* (1895) he forgot whatever he may have known about her; in O'Grady she is 'a
queen of the infernal regions', and 'a great sourceress'   *ulalu*: a cry of wonder or lamentation

P. 29 'Fergus and the Druid'   *Fergus*: see notes on 'To the Rose upon the Rood of Time', p.
313   *Red Branch kings*: the heroes who served Conchubar king of Ulster at his court Emain
Macha. Yeats also spelt his name Conhor, Conchobar and Concobar   *quern*: apparatus for
grinding corn, usually two circular stones, the upper turned by hand   *slate-coloured thing*: the bag
of dreams of 1.29

P. 30 'Cuchulain's Fight with the Sea' See notes on 'To the Rose upon the Rood of Time', p.
313. This poem is based upon the account in Jeremiah Curtin, *Myths and Folk-Lore of Ireland*
(1890), pp. 304–26   *Emer*: Emer of Borda, the daughter of Forgael (or Forgall), Cuchulain's
wife; though Yeats here may have meant Aoife, mother of Cuchulain's son Conlaech   *rad-
dling*: dyeing   *one . . . like a bird*: Cuchulain's young mistress Eithne Inguba   *her son*: called
Finmole in early versions of the poem   *herd*: herdsman, cattle herd   *The Red Branch*:
Conchubar and his army. See notes on 'The Madness of King Goll', p. 319   *Cuchulain*: see
notes on 'To the Rose upon the Rood of Time', p. 313   *Cuchulain I . . . son*: the original
version read 'I am Finmole mighty Cuchulain's son'   *sweet-throated maid*: Eithne
Inguba   *horses of the sea*: the waves

P. 33 'The Rose of Battle'   *Rose*: see notes on 'To the Rose upon the Rood of Time', p. 313

P. 34 'Who goes with Fergus'   *Fergus*: see notes on 'The Rose upon the Rood of Time', p.
313   *brazen cars . . . wood*: presumably he is using his chariot for hunting in the woods – a
place of escape from the cares of kingship where the young man may also escape from 'love's
bitter mystery'

P. 35 'Into the Twilight'   *Eire*: see notes on 'To the Rose on the Rood of Time', p. 313

P. 35 'The Valley of the Black Pig'   Yeats's first note on the poem read:

> The Irish peasantry have for generations comforted themselves, in their misfortunes, with
> visions of a great battle, to be fought in a mysterious valley called, 'The Valley of the Black
> Pig,' and to break at last the power of their enemies. A few years ago, in the barony of
> Lisadell, in County Sligo, an old man would fall entranced upon the ground from time to
> time, and rave out a description of the battle; and I have myself heard [it] said that the girths
> shall rot from the bellies of the horses, because of the few men that shall come alive out of the
> valley.

He thought that the Battle of the Black Pig would not be as nationalists thought, between
Ireland and England, but an Armageddon 'which would quench all things in Ancestral
darkness again'. There is a longer note in *WR*, quoted *NC*, pp. 69–72   *cromlech*: a prehistoric
structure of stones, usually consisting of one large stone resting upon several upright
stones   *grey cairn*: possibly the great cairn of stones upon the summit of Knockarea (*Irish*, Hill
of the Kings), Co. Sligo, reputedly the burial place of Queen Maeve of Connacht, but more
likely that of Eoghan Bel, the last pagan king of Connacht

P. 36 'The Secret Rose'   Yeats's note reads:

> I find that I have unintentionally changed the old story of Conchobar's death. He did not
> see the crucifix in a vision, but was told about it. He had been struck by a ball, made of the
> dried brain of a dead enemy, and hurled out of a sling; and this ball had been left in his head,

and his head had been mended, the Book of Leinster says, with thread of gold because his hair was like gold. Keating, a writer of the time of Elizabeth, says: 'In that state did he remain seven years, until the Friday on which Christ was crucified, according to some historians; and when he saw the unusual changes of the creation and the eclipse of the sun and the moon at its full, he asked of Bucrach, a Leinster Druid, who was long with him, what was it that brought that unusual change upon the planets of Heaven and Earth. "Jesus Christ, the son of God," said the Druid, "who is now being crucified by the Jews." "That is a pity," said Conchobar; "were I in his presence I would kill those who were putting him to death." And with that he brought out his sword, and rushed at a woody grove which was convenient to him, and began to cut and fell it; and what he said was, that if he were among the Jews that was the usage he would give them, and from the excessiveness of his fury which seized upon him, the ball started out of his head, and some of the brain came after it, and in that way he died. The wood of Lanshraigh, in Feara Rois, is the name by which that shrubby wood is called.'

I have imagined Cuchullain meeting Fand 'walking among flaming dew.' The story of their love is one of the most beautiful of our old tales. Two birds, bound one to another with a chain of gold, came to a lake side where Cuchullain and the host of Uladh was encamped, and sang so sweetly that all the host fell into a magic sleep. Presently they took the shape of two beautiful women, and cast a magical weakness upon Cuchullain, in which he lay for a year. At the year's end an Aengus, who was probably Aengus the master of love, one of the greatest of the children of the goddess Danu, came and sat upon his bedside, and sang how Fand, the wife of Mannannan, the master of the sea, and of the islands of the dead, loved him; and that if he would come into the country of the gods, where there was wine and gold and silver, Fand, and Laban her sister, would heal him of his magical weakness. [In 'Mortal Help' Cuchullain 'won the goddess Fand for a while by helping her married sister and her sister's husband to overthrow another nation of the Land of Promise' (M 9).] Cuchullain went to the country of the gods, and, after being for a month the lover of Fand, made her a promise to meet her at a place called 'the Yew at the Strand's End,' and came back to the earth. Emer, his mortal wife, won his love again, and Mannannan came to 'the Yew at the Strand's End,' and carried Fand away. When Cuchullain saw her going, his love for her fell upon him again, and he went mad, and wandered among the mountains without food or drink, until he was at last cured by a Druid drink of forgetfulness.

I have founded the man 'who drove the gods out of their Liss,' or fort, upon something I have read about Caolte after the battle of Gabra, when almost all his companions were killed, driving the gods out of their Liss, either at Osraighe, now Ossory, or at Eas Ruaidh, now Asseroe, a waterfall at Ballyshannon, where Ilbreac, one of the children of the goddess Danu, had a Liss. I am writing away from most of my books, and have not been able to find the passage; but I certainly read it somewhere. [But maybe I only read it in Mr Standish O'Grady, who has a fine imagination, for I find no such story in Lady Gregory's book. (CW, 1).]

I have founded 'the proud dreaming king' upon Fergus, the son of Roigh, the legendary poet of 'the quest of the bull of Cualg[n]e,' as he is in the ancient story of Deirdre, and in modern poems by Ferguson. He married Nessa, and Ferguson makes him tell how she took him 'captive in a single look.'

> 'I am but an empty shade,
> Far from life and passion laid;
> Yet does sweet remembrance thrill
> All my shadowy being still.'

Presently, because of his great love, he gave up his throne to Conchobar, her son by another, and lived out his days feasting, and fighting, and hunting. His promise never to refuse a feast from a certain comrade, and the mischief that came by his promise, and the vengeance he took afterwards, are a principal theme of the poets. I have explained my imagination of him in 'Fergus and the Druid,' and in a little song in the second act of 'The Countess Kathleen.'

I have founded him 'who sold tillage, and house, and goods,' upon something in 'The Red Pony', a folk tale in Mr Larmine's *West Irish Folk Tales*. A young man 'saw a light before him on the high road. When he came as far, there was an open box on the road, and a light coming up out of it. He took up the box. There was a lock of hair in it. Presently he had to go to become the servant of a king for his living. There were eleven boys. When they were going out into the stable at ten o'clock, each of them took a light but he. He took no candle at all with him. Each of them went into his own stable. When he went into his stable he opened the box. He left it in a hole in the wall. The light was great. It was twice as much as in the other stables.' The king hears of it, and makes him show him the box. The king says, 'You must go and bring me the woman to whom the hair belongs.' In the end, the young man, and not the king, marries the woman. (*WR*)

Rose: see notes on 'To the Rose upon the Rood of Time', p. 313   *the Holy Sepulchre*: where Jesus Christ was buried in Jerusalem   *great leaves*: the Rosicrucian emblem of the four-leaved rose   *the crowned Magi*: the three wise men or kings who came from the East to see the infant Jesus. The Magi were priests in Persia   *Pierced Hands . . . Rood*: the hands of Christ nailed to the rood, or cross   *him/Who*: Cuchulain   *Emer*: Cuchulain's wife   *liss*: an enclosed space, later a mound inhabited by supernatural beings   *a woman . . . loveliness*: the poem was written to Maud Gonne   *thy great wind*: probably marking the end of the world. The poem was written out of Yeats's desire to blend Christian and pagan imagery – and ideas. Yeats's idea of an Order of Celtic mysteries contained the suggestion of some revelation (and with it the achievement of understanding between himself and Maud Gonne. See 1.25 of the poem). A passage in *A*, p. 254, recounts that he had an unshakable conviction

> that invisible gates would open as they opened for Blake, as they opened for Swedenborg, as they opened for Boehme, and that this philosophy would find its manuals of devotion in all imaginative literature and set before Irishmen for special manual an Irish literature which, though made by many minds, would seem the work of a single mind, and turn our places of beauty or legendary association into holy symbols. I did not think this philosophy would be altogether pagan, for it was plain that its symbols must be selected from all those things that have moved men most during many, mainly Christian, centuries.

P. 37   'He mourns for the change that has come upon Him and His Beloved, and longs for the End of the World'   Yeats's first note on the poem (see *NC*, pp. 55–6 quoting the fuller note in *WR*) described how in the Irish story of Usheen's journey to the Islands of the Young (told in 'The Wanderings of Oisin') Usheen sees amid the waters a hound with one red ear following a deer with no horns; and other persons in other old Celtic stories see 'the like images of the desire of the man, and of the desire of the woman "which is for the desire of the man", and of all desires that are as these. The man with the wand of Hazel may well have been Aengus, Master of Love [see 'The Song of Wandering Aengus' and notes on it, p. 351]; and the boar without bristles is the ancient Celtic image of the darkness which will at last destroy the world as it destroys the sun at nightfall in the west.' (See 'The Valley of the Black Pig', and notes on it, p. 320)

P. 37 'The Withering of the Boughs' *Echtge*: she was said to have been a goddess, of the Tuatha de Danaan. See notes on 'The Madness of King Goll', p. 319. Here Echtge is Slieve Aughty (*Irish*, Echtge's Mountain) a range of mountains running between Co. Galway and Co. Clare *Danaan kind*: see note on Invar Amargin, 'The Madness of King Goll', p. 319   *swans . . . Coupled with golden chains*: in Irish legend Baile and Aillinn were lovers, but Aengus the god of love, wanting them to be happy in his own land among the dead, told each the other was dead, and both died of a broken heart. When dead they took the shape of swans linked with a golden chain. See 'Baile and Aillinn', *PNE*, poem 377/*CP*, pp. 459–65   *A king and queen*: Baile and Aillinn

P. 38 'The Harp of Aengus' *Edain . . . Midhir's hill . . . tower of glass*: Yeats's note to *Baile and Aillinn* (1902) reads:

> Midhir was a king of the Sidhe, or people of faery, and Etain his wife, when driven away by a jealous woman, took revenge once upon a time with Aengus in a house of glass, and there I have imagined her weaving harp-strings out of Aengus's hair. I have brought the harp-strings into 'The Shadowy Waters' where I interpret the myth in my own way

Edain sought refuge with Aengus, at his house, the tumulus at New Grange, Co. Louth, having been transformed into the shape of a purple fly; he carried her round in a cage, described by John Rhys, *Lectures on the Origin and Growth of Religion as Illustrated by Celtic Heathendom* (2nd ed., 1892), p. 145, as a glass grianan or sun bower where she fed 'on fragrance and the bloom of odoriferous flowers'. Fuamnach found out where Edain was, conjured a wind to blow her out of the glass house and, after being blown about for 1012 years, she was swallowed by a woman, who became pregnant and bore a second Edain. She then married Eochaid the Ploughman. See 'The Two Kings' and notes on it, p. 343   *Druid*: here means magical; see notes on 'To the Rose upon the Rood of Time', p. 313

P. 39 'The Grey Rock' The Grey Rock (*Irish*, Craigh Liath) is near Killaloe, Co. Clare, the home of Aoibhell in Irish fairy legend. She offered Dubhlaing O'Hartagan two hundred years with her on condition he did not join his friend Murchad (Murrough) son of King Brian Boru, in the Battle of Clontarf, North of Dublin, where the Dantes were defeated in 1014. O'Hartagan refused her offer and was killed in the battle. There are several Irish sources for the story, and Yeats may have drawn on Nicholas O'Kearney's 'The Festivities at the House of Conan', *Trans. Ossianic Society* II 1856, 98–102, though it is included in Lady Gregory, *Gods and Fighting Men* (1904) which he read and praised   *Poets . . . Cheshire Cheese*: a group of poets calling themselves the Rhymers' Club used to meet in the Cheshire Cheese, a chop house in Fleet Street, London; several of them were interested in Irish literature   *Goban*: Gobniu, the Celtic god, famous for his ale, which conferred immortality on those who drank it; he was a smith and a mason   *Slievenmaon*: a mountain in Co. Tipperary (*Irish*, the Mountain of the Women) where the Bodb Derg, a king of the Tuatha de Danaan, had his palace   *one . . . like woman made*: Aoife, a woman of the Sidhe   *a dead man*: O'Hartagan   *a woman*: Maud Gonne   *lout*: a word used by Yeats to describe John MacBride, cf. 'Easter 1916'   *wine or women*: possibly references to Lionel Johnson (1867–1902) and Ernest Dowson (1867–1900), described by Yeats as 'the one a drunkard, the other a drunkard and mad about women' (*M*, p. 331), who are mentioned in l.62, see *NC*, p. 122   *The Danish troop . . . King of Ireland's dead*: Brian Boru and his son Murchad died in the battle which destroyed the power of the Norsemen, who had begun to invade the British Isles from about 800 onwards, virtually controlling Ireland by 977   *an unseen man*: O'Hartagan   *a young man*: O'Hartagan   *Aoife*: Aoife was a Scottish warrior queen, the mother of Cuchulain's son; but the Aoife of this poem is a woman of the Sidhe, probably Aoibhell of Craig Liath, the fairy mistress, elsewhere described by Yeats as a 'malignant phantom'   *two hundred years*: see general note on the poem above   *that rock-born, rock-wandering foot*: Maud Gonne is being compared to this fairy   *loud host*: possibly a reference to Yeats's being unpopular with Irish nationalists because of, *inter alia*, his accepting a British civil list pension of £150 a year in 1910 and his stance in the controversies over the *'Playboy'* and Lane's pictures. See notes on 'On those that hated "the Playboy of the Western World"', 1907', p. 381 and on 'To a Wealthy Man . . . Pictures', p. 382

Section 4: FRIENDS AND FRIENDSHIP

P. 45   'Friends'   *One*: Mrs Olivia Shakespear (1867–1938) whom Yeats first met in 1894 in London. He wrote that for more than forty years she was the centre of his life in London, and during that time they never had a quarrel, 'sadness sometimes, but never a difference'. Those of his letters to her which survive often provide useful comment on his reading and on what he was writing   *fifteen . . . years*: they had a love affair in 1896. See Hone, *W. B. Yeats 1865–1937* (1942), pp. 123–5, and Jeffares, *Yeats: Man and Poet* (1962), pp. 100–3   *And one*: Lady Augusta Gregory (1852–1932) the Irish playwright and translator, whom Yeats first met in 1896, and whose house in Co. Galway, Coole Park, he visited in succeeding summers. She became his ally in the movement to create an Irish theatre, and got him to help her in collecting folklore   *changed me*: she created conditions at Coole Park in which he could work efficiently during the summers he spent there, providing an ordered regime and lending him money (which he repaid out of the proceeds of American lecture tours) so that he did not need to write journalism   *Labouring in ecstasy*: possibly a reference to Yeats's first tour in Italy in 1907 with Lady Gregory and her son Robert, which introduced him to the achievements of Italian Renaissance art and architecture; the summers at Coole (see 'Coole Park, 1929' and 'Coole Park and Ballylee, 1931') afforded an Irish parallel to Urbino's court. See notes on 'The People', p. 316   *her that took*: Maud Gonne, whom Yeats first met in 1889   *eagle look*: Yeats associated this with active rather than contemplative people. Maud Gonne said to him that she hated talking about herself (see notes on 'Adam's Curse', p. 314)

P. 46   'To a Child dancing in the Wind'   *shore*: the poem was written when Yeats was visiting Maud Gonne MacBride at Les Mouettes, her house at Colville, Calvados, in Normandy   *you*: Iseult Gonne (1895–1963) Maud Gonne's daughter by Lucien Millevoye, a French newspaper editor and Boulangist

P. 46   'The New Faces'   *You*: Lady Gregory whom Yeats first met in 1896; he was then thirty-one, she forty-five   *catalpa tree*: in the garden at Coole Park   *tread/Where*: Coole Park

P. 47   'Two Years Later'   *you*: Iseult Gonne, Maud Gonne's daughter. See notes on 'To a Child dancing in the Wind', p. 324   *your mother*: Maud Gonne

P. 47   'Upon a Dying Lady' 'Her Courtesy'   The first of seven poems Yeats wrote, between January 1912 and July 1914, about Mabel Beardsley (sister of the artist Aubrey Beardsley), who married an actor, George Bealby Wright. She died of cancer in her early forties   *a wicked tale*: Yeats told Lady Gregory in a letter of 8 January 1913 that when he visited her 'she began telling improper stories and inciting us (there were two men besides myself) to do the like. At moments she shook with laughter.'   *broken-hearted wit . . . saints . . . Petronius Arbiter*: Yeats wrote to Lady Gregory of her strange charm, the pathetic gaiety with which she faced death; in a letter of 11 February he described her 'putting aside any attempts to suggest recovery . . .

Till one questions her she tries to make one forget that she is ill'   *Petronius Arbiter*: a Roman writer (1st century AD) supposed to be the Gaius Petronius known as *Arbiter elegantiae* at the court of the Emperor Nero, believed to be the author of the satirical romance *Satirae*

P. 48   'To a Friend whose Work has come to Nothing'   *defeat*: the poem was written to Lady Gregory and probably refers to the final decision of Dublin Corporation about the Lane pictures (see notes on 'To a wealthy Man . . . Pictures', p. 382   *one/Who*: William Martin Murphy (1844–1919), proprietor of two Dublin newspapers, the *Irish Independent* and the *Evening Herald*, a highly successful businessman whom Yeats disliked as typical of contemporary commercially-minded middle-class Ireland. See 'To a Shade' with its 'old foul mouth'

P. 48   'To a Young Girl'   *my dear*: Iseult Gonne   *your own mother*: Maud Gonne. See notes on 'To a Child dancing in the Wind', p. 324

P. 49   'In Memory of Major Robert Gregory'   This is one of four poems (the others are 'Shepherd and Goatherd', 'An Irish Airman foresees his Death', and 'Reprisals') that Yeats wrote in memory of Lady Gregory's only child, Major Robert Gregory, RFC, MC, Legion d'honneur, who was killed in action on the Italian front, 23 January 1918. Sometime afterwards it was learned that he had been shot down in error by an Italian pilot   *almost settled in our house*: the poem was written when Yeats and his wife (he married Georgie Hyde-Lees on 20 October 1917) were staying at Ballinamantane House, lent to them by Lady Gregory while they were supervising alterations to 'our house', Thoor Ballylee, the Norman tower and two adjoining cottages which Yeats bought for £35 in 1917, in which he and his family spent their summers until 1929   *turf*: peat   *ancient tower*: the tower became a potent symbol in Yeats's poetry. See, for instance, 'The Tower' and 'Meditations in Time of Civil War'   *narrow winding stair*: the stone staircase, associated in Yeats's mind with the spiral of the gyres. See notes on 'Demon and Beast', p. 333 and on 'The Second Coming', p. 366   *Discoverers . . . forgotten truth*: those interested in the occult tradition   *Lionel Johnson*: Yeats met him in 1888 or 1889; he was a member of the Rhymers' Club (see notes on 'The Grey Rock', p. 323)   *his learning*: he had a large library and impressed Yeats by his 'knowledge of tongues and books'   *courteous*: Yeats envied Johnson his social poise; he did not discover till much later that Johnson invented many of the conversations he reported that he had had with famous men   *falling . . . sanctity*: the 'falling' may be ambiguous; it may refer to his excessive drinking, or to his theological outlook – 'I am one of those who fall', he wrote in his poem 'Mystic and Cavalier' or to both   *John Synge*: John Millington Synge (1871–1909) Irish dramatist, poet and essayist, studied Irish and Hebrew at Trinity College Dublin, then music in Germany. His plays include *In the Shadow of the Glen, Riders to the Sea, The Well of the Saints* and *The Tinkers' Wedding*; see notes on 'On those that hated "The Playboy of the Western World"', 1907', p. 381   *dying*: Synge died of Hodgkin's disease. Yeats thought some of his poems were written in expectation of early death (*E & I*, p. 307)   *long travelling*: perhaps 'into the world beyond himself' (*A*, p. 344)   *desolate stony place*: Co. Galway, which Synge visited in 1898, 1899, 1900 and 1901. He wrote *The Aran Islands* (1906); and his plays *Riders to the Sea* and *The Playboy of the Western World* (1907) owe much to his various stays there   *Passionate and simple*: the islands were remote, the inhabitants Irish-speaking, believers in the miraculous and supernatural, often near to sudden death in their battles with the elements, and possessed of a wildness Synge found very appealing   *George Pollexfen*: Yeats's maternal uncle (1839–1910) who lived in Sligo, a pessimistic hypochondriac   *muscular youth*: he had been a successful rider in steeple-chases   *Mayo men*: Co. Mayo, south of Co. Sligo   *by opposition, square and trine*: astrological terms for heavenly bodies, respectively separated by 180°, 90° and 120°   *sluggish and contemplative*: George Pollexfen became interested in astrology and symbolism   *Our Sidney*: Sir Philip Sidney (1554–86), the Elizabethan courtier, soldier and author of a pastoral romance, the *Arcadia* (1590); completed 1598, *Apologie for Poetrie* (1591) and the sonnets and songs of *Astrophel and Stella* (1591). He died in battle near Zutphen in Holland. The parallels between his versatile life and Gregory's are continued in succeeding stanzas   *all things*: Robert Gregory had encouraged Yeats to buy the tower and had made several drawings of it   *When . . . he would ride . . . feet*: these lines were added at the request of Gregory's widow   *Galway*: Co. Galway, in the west of Ireland   *Castle Taylor*: an early nineteenth-century big house belonging to the Persse family, incorporating a former Norman keep   *Roxborough*: between Longhrea and Gort, Co. Galway, where Lady Gregory (*née* Persse) was brought up   *Esserkelly*: *Irish* Ceallagh's Hermitage (after Saint Celleagh), near Ardrahan, Co. Galway   *Mooneen: Irish*, the little bog; near Esserkelly   *a great painter*: some of his work is reproduced in *Robert Gregory 1881–1918*, ed. Colin Smythe, 1981

P. 48   'To a Young Beauty'   *Dear fellow-artist*: the poem was written to Iseult Gonne   *every Jack and Jill*: Yeats disliked Iseult Gonne's bohemian friends in London and Dublin; she married Francis Stuart early in 1920   *Ezekiel's cherubim*: see the Bible, Ezekiel IX, 3; X 2, 6, 7, 14, 16, 19; XI, 22; XXVIII, 16; XLI, 18. Ezekiel was a prophet who lived in the sixth century BC   *Beauvarlet*: Jacques Firmin Beauvarlet (1751–97), a mediocre French painter and engraver   *Landor and . . . Donne*: Walter Savage Landor (1775–1864), a polished minor poet, whom Yeats read between 1914 and 1916. He wrote verse throughout most of his life; his principal prose work was *Imaginary Conversations* (1824–9). John Donne (1571/2–1631), the metaphysical poet, whom Yeats read in Professor Grierson's edition of 1912; he appreciated how 'the more precise and learned the thought the greater the beauty, the passion' of his poetry. In Landor he appreciated the metaphysical paradox of 'the most violent of men' using his intellect to disengage a 'visionary image of perfect sanity'

P. 53   'Michael Robartes and the Dancer'   *He*: probably represents Yeats's views, *She* Iseult Gonne's (see notes on 'To a Child dancing in the Wind', p. 324)   *this altar-piece*: probably 'Saint George and the Dragon', in the National Gallery, Dublin, ascribed to Bordone (*c.* 1500–71)   *Athena*: Pallas Athene/Athena, Greek goddess, patron of arts and crafts   *Paul Veronese*: cognomen of Paolo Cagliari (1525–88), Venetian painter; he settled in Venice in 1535   *lagoon*: at Venice   *Michael Angelo's Sistine roof*: Michaelangelo Buonarroti (1475–1564) the Italian artist who painted the roof of the Sistine Chapel in the Vatican at Rome from 1508–12. His 'Morning' (known also as 'The Dawn') and 'Night' are statues in the Medici Chapel at Florence which Yeats saw on his visit there in 1907

P. 55   'All Souls' Night'   *Christ Church bell*: Christ Church, Oxford. Yeats was living in Broad Street, Oxford, when he wrote the poem. All Souls' Night is the feast on which the Roman Catholic Church on earth prays for the souls of the departed who are still in Purgatory; the poem, Yeats said, was written in a moment of exaltation   *Horton's the first*: William Thomas Horton (1864–1919) a mystical painter and illustrator, an Irvingite and a member of the Order of the Golden Dawn, for whose *A Book of Images* (1898) Yeats wrote a preface   *platonic love . . . his lady died*: Amy Audrey Locke (1881–1916), with whom Horton lived platonically   *of her or of God*: in *AV* (1925), p. x Yeats remarked that Horton survived Audrey Locke 'but a little time during which he saw her in apparition and attained through her certain of the traditional experiences of the saint'   *companionable ghost*: Yeats wrote to Horton after Miss Locke's death 'the dead are not far from us . . . they cling in some strange way to what is most deep and still in us'   *Florence Emery*: Florence Farr Emery (1869–1917), an actress and member of the Order of the Golden Dawn, first met Yeats in 1890; she produced his *The Land of Heart's Desire* in 1894, and acted Aleel in his *The Countess Cathleen* in 1899. She recited Yeats's poems to the psaltery, an instrument similar to a lyre but with a trapezoidal sounding board; it originated in the Middle East but was popular in Europe in the middle ages   *teach a school . . . dark skins*: she left England in 1912 to teach at Ramanathan College in Ceylon   *foul years*: she died of cancer   *some learned Indian*: probably Sir Ponnambalam Ramanathan who founded the college where she taught   *Chance and Choice*: see notes on 'Solomon and the Witch', p. 355   *MacGregor*: MacGregor Mathers (1854–1918), originally Samuel Liddle Mathers, who studied occultism in London from 1885. Yeats met him possibly in 1887 (see *A*, pp. 182–3), certainly not later than 1890   *estranged*: he was a founder of the Order of the Golden Dawn; Yeats and he quarrelled over matters connected with the Order in 1900

P. 58   'In Memory of Eva Gore-Booth and Con Markievicz'   *Lissadell*: Irish Lios a Daill, the Courtyard or Fort of the Blind Man, the Gore-Booth house in Sligo where Yeats visited the Gore-Booth sisters in the winter of 1894–5   *One a gazelle*: Eva (1870–1926), who wrote poetry, worked for the women's suffrage movement and was strongly committed to social work   *the older . . . death*: for her part in the 1916 Rising. Constance was born in 1868. See notes on 'Easter 1916', p. 384 and 'On a Political Prisoner', p. 385 for details of her political career   *lonely years*: her friend James Connolly was shot after the Easter rising; her husband Casimir had left Dublin for his estates in the Ukraine in 1913 and never lived in Dublin again; her stepson Stasko left to join his father in 1915; her daughter Maeve Alys was estranged from her (they met again in America in 1922). Her husband and Stasko arrived from Warsaw to see her a few days before her death in Dublin in 1927   *old Georgian mansion*: Lissadell, built in 1832 to the design of Francis Goodwin (1784–1835)   *shadows*: as they were both dead   *gazebo*: there are three possible meanings: a summer house; to make a gazebo of yourself (in Hiberno-English) is to make yourself ridiculous; and a place to look from

P. 59   'Coole Park, 1929'   A prose draft of the poem reads:

Describe house in first stanza. Here Synge came, Hugh Lane, Shaw[e] Taylor, many names. I too in my timid youth. Coming and going like migratory birds. Then address the swallows fluttering in their dream like circles. Speak of the rarity of circumstances that bring together such concords of men. Each man more than himself through whom an unknown life speaks. A circle ever returning into itself.

an aged woman: Lady Gregory (1852–1932). See notes on 'Friends', p. 324   *her house*: Coole Park near Gort, Co. Galway   *Hyde*: Dr Douglas Hyde (1860–1949) Irish poet, translator and scholar, founder of the Gaelic League, first President of Ireland (1938–45). Yeats remarked in *Dramatis Personae* that Hyde had given up verse writing because it affected his lungs or his heart (see *A*, pp. 439–40)   *one that ruffled*: Yeats himself   *slow man . . . Synge*: John Millington Synge; see notes on 'In Memory of Major Robert Gregory', p. 325   *Shawe-Taylor and Hugh Lane*: both nephews of Lady Gregory. Shawe-Taylor (1866–1911) seemed to Yeats to have 'the energy of swift decision, a power of sudden action'. He called a Land Conference which, in effect, settled the land question. For Lane, see notes on 'To a wealthy man . . . Pictures', p. 382   *compass-point*: swallows often fly around a turning point such as a steeple or high building   *rooms and passages . . . gone*: The Forestry Department took over the estate during Lady Gregory's life; she rented the house from the Department, which sold it after her death, the purchaser demolishing it

P. 60   'For Anne Gregory'   *Anne Gregory*: Lady Gregory's second grandchild (*b.* 1911); the eldest was Richard, the youngest Catherine

P. 60   'The Results of Thought'   *companion*: Mrs Shakespear. See notes on 'Friends', p. 324   *One dear . . . woman*: Lady Gregory. See notes on 'Friends', p. 324

P. 61   'Beautiful Lofty Things'   *O'Leary's noble head*: see notes on 'September 1913', p. 383   *my father . . . head thrown back*: John Butler Yeats (1839–1922) attended the debate held on 4

February 1907 in the Abbey Theatre on the issues arising out of the riots about Synge's *The Playboy of the Western World*. The account of the incident given by Yeats's father, in *Letters to His Son W. B. Yeats and Others* (1944), p. 214, is somewhat different but no less vivid   *Standish O'Grady . . . drunken audience*: Standish James O'Grady (1866–1928), Irish historian and novelist, sometimes called the father of the Irish literary revival. The speech was made at a dinner given by the editor of the Dublin *Daily Express* in honour of the Irish Literary Theatre on 11 May 1899, described by Yeats, *A*, pp. 423–4   *Augusta Gregory . . . blinds drawn up*: Lady Gregory on being threatened in 1922 by one of her tenants showed him how easy it would be to shoot her through her unshuttered window if he wanted to use violence. See *Lady Gregory's Journals* (1978) I, p. 337   *Maud Gonne . . . Howth station*: a memory going back to their walks at Howth (see note on 'The Ballad of Moll Magee', p. 329), possibly to the first occasion when Yeats proposed to her on 4 August 1891   *Pallas Athena*: see notes on 'Michael Robartes and the Dancer', p. 326 and 'A Thought from Propertius', p. 375. When Yeats first met Maud Gonne he thought she seemed to suit the commendation of the Roman poet Virgil: 'She walked like a goddess'. See *A*, pp. 123, 364   *the Olympians*: in Greek mythology the Gods, who dwelt upon Mount Olympus

P. 62   'The Municipal Gallery Re-visited'   In *A Speech and Two Poems* (1937) Yeats described a visit he made in August 1937 to the Municipal Gallery of Modern Art in Dublin:

> For a long time I had not visited the Municipal Gallery. I went there a week ago and was restored to many friends. I sat down, after a few minutes, overwhelmed with emotion. There were pictures painted by men, now dead, who were once my intimate friends. There were the portraits of my fellow-workers; there was that portrait of Lady Gregory, by Mancini, which John Synge thought the greatest portrait since Rembrandt; there was John Synge himself; there, too, were portraits of our Statesmen; the events of the last thirty years in fine pictures: a peasant ambush, the trial of Roger Casement, a pilgrimage to Lough Derg, event after event: Ireland not as she is displayed in guide book or history, but, Ireland seen because of the magnificent vitality of her painters, in the glory of her passions.
>
> For the moment I could think of nothing but that Ireland: that great pictured song. The next time I go, I shall stand once more in veneration before the work of the great Frenchmen. It is said that an Indian ascetic, when he has taken a certain initiation on a mountain in Tibet, is visited by all the Gods. In those rooms of the Municipal Gallery I saw Ireland in spiritual freedom, and the Corots, the Rodins, the Rousseaus were the visiting gods.

An ambush . . . pilgrims: the first a painting by Sean Keating (1889–1977) 'The Men of the West'; the second 'St. Patrick's Purgatory' (see notes on 'The Pilgrim', p. 331) by Sir John Lavery (1856–1941)   *Casement upon trial*: Lavery's 'The Court of Criminal Appeal' see notes on 'The Ghost of Roger Casement', p. 386   *Griffith*: Lavery's 'Arthur Griffith' see notes on 'On those that hated "The Playboy of the Western World"', 1907', p. 381   *Kevin O'Higgins*: Lavery's 'Kevin O'Higgins'. See note on 'Death', p. 378   *soldier . . . Tricolour*: Lavery's 'The Blessing of the Colours'   *a woman's portrait*: probably 'Lady Charles Beresford' by John Singer Sargent (1856–1925); she was the wife of Baron Beresford of Metemmeh and Curraghmore, Co. Waterford   *Heart-smitten . . . my heart recovering*: at the time of the visit Yeats was suffering from heart-trouble   *Augusta Gregory's son*: 'Robert Gregory' by Charles Shannon (1863–1937)   *Hugh Lane*: probably Sargent's 'Sir Hugh Lane'. He was 'the onlie begetter' (a phrase from the Dedication to Shakespeare's *Sonnets*) because of his dedication to great art and his gift of paintings to Dublin (see notes on 'To a Wealthy Man . . . Pictures', p. 382). Until a rapprochement was reached in 1959 over the Lane pictures between the British and Irish governments, part of the Municipal Gallery was left empty to receive them   *Hazel Lavery living and dying*: the 'living' may be Lavery's 'Portrait of Lady Lavery', but there are two other paintings of her by Lavery which could have been intended; 'Hazel Lavery at her easel' is the most likely; the 'dying' portrait is 'It is finished' – 'The Unfinished Harmony' by Lavery. Lady Lavery died in 1935   *Mancini's portrait*: 'Lady Gregory' by Antonio Mancini (1852–1930), an Italian artist. For Lady Gregory see note on 'Friends', p. 324, for Synge, see note on 'Coole Park, 1929', p. 327   *Rembrandt*: the famous Dutch painter and etcher, Rembrandt van Rijn (1606–69)   *my medieval knees*: Yeats was pleased that the Swedish Royal Family thought (when he visited Stockholm to receive the Nobel Prize in 1923) that he had the manners of a courtier   *that women, that household*: Lady Gregory, Coole Park   *its end*: the family, the house, the way of life, did not prove deep-rooted, though Lady Gregory thought of preserving the place for her grandson once her son Robert was killed; but his family moved to England   *No fox . . . badger swept . . . Spenser*: from 'the Ruins of Time' by Edmund Spenser (1552?–99) part of which poem Yeats had included in his 1906 edition of *Poems of Spenser*: 'He [the Earl of Leicester] is now gone, the whiles the Foxe is crept/Into the hole, the which the badger swept'. The comparison between the 'great Earl' of Leicester and Lady Gregory is implicit   *John Synge . . . I . . . Gregory*: they are linked by their work for the Abbey Theatre, as writers and Directors, and by their delight in history and tradition   *Antaeus-like*: the giant Antaeus, son of Poseidon and Earth, in Greek mythology, grew stronger whenever he came in contact with the earth   *noble and beggarman*: Yeats mentions Lady Gregory quoting from Aristotle 'to think like a wise man, but express oneself like the common people'   *here's John Synge*: 'John M. Synge' by Yeats's father, John Butler Yeats. See notes on 'In Memory of Major Robert Gregory', p. 325

Section 5: IRISH CHARACTERS AND PLACES

P. 67   'The Ballad of Moll Magee'   A poem derived from a sermon preached at Howth where the Yeats family lived (1881–5), then a fishing village, now a suburb, situated on the northern side of the headland and peninsula forming the northern arm of Dublin Bay   *saltin' herrings . . . shed*: one pier of Howth Harbour was lined with salting sheds   *Kinsale*: fishing port in Co. Cork   *boreen*: Irish lane, small road   *keening'*: mourning, uttering the keen for the dead, usually at wakes and funerals (*Irish* caoinim, I wail)   *she*: presumably the dead child

P. 69   'The Lamentation of the Old Pensioner' (and its revised version)   This is another drastically rewritten poem, which Yeats described as 'little more than a translation into verse of the very words of an old Wicklow peasant'. Yeats's 'A Visionary', *The Celtic Twilight* (1893), gives an account of the conversation between the peasant and Yeats's friend Æ, the poet and mystic George Russell, in which the 'very words' were used, as the two walked at night on the Two Rock Mountain, south west of Dublin   *fret*: Irish for doom

P. 70   'The Lake Isle of Innisfree'   Yeats wrote this poem when living in Bedford Park, London; he was reminded by hearing a little tinkle of water and seeing a fountain in a shop window which balanced a little ball upon its jet, of a day-dream of living on Innisfree (*Irish* Inisfraoich, Heather Island), an island in Lough Gill, Co. Sligo, in imitation of the American author Henry David Thoreau (1817–62) some of whose *Walden* (1854) his father John Butler Yeats had read to him. He was also attracted to the island because of its association with local legends. See notes on 'The Danaan Quicken Tree', p. 357   *I will arise*: an echo of Luke XV. 18:

'I will arise and go to my father'   *night and day*: an echo of Mark V.5: And always, night and day, he was in the mountains

P. 70   'The Fiddler of Dooney'   *Dooney*: a rock on the shore of Lough Gill, Co. Sligo   *Kilvarnet*: a townland near Ballinacarrow, Co. Sligo   *Mocharabuiee*: the townland of Magheraboy (*Irish* Machaire Bui, Yellow Plain), south west of Sligo. A note was added to the second edition of *Collected Poems* (1950) by Mrs W. B. Yeats saying the word was pronounced as if spelt 'Mockrabwee'   *Sligo fair*: held in Sligo town where Yeats spent much of his childhood in the house of his maternal grandparents, the Pollexfens, who were local merchants and shipowners. See notes on 'Introductory Rhymes', p. 331   *Peter*: Saint Peter, who keeps the gate of heaven

P. 71   'Red Hanrahan's Song about Ireland'   *Red Hanrahan*: a character Yeats invented; he appears in his early short stories. See also 'The Tower', p. 148   *Cummen Strand*: on the shore of the estuary, on the road from Sligo to Strandhill   *left hand*: the left-hand side, regarded as unlucky   *Cathleen, the daughter of Houlihan*: in popular tradition she personifies Ireland; the poem was written to Maud Gonne who played the part of Cathleen in Yeats's play *Cathleen ni Houlihan* (1902). This poem may owe something to a poem 'Kathleen-ny-Houlahan' by James Clarence Mangan   *Knocknarea . . . stones . . . Maeve*: Knocknarea (*Irish* Cnoc na Riaghadh or Cnoc na Riogh, differently translated as the hill of the king and the hill of the executions. Eoghan Bel, the last king of pagan Connacht, was buried there, until his enemies reburied his body near Sligo), is a mountain in Co. Sligo; the cairn on its summit is popularly reputed to be the grave of Queen Maeve of Connaught, but it is more likely she was buried at Cruachan, Co. Roscommon   *kissed the . . . feet*: Yeats described how Maud Gonne's great height made her, when playing the role of Cathleen, 'seem a divine being fallen into a mortal infirmity' (*NC*, p. 94)   *Clooth-na-Bare*: Yeats wrote in 'The Untiring Ones', *The Celtic Twilight* (see *M*, pp. 77–9):

> Such a mortal too was Clooth-na-Bare [his footnote read 'Doubtless Clooth-na-Bare should be Cailleac Beare, which would mean the old Woman Beare. Beare or Bere or Verah or Dera or Dhera was a very famous person, perhaps the Mother of the Gods herself. Standish O'Grady found her, as he thinks, frequenting Lough Leath, or the Grey Lake on a mountain of the Fews. Perhaps Lough Ia is my mishearing or the story teller's mispronunciation of Lough Leath, for there are so many Lough Leaths] who went all over the world seeking a lake deep enough to drown her faery life, of which she had grown weary, leaping from hill to lake and lake to hill, and setting up a cairn of stones wherever her feet lighted, until at last she found the deepest water in the world in little Lough Ia, on the top of the Birds' Mountain at Sligo.
>
> The two little creatures may well dance on [they were faeries, one like a young man, the other like a young woman], and the woman of the log and Clooth-na-Bare sleep in peace, for they have known untrammelled hate and unmixed love, and have never wearied themselves with 'yes' and 'no', or entangled their feet with the sorry net of 'maybe' and 'perhaps'. The great winds came and took them up into themselves.

Rood: the cross on which Christ was crucified

P. 72   'The Wild Swans at Coole'   *The trees . . . paths . . . the water*: the lake and its surroundings at Coole Park, Co. Galway. They are well described in Lady Gregory, *Coole* (1931)   *nine and fifty*: there *were* 59 swans there when Yeats wrote the poem, in a mood of intense depression   *nineteenth autumn*: these lines do not refer to Yeats's first brief visit to Coole in the summer of 1896, but to 1897 when he stayed from summer to autumn there. He was fifty-one when he wrote the poem   *trod with a lighter tread*: Yeats regarded 1897 as a crucial year in his life; he was then thirty-two and was involved, as he put it in *A*, pp. 399ff., in his 'miserable love affair, that had but for one brief interruption absorbed my thoughts for years past and would for some years yet. My devotion might as well have been offered to an image in a milliner's window, or to a statue in a museum, but romantic doctrine had reached its extreme development'. His health was undermined, his nerves wrecked, but Lady Gregory had set him to work again   *Their hearts . . . old*: Yeats was troubled by the death of his love for Maud Gonne. He had proposed to her in 1916, after her husband was executed, but was refused again. He may also have felt Iseult Gonne, to whom he proposed marriage in 1916 and 1917, would regard him as old   *among what rushes*: in 1928 Yeats recorded that, for the first time in his thirty years' knowledge of the lake, swans had built a nest at Coole

P. 73 'The Pilgrim'   *Lough Derg's . . . island*: the poem deals with one of Ireland's main pilgrimages, to Lough Derg, on the borders of Co. Fermanagh and Co. Donegal. St Patrick's Purgatory is situated on an island there, its cave of vision is where the saint (see notes on 'The Wanderings of Oisin', p. 341 and see 'The Dancer at Cruachan and Cro. Patrick') is reputed to have fasted and received a vision of the next world   *Stations*: the stations of the cross, usually fourteen stages representing Christ's passion and crucifixion   *black ragged bird*: Yeats had read several accounts of the history of the pilgrimage in which a mysterious black bird, thought to be an evil spirit, probably an old heron, terrified pilgrims. See A. Norman Jeffares, 'A great black ragged bird', *Hermathena*, CXVIII, 1974, 69–81

Section 6: THE POET'S FAMILY

P. 77 'Introductory Rhymes'   *old fathers*: Yeats's ancestors. The poem was provoked by the Irish novelist George Moore's (1852–1933) mocking remarks in portions of *Vale*, published in the *English Review* in 1914, on Yeats's 'own class: millers and shipowners on one side and on the other a portrait-painter of distinction'. At the time Yeats had become interested in his family's history   *Old Dublin merchant*: probably Benjamin Yeats (1750–95) Yeats's great-great-grandfather, a wholesale linen merchant (the first of the Yeats family to live in Ireland was Jervis Yeats (*d*. 1712) a linen merchant of Yorkshire stock)   *ten and four*: Yeats's note of 1914 reads ' "Free of the ten and four" is an error I cannot now correct without more rewriting than I have a mind for. Some merchant in Villon, I forget the reference, was "free of the ten and four" [Francois Villon (1531–?) wrote, in 'Epistre a ses amis', 'nobles hommes, francs de quart et de dix' (Noblemen free of the quarter and the tenth), a reference to different taxes]. Irish merchants exempted from certain duties by the Irish Parliament were, unless memory deceives me again, for I am writing away from books, "free of the eight and six".' Irish merchants were originally not required to pay import duties until their merchandise was sold to retailers; under a new system in the eighteenth century merchants who had been wholesalers under the earlier system had allowances of 10 per cent on all wine and tobacco and 6 per cent on all other goods. Benjamin Yeats was listed in a Dublin directory as 'free of the six and ten per cent tax at Custom-house, Dublin' from 1783 to 1794   *country scholar . . . Emmet's friend*: Yeats's great-grandfather, the Rev. John Yeats (1774–1846), Rector of Drumcliff, Co. Sligo from 1805–46. He was a friend of Robert Emmet (1778–1803), who led a rebellion in 1803. It failed and he was executed. John Yeats was suspected of supporting it and was imprisoned for a few hours   *to the poor*: he was known for his charity   *Merchant and scholar*: Benjamin and the Rev. John Yeats   *huckster's loin*: Yeats is drawing a difference between his ancestors – 'merchants' – and the new middle class of Ireland – 'huckster', a contemptuous word   *soldiers*

. . . *a Butler or an Armstrong*: Benjamin Yeats married Mary Butler (1751–1834) in 1773; she was a member of the great Ormonde family which came to Ireland in the twelfth century: the Yeats family set great store by his connection, frequently using Butler as a Christian name. Grace Armstrong (1774–1864) married William Corbet (1757–1824) and their daughter Jane Grace Corbet (1811–76) married the Rev. William Butler Yeats (1806–62), the poet's grandfather. Both Butler and Armstrong families had strong military traditions *Boyne*: on 1 July 1690, in the Battle of the Boyne (a river flowing into the sea at Drogheda on the east coast of Ireland about 40 miles north of Dublin) James II (1633–1701) was defeated by William of Orange, William III (1650–1702) *Old merchant skipper*: William Middleton (1770–1832) Yeats's maternal great-grandfather, sea captain and smuggler, who had a depot in the Channel Islands, traded to South America, and developed cargo traffic between Sligo and the Iberian peninsula *silent and fierce old man*: William Pollexfen (1811–92), the poet's maternal grandfather, a sea captain and merchant, who had run away to sea as a boy. Yeats gives an account of his silences and fierceness in *A*, 6ff *wasteful virtues*: possibly an implicit contrast between the Middleton relatives in Sligo and the Pollexfens; the former 'had not the pride and reserve, the sense of decorum and order, the instinctive playing before themselves that belongs to those who strike the popular imagination' (*A*, p. 17) *barren passion's sake*: Yeats's unrequited love for Maud Gonne *forty-nine*: Yeats was born on 13 June 1865; the poem was first published on 25 May 1914

P. 77 'To be carved on a stone at Thoor Ballylee' *Gort*: the tower was about four miles from the village of Gort, Co. Galway *George*: Bertha Georgie Hyde-Lees (1894–1968), whom Yeats married on 20 October 1917 *all is ruin*: the tower fell into disrepair after Yeats's death but has been restored

P. 78 'A Prayer for my Daughter' Yeats's daughter Anne Butler Yeats was born in Dublin on 26 February 1919; this poem was begun shortly after that and finished at Yeats's tower, Thoor Ballylee, in June 1919 *Gregory's wood*: Yeats's tower was near Lady Gregory's estate, Coole Park; it was purchased in 1768 by Robert Gregory, the first of the family to live there *Atlantic*: to the west of the tower *Helen*: Helen of Troy, associated earlier with Maud Gonne *great Queen*: Aphrodite, the Greek goddess of love; born of the sea (Aphros = foam), hence fatherless *bandy-legged smith*: her husband was Hephaestus, God of Fire; he was lame *Horn of Plenty*: Zeus, chief of the Greek gods, was suckled by the goat, Amalthea. Her horns flowed with nectar and ambrosia: one broke off and she gave it to him. The cornucopia is an image of plenty *played the fool . . . beauty's very self*: probably a reference to Yeats's love for Maud Gonne *a poor man . . . glad kindness*: the poor man is Yeats; the glad kindness a reference to his marriage *Prosper but little*: perhaps a reference to Maud Gonne and Constance Markievicz having been imprisoned in Holloway Gaol in May 1918 *the loveliest woman born*: Maud Gonne, hinted at in the fourth stanza; the parallels are implicit between Helen's, Aphrodite's and Maud's choice of partners

P. 80 'Under Saturn' *saturnine*: born under the influence of the planet Saturn, gloomy *lost love*: for Maud Gonne *the wisdom . . . you brought*: perhaps a reference to Mrs Yeats's share in *A Vision*; she began automatic writing shortly after their marriage and the scripts form part of *A Vision*. See 'Introduction to "A Vision" ', *AV* (1937), pp. 8–25 *the comfort*: Yeats enjoyed living in Oxford; the house that he and Mrs Yeats occupied, in Broad Street, has since been demolished. After his marriage he gave up the rooms he had rented in 18 Woburn Buildings (they have been preserved and are now 5 Woburn Walk) for twenty years. The Merrion Square House, no. 82, in Dublin was not bought until February 1922 *an old cross Pollexfen*: William Pollexfen, Yeats's maternal grandfather. See notes on 'Introductory Rhymes', above *a Middleton*: one of Yeats's maternal grandmother's relatives living in Sligo *a red-haired Yeats*:

the Reverend William Butler Yeats (1806–62), Yeats's great-grandfather, the Rector of Tullylish, Co. Down.

P. 81 'Father and Child' This poem was numbered I in *AWYO* in *WS* (1929) *She*: Anne Yeats, Yeats's daughter, see notes on 'A Prayer for My Daughter', p. 332 *strike the board*: an echo of George Herbert's 'The Collar': 'I struck the board and cried "no more".' *a man*: Fergus Fitzgerald, whose appearance was praised by Anne. Both she and Fergus were children at the time, Anne seven or eight years old.

P. 81 'Are you Content?' *He that in Sligo . . . stone Cross*: Rev. John Yeats, who was Rector of Drumcliff, Co. Sligo, from 1805 till his death in 1846. See notes on 'Introductory Rhymes', p. 331. The old stone cross still stands in the churchyard, where Yeats himself is buried; the three-storied rectory, now demolished, was on the opposite side of the road *That red-headed rector*: Rev. William Butler Yeats, curate at Moira, Co. Down, before becoming Rector of Tullylish, near Portadown. On retirement he lived at Sandymount *Sandymount Corbets*: Yeats's great-uncle Robert Corbet (*d.* 1872) lived at Sandymount Castle, outside Dublin on the south side of Dublin bay. See note on 'Introductory Rhymes', p. 331 *William Pollexfen . . . The smuggler Middleton . . . Butlers far back*: see notes on 'Introductory Rhymes' p. 331 *an old hunter talking with God*: the words come from *Pauline* (1833) by Robert Browning (1812–89)

Section 7: MOODS AND MEDITATIONS

P. 85 'The Cold Heaven' *love crossed long ago*: his unrequited love for Maud Gonne *out of all sense*: an ambiguous expression meaning beyond what is capable of being sensed as well as beyond the limits of common sense

P. 85 'The Dawn' *that old queen measuring a town*: the town was Emain Macha, the capital of Ulster, the northern province of Ireland, situated about two miles from modern Armagh (*Irish* Ard Macha, Macha's Hill). Emain Macha means the twins of Macha, a horse-goddess, who bore them on this site. Yeats got the story of her measuring the circuit of the town with 'the pin of a brooch' from Standish James O'Grady, *History of Ireland: Critical and Philosophical* I (1881) p. 181, where it is 'the spear' of her brooch, or else from Edward Rogers, *Memoir of Armagh Cathedral* (1882) *Babylon*: a city in Mesopotamia, capital of the Chaldee empire *the glittering coach*: presumably the chariot of Phoebus, the sun God

P. 86 'A Meditation in Time of War' *artery*: cf. Blake's poem 'Time' with its 'pulsation of the artery' and cf. also this prose passage from Yeats's 'Anima Mundi', *M*, p 357:

When all sequence comes to an end, time comes to an end, and the soul puts on the rhythmic or spiritual body or luminous body and contemplates all the events of its memory and every possible impulse in an eternal possession of itself in one single moment. That condition is alone animate, all the rest is fantasy, and from thence come all the passions, and, some have held, the very heat of the body.

P. 86 'Demon and Beast' The poem describes a momentary state of aimless joy *perned in the gyre*: to pern is to move in a circular spinning movement. Yeats's note (*CP*, p. 163) tells how when he was a child in Sligo he could see a little column of smoke from 'the pern mill' and was told pern was another name for the spool on which thread was wound. Gyre is used to describe a whirling spiral or circular motion; when Yeats used the word in *A Vision* he meant

A line is the symbol of time and it expresses a movement . . . [it] symbolises the emotional subjective mind. . . . A plane cutting the line at right angles constitutes, in combination with the moving line, a space of three or more dimensions, and is the symbol of all that is objective, and so . . . of intellect as opposed to emotion. Line and plane are combined in a gyre, and as one tendency or the other must always be stronger, the gyre is always expanding or contracting. For simplicity of representation the gyre is drawn as a cone. Sometimes this cone represents the individual soul . . . sometimes general life . . . understanding that neither the soul of man nor the soul of nature can be suppressed without conflict . . . we substitute for this cone two cones. (AV (1925), p. 129)

There are thus four gyres, two expanding, two narrowing, the apex of each cone coinciding with the base of the other:

When, however, a narrowing and widening gyre reach their limit, the one the utmost contraction the other the utmost expansion, they change places, point to circle, circle to point, for this system conceives the world as catastrophic, and continue as before, one always narrowing, one always expanding, and yet bound for ever to one another. (AV (1925), p. 131)

In a note included in *Michael Robartes and the Dancer* (1920) [published 1921] Yeats wrote

. . . The figure while the soul is in the body, or suffering from the consequences of that life, is frequently drawn as a double cone, the narrow end of each cone being in the centre of the broad end of the other.

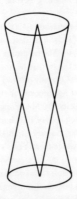

It had its origin from a straight line which represents, now time, now emotion, now subjective life, and a plane at right angles to this line which represents, now space, now intellect, now objective life; while it is marked out by two gyres which represent the conflict, as it were, of plane and line, by two movements, which circle about a centre because a movement outward on the plane is checked by and in turn checks a movement onward upon the line; & the circling is always narrowing or spreading, because one movement or other is always the stronger. In other words, the human soul is always moving outward into the objective world or inward into itself; & this movement is double because the human soul would not be conscious were it not suspended between contraries, the greater the contrast the more intense the consciousness. The man, in whom the movement inward is stronger than the movement outward, the man who sees all reflected within himself, the subjective man, reaches the narrow end of a gyre at death, for death is always, they contend, even when it seems the result of accident, preceded by an intensification of the subjective life; and has a moment of revelation immediately after death, a revelation which they describe as his being carried into the presence of all his dead kindred, a moment whose objectivity is exactly equal to the subjectivity of death. The objective man on the other hand, whose gyre moves outward, receives at this moment the revelation, not of himself seen from within, for that is impossible to objective man, but of himself as if he were somebody else. This figure is true also of history, for the end of an age, which always receives the revelation of the character of the next age, is represented by the coming of one gyre to its place of greatest expansion and of the other to that of its greatest contraction. At the present moment the life gyre is sweeping outward, unlike that before the birth of Christ which was narrowing, and has almost reached its greatest expansion. The revelation which approaches will however take its character from the contrary movement of the interior gyre. All our scientific, democratic, fact-accumulating, heterogeneous civilization belongs to the outward gyre and prepares not the countinuance of itself but the relevation as in a lightning flash, though in a flash that will not strike only in one place, and will for a time be constantly repeated, of the civilisation that must slowly take its place. This is too simple a statement, for much detail is possible.

Their symbolic meaning can be seen best in 'The Second Coming'. In 'Demon and Beast' the gyre can be explained in *AV*'s terminology as being between hatred and desire, but in the third stanza it seems to be used merely to describe the movement of the seagull. For a fuller discussion see Jeffares, 'Gyres in the Poetry of W B Yeats', *The Circus Animals* (1970), pp. 103–14   *Luke Wadding*: an Irish Franciscan (1588–1657) who became president of the Irish College at Salamanca; the portrait by José Ribera (1588–1652), the Spanish painter, is in the National Gallery of Ireland, Dublin   *Ormondes*: portraits of titled members of the Butler family in the National Gallery, Dublin. Yeats was proud of his family's link with the Butler family; see notes on 'Introductory Rhymes', p. 331   *Stafford*: Sir Thomas Wentworth, 1st earl of Strafford (1593–1641), Lord Deputy of Ireland (1632–40). His portrait is in the National Gallery, Dublin   *the Gallery*: the National Gallery of Ireland, in Merrion Square, Dublin   *the little lake*: in St Stephen's Green, Dublin. When he wrote the poem Yeats and his wife were living in 73 St Stephen's Green, Maud Gonne MacBride's house   *absurd . . . bird*: one of the many ducks on the lake   *barren Thebaid*: in upper Egypt where Egyptian monasticism flourished; its barren nature was emphasised in two books on early Christian monasticism by Rev. J. O. Hannay, which Yeats had read   *Mareotic sea*: one of the five regions known for monasticism; Shelley's witch of Atlas glided down the Nile 'By Moeris and the Mareotid lakes'   *exultant Anthony*: St Anthony of Coma (?240–c. 345), whose enthusiasm was described in J. O. Hannay, *The Spirit and Origin of Christian Monasticism* (1903), p. 101   *twice a thousand more*: monasticism spread rapidly under St Anthony's influence   *the Caesars . . . thrones*: the Caesars, the emperors of Rome; the name was taken from Caius Julius Caesar (?102–44BC). Yeats had read in the German historian Theodor Mommsen (1817–1903) the theory that from Julius Caesar on the Roman State became a dead thing, a mere mechanism. To Yeats Christianity was the antithesis of the classical world. Cf. 'Whence had they come?' with its line 'the hand and lash that beat down frigid Rome'

P. 88   'The Wheel'   This poem was written directly on to a piece of notepaper in the Euston

Hotel, London, when Yeats was waiting to board the Irish mail train which ran from Euston to Holyhead

P. 88 'Meditations in Time of Civil War' The 'civil war' is the Irish civil war, 1922–3, between the newly established Irish Free State Government and those Republicans who rejected the Anglo-Irish Treaty, signed in London on 6 December 1921, ratified by the Irish Parliament on 7 January 1922 I *'Ancestral Houses' The abounding . . . jet*: a symbol used by Yeats for delight in living   *gardens . . . the peacock strays*: peacocks, symbols of immortality, were sacred to Juno and usually accompanied her; here Yeats is remembering Lady Ottoline Morrell's house and gardens at Garsington, near Oxford   *Juno*: Queen of the Gods in Roman mythology II *'My House'* This poem describes Yeats's tower in Co. Galway, Thoor Ballylee   *symbolic rose*: see notes on 'To the Rose upon the Rood of Time', p. 313   *Chamber arched with stone*: Yeats's bedroom on the first floor of the castle, also used as a study   *Il Penseroso's Platonist*: see notes on 'The Phases of the Moon', p. 364   *Benighted travellers*: possibly a memory of Samuel Palmer's illustration to Milton's poem, and of Shelley's *Prince Athanase*. See notes on 'The Phases of the Moon', p. 364   *My bodily heirs*: Anne Butler Yeats, born 26 February 1919, and Michael Butler Yeats, born 22 August 1921 III *'My Table' Sato's gift*: Junzo Sato, then Japanese Consul at Portland, Oregon, came to see Yeats and his wife when Yeats was lecturing there in 1920. He had read Yeats's poetry in Japan and heard his lecture in Portland:

> . . . He had something in his hand wrapped up in embroidered silk. He said it was a present for me. He untied the silk cord that bound it and brought out a sword which had been for 500 years in his family. It had been made 550 years ago and he showed me the maker's name upon the hilt. I was greatly embarrassed at the thought of such a gift and went to fetch George [Mrs Yeats], thinking that we might find some way of refusing it. When she came I said 'But surely this ought always to remain in your family?' He answered 'My family have many swords.' But later he brought back my embarrassment by speaking of having given me 'his sword'. I had to accept it but I have written him a letter saying that I 'put him under a vow' to write and tell me when his first child is born – he is not yet married – that I may leave the sword back to his family in my will.

Chaucer . . . had not . . . forged: Geoffrey Chaucer (?1340/5–1400) the poet *had* drawn breath if the sword was made 500 years before but the figure is a round one   *Juno's peacock*: see note on 1.25, above. In *AV* a peacock's scream symbolises the end of a civilisation   IV *'My Descendants' fathers*: probably Yeats's father, grandfather and great-grandfather, all educated at Trinity College, Dublin (of which Yeats himself became an honorary graduate in 1922)   *a woman and a man*: his children, Anne and Michael   *Primum Mobile*: in the Ptolemaic system, the outermost sphere supposed to revolve around the earth from east to west in twenty-four hours, carrying with it the contained spheres of fixed stars and planets – a prime source of motion   *an old neighbour's friendship*: that of Lady Gregory, the tower being near Coole Park   *a girl's love*: that of Mrs Yeats   V *'The Road at My Door' Irregular*: a member of the Irish Republican Army, which was opposed to the signing of the Treaty. Yeats's note read:

> These poems were written at Thoor Ballylee in 1922, during the civil war. Before they were finished the Republicans blew up our 'ancient bridge' one midnight. They forbade us to leave the house, but were otherwise polite, even saying at last 'Goodnight, thank you', as though we had given them the bridge.

Falstaffian: from Sir John Falstaff, the comic fat knight in several of Shakespeare's plays   *Lieutenant and his Men . . . half dressed*: 'Free Staters', members of the new national army loyal to the Provisional Government; green uniforms had not yet been issued to these troops   VI *'The Stare's Nest by My Window'*

> I was in my Galway house during the first months of civil war, the railway bridges blown up and the roads blocked with stones and trees. For the first week there were no newspapers, no reliable news, we did not know who had won nor who had lost, and even after newspapers came, one never knew what was happening on the other side of the hill or of the line of trees. Ford cars passed the house from time to time with coffins standing upon end between the seats, and sometimes at night we heard an explosion, and once by day saw the smoke made by the burning of a great neighbouring house. Men must have lived so through many tumultuous centuries. One felt an overmastering desire not to grow unhappy or embittered, not to lose all sense of the beauty of nature. A stare (our West of Ireland name for a starling) had built in a hole beside my window and I made these verses out of the feeling of the moment:

> > The bees build in the crevices
> > Of loosening masonry, and there
> > The mother birds bring grubs and flies,
> > My wall is loosening; honey bees,
> > Come build in the empty house of the stare.

> > We are closed in, and the key is turned
> > On our uncertainty; somewhere
> > A man is killed, or a house is burned,
> > Yet no clear fact to be discerned:
> > Come build in the empty house of the stare.

> That is only the beginning but it runs on in the same mood. Presently a strange thing happened. I began to smell honey in places where honey could not be, at the end of a stone passage or at some windy turn of the road, and it came always with certain thoughts. When I got back to Dublin I was with angry people who argued over everything or were eager to know the exact facts: in the midst of the mood that makes realistic drama.

VII *'I See Phantoms of Hatred and of the Heart's Fullness and of the Coming Emptiness'*   *Jacques Molay*: Jacques de Mólay (1244–1314), Grand Master of the Templars, was arrested for heresy in 1307 and burned alive in Paris on 14 March 1314. Yeats's explanation of the line is:

> . . . A cry for vengeance because of the murder of the Grand Master of the Templars seems to me fit symbol for those who labour from hatred, and so for sterility in various kinds. It is said to have been incorporated in the ritual of certain Masonic societies of the eighteenth century, and to have fed class-hatred.

Magical unicorns bear ladies: probably a memory of Gustave Moreau's (1825–99) painting *Ladies and Unicorns*, a copy of which hung in Yeats's house in Dublin   *brazen hawks*: Yeats's note explained that

I suppose that I must have put hawks into the fourth stanza because I have a ring with a hawk and a butterfly upon it, to symbolise the straight road of logic, and so of mechanism, and the crooked road of intuition: 'For wisdom is a butterfly and not a gloomy bird of prey.'

P. 94   'Among School Children'   A prose draft written about 14 March 1926 reads

. . . 'Topic for poem — School children and the thought that live [life] will waste them perhaps that no possible life can fulfill our dreams or even their teacher's hope. Bring in the old thought that life prepares for what never happens'.

the long schoolroom: In St Otteran's School, Waterford, visited by Yeats in February 1926. This school was run on the principles suggested by Maria Montessori (1870–1952), an Italian doctor and educationalist, author of *The Montessori Method* (1912; rev. ed. 1919), to create spontaneity and neatness in children   *a kind old nun*: the Mistress of Schools, Rev. Mother Philomena   *public man*: Yeats, then a Senator of the Irish Free State and a Nobel Prize winner   *Ledaean body*: Maud Gonne's (the link is that which Yeats used to symbolise her through Leda's daughter Helen). Leda suggests the story of the eggs, cited in *AV* (1925):

. . . I imagine the annunciation that founded Greece as made to Leda, remembering that they showed in a Spartan temple, strung up to the roof as a holy relic, an unhatched egg of hers; and that from one of her eggs came Love and from the other War.

This leads to Plato's *Symposium*, 190, in which Aristophanes (*c*.450–385BC), the Greek playwright, argues that man was originally double in a nearly spherical shape until Zeus divided him in two, like a cooked egg cut in half. Love is an attempt to regain the unity   *Her present image*: Maud Gonne's appearance at the time of the poem   *Quattrocento finger*: a fifteenth-century Italian artist; probably Yeats had Leonardo da Vinci (1452–1519) in mind; the version of the poem printed in the *London Mercury* in 1927 had 'Da Vinci finger'   *Honey of generation*: Yeats wrote in a note that he had taken the phrase from Porphyry's essay on *The Cave of the Nymphs* but that he found 'no warrant in Porphyry for considering it the drug that destroys the "recollection" of pre-natal freedom. He blamed a cup of oblivion given in the zodiacal sign of cancer'. See note on 'some Platonist' in 'Nineteen Hundred and Nineteen', p. 345 Porphyry's work is a commentary on the symbolism of Homer's *Odyssey*, and the 'honey' was stored by bees in a cave (in Book 13) via which Odysseus had to return to Ithaca   *Plato . . . scare a bird*: Yeats wrote to Mrs Shakespear on 24 September 1926 to describe this stanza as a fragment of his last curse on old age: 'It means that even the greatest men are owls, scarecrows, by the time their fame has come. Aristotle, remember, was Alexander's tutor, hence the taws (form of birch) . . . Pythagoras made some measurements of the intervals between notes on a stretched string'. Plato (*c*.429–347), the Athenian philosopher, developed the theory of ideas of forms: these are the true objects of knowledge, timeless, unchanging universal examples of transient finite particulars or objects of the impressions of sense. Unphilosophical man at the mercy of his sense impressions is like a prisoner in a cave who mistakes shadows on the wall for reality. 'Paradigm' was a word used by Thomas Taylor for an archetype, for the Platonic idea of essence   *king of kings*: Alexander the Great (356–323BC) was tutored by Aristotle (384–322BC), the Greek philosopher, a pupil of Plato   *Pythagoras*: another Greek philosopher (*fl*. 6th century BC) born in Samos, to whom the doctrine of the transmigration of souls is attributed; he and his school at Crotona were known for their investigations into the relations of numbers

P. 97 'A Dialogue of Self and Soul' I *ancient stair*: of Thoor Ballylee *the star*: Ursa minor, the pole star *Sato's blade*: see note on I. 'Meditations in Time of Civil War', p. 336 *Montashigi*: Bishu Osafune Motoshigi lived in the period of Oei (1394–1428) II *blind man's ditch . . . men*; see Matthew XV.14 and Luke VI.39 for the blind leading the blind and falling into the ditch *a proud woman*: a reference, no doubt, to his own passion for Maud Gonne

P. 99 'Vacillation' I Yeats sent the first section to Mrs Shakespear in late November 1931

> . . . I went for a walk after dark and there among some great trees became absorbed in the most lofty philosophical conception I have found while writing *A Vision*. I suddenly seemed to understand at last and then I smelt roses. I now realised the nature of the timeless spirit. Then I began to walk and with my excitement came – how shall I say? – that old glow so beautiful with its autumnal tint. The longing to touch it was almost unendurable. The next night I was walking in the same path and now the two excitements came together. The autumnal image, remote, incredibly spiritual, erect, delicate featured, and mixed with it the violent physical image, the black mass of Eden. Yesterday I put my thoughts into a poem which I enclose, but it seems to me a poor shadow of the intensity of the experience.

extremities: this first section relates to the poet William Blake's ideas about contraries. Yeats dealt with them in his and Edwin Ellis's 1893 edition of Blake and he pencilled the following passage in Denis Saurat's *Blake and Modern Thought* (1929):

> With contraries there is no progression. Attraction and Repulsion, Love and Hate, are necessary to Human existence. From these contraries spring what the religious call Good and Evil. Good is the passive that obeys Reason. Evil is the active springing from Energy. Good is Heaven – Evil is Hell.

II *A tree there is*: this derives from Lady Charlotte Guest's translation of the *Mabinogion* (1877), p. 109: 'A tall tree by the side of the rise, one half of which was in flames from the root to the top, and the other half was green and in full leaf' *Attis*: Attis was a vegetation god in Greek legend; to prevent him marrying someone else Cybele the earth mother drove him to frenzy and he castrated himself. Yeats read Sir James Frazer's *The Golden Bough* (1890) I, 297–9 and *Attis, Adonic and Osiris*, 219–49 in which the effigy of Attis was hung on to a sacred pine tree as an image of his coming to life again in the form of a tree *trivial days*: possibly a reference to Yeats's administrative work at the Abbey Theatre III *Lethean foliage*: Lethe meant oblivion in Greek. The waters of Lethe, a river in Hades, were drunk by souls about to be reincarnated so that they forgot their past lives *fortieth*: Yeats was forty in 1905, by which time he had settled into his new bare style of poetry. But 1905 must have been a testing year, for in it Maud Gonne won a legal separation from her husband, but not the divorce she had sought IV *fiftieth year*: Yeats was fifty in 1915–16. In 'Anima Mundi', M, pp. 364–5, Yeats wrote

> At certain moments, always unforeseen, I become happy, most commonly when at hazard I have opened some book of verse. Sometimes it is my own verse when, instead of discovering new technical flaws, I read with all the excitement of the first writing. Perhaps I am sitting in some crowded restaurant, the open book beside me, or closed, my excitement having over-brimmed the page. I look at the strangers near as if I had known them all my life, and it seems strange that I cannot speak to them: everything fills me with affection, I have no longer any fears or any needs; I do not even remember that this happy mood must come to an end. It seems as if the vehicle had suddenly grown pure and far extended and so luminous that the images from *Anima Mundi*, embodied there and drunk with that

sweetness, would, like a country drunkard who has thrown a wisp into his own thatch, burn up time.

It may be an hour before the mood passes, but latterly I seem to understand that I enter upon it the moment I cease to hate. I think the common condition of our life is hatred – I know that this is so with me – irritation with public or private events or persons.

VI *Chou*: probably the Chinese statesman and author Chou-Kung (*d*. 1105BC), known as the Duke of Chou   *Babylon*: see note below on 'Two Songs from a Play', p. 368   *Nineveh*: the capital of the Assyrian Empire   VII *Isaiah's coal*: in the Bible, Isaiah, VI, 6–7, the prophet Isaiah is purified by an angel who applies a live coal taken from the altar to his lips   VIII *Von Hügel*: Baron Friederich von Hügel (1852–1925) whose *The Mystical Element of Religion* (1908) Yeats had been reading   *Saint Teresa*: Saint Teresa, a Carmelite nun. See note on 'Oil and Blood', p. 358   *self-same hands*: of the embalmers who embalmed Saint Teresa (a modern saint)   *Pharaoh's mummy*: the bodies of the Pharaohs of Egypt were mummified   *the lion and the honeycomb . . . Scripture*: in the Bible, Judges XIV, 5–18 Samson kills a lion and gets honey from its carcase. He made up a riddle 'Out of the eater came forth what is eaten and out of the strong what is sweet'. He told the answer to his wife and she was exposed by revealing it.

P. 102   'Crazy Jane on God'   This poem was first numbered V in *WMP* in *WS* (1933)   *All things remain*: A passage in Yeats's 'Anima Mundi', *M*, p. 354, deals with the idea

> Spiritism, whether of folk-lore or of the séance-room, the visions of Swedenborg, and the speculation of the Platonists and Japanese plays, will have it that we may see at certain roads and in certain houses old murders acted over again, and in certain fields dead huntsmen riding with horse and hound, or ancient armies fighting above bones or ashes.

See also Yeats's Introduction to *The Words Upon the Window Pane*, *E*, pp. 368–9:

> . . . the Irish countrywoman did see the ruined castle lit up, the bridge across the river dropping . . .

Armoured horses neigh: 'Cracked Mary', in Yeats's note to *The Pot of Broth* (1902), sometimes saw 'unearthly riders on white horses coming through stony fields to her hovel door in the night time (see notes on 'Crazy Jane and the Bishop', p. 355)   *a house . . . lit up*: probably Castle Dargan, near Sligo. The image recurs in Yeats, and may be traceable to an experience recorded in *A*, p. 77

P. 103   'Old Tom Again'   This poem was first numbered XXIX in *WMP* in *WS* (1933). Tom is presumably a figure in other poems of *WMP*, 'Tom the Lunatic' and 'Tom at Cruachan', possibly a reflection of 'Tom Fool', or 'Tom O'Bedlam', a name formerly given to inmates of Bedlam Hospital, a lunatic asylum in London, allowed out to beg for money for their keep. See also the fool in Shakespeare's *King Lear*

P. 103   'Stream and Sun at Glendalough'   *Glendalough*: see notes below on 'Under the Round Tower', p. 361

P. 104   'The bravest from the gods but ask'   This poem was included in Yeats's *W & B*

P. 104   'A Bronze Head'   A poem prompted by a plaster cast painted bronze, of the head of Maud Gonne MacBride, by Laurence Campbell RHA, in the right of the entrance at the Municipal Gallery of Modern Art, Dublin   *dark tomb-haunter*: probably a reference to Maud Gonne MacBride's habit of attending funerals (on political occasions); she constantly wore long black flowing clothes and a veil in old age   *Profound McTaggart*: John McTaggart Ellis McTaggart

(1866–1925), a Cambridge philosopher; his commentaries on Hegel led to his own *Nature of Existence* (I, 1921, II & III, 1927). Yeats read his *Studies in Hegelian Cosmology* (1901), his *Human Immortality and Pre-Existence* (1915) and *The Nature of Existence* (1921)

Section 8: IRISH NARRATIVE POEMS

P. 109 'The Wanderings of Oisin' Book I *S Patrick*: see notes on 'Ribh at the Tomb of Baile and Aillinn', p. 356 and on 'The Pilgrim', p. 331. Patrick was largely responsible for introducing Christianity to Ireland *You*: In Irish mythology Oisin (in *Irish* the little fawn), son of Finn MacCool and Saeve (of the Sidhe). Yeats describes him as the poet of the Fenian cycle of tales *a demon thing*: Niamh, daughter of Aengus and Edain; her name means beauty or brightness *Caoilte*: Caoilte MacRonan, Finn's favourite warrior. See notes on 'The Secret Rose', p. 320 *Conan*: Conan Mail, the baldheaded, another of Finn's warriors, a braggart whom Yeats described as the Thersites of the Fenian cycle (Thersites was the most querulous and ill-favoured of the Greeks who fought in the Trojan War) *Finn*: Finn MacCool (*Irish* Fionn mac Cumhaill), the main figure in the Fenian cycle, leader of the Fenians *Bran, Sceolan and Lomair*: Bran and Sceolan were hounds, but also cousins of Finn, his maternal aunt Uirne having been transformed into a bitch when pregnant; Lomair was one of the three whelps of Bran and Sceolan *Firbolgs*: supposedly prehistoric invaders of Ireland. Yeats described them as an early race who warred upon the Fomorians or Fomoroh (see notes on 'The Madness of King Goll', p. 319) before the coming of the Tuatha de Danaan *burial-mounds*: Yeats thought that Firbolg kings killed at the Battle of Southern Moytura (*Irish* Magh Tuiridh, the plain of the pillars, or Magh Turach, the towered plain), near Lough Arrow, Co. Sligo, where the Tuatha de Danaan defeated them, were buried under cairns at Beltra Strand near Ballisodare, Co. Sligo. Eochaid MacEirc, the Firbolg King, left the battle to get a drink; the Tuatha de Danaan (see notes on 'The Madness of King Goll', p. 319) hid all the rivers and streams so he travelled to Beltra Strand (*Irish* Traigh Eothail) and was killed there with other Firbolgs. Yeats added that it was by their graves that Oisin and his companions were riding *Cairn-heaped . . . hill . . . Maeve*: the cairn on Knocknarea, a mountain in Sligo, is the reputed burial place of Maeve, a queen in the Red Branch cycle of Tales. See notes on 'Red Hanrahan's song about Ireland', p. 330 *findrinny*: (*Irish* fiondruine, an alloy) literally white-bronze. Yeats called it this in his notes of 1895, but red-bronze in a revised note of 1899 *Oscar's pencilled . . . Gabhra's . . . plain*: Oscar was Oisin's son; he was killed at the battle of Gabhra (near Garristown, in north Co. Dublin) in 824, in which, Yeats remarked, 'the power of the Fenians was broken', hence the pencilled urn is an image presumably covered by ravens eating the dead bodies, from Sir Samuel Ferguson's (1810–86) 'Aideen's Grave': 'A cup of bodkin pencill'd clay Holds Oscar' which presumably means that a pattern was imposed by a bodkin on the pottery urn containing Oscar's ashes *Aengus . . . Edain . . . Niamh*: see note on 'Under the Moon', p. 314. Edain was 'a legendary queen who went away and lived among the Shee'. She was lured away by Midhir who wooed her through King Eochaid's brother Ardan, and won the right to kiss her after defeating her husband in a game of chess, whereupon he took her away through the roof. See notes on 'The Two Kings', p. 343 (which deals with part of the tale). For Niamh see note above on *a demon thing* and also note on 'Under the Moon', p. 314 *birds of Aengus*: four birds that he made out of his kisses, that fluttered round his head *Danaan*: of the Tuatha de Danaan; see notes on 'The Madness of King Goll', p. 319 *brazen bell*: he was reputed to have introduced oblong iron bells into Ireland *Fenians*: the 'great military order of which Finn was chief   *a hornless deer* . . . *hair*: one of Yeats's sources was Brian O'Looney's translation of Michael Comyn's 'The Lay of Oisin in the Land of Youth', *Transactions of the Ossianic Society* IV (1859) 21–5, 117–18, 249, in which this passage occurs:

> We saw also, by our sides
> A hornless fawn leaping nimbly
> And a red-eared white dog,
> Urging it boldly in the chase.
> We beheld also, without fiction
> A young maid on a brown steed,
> A golden apple in her right hand,
> And she going on top of the waves.
> We saw after her,
> A young rider on a white steed.

Almhuin's hosting hall: Finn's home and the Fenian headquarters at the Hill of Allen in Co. Kildare   *Druid*: magical, see notes on 'To the Rose upon the Rood of Time', p. 313 and on 'Fergus and the Druid', p. 320   *this strange human bard*: Oisin   Book III Niamh and Oisin leave the islands of Dancing and Victories for the Island of Forgetfulness   *Fenians . . . Bran, Sceolan and Lomair*: see notes on Book I above   *bell-branch . . . Sennachies*: Yeats glossed this as 'a legendary branch whose shaking cast all men into a gentle sleep'. In the Irish legend Cormac MacArt gained the branch after giving an unknown warrior three requests; he thus loses his wife, son and daughter; the stranger, however, is Mannannan MacLir (God of the Sea) and the family is reunited. A sennachy (*Irish* Seanchai), a reciter of old lore, a story-teller   *the demon . . . hammer . . . Conchubar*: Culann the Smith, who made it for Conchubar   *Kings of the Red Branch*: heroes in the Red Branch, Ulster cycle of tales   *Blanid*: Yeats's note calls her the heroine of a beautiful and sad story told by Keating. In Geoffrey Keating's (*c.* 1570–*c.* 1650) *History of Ireland* II 224–25, Blanid, daughter of the Lord of Manainn, was claimed as a prize by Curaoi, son of Daire, who assisted Cuchulain in the sacking of Manainn. She was carried off, despite Cuchulain's refusal and vain attempt to retrieve her; she later conspired with Cuchulain to murder Curaoi but was killed in revenge by his harper Feircheirtne. Keating drew upon the tale of *The Death of Cu-Roi mac Daire*   *MacNessa*: Conchubar, son of Ness   *Fergus feastward . . . Cook Barach*: see notes on 'Fergus and the Druid', p. 320. Fergus acted as safe-conduct for Naoise and Deirdre and Naoise's brothers but they were murdered by Conchubar's men when Fergus was invited (on Conchubar's orders) to a feast by Barach. Fergus was under *geasa* (an Irish term akin to tabu, a bond that could not be broken) and could not refuse to go to the feast. The story is told in Yeats's play *Deirdre* (1907)   *Balor*: a Fomorian King, whom Yeats described as 'the Irish Chimaera, the leader of the hosts of darkness at the great battle of good and evil, life and death, light and darkness, which was fought out on the strands of Moytura [the second battle] near Sligo'. In Greek mythology the chimaera was a monster, part lion, part goat and part dragon   *Grania*: Yeats's account of Grania came from Standish O'Grady's version of the tale in *Transactions of the Ossianic Society* 3 (1857), in which Grania returns to Finn whom she left for Diarmid (in other versions she urges her children to take vengeance on Finn); his note reads:

> A beautiful woman, who fled with Dermot to escape from the love of aged Finn. She fled from place to place over Ireland, but at last Dermot was killed at Sligo upon the seaward point of Benbulben and Finn won her love and brought her, leaning upon his neck, into the assembly of the Fenians, who burst into inextinguishable laughter.

Conan: Conan Maol, see note above on I, l. 13   *Meredian isle*: an imaginary island in the middle of the earth   *keened*: see note on 'The Ballad of Moll Magee', p. 329   *Rachlin . . . Bera of ships*: Rathlin island, off the coast of Co. Antrim; Bere or Beare Island, Co. Cork (supposedly named after Beara, a Spanish princess, the wife of Eoghan Mor, a king of Munster who reputedly gained power in the southern half of Ireland from Conn the Hundred Fighter (*Irish* Conn Cetchathach, Conn of the Hundred Battles)   *rath*: an Irish fort or dwelling   *the straw-death*: death in bed   *Crevroe . . . Knockfefin*: possibly *Irish* Craobh Ruadh, the Red Branch, the building at Emain Macha (see notes on 'The Dawn', p. 333) where the Red Branch heroes lived. According to James P. McGarry, *Place Names in the Writings of William Butler Yeats* (1976) pp. 61–2, Knockfefin may be Sliab-na-mBan-Femhinn, the mountain of the women of Feimhenn or Femen, now Slievenamon, Co. Tipperary. It was a fairy palace, called Sid ar Femen, the home of Bodb-Derg, son of Dagda, in which the Sidhe enchanted Finn MacCool. The late Padraic Colum thought that Crevroe and Knockfefin, the names of small townlands in Co. Sligo, were what Yeats had in mind   *Maeve*: see note on I, ll. 17–18   *stones of wide Hell*: Yeats commented that

> In the older Irish books Hell is always cold, and this is probably because the Fomoroh, or evil powers, ruled over the north and the winter. Christianity adopted as far as possible the Pagan symbolism in Ireland as elsewhere, and Irish poets, when they became Christian, did not cease to speak of 'the cold flagstone of Hell'. The folk-tales, and Keating in his description of Hell, make use, however, of the ordinary fire symbolism.

P. 128 'The Old Age of Queen Maeve'   *Maeve*: queen of Connacht, who is a major figure in the Irish epic tale the *Tain Bo Cuailgne*, the cattle raid of Cooley   *Cruachan*: her palace at Cruachan in Co. Roscommon; the action of the *Tain* begins and ends there   *praise another, praising her*: Yeats had been picturing Maud Gonne while praising Maeve's beauty   *Druid*: here magical; see notes on 'To the Rose upon the Rood of Time', p. 313 and on 'Fergus and the Druid', p. 320   *Sidhe*: Yeats's note on them in *CP* calls them 'the gods of ancient Ireland, the Tuatha de Danaan, or the Tribes of the goddess Dana, or the Sidhe, from Aes Sidhe or Sluagh Sidhe, the people of the Faery Hills . . . Sidhe is also Gaelic for wind, and certainly the Sidhe have much to do with the wind'   *White-Horned Bull . . . Brown Bull*: in the prelude, the 'Pillow Talk' added (in the eleventh century) to the *Tain Bo Cuailgne*, Maeve invades Ulster to capture the Brown Bull of Cooley, angered that her white-horned bull had gone over to her husband's herds   *Ailell*: Maeve's husband   *Fergus, Nessa's husband*: see notes on 'Fergus and the Druid', p. 320   *Magh Ai*: a plain in Co. Roscommon   *the Great Plain*: the great plain of the other world; in Yeats's note to *Baile and Aillinn* (1902) he described it as the Land of the Dead and of the Happy, and remarked that it was also called 'The Land of the Living Heart', and many beautiful names besides   *Aengus*: see note on 'The Song of Wandering Aengus', p. 351   *the children of the Maines*: usually taken to be the children of Maeve and Ailill. There were seven or eight of them. But her grandchildren are mentioned in l. 109 and may be the children of Maeve's son Maines, married to Ferbe, and killed by Conchubar   *Bual's hill . . . Caer*: Ethal Anbual, from the Sidhe of Connaught; he was father of Caer   *of the birds*: see notes on 'The Wanderings of Oisin' I, p. 341   *Friend*: Maud Gonne   *that great queen*: Maeve

P. 132 'The Two Kings'   *Eochaid . . . Tara*: Eochaid the Ploughman (*Irish* Eochaid Airem) was High King of Ireland. Yeats remarked in a note of 1913 the 'Eochaid is pronounced "Yohee" '. The seat of the High Kings was Tara, Co. Meath   *his queen*: Edain. See notes on 'The Harp of Aengus', p. 323. In the original tale she married Eochaid when re-born; but Midhir (Midir) by winning a board-game (of chess) in play with Eochaid wins the right to kiss her. He and she

then fly out of the smoke hole of the king's house and return to the fairy mounds, which Eochaid digs up to get her back. He is tricked into accepting her (identical) daughter as his wife, but Edain remains with Midhir. See notes on 'The Wanderings of Oisin', p.
341 *African Mountains of the Moon*: the Ruwenzori, in Ruanda *Ardan*: he is called Ailill Anguba in the original tale, to be found in *The Yellow Book of Lecan* and *The Book of the Dun Cow*. Yeats may have read it in R. I. Best's translation of H. Arbois de Jubainville's *The Irish Mythological Cycle and Celtic Mythology* (1903) *Ogham*: an ancient alphabet of twenty characters *Loughlan waters*: Norse waters *man . . . unnatural majesty*: Midhir, King of the Sidhe *your husband . . . being betrayed*: see notes on 'The Harp of Aengus', p. 323 and on l. 2 above *Thrust him away*: in the original tale she returns to Midhir and the land of Faery

Section 9: ANGLO-IRISH ATTITUDES

P. 141 'An Irish Airman foresees his Death' *I know*: Robert Gregory (see notes on 'In Memory of Major Robert Gregory', p. 325) *Those that I fight*: the Germans *Those that I guard*: presumably the English *Kiltartan Cross*: near Coole, Co. Galway. Lady Gregory's style in her translations is sometimes known as Kiltartan.

P. 141 'Nineteen Hundred and Nineteen' This poem arose out of 'some horrors at Gort', Co. Galway, during the period when guerrilla warfare waged by the Irish Republican Army was countered by the activities of the British forces, notably the Auxiliaries and the Black-and-Tans *an ancient image*: probably the olive wood statue of Athena in the Erechtheum on the Acropolis at Athens *Phidias's ivories*: Phidias (*c.* 490–423 BC) the famous Athenian sculptor, was commissioned by Pericles to execute the main statues in Athens. He was responsible for the Parthenon and the Propylaea; his gold and ivory Athena at Athens and his Zeus at Olympia were considered his best works *golden grasshoppers and bees*: Yeats's sources were probably the Greek historian Thucydides (*c.* 460–*c.* 400 BC) who describes golden grasshoppers used as brooches, and Walter Pater, who mentions the 'golden honeycomb' of Daedalus in his *Greek Studies: a Series of Essays* (1895) *we thought*: in a speech of 2 August 1924 Yeats described the general belief in the 1880s that the world was growing better *no cannon*: these lines relate to Isaiah II.4: And they shall beat their swords into plowshares and their spears into pruning hooks: nation shall not lift up sword against nation neither shall they learn war any more.' Cf. Micah IV.3 and Joel III.10 (where the plowshares are beaten into swords) *unless a little powder burned*: probably a reference to parades and reviews before the 1914–18 war. In his speech of 2 August 1924 Yeats retailed how an English Member of Parliament described troops marching past in a Review in one of the London parks as a fine sight 'but it is nothing else, there will never be another war' and Yeats added ' "There will never be another war", that was our opium dream' *dragon-ridden . . . scot-free*: a reference to atrocities committed in the pre-Treaty fighting in Ireland by Auxiliaries and Black-and-Tans in the Gort area of Co. Galway, when a Mrs Ellen Quinn was killed and the Longhnane brothers murdered and mutilated. See *Lady Gregory's Journals 1916–1930*, ed. Lennox Robinson (1946) pp. 129–46 *that country round*: the poet is linking the burning of 'big' houses in Ireland, unthinkable before the fighting between the IRA and the British Army, with the destruction of the artefacts in Athens II *Loie Fuller's Chinese dancers*: Loie Fuller (1862–1928), an American dancer, had a troupe of Japanese dancers; she danced 'in a whirl of draperies manipulated on sticks' at the Folies Bergère in the eighteen-nineties *Platonic Year*: this is discussed at length by Yeats in *AV* (1937) pp. 245–54; see also *AV* (1925), pp. 154–5 where he based his ideas on Pierre Duhem, *Le Système de Monde*

(1913) and used Cicero's (see notes on 'Mad as the Mist and Snow', p. 316) definition of the Great Year when the whole of the constellations return to the positions from which they once began, 'thus after a long interval remaking the first map of the heavens'   *mythological poet*: probably Shelley, in *Prometheus Unbound* (1820) II, 5, 72–4: 'My soul is like an enchanted boat,/Which, like a sleeping swan, doth float/Upon the silver waves of thy sweet singing'   *Some Platonist affirms*: possibly Thomas Taylor (1758–1835) a scholar known as 'The Platonist', who in his translation of Porphyry's *De Antro Nympharum* (*The Cave of the Nymphs*) alluded to departed souls being ignorant of their earthly lives once they have crossed the River Styx but adds that 'by means of the blood departed spirits recognise material forms, and recollect their pristine condition on the earth'   *some few . . . are garlanded*: Yeats's note read.

The country people see at times certain apparitions whom they name now 'fallen angels', now 'ancient inhabitants of the country' and describe as riding at whiles 'with flowers upon the heads of the horses'. I have assumed in the sixth poem that these horsemen, now that the times worsen, give way to worse. My last symbol, Robert Artisson, was an evil spirit much run after in Kilkenny at the start of the fourteenth century. Are not those who travel in the whirling dust also in the Platonic Year? – May 1921 (This version follows the text in *The Dial*, September, 1921)

Herodias' daughters: in a note on his poem 'The Hosting of the Sidhe' in *CP* Yeats wrote that Sidhe is the Gaelic for wind (see note on 'The Old Age of Queen Maeve, p. 343) and that the Sidhe journey in whirling winds, the winds that were called the dance of the daughters of Herodias in the Middle Ages, Herodias doubtless taking the place of some old goddess   *Robert Artisson . . . Lady Kyteler*: see note on 'some few' above. Yeats read the *History of the Diocese of Ossory* and the MS accounts in the British Library of the trial of Dame Alice Kyteler for witchcraft; she was of a good family that had been settled in the city of Kilkenny for many years. She had been married four times – she was supposed to have poisoned her first three husbands – and was charged with being the head of a band of sorcerers and with having an incubus, a demon named Robin, son of Art. The sacrifice to an evil spirit is said to have consisted of nine red cocks and nine peacocks' eyes

P. 146   'The Tower'   1 *Decrepit age*: he was sixty; he had been seriously ill in the autumn of 1924   *Ben Bulben's back*: a mountain north of Sligo   *the Muse*: presumably of poetry. There were nine muses in Greek mythology; Clio, of History; Melpomene, of Tragedy; Thalia, of comedy; Euterpe of Music, Terpsichore, of dance; Erato, of love/poetry; Calliope, of epic poetry; Urania, of astronomy, and Polyhymnia, of eloquence and imitation   *Plato and Plotinus*: Yeats's note (*CP* p. 533) read:

When I wrote the lines about Plato and Plotinus I forgot that it is something in our own eyes that makes us see them as all transcendence. Has not Plotinus written: 'Let every soul recall, then, at the outset the truth that soul is that author of all living things, that it has breathed the life into them all, whatever is nourished by earth and sea, all the creatures of the air, the divine stars in the sky; it is the maker of the sun; itself formed and ordered this vast heaven and conducts all that rhythmic motion – and it is a principle distinct from all these to which it gives law and movement and life, and it must of necessity be more honourable than they, for they gather or dissolve as soul brings them life or abandons them, but soul, since it never can abandon itself, is of eternal being?'

For Plato, see notes on 'Among School Children', p. 338; Plotinus (205–270) one of the first

Neoplatonic philosophers, was probably born in Egypt; he settled in Rome in 244, and died at Minturnae. His pupil Porphyry arranged his 54 books in six groups of nine books or *Enneads*   II *the battlements*: of Yeats's tower   *Mrs French*: 'She lived at Peterswell in the eighteenth century', Yeats commented, 'and was related to Sir Jonah Barrington who described the incident of the ears and the trouble that came of it'. The story is told in Sir Jonah Barrington's (1760–1834) *Personal Sketches of his own Time* (2 vols, 1827; 1832)   *when I was young/A peasant girl*: in his essay 'Dust hath closed Helen's eye' of 1900 (included in *The Celtic Twilight* (1893), *M*, pp. 22–30) Yeats wrote of Mary Hynes and how her memory was 'still a wonder by turf fires'; she died sixty years before he wrote the essay (she was found dead in Mooneen, the little bog, near Esserkelly, Co. Galway)   *a song*: the Irish folk poet and travelling fiddler Antony Raftery (*c.* 1784–1835) who spent most of his life in the Gort and Loughrea districts of Galway; his poems were collected and edited by Douglas Hyde in 1903. Yeats gives the Irish poem Raftery wrote on Mary Hynes (in Lady Gregory's translation) in his essay (*M*, pp. 24–5; *NC*, pp. 262–3)   *that rocky place*: it is an area of limestone   *certain men . . . bog of Cloone*: Yeats reported the old weaver's memories in his essay:

> There was a lot of men up beyond Kilbecanty one night sitting together drinking, and talking of her, and one of them got up and set out to go to Ballylee and see her; but Cloone Bog was open then, and when he came to it he fell into the water, and they found him dead there in the morning.

Homer: the connection is a double one. Raftery was blind and so was Homer. Each sang of a woman who was spoken of in the same way by the old: Yeats wrote in *BS* of his speaking to old men and women who remembered Mary Hynes and 'they spoke of her as the old men upon the wall of Troy spoke of Helen, nor did man and woman differ in their praise' (*A*, p. 561)   *Helen*: Mary Hynes resembled her, see note on l.37. And Helen is a symbol for Maud Gonne. This leads on to the poet himself in lines 56ff. See notes on 'The Sorrow of Love', p. 350   *moon and sunlight*: the same symbolism is used in 'The Man who dreamed of Faeryland'   *Hanrahan*: he was a character invented by Yeats who appears in his *Stories of Red Hanrahan* (1904) and *The Secret Rose* (1907), ll. 57–73 retells the story 'Red Hanrahan', leaving out the fact that Hanrahan was journeying to his sweetheart Mary Lavelle when he met the old man in the old bawn, but describing his pursuit of the phantom hare and horses. Hanrahan is probably modelled on the Irish poet Eoghan Ruadh O'Suilleabhan (1748–84) whose wandering life as labourer, schoolmaster and poet is mirrored in some of his poems, edited in 1907 by Father Padraig O'Duinnin. He served in the navy and army and died of fever after being wounded in a brawl   *bawn*: usually a fortified enclosure   *a man . . . so harried*: this bankrupt owner of the tower lived about a hundred years earlier. Yeats's note adds that 'According to one legend he could only leave the castle upon a Sunday because of his creditors, and according to another he hid in the secret passage' (*CP*, p. 532)   *for centuries*: Yeats's tower was a medieval building owned by the de Burgo family, mentioned in 1385 as Islandmore Castle, the property of Edward Ulrick de Burgo   *images . . . wooden dice*: 'The ghosts have been seen', Yeats commented, 'at their game of dice in what is now my bedroom'   *Great Memory*: this contained archetypal images, which are transmitted from generation to generation; it is discussed in Yeats's 'Anima Mundi', in *Per Amica Silentia Lunae* (see *M*, pp. 343–66)   *half-mounted*: the bankrupt owner of the tower; the phrase implies his lack of social standing   *beauty's . . . celebrant*: the poet Raftery   *the red man*: Hanrahan   *an ear*: that of Dennis Bodkin, the 'insolent farmer' of l.31 (who lost both his ears in Sir Jonah Barrington's account)   *the man drowned*: the man of l.48   *old lecher*: Hanrahan   *woman lost*: presumably Maud Gonne   III *spat on . . . spat*: a private joke, referring to friends of Yeats, whom he called 'Spit, spat, and spat on'   *the people of Burke and Grattan*: Edmund Burke (1729–97), Irish author, politician, and orator who fought for the freedom of the House of Commons from the control of George III, for the emancipation of the American Colonies; of India from the misgovernment of the East India Company; of Irish trade, the Irish parliament and Irish Catholics; and against the atheistical Jacobin excesses of the French Revolution. Henry Grattan (1746–1820), Irish patriot, parliamentarian and orator; a Protestant who fought for Catholic Emancipation, he was unable to persuade the Irish parliament to share his own largeness of vision. He carried an address demanding legislative independence for Ireland (1782); the Parliament known as 'Grattan's Parliament' sat during one of Ireland's brief spells of prosperity. He opposed the Union in 1800   *fabulous horn*: see notes on 'A Prayer for my Daughter', p. 332   *when the swan*: Yeats's note reads:

In the passage about the Swan in Part III I have unconsciously echoed one of the loveliest lyrics of our time – Mr Sturge Moore's 'Dying Swan'. I often recited it during an American lecturing tour, which explains the theft.

THE DYING SWAN

O silver-throated Swan
Struck, struck! A golden dart
Clean through thy breast has gone
Home to thy heart.
Thrill, thrill, O silver throat!
O silver trumpet, pour
Love for defiance back
On him who smote!
And brim, brim o'er
With love; and ruby-dye thy track
Down thy last living reach
Of river, sail the golden light –
Enter the sun's heart – even teach,
O wondrous-gifted Pain, teach thou
The god to love, let him learn how.

learned Italian things: such as the writings of Dante and Castiglione, the work of the Italian painters and sculptors he had seen on his visits to Italy. Cf. 'To a Wealthy Man . . . Pictures' and 'The People' and notes on them   *stones of Greece*: particularly the sculptures in the British Museum. Yeats read various books on classical sculpture, and refers to Greek sculpture on several occasions in *A Vision*   *loophole*: in the tower   *make my soul*: an expression in common use in Ireland, to prepare for death

P. 152   'Blood and the Moon'   *this place*: Thoor Ballylee   *cottages*: the two cottages adjoining the tower   *Half dead at the top*: the tower was never completely restored; one room remained empty at the top. The phrase probably derives from Swift's remark made when gazing 'at a noble tree, which in its uppermost branches was much withered and decayed. Pointing at it, he said "I shall be like that tree, I shall die at [the] top." ' (cited by Edward Young, *Works* (1798) III, 196)   II *Alexandria's . . . beacon tower*: the Pharos, the lighthouse (built by King Ptolemy Philadelphus on the island of Pharos) was one of the seven wonders of the world   *Babylon's*: see notes on 'Two Songs from a Play', p. 368   *Shelley . . . towers*: Shelley referred to thought's crowned powers in *Prometheus Unbound* (1820) IV, 103   *Goldsmith*: Oliver Goldsmith (1728–74), the Irish writer   *The Dean*: Jonathan Swift (1667–1745), Irish writer and Dean of St Patrick's Cathedral, Dublin   *Berkeley*: George Berkeley (1685–1753), Irish philosopher, Bishop of Cloyne, Co. Cork. See notes on 'The Seven Sages', p. 348   *Burke*: Edmund Burke (1729–97) Irish politician, author and orator. See notes on 'The Tower' III, p. 347   *honey-pot*: probably a reference to Goldsmith's essays and humorous verse in *The Bee* (1759)   *the State a tree . . . a dream*: Yeats thought Burke was the first to say (in his *Reflections*, *Works* II, 357) that a nation is a tree, Berkeley the first to say the world is a vision   *pragmatical . . . pig*: possibly the phrase reflects upon Yeats's experiences when chairing the Commission which was responsible for Ireland's coinage; the artist was asked to alter the shape of the pig on the halfpenny coin to a shape which was better for merchandising 'but less living' ('What We Did or Tried to Do' *Coinage of Saorstat Eireann* (1928), pp. 1–7). See Hugh Kenner, *A Colder Eye. The Modern Irish Writers* (1983), pp. 44–5   *Saeva Indignatio*: the Latin phrase, meaning fierce or savage indignation, is from the epitaph Swift wrote for his own tomb in St Patrick's Cathedral, translated by Yeats as 'savage indignation' in 'Swift's Epitaph'   *Tortoiseshell butterflies, peacock butterflies*: they entered the top room of the tower by the loopholes and died against the window panes   *Half dead*: see note on l. 12 above

P. 154   'The Seven Sages'   *my great-grandfather . . . my great-grandfather's father*: Yeats is involved in a search for his intellectual ancestry among the Anglo-Irish of the eighteenth century. Cf. his remarks in *Pages from a Diary written in Nineteen Hundred and Thirty* (1944):

> How much of my reading is to discover the English and Irish originals of my thought, its first language, and, where no such originals exist, its relation to what original did. I seek more than idioms, for thoughts become more vivid when I find they were thought out in historical circumstances which affect those in which I live, or, which is perhaps the same thing, were thought first by men my ancestors may have known. Some of my ancestors may have seen Swift, and probably my Huguenot grandmother who asked burial near Bishop King spoke both to Swift and Berkeley. (*E*, p. 293)

Edmund Burke: see notes on 'The Tower' III, p. 347   *Henry Grattan*: see notes on 'The Tower' III, p. 347   *Oliver Goldsmith*: see notes on 'Blood and the Moon' II, above   *Bishop of Cloyne*: George Berkeley (see notes on 'Blood and the Moon' II, above) believed strongly in the medicinal properties of tar-water, extolled in his *Siris* (1744)   *Stella*: Swift's (see note on 'Blood and the Moon' II, above) name for Esther Johnson whom he first met at Moor Park, Sir William Temple's house in England. His *Journal to Stella* consists of the letters he wrote to her and her friend Rebecca Dingley during 1710–13. Their close Platonic friendship lasted till Stella's death; the best account of her is Swift's one, written at the time of her death. She is buried in St Patrick's Cathedral, Dublin   *Burke was a Whig*: so, initially, was Swift; both men had a strong conservative sense; Swift aided the Tory Ministry in London till its collapse, Burke, disturbed by the violent excesses of the French Revolution, sided with the Tories   *great melody*: see note on Burke 'The Tower' III, p. 347   *roads full of beggars, cattle . . .*: Goldsmith's poem 'The Deserted Village' depicts the evil effects of rural depopulation

P. 156   'Remorse for Intemperate Speech'   *knave and fool*: a reference to Yeats's early work as a nationalist   *Fit audience*: possibly the friends he made after he was thirty, such as Lady Gregory and Synge, and others in England

P. 156   'Parnell's Funeral'   *Great Comedian*: Daniel O'Connell (1775–1847), Irish politician responsible for Catholic Emancipation in 1929: he is the great comedian in contrast to the tragedian Parnell   *Parnell's Funeral*: for Charles Stewart Parnell (1846–91); see notes below on 'To a Shade', p. 383 and 'Come gather round me, Parnellites', p. 385   *a brighter star*: the star of which Maud Gonne told Yeats, which fell as Parnell's body was lowered into the grave at Glasnevin cemetery, Dublin   *the Cretan barb*: this is explained by Yeats in 'The Stirring of the Bones' (*A*, pp. 372–5; quoted *NC*, p. 406) in a passage he annotated very fully. He described a vision he had of a galloping centaur, and a moment later a naked woman standing on a pedestal shooting an arrow at a star; and he interpreted it as akin to the mother goddess (the 'Great Mother', cf. l. 13) whose priestess shot an arrow at a child whose death symbolised the death and resurrection of the tree-spirit or Apollo. She was depicted on some fifth century BC Cretan coins sitting in the heart of a branching tree   *Sicilian coin*: presumably for the Cretan coins mentioned to Yeats by Vacher Burch, who directed him to G. F. Hill, *A Handbook of Greek and Roman Coins* (1899), p. 163, which illustrates the coin showing the Cretan goddess in the tree   *strangers . . . Emmet, Fitzgerald, Tone*: those who killed them were not Irish people. See notes on 'September 1913', p. 383   *popular rage*: the difference is that now Irish people themselves have attacked their own leader, Parnell   *Hysterica passio*: hysteria; from Shakespeare's *King Lear* II, 4, 56, 'Hysterica passio, down, thou climbing sorrow'   *dragged this quarry down*: Parnell, whose leadership of the Irish party was repudiated after his adulterous relationship with Mrs O'Shea became known. For the image see note on 'To a Shade', p. 383   *devoured his heart*: Parnell is envisaged as the sacrificial victim, the God devoured in a ritual   *Come, fix*: Yeats is presumably challenging those nationalists who spurned Parnell   *the rhyme rats hear*: possibly a reflection of the belief that Irish poets could rhyme rats to death, or make them migrate by power of their poetry. The poet Seanchan Torpest killed 10 rats in King Guaire's palace at Gort, Co. Galway by speaking poetry against them   II *de Valéra*: Eamonn de Valéra (1882–1975) sentenced to death in 1916, sentence commuted to penal servitude for life, released in 1917; opposed the Treaty of 1922, president of the Executive Council of the Irish Free State after 1932 election until 1948, re-elected 1951–4, 1957–9, President of Ireland 1959–73   *Cosgrave*: William T. Cosgrave (1880–1965), President of the Executive Council of the Irish Free State (1922–32), member of Dail Eireann (1922–44). He was sentenced to death in 1916, the sentence commuted to penal servitude for life; released in 1917, he succeeded Arthur Griffith as Acting Chairman of the provisional Irish Government in 1922   *O'Higgins*: Kevin O'Higgins (1892–1927); see notes on 'Death', p. 378   *O'Duffy*: Eoin O'Duffy (1892–1944), joined IRA in 1917, became first Commissioner of the Civic Guard in 1922, dismissed by de Valéra in 1933, leader of the Blue Shirt organisation July 1933, became President of Fine Gael Party, September 1933 – resigned 1934; in 1936 organised an Irish Brigade to fight for the Nationalists in the Spanish Civil War   *Jonathan Swift*: see note on 'Blood and the Moon' II, p. 348   *bitter wisdom*: possibly a reference to Swift's *Discourse of the Contests and Dissentions between the Nobles and the Commons in Athens and Rome* (1701). Yeats thought Swift argued that the health of all states depends upon a right balance between the one, the few and the many. See his *E*, p. 357, quoted *NC*, pp 413–14

P. 158   'The Curse of Cromwell'   *Cromwell's . . . murderous crew . . . into the clay*: Yeats regarded Cromwell as 'the Lenin of his day'. After the execution of Charles I Oliver Cromwell (1599–1658) spent nine months in Ireland, sacked Drogheda and Wexford, and left bitter memories of the cruelty of his campaign and the ruthlessness of his settlement, which through an Act of 1652 brought almost every Irish landlord under condemnation. They were ordered to move to Clare or Connaught to make way for new settlers from England. In 1641 the majority of landlords had been Roman Catholics; after the Cromwellian Settlement the majority were Protestants. In this poem the lovers, dancers, tall men, swordsmen and horsemen are

presumably those who suffered from Cromwell's activities. The phrase 'beaten into the clay'
comes from a translation by Frank O'Connor [Michael O'Donovan (1903–66)] of the Irish
poem 'Kilcash': 'the earls, the lady, the people beaten into the clay' *an old beggar. . . crucified
. . .* Yeats is echoing the Irish poet Egan O'Rahilly's (1670–1726) 'Last Lines', as translated by
Frank O'Connor, except for 'served', which is 'followed' in O'Connor's version (but see C. C.
W. Quin, 'W. B. Yeats and Irish Tradition', *Hermathena* XCVII, 1963, p. 16 which translates
the Irish as 'Loyal Service, ere Christ died, my fathers gave') in *The Wild Birds Nest: Poems from*
the Irish (1932), p. 23 *the Spartan boy's*: in Plutarch's (*c.* 46–*c.* 120) life of Lycurgus the story is
told of a Spartan stealing a fox, concealing it under his clothes and, when apprehended, letting
it gnaw him to death rather than be detected in thaft *great house . . . ruin*: cf. notes on 'Crazy
Jane on God', p. 340

Section 10: LOVE AND SEX

P. 163 'Ephemera' *other loves*: a reference to reincarnation. Yeats regarded the doctrine as
hypothetical, 'the most plausible of the explanations of the world', but we added 'can we say
more than that?'
P. 164 'The Falling of the Leaves' Yeats wrote in 1907 that he sometimes composed his poetry
to 'a remembered air', and added that he spoke the verses that begin 'Autumn is over the long
leaves that love us' to some traditional air, though he 'could not tell that air or any other on
another's lips' (*E & I* p. 21)
P. 164 'The Pity of Love' ll.4–8 of the first printed version of the poem, in *CK*, ran:

> The stars of God where they move,
> The mouse-grey waters on flowing,
> The clouds on their journey above,
> And the cold wet winds ever blowing,
> All threaten the head that I love

P. 164 'The Sorrow of Love' (and its revised version) This is one of the best known examples of
Yeats rewriting his poems *A girl*: the revised version associates the poem with Helen of Troy
and implicitly, through her, with Maud Gonne *Odysseus*: son of Laertes, king of Ithaca; a
former suitor of Helen of Troy, married to Penelope, he was one of the leaders of the Greek
expedition to recover Helen from Troy where she had gone with Paris, son of Priam, king of
Troy, leaving her husband Menelaus king of Sparta. After the sack of Troy which the Greeks
had besieged for ten years Odysseus took nearly ten years to return to Ithaca; his adventures are
told in Homer's *Odyssey* *Priam*: the son of Laomedon, he was the last king of Troy and father
of many children, among them Hector, Paris and Cassandra. He was killed by Neoptolemus,
the son of Achilles, during the taking of Troy.
P. 165 'The White Birds' Yeats added a note after the title in the first printing: 'The birds of
fairyland are said to be white as snow. The Danaan Islands are the islands of the fairies'. The
poem was written to Maud Gonne, see *NC*, p. 32 *meteor . . . flee*: because meteors cannot be
seen for long *blue star of twilight*: Venus *Danaan Shore*: Yeats glossed it as 'Tier-nan Oge, or
fairyland', *Irish* Tir na nOg, the Land of the Young, meant a vaguely conceived afterworld
inhabited by fairies; if mortals were brought there they shared in the everlasting youth of the
fairy people *the rose and the lily*: the rose is a feminine symbol, the lily masculine

P. 166 'The Lover tells of the Rose in his Heart' *your image*: Maud Gonne's *a green knoll apart*: possibly a reference to the island on Lough Key, Co. Roscommon, where Yeats dreamed of creating a Celtic order of mysteries, a dream shared with Maud Gonne, among others

P. 166 'The Song of Wandering Aengus' The poem was suggested to Yeats by a Greek folk song, probably 'The Three Fishes', *Greek Folk Poesy* (1896); the folk belief of Greece seemed very like that of Ireland to him and he thought 'of Ireland and of the spirits that are in Ireland' (*WR*) when he wrote the poem. Aengus he described (in 1895) as 'the God of youth, beauty and poetry'. In a note of 1899 he said that the Tribes of the Goddess Danu (the Tuatha de Danaan, see notes on 'The Madness of King Goll', p. 319 and on 'The Old Age of Queen Maeve', p. 343) 'can take all shapes and those that are in the waters take often the shape of fish'. There are other Irish sources for the poem, Samuel Lover's 'The White Trout', *Legends and Stories of Ireland* (nd), pp. 23–31, and Standish Hayes O'Grady's edition of the story of Diarmuid and Grainne, who when fleeing from Grainne's husband Finn, meet Aengus, who provides them with a fish to eat by going into a wood, plucking a rod from a quicken tree and fishing with a holly berry for bait *hazel wood . . . hazel wand*: Yeats commented that the hazel tree was the Irish Tree of Life or Knowledge, and was doubtless in Ireland the tree of the heavens *glimmering girl . . . apple blossom*: Yeats described his first meeting with Maud Gonne thus: 'Her complexion was luminous, like that of apple blossom through which the light falls and I remember her standing that first day by a great heap of such blossoms in the window' (*A*, p. 123) *the silver apples . . . the golden apples*: the imagery may derive from a description of May day festivals in Ireland given in Lady Wilde's *Ancient Cures, Charms and Usages* (1890) pp. 101–2. See note on 'The Man who Dreamed of Faeryland', p. 357, and for fuller discussion of the golden and silver imagery, *NC*, p. 35

P. 167 'He bids his Beloved be at Peace' Yeats's note to the poem in *WB* reads:

> November, the old beginning of winter, or of the victory of the Fomor, or powers of death, and dismay, and cold, and darkness, is associated by the Irish people with the horse-shaped Púcas, who are now mischievous spirits, but were once Fomorian divinities. I think that they may have some connection with the horses of Mannannan, who reigned over the country of the dead, where the Fomorian Tethra reigned also; and the horses of Mannannan, though they could cross the land as easily as the sea, are constantly associated with the waves. Some neo-platonist, I forget who [probably Thomas Taylor (1758–1835) 'the Platonist'], describes the sea as a symbol of the drifting indefinite bitterness of life, and I believe there is like symbolism intended in the many Irish voyages to the islands of enchantment, or that there was, at any rate, in the mythology out of which these stories have been shaped. I follow much Irish and other mythology, and the magical tradition, in associating the North with night and sleep, and the East, the place of sunrise, with hope, and the South, the place of the sun when at its height, with passion and desire, and the West, the place of sunset, with fading and dreaming things.

The North: see notes on 'The Madness of King Goll', p. 319 *Beloved*: the poem was written to Yeats's friend, Mrs Shakespear

P. 168 'He Gives His Beloved Certain Rhymes' This poem appeared in a story 'The Binding of the Hair' which was based 'on some old Gaelic legend'. A certain man swears to sing the praise of a certain woman, his head is cut off and the head sings. This poem is the song of the head *You*: the poem may have been written to Mrs Shakespear

P. 168 'The Travail of Passion' This poem was written to 'Diana Vernon' (Mrs Shakespear; see notes on 'Friends', p. 324 *Kedron*: spelt Kidron in early versions; it is the brook flowing between Jerusalem and the Mount of Olives. The poem has other biblical imagery: Christ's crown of plaited thorns; *the via dolorosa*, the way crowded with bitter faces; the wounds; and the sponge filled with vinegar

P. 169 'He remembers Forgotten Beauty' This poem was originally entitled 'O'Sullivan Rua to Mary Lavelle'; it became 'Michael Robartes remembers Forgotten Beauty' in *WR*

P. 169 'He reproves the Curlew' *water in the West*: possibly an echo of the Neoplatonist mentioned in Yeats's note on 'He bids his Beloved be at Peace', p. 351. The West is the region of 'fading and dreaming things' *long heavy hair*: cf. 'He bids his Beloved be at Peace', l. 10; this poem was probably also written to Mrs Shakespear *wind*: a symbol of vague desires, vague hopes

P. 170 'He hears the Cry of the Sedge' In *WR* Yeats wrote a note to cover this poem, 'The Poet pleads with the Elemental Powers' (*PNE*, poem 72; *CP*, p. 80) and 'He thinks of his Past Greatness when a Part of the Constellations of Heaven' (*PNE*, poem 75; *CP*, p. 81):

The Rose has been for many centuries a symbol of spiritual love and supreme beauty. The Count Goblet D'Alviella thinks that it was once a symbol of the sun, – itself a principal symbol of the divine nature, and the symbolic heart of things. The lotus was in some Eastern countries imagined blossoming upon the Tree of Life, as the Flower of Life, and is thus represented in Assyrian bas-reliefs. Because the Rose, the flower sacred to the Virgin Mary, and the flower that Apuleius' adventurer ate when he was changed out of the ass's shape and received into the fellowship of Isis, is the western Flower of Life, I have imagined it growing upon the Tree of Life. I once stood beside a man in Ireland when he saw it growing there in a vision, that seemed to have rapt him out of his body. He saw the garden of Eden walled about, and in the top of a high mountain, as in certain medieval diagrams, and after passing the Tree of Knowledge, on which grew fruit full of troubled faces, and through whose branches flowed, he was told, sap that was human souls, he came to a tall, dark tree, with little bitter fruits, and was shown a kind of stair or ladder going up through the tree, and told to go up; and near the top of the tree, a beautiful woman, like the Goddess of Life associated with the tree in Assyria, gave him a rose that seemed to have been growing upon the tree. One finds the Rose in the Irish poets, sometimes as a religious symbol, as in the phrase, 'the Rose of Friday,' meaning the Rose of austerity, in a Gaelic poem in Dr Hyde's *Religious Songs of Connacht*, and, I think, was a symbol of woman's beauty in the Gaelic song, 'Roseen Dubh'; and a symbol of Ireland in Mangan's adaptation of 'Roseen Dubh,' 'My Dark Rosaleen,' and in Mr Aubrey de Vere's 'The Little Black Rose.' I do not know any evidence to prove whether this symbol came to Ireland with mediaeval Christianity, or whether it has come down from Celtic times. I have read somewhere that a stone engraved with a Celtic god, who holds what looks like a rose in one hand, has been found somewhere in England; but I cannot find the reference, though I certainly made a note of it. If the Rose was really a symbol of Ireland among the Gaelic poets, and if 'Roseen Dubh' is really a political poem, as some think, one may feel pretty certain that the ancient Celts associated the Rose with Eire, or Fotla, or Banba – goddesses who gave their names to Ireland – or with some principal god or goddess, for such symbols are not suddenly adopted or invented, but come out of mythology.

I have made the Seven Lights, the constellation of the Bear, lament for the theft of the Rose, and I have made the Dragon, the constellation Draco, the guardian of the Rose, because these constellations move about the pole of the heavens, the ancient Tree of Life in many countries, and are often associated with the Tree of Life in mythology. It is this Tree of Life that I have put into the 'Song of Mongan' under its common Irish form of a hazel; and, because it had sometimes the stars for fruit, I have hung upon it 'The Crooked Plough' and the 'Pilot star', as Gaelic-speaking Irishmen sometimes call the Bear and the North star. I have made it an axle-tree in 'Aedh ['Aedh', 'Mongan' and 'Hanrahan' were replaced by 'He' in the titles of several poems in *The Wind Among the Reeds* (1899). For Aedh see glossary] hears the Cry of the Sedge', for this was another ancient way of representing it.

this desolate lake: probably the lake of Coole Park, Co. Galway, Lady Gregory's house   *sedge*: an echo of Keats's line 'The Sedge is withered from the lake' in 'La Belle Dame sans Merci'   *banners*: possibly a reference to the initiation ceremony of the Order of the Golden Dawn   *will not lie . . . your beloved*: the poem was written to Maud Gonne at a time of strain and sorrow; in an unpublished autobiography Yeats wrote

> Since my mistress had left me no other woman had come into my life and for nearly seven years none did. I was tortured with sexual desire and disappointed love. Often as I walked in the woods at Coole it would have been a relief to have screamed aloud.

P. 170   'He thinks of his Past Greatness when a Part of the Constellations of Heaven'   Yeats's note reads [the poem was originally titled 'Mongan thinks . . .']:

> Mongan, in the old Celtic poetry, is a famous wizard and king who remembers his passed lives. 'The Country of the Young' is a name in the Celtic poetry for the country of the gods and of the happy dead. The hazel tree was the Irish tree of Life or of Knowledge, and in Ireland it was doubtless, as elsewhere, the tree of the heavens. The Crooked Plough and the Pilot Star are translations of the Gaelic names of the Plough and the Pole star.

Country of the Young: see the note on 'The White Birds', p. 350

P. 171   'He wishes for the Cloths of Heaven': Yeats described 'The Cap and Bells' as the way to win a lady, but this poem as the way to lose one. See Joseph Hone, *W. B. Yeats 1865–1939* (1942) p. 152.

P. 171   'The Arrow'   *your beauty*: Maud Gonne's   *this arrow*: possibly an echo of a line in Blake's 'Preface to Milton': 'Bring me my arrows of desire'   *apple blossom*: see note on 'The Song of Wandering Aengus', p. 351   *This beauty's kinder . . . the old*: Yeats had first met Maud Gonne in 1889; the poem was written in 1901

P. 171   'O do not love too long'   *so much at one*: Yeats's friendship with Maud Gonne   *she changed*: probably a reference to Maud Gonne's marriage to John MacBride in 1903. The poem is similar to 'Never give all the Heart'

P. 172   'Never give all the Heart'   *never give*: the poem is reminiscent of Blake's 'Love Secret':

> Never seek to tell they love
> Love that never told can be;
> For the gentle wind doth move
> Silently, invisibly.
>
> I told my love, I told my love,
> I told her all my heart,
> Trembling, cold, in ghastly fears
> Ah! she did depart!

deaf and dumb and blind: A description of the effect of the poet's hopeless passion for Maud Gonne   *and lost*: a reference to Maud Gonne's marriage

P. 172 'Words' *cannot understand*: Maud Gonne, about whom the poem is written, frequently reproached Yeats for not turning his art into nationalist propaganda; she hoped the literary movement would aid the policies of the Sinn Fein movement. The poem was first written in prose in Yeats's Diary:

> To-day the thought came to me that P.I.A.L. [Maud Gonne] never really understands my plans, or nature or ideas. Then came the thought – what matter? How much of the best I have done and still do is but the attempt to explain myself to her? If she understood I should lack a reason for writing, and one can never have too many reasons for doing what is so laborious.

P. 173 'Reconciliation' *You*: Maud Gonne *the day when . . . you went from me*: Yeats received the news of her marriage just before giving a lecture; he gave the lecture but never knew what he said in it *kings . . . things*: probably the plays *On Baile's Strand* (1904), *The King's Threshold* (1904), *The Shadowy Waters* (1906), and *Deirdre* (1907) *the pit*: the grave

P. 174 'No Second Troy' *her*: Maud Gonne *of late*: after the break-up of her marriage in 1905 Maud Gonne withdrew from public life *of late . . . ignorant men . . . most violent ways*: Yeats had been deeply disturbed by the street riots in Dublin in 1897, in part sparked off by Maud Gonne's demagogic oratory. She was not averse to violence and before her marriage became increasingly involved in anti-British activity *little streets . . . great*: Yeats had come to distrust the 'little semi-literary and semi-political clubs and societies' out of which the Sinn Fein movement grew; he thought that the nationalists with whom he had associated in the 1890s were 'because of their poverty, their ignorance, their superstitious piety' subject to 'all kinds of fear'. See 'Easter 1916' for the generally mocking attitude he had developed towards the Irish political nationalists; he had become depressed by attacks on the Abbey Theatre and the treatment of Sir Hugh Lane's offer of his pictures to Dublin *tightened bow*: see notes (on Blake's imagery) on 'The Arrow', p. 353 *not natural . . . most stern*: Yeats described Maud Gonne as looking as if she were a classical goddess; her beauty, 'backed by her great stature' [she was nearly six feet in height] was solitary. Cf. notes on 'Beautiful Lofty Things', p. 328 *Troy*: she was, like Helen of Troy (whose running away with Paris ultimately caused the ruin of the city), beyond blame

P. 174 'Against Unworthy Praise' *knave nor dolt*: possibly a reference to the behaviour of the audience in the Abbey Theatre in 1907 when disturbances over Synge's play *The Playboy of the Western World* occurred *for a woman's sake*: in his unpublished Diary, section 10, Yeats wrote 'How much of the best that I have done and still do is but the attempt to explain myself to her' *self-same dolt and knave*: see the notes on 'The People', p. 316, about Maud Gonne's experience at the Abbey Theatre

P. 175 'Fallen Majesty' *she*: Maud Gonne *crowds gathered*: a reference to her demagogic oratorical power *even old men's eyes*: those old men may be the older nationalists (of John O'Leary's temper) who disapproved of the more violent attitudes with which Maud Gonne sympathised, and which her speeches reinforced. Cf. the reference in 'No Second Troy' to her teaching to ignorant men 'most violent ways' *what's gone*: the spectacle of Maud Gonne as a public figure; she virtually retired from public life after her marriage broke down. Yeats may be remembering in particular the crowds which attended meetings (in 1897 and 1898) of the Association formed to commemorate the revolution of 1798

P. 176 'When Helen Lived' *topless towers . . . Helen*: of Troy. Cf. Marlowe, *Dr Faustus* V.i

> Was this the face that launched a thousand ships
> And burnt the topless towers of Ilium?

And cf. notes on 'Long-legged Fly', p. 371   *A word and a jest*: Yeats's work for the literary revival and the theatre, theoretically for Maud Gonne's sake; he dreamed a thought on 6 July 1909: 'Why should we complain if men ill-treat our Muses, when all that they gave to Helen while she still lived was a song and a jest?' (*A*, p. 521)

P. 176 'Her Praise' *She is foremost*: the poem is about Maud Gonne, see the note on 'Fallen Majesty', p. 354   *the long war*: which began in August 1914; many people in Britain thought it would be over in a few months, and Yeats wrote the poem in January 1915   *among the poor*: Maud Gonne was well known for her charity among the poor of Dublin

P. 177 'Presences' *One is a harlot*: possibly a reference to Mabel Dickinson. See Joseph Hone, *W. B. Yeats, 1865–1939*, p. 301 for the reason   *a child*: Iseult Gonne   *a queen*: Maud Gonne

P. 177 'Owen Aherne and his Dancers' the first part of this poem was written four days after Yeats's marriage, the second three days later, Owen Aherne is the name of an invented character, described in 'The Tables of the Law' (*M*, pp. 293–4); he is also in 'The Phases of the Moon' *Norman upland*: Yeats proposed marriage to Iseult Gonne in 1916 and 1917 in Normandy. The poem describes his feelings in 1917, but the 'unsought' could refer to Iseult proposing to him at the age of fifteen and being rejected 'because there was too much Mars in her horoscope' *that young child*: Iseult Gonne, to whom he delivered an ultimatum when accompanying her and her mother Maud Gonne MacBride to London from France in September 1917. She must make up her mind within a week: if she did not marry him he would marry someone else, whom he had known for several years and who was willing to marry him. Iseult refused and he married Georgie Hyde-Lees on 20 October 1917 *the woman at my side*: his wife, whose automatic writing began *AV* and released much of the poet's tension and unhappiness. He wrote to Lady Gregory on 29 October 1917 'From being more miserable than I ever remember since Maud Gonne's marriage I became extremely happy. That sense of happiness has lasted ever since'

P. 178 'Solomon and the Witch' *that Arab lady*: the Queen of Sheba, in Arabia, visited Solomon, King of the Hebrews (*c*.972–*c*.932 BC), according to the Bible I, Kings X 1–13. There is another account of the visit in the *Kebra Negast*   *Solomon*: the poem is about Yeats and his wife, but deals with the possible annihilation of time through a perfect union of lovers *A cockerel*: possibly the Hermetic cock, the harbinger of the cycles, in the Tree of Life (see 'The Two Trees') *the Fall*: the Fall of Man brought about when Adam and Eve ate the forbidden fruit (the 'brigand apple') of the Tree of Knowledge *Choice and Chance*: Yeats wrote a long note on Chance and Choice in *Four Plays for Dancers* (1921) quoted in *NC*, pp. 218–20

P. 180 'A Last Confession' This poem is numbered IX in *AWYO* in *WS* (1929)

P. 180 'Parting' This poem is numbered VII in *AWYO* in *WS* (1929)

P. 181 'First Love' This poem is numbered I in *AMYO* and is probably a description of the poet's youthful love for Maud Gonne. The 'Heart of stone' echoes an image in 'Easter 1916'

P. 182 'The Mermaid' This poem is numbered III in *AMYO*, *TT* (1928) and refers to Yeats's brief relationship with Mrs Shakespear in 1896

P. 182 'Consolation' This poem is numbered V in *AWYO* in *WS* (1929)

P. 183 'Crazy Jane and the Bishop' This poem was first numbered I in *WMP* in *WS* (1933) *Crazy Jane*: this name was substituted for 'Cracked Mary', an old woman who lived in a cottage near Gort and was, according to Yeats, 'the local satirist and a really terrible one'. She had 'an amazing power of audacious speech' *Jack the Journeyman*: a character in Yeats's play *The Pot of Broth* (1902). In a note he said that the words and air of the tramp's song in the play came from 'Cracked Mary'

P. 184 'Girl's Song' This poem was first numbered VIII in *WMP* in *WS* (1933)

P. 184 'Lullaby' This poem was first numbered XVI in *WMP* in *WS* (1933). *Paris . . . Helen*:

Paris was a son of Priam, king of Troy, and his wife Hecuba, who was exposed on Mount Ida as it was prophesied he would bring ruin on his country. He was brought up by shepherds, and lived with Oenone, a nymph, until he was appointed to award the prize for beauty to one of the three goddesses, Hera, Athene and Aphrodite. Aphrodite offered him the fairest woman in the world if she gained the prize. Afterwards Paris visited Sparta and persuaded Helen, the wife of King Menelaus, to elope with him. This caused the Greek siege of Troy in which Paris was mortally wounded by an arrow. He was brought to Oenone, but it was too late for her to cure him and in her grief she committed suicide   *Tristram*: in the medieval romance he is sent to Ireland to bring Isolde to Cornwall to be King Mark's bride. He had fallen in love with her on a previous visit to Ireland   *potion's work*: a potion that Tristram and Isolde drink unwittingly makes their love inevitable   *Eurotas*: the main river in Sparta   *holy bird*: Zeus who took the shape of a swan. Cf. 'Leda and the Swan'   *Leda*, the wife of Tyndareus, king of Sparta, was bathing in the Eurotas when Zeus saw her. She bore Castor and Pollux and Helen to Zeus. Maud Gonne is described as having a 'Ledaean body' in 'Among School Children'

P. 185   'After Long Silence'   This poem was first numbered XVII in *WMP* in *WS* (1933)   *young . . . ignorant*: the poem is about Yeats and Mrs Shakespear

P. 185   'Her Triumph'   This poem was numbered IV in *AWYO* in *WS* 1929   *the dragon's will . . . Saint George . . . Perseus*: the image may derive from 'Saint George and the dragon' a painting ascribed to Paris Bordone (1500–71) in the National Gallery, Dublin, or from Cosimo Tura's (1430–95) 'St George and the dragon' which Yeats saw in Ferrara in 1907. He had a reproduction of the Tuscan artist Perino del Vaga's (Pietro-Buonaccorsi, 1500–47) 'Andromeda and Persius'. Saint George, patron of chivalry, guardian saint of England and Portugal, was probably tortured and put to death by Diocletian at Nicomedia in 303 (or suffered martyrdom at Lydda in Palestine *c*.250). He is sometimes confused with George of Cappadocia, an army contractor who became Archbishop of Alexandria and was torn in pieces by a mob in 361. Common to the legends of George and Perseus is the killing of a dragon (Perseus was a Greek mythological hero, son of Zeus and Danae; he killed the Gorgon, and later rescued Andromeda, exposed on a rock to a dragon that was about to devour her).

P. 186   'Crazy Jane talks with the Bishop'   This poem was first numbered VI in *WMP* in *WS* (1933)   *excrement*: possibly an echo of Blake's line in *Jerusalem*: 'For I will make their places of love and joy excrementitious'

P. 186   'Ribh at the Tomb of Baile and Aillinn'   This poem was numbered 1 in the series *Supernatural Songs* in *KGCT* 1934) and in *FMIM* (1935). Yeats wrote to Mrs Shakespear on 24 July 1934 that he had:

. . . another poem in my head where a monk reads his breviary at midnight upon the tomb of long-dead lovers on the anniversary of their death, for on that night they are united above the tomb, their embrace being not partial but a conflagration of the entire body and so shedding the light he reads by.

me: Ribh is an imaginary character, described by Yeats in the preface to *A Full Moon in March* (1935) as a hermit, an imaginary critic of Ireland's patron saint, Patrick (died *c*.490; author of *Confessions*, *Epistle to Coroticus* and the hymn the *Breastplate of St Patrick*). Ribh's Christianity, Yeats remarked, 'came perhaps from Egypt like much early Irish Christianity echoes pre-Christian thought'   *Baile and Aillinn*: legendary Irish lovers; see notes on 'The Withering of the Boughs', p. 323   *apple and yew*: a yew tree grew where Baile's body lay, a wild apple where Aillinn's; their love stories were written on boards made of yew and apple   *the intercourse of angels*: Yeats probably got this idea from Emmanuel Swedenborg, the Swedish mystic writer, whose saying that the sexual intercourse of the angels is 'a conflagration of the whole being' he mentioned twice in letters to Mrs Shakespear (of 21 February and 9 March 1933) *Lies in a circle*: to indicate the perfect harmony of the lovers

P. 187 'The Wild Old Wicked Man' this poem was written in 1937 when Yeats was considering going to India, accompanied by Lady Elizabeth Pelham. See his letters to Shri Bhagwan Hamsa of 12 March, and to Shri Purohit Swami of 21 March and 15 May 1937, quoted in Shankar Mokashi-Punekar, *The Later Phase in the Development of W. B. Yeats* (1966) pp. 264–5 *girls . . . on the seashore*: probably a memory of stories told to him by a boy in Sligo. See *A*, p. 75 *warty lads*: Yeats wrote to Dorothy Wellesley on 22 May 1936 to tell her that he had written to Laura Riding that 'poets were good liars who never forgot that the Muses were women who liked the embrace of gay warty lads. I wonder if she knows that warts are considered by the Irish peasantry a sign of sexual power?' *Letters on Poetry to Dorothy Wellesley* (1964) p. 63

Section 11: THE SUPERNATURAL

P. 193 'The Stolen Child' The places, Yeats explained in *Fairy and Folk Tales of the Irish Peasantry* (1888), are around Sligo. 'Further Rosses is a very noted locality. There is here a little point of rocks where, if anyone falls asleep, there is a danger of their waking silly, the fairies having carried off their souls' *Sleuth Wood*: a wood on the south of Lough Gill, to the south east of Sligo *Rosses*: Rosses Point, a seaside village to the north-west of Sligo *Glen-Car*: the valley of the standing monumental stone (*Irish* Gleann an Chairthe), north east of Sligo

P. 195 'The Man who dreamed of Faeryland' *Dromohair*: this is spelt as Dromahair and Drumahair also, a village in Co. Leitrim *world-forgotten isle*: akin to the first island paradise to which Niamh brings Oisin in 'The Wanderings of Oisin' *Lissadell*: a barony in Co. Sligo; Lissadell House, home of the Gore-Booth family is there. As a young man Yeats became friendly with the Gore-Booth sisters, Constance and Eva. See 'In Memory of Eva Gore-Booth and Con Markievicz', p. 327 and 'On a Political Prisoner', p. 385 *money cares and fears*: Yeats spent many summers in his twenties in Sligo through lack of funds, staying with his mother's family, the Pollexfens, and later with his uncle George Pollexfen *hill*: the hill of Lugnagall (*Irish* the Hollow of the Foreigners), a townland in Glencar valley, Co. Sligo *golden or silver skies*: Yeats often uses the golden/silver contrast symbolically, describing the solar principle in his *A*, p. 371, as 'elaborate, full of artifice, all that resembles the work of a goldsmith', the lunar being 'simple, popular traditional, emotional' See *NC*, pp. 35–6 *Scanavin*: a well in Co. Sligo *spired*: circled, twisted spirally. cf. 'gyring, spiring' in 'The Two Trees', and 'gyring down and perning there' in 'Demon and Beast'

P. 196 'The Danaan Quicken Tree' The note accompanying the poem in *The Bookman* May 1893 ran:

> It is said that an enchanted tree grew once on the little lake-island of Innisfree, and that its berries were, according to one legend, poisonous to mortals, and according to another, able to endow them with more than mortal powers. Both legends say that the berries were the food of the *Tuatha de Danaan*, or faeries. Quicken is the old Irish name for the mountain ash. The Dark Joan mentioned in the last verse is a famous faery who often goes about the roads disguised as a clutch of chickens. Niamh is the famous and beautiful faery who carried Oisin into faeryland. *Aslanga Shee* means faery host.

Innisfree: see notes on 'The Lake Isle of Innisfree', p. 329   *hurley*: an Irish game, played with a ball and hurley sticks, somewhat similar to hockey   *Aslauga Shee*: The (fairy) host of the mound (*Irish* an sluagh sidhe)

P. 197   'The Host of the Air'   Yeats heard the story on which this ballad is founded from an old woman at Ballisodare, Co. Sligo. She repeated an Irish poem on the subject and then translated it for him. He always regretted not having written it down. He added in a note that 'anyone who tastes fairy food and drink is glamoured and stolen by the fairies. This is why Bridget gets O'Driscoll to play cards. "The Folk of the Air" is a Gaelic name for the fairies.' Yeats wrote a long note on fairies stealing away humans in *WR*. See 'The Harp of Aengus' for Midhir's appeal to the mortal Etain to come away with him. 'The Two Kings' also deals with the subject.   *Hart Lake*: a lake in the Ox mountains, six or seven miles west of Ballisodare, Co. Sligo   *Bridget his bride*: Yeats used the same material in a story 'Kidnappers' (*M*, pp. 73 ff) in which the fairies steal the bride as a wife for their chief   *the bread and wine had a doom*: Bridget sets her husband to play cards so that he will not eat or drink anything   *one bore Bridget . . . away*: the fairy chief.

P. 199   'To Some I have talked with by the Fire'   *Danaan*: see note on 'The Madness of King Goll', p. 319

P. 199   'Out of sight is out of mind'   This is a poem from Yeats's story 'The Wisdom of the King' (*M*, pp. 165 ff) in which hawk women recite human sins before giving a prince wisdom

P. 200   'The Unappeasable Host'   *Danaan*: see notes on 'The Madness of King Goll', p. 319   *North*: the north wind, used, Yeats remarked in *WR*, 'as a symbol of vague desires and hopes, not merely because the Sidhe [faeries] are in the wind, or because the wind bloweth as it listeth, but because mind and spirit and vague desire have been associated everywhere'   *ger-eagle*: geier eagle, used in the Bible (Lev. XI 18 and Deut. XIV 17) to translate raham, Hebrew for a vulture   *flaming West*: Yeats associated the West, the place of sunset, with fading and dreaming things   *Mother Mary*: the Virgin Mary, mother of Jesus Christ

P. 200   'The Mountain Tomb'   Yeats was a member of the Order of the Golden Dawn, a Rosicrucian order. Christian Rosenkreutz (1378–?) allegedly founded the Rosicrucians in 1459–84, first mentioned in 1614. In *E & I*, pp. 196–7, Yeats tells how 'the old tradition' had it that his followers

> . . . wrapped his imperishable body in noble raiment and laid it under the house of their Order, in a tomb containing the symbols of all things in heaven and earth, and in the waters under the earth, and set about him inextinguishable magical lamps, which burnt on generation after generation, until other students of the Order came upon the tomb by chance. . . .

In vain, in vain: the symbolism of the tomb is used to describe Yeats's own times, showing the futility of housing a body that does not reveal wisdom. Cf. *E & I*, p. 196:

> It seems to me that the imagination has had no very different history during the last two hundred years, but has been laid in a great tomb of criticism, and had set over it inextinguishable magical lamps of wisdom and romance, and has been altogether so nobly housed and apparelled that we have forgotten that its wizard lips are closed, or but opened for the complaining of some melancholy and ghostly voice. . . .

P. 201   'Oil and Blood'   *odour of violet*: Saint Teresa's (1515–82) body was described, when her tomb was opened, as exuding miraculous oil and smelling of violets. Yeats had read several books about her, notably Lady Alice Lovat's *The Life of Saint Teresa* (1911), p. 606, which describes how the body of the saint was intact, 'her flesh white and soft, as flexible as when she was buried, and still emitted the same delicious and penetrating smell. Moreover her limbs exuded a miraculous oil which bore a similar perfume and embalmed the air and everything with which it came into contact' *the vampires*: Yeats read and enjoyed Bram Stoker's (1847–1912) horror novel *Dracula* (1897) and Sheridan le Fanu's (1814–73) vampire story *Carmilla*, included in his *In a Glass Darkly* (1872)

P. 201 'Cuchulain Comforted' Dorothy Wellesley gave an account of Yeats reading the prose theme of the poem in *Letters on Poetry from W. B. Yeats to Dorothy Wellesley* (1940; 1964), p. 193:

A shade recently arrived went through a valley in the Country of the Dead; he had six mortal wounds, but had been a tall, strong, handsome man. Other shades looked at him from among the trees. Sometimes they went near to him and then went away quickly. At last he sat down, he seemed very tired. Gradually the shades gathered round him, and one of them who seemed to have some authority among the others laid a parcel of linen at his feet. One of the others said: 'I am not so afraid of him now that he is sitting still. It was the way his arms rattled'. Then another shade said: 'You would be much more comfortable if you would make a shroud and wear it instead of the arms. We have brought you some linen. If you make it yourself you will be much happier, but of course we will thread the needles. We do everything together, so everyone of us will thread the needles, so when we have laid them at your feet you will take whichever you like best.' The man with the six wounds saw that nobody had ever threaded needles so swiftly and so smoothly. He took the threaded needles and began to sew, and one of the shades said: 'We will sing to you while you sew; but you will like to know who we are. We are the people who run away from the battles. Some of us have been put to death as cowards, but others have hidden, and some died without people knowing they were cowards.' Then they began to sing, and they did not sing like men and women, but like linnets that had been stood on a perch and taught by a good singing master.

a man . . . six . . . wounds: Cuchulain. See note on 'Cuchulain's Fight with the Sea', p. 320. The six who gave him the fatal wounds were themselves killed by Conall Caernach, the Victorious, one of the twelve chief warriors of the Red Branch *shrouds*: possibly a reflection of Plato's myth of Er in *The Republic*, where unborn souls have lots and samples of life put before them

Section 12: FROM THE PLAYS

P. 205 'I am come to cry with you, woman' This is part of a song sung by the Old Woman in Yeats's early play *Cathleen Ni Houlihan* (1902?) His interpretation of the play was given in *The United Irishman*, 5 May 1902:

My subject is Ireland and its struggle for independence. The scene is laid in the West of Ireland at the time of the French landing. I have described a household preparing for the wedding of the son of the house. Everyone expects some good thing from the wedding. The bridegroom is thinking of his bride, the father of the fortune which will make them all more prosperous, and the mother of a plan of turning this prosperity to account by making her youngest son a priest, and the youngest son of a greyhound pup the bride promised to give him when she marries. Into this household comes Kathleen Ni Houlihan herself, and the bridegroom leaves his bride, and all the hopes come to nothing. It is the perpetual struggle of the cause of Ireland and every other ideal cause against private hopes and dreams, against all that we mean when we say the world. I have put into the mouth of Kathleen Ni Houlihan verses about those who have died or about to die for her, and these verses are the key of the rest. She sings of one yellow-haired Donough in stanzas that were suggested to me by some old Gaelic folk-song.

The full twelve lines of the song followed. The first four lines in the text of the play run:

> I will go cry with the woman,
> For yellow-haired Donough is dead,
> With a hempen rope for a neckcloth,
> And a white cloth on his head, –

In the play the old woman sings the first four lines; when asked by Michael what she is singing about she answers 'singing I am about a man I knew one time, yellow-haired Donough that was hanged in Galway', and then sings the rest of the song which is included in *PNE* under the title 'I am come to cry with you, woman'. The folksong 'Flaxen-haired Donough' (*Irish* Donnchadh Ban) was the source for the song; it is sometimes thought to have been composed by Anthony Raftery (*c.* 1784–1835), the blind poet of Mayo. See notes on 'The Tower', p. 346   *Enniscrone*: *Irish* Inis Crabhann, the promontory of Crone, a seaside village of Co. Sligo, five miles from Ballina

P. 205 'The four rivers that run there' A song from Yeats's play *The King's Threshold* (1904)   *all the fowls of the air*: possibly an echo of lines in the song in *Tommy Thumb's Pretty Song Book* (*c.* 1744):

> All the birds of the air fell a-sighing and a-sobbing
> When they heard of the death of poor Cock Robin

P. 206 'Nothing that he has done' A song from Yeats's play *The Green Helmet* (1910); it is sung by Emer about Cuchulain. For Cuchulain and Emer see notes on 'Cuchulain's Fight with the Sea', p. 320

P. 206 'The Mask' This is a lyric from Yeats's play *The Player Queen* (1922), in which the man speaks lines 1–2, 6–7 and 11–12, and the woman replies to him   *that mask*: Yeats described 'the Mask' as 'an emotional antithesis' to all that comes out of the internal nature of subjective men

P. 207 'A Song from "The Player Queen" ' In Yeats's play *The Player Queen* (1922) an actress, Decima, introduces the song which her husband Septimus, a poet, has made; she says that it is the only song of the mad singing daughter of a harlot: 'My father was a drunken sailor waiting for the full tide, and yet she thought her mother had foretold that she would marry a prince and become a great queen'

P. 208 'I call to the eye of the mind' The opening song sung by the second and third musicians from Yeats's play *At the Hawk's Well* (1917); originally entitled 'At the Hawk's Well or waters of immortality' in June 1917, it was the first of Yeats's *Four Plays for Dancers* (1921), written under the influence of Japanese Nōh drama, in which he aimed at a lyric intensity of 'rhythm, balance, pattern, images', a drama where character 'grows less and sometimes disappears'. The play was first performed in Lady Cunard's drawing room at Cavendish Square, London, on 2 April 1916   *A mother . . . son*: this stanza's thought is later echoed in 'Among School Children', stanza V

P. 208   'He has lost what may not be found'   A song sung by the musicians in Yeats's play *At the Hawk's Well* (1917), after Cuchulain has been led away (see notes on 'Cuchulain's Fight with the Sea', p. 320) from the well at the moment the water rises in it and so loses his chance to become immortal

P. 209   'At the grey round of the hill'   A song sung by the three musicians at the close of Yeats's play *The Dreaming of the Bones* (1919), the conception of which was derived 'from the world-wide belief that the dead dream back, for a certain time, through the more personal thoughts and deeds of life'   *Music of a lost kingdom*: probably to be associated with the supernatural music of the Irish fairy world, and with the music made by the spirits of the dead   *Clare-Galway*: a townland (*Irish* Baile an Chlair) in Co. Galway   *Carry it*: Yeats quoted Henry More's *The Immortality of the Soul* in 'Swedenborg Mediums and the Desolate Places' (See *E*, p, 64), which describes the graceful dancing and melodious singing and playing of the spirits of the dead 'as if we should imagine air itself to compose lessons and send forth musical sounds without the help of any terrestrial instrument'   *moidered*: (or moithered) worried, bothered   *cat-headed bird*: like the man-headed birds of *The Shadowy Waters*, they are the spirits of the dead, according to F. A. C. Wilson, *Yeats's Iconography* (2nd ed. 1969), pp. 230–1

P. 210   'A woman's beauty . . . bird'   A song from Yeats's *The Only Jealousy of Emer* (1919); it is sung by the First Musician and begins the play   *Archimedes*: the Greek mathematician, scientist and inventor (*c*. 287–212 BC); he was born in Syracuse and died in the capture of the city by the Romans

P. 211   'O, but the mockers' cry'   A song sung by the First Musician in Yeats's play *Calvary* (1920)

P. 211   'Lonely the sea-bird lies at her rest'   The concluding song in Yeats's play *Calvary* (1920)   *ger-eagle*: see notes on 'The Unappeasable Host', p. 358

P. 212   'O, but I saw a solemn sight'   The concluding song in Yeats's play *The King of the Great Clock Tower* (1935). See notes on 'Crazy Jane on God', p. 340   *Castle Dargan*: see notes below on 'The poet, Owen Hanrahan, undere a bush of may', p. 378

P. 212   'I sing a song of Jack and Jill'   A song from Yeats's play *A Full Moon in March* (1935)   *murdered*: the nursery rhyme 'Jack and Jill' does not involve murder as does this song, in which the second attendant sings as the severed head of the Swineherd

Section 13: IDIOSYNCRASIES AND GROTESQUERIES

P. 217   'Running to Paradise'   *skelping*: beating   *bare heel*: as a young man Yeats used to ink his heels to hide the holes in his socks   *old sock full*: of money

P. 218   'The Peacock'   *Three Rock*: Three Rock Mountain, overlooking Dublin

P. 218   'The Cat and the Moon'   *Minnaloushe*: the black Persian cat in the Gonne household, Les Mouettes at Colleville, near Calvados in Normandy where Yeats was staying when he wrote the poem

P. 219   'Under the Round Tower'   *Billy Byrne*: William Byrne, a Catholic gentleman from Ballymanus, Co. Wicklow, who was a member of the Leinster Directory of the United Irishmen; he was captured and hanged in 1798. He was a legendary figure in Glendalough, Co. Wicklow, where the poet and his wife stayed in March 1918 at the Royal Hotel   *great-grandfather's battered tomb*: in the graveyard at Glendalough (*Irish* the Glen of the Two Lakes), in which the pencil-shaped round tower is situated, as well as the stone crosses and ruined churches, part of the monastery established by St Kevin (*d*.618) which became a monastic school and place of pilgrimage. There are many Byrnes and O'Byrnes buried in this graveyard   *sun and moon*: the 'golden king and that wild lady' echo the imagery of 'The Man who dreamed of Faeryland'. Here they symbolise the continuous oscillation representative, in *AV*, of the horizontal movement of the historical cones; see Book V of *AV* 1937)   *the round tower*: one of the many pencil-shaped stone towers originally built in Ireland as a defence against Scandinavian raiders from about the ninth to the thirteenth centuries

P. 220   'Another Song of a Fool'   *butterfly*: the butterfly symbolises the wisdom of wide-ranging thought in 'Tom O'Roughley'. The butterflies also appear in 'Blood and the Moon' III

P. 221   'Crazy Jane Reproved'   *Europa*: in Greek mythology Europa the daughter of Agenor, King of Phoenicia, was loved by Zeus who assumed the shape of a bull and carried her off to Crete; there she became the mother of Minos, Sarpedon and Rhadamanthus

P. 221   'A Statesman's Holiday'   *No Oscar*: probably Oscar Wilde (1854–1900), Irish author and wit, whom Yeats regarded as 'the greatest talker of his time'   *Avalon*: see note on 'Under the Moon', p. 314   *Lord Chancellor . . . sack*: in the House of Lords the Lord Chancellor sits upon a wool sack. Here Yeats probably means F. E. Smith (1872–1930), Earl of Birkenhead, who was Lord Chancellor from 1919–22; a brilliant orator, he supported Lord Carson's (there may be a link here with Wilde, whom Carson cross-examined brilliantly in Wilde's action of 1895 against the Marquis of Queensberry) resistance to Home Rule in 1914; he appeared for the Crown in the Casement trial; and played a major part in the Irish settlement of 1921   *Commanding officer*: probably Sir Hubert Gough (1870–1963); as commanding officer of the Third Cavalry Brigade based on the Curragh, Co. Kildare, he was leader of the 'Curragh mutiny'; refusing to promise to fight against the Ulster Volunteers, he resigned his commission   *de Valéra*: see note on 'Parnell's Funeral', p. 349   *the King of Greece*: George II (1890–47) who returned to Greece in 1925   *made the motors*: probably William Richard Morris (1887–1963), created Lord Nuffield, who manufactured Morris cars at Cowley, Oxford   *Montenegrin*: Montenegro is a state in what became Yugoslavia after the 1914–18 war.

P. 222   'High Talk'   *high stilts*: the stilts were stolen, as he told Dorothy Wellesley, *Letters on Poetry from W. B. Yeats to Dorothy Wellesley*, p. 182. He may refer here to his earlier creation of a poetic mythology. (He described how the later Celtic twilight writers stole his 'cloak' in 'A Coat'.) At the end of the 1890s, he thought, 'we all got down off our stilts'   *piebald ponies*: probably a memory of some circus visiting Sligo   *patching old heels*: repairing socks   *Malachi Stilt-Jack*: possibly a memory of some figure from Yeats's youth in Sligo. Malachi was a minor Hebrew prophet, author of the last book of the Old Testament; St Malachy (1095–1148) was an Irish saint and Malachy is used as a Christian name in Ireland   *sea-horses*: the waves

P. 223   'Crazy Jane on the Mountain'   *Bishop . . . Crazy Jane*: see note on 'Crazy Jane and the Bishop', p. 355   *A King . . . cousins . . . cellar . . . throne*: George V (1865–1936) King of England, whose cousins were Nicholas II (1868–1918), last Czar of Russia, and his family, brutally murdered at Ekaterinburg in July 1918. Yeats wrote that King George V asked that the Russian Royal family should be brought to England but the Prime Minister refused, fearing the effect on the working class. He added that the story might have been 'no more true than other stories spoken by word of mouth' (*E*, pp. 442–3). For a recent, more authoritative view of the matter, see Kenneth Rose, *King George V* (1983)   *Great-bladdered Emer*: Emer, Cuchulain's wife (see notes on 'Cuchulain's Fight with the Sea', p. 320, and 'To the Rose upon the Rood of Time', p. 313). Yeats thought there was a fragment from an early version of the Irish story 'The Courting of Emer' in which Emer was chosen for the strength and volume of her bladder, a sign of vigour

Section 14: ARCADIAN AND INDIAN POEMS

P. 227 'The Song of the Happy Shepherd' *Arcady*: a region in the Peloponnesus, in Southern Greece, a rustic paradise in pastoral tradition *Grey Truth . . . now . . . painted toy*: nineteenth-century science. See Hugh Kenner, *A Colder Eye. The Modern Irish Writers* (1983), p. 95, who suggests that Truth inheres in a toy 'a wheel kept spinning by a thumb-driven plunger, a little tin wheel on which seven painted colours blur before your eyes into grey as Newton prescribed' *Chronos*: Greek for time; Cronos or Kronos, one of the Titans, was identified with Time *Rood*: the cross on which Jesus Christ was crucified *starry men*: astronomers *optic glass*: telescope (an echo of Milton's association of the 'optic glass' with Galileo, the 'Tuscan artist', *Paradise Lost* I, 286–91) *rewarding*: a better reading is 'rewording' from *Poems* (1895) *sooth*: truth *poppies*: a reference to their narcotic properties

P. 228 'The Sad Shepherd' This poem was entitled 'Miserrimus' (the most miserable man) when first published. This was the title of a tale of terror, published in 1832 and dedicated to William Goodwin (1756–1836) by E. M. Reynolds.

P. 229 'The Indian to his Love' *peahen's dance*: Yeats replied to a critic's objection that peahens do not dance that they dance 'throughout the whole of Indian poetry' (*L*, p. 109)

P. 230 'Mohini Chatterjee' *the Brahmin*: Mohini Chatterjee was a Bengali Brahmin, one of the earliest members of the Theosophical Society in India, whom Yeats and his friends in the Hermetic Society in Dublin invited to lecture to them in 1885 or 1886 *Pray for nothing*: Mohini Chatterjee thought prayer was 'too full of hope, of desire, of life, to have any part in that acquiesence that was his beginning of wisdom' *these, or words like these*: an early poem 'Kanva on Himself', in *The Wanderings of Oisin* (1889), also gave the Brahmin's reply in verse (which Yeats also put in a note; the Brahmin said that 'One should say, before sleeping: "I have lived many lives, I have been a slave and a prince. Many a beloved has sat upon my knees and I have sat upon the knees of many a beloved. Everything that has been shall be again" ')

P. 231 'Meru' This poem was included unnumbered in the series *Supernatural Songs* in *KGCT* (1934); it was numbered XII in *FMIM* (1935). In the poem the hermits learn the truth that man destroys what he creates, that civilisation succeeds civilisation. Yeats wrote it when he was about to begin his Introduction to Bhagwan Shri Hamsa's *The Holy Mountain: Being the Story of a Pilgrimage to Lake Manas and of Initiation on Mount Kailas in Tibet* (1934), translated by Shri Purohit Swami (1882–?) *Mount Meru . . . Everest*: a friend of the Swami had been ordered in a meditation to seek *Turiya*, the greater or conscious Samadhi at Mount Kailas, the twin of the legendary Meru, the centre of Paradise in Hindu mythology. Mount Everest is in the Himalayas, on the border of Tibet and Nepal

Section 15: THE THOUGHT OF *A VISION*

P. 235 'The Two Trees' *the holy tree*: the Sephirotic tree of the Cabbala and the Tree of Knowledge. See *NC*, pp. 38–40. Yeats wrote about the Tree of Life seen by a young Irish woman cast into a trance, and of the description of it in *The Book of Concealed Mystery* (translated by his then friend MacGregor Mathers (1854–1918) in *The Kabbalah Unveiled* (1887)) as having birds lodging in its branches; 'the souls and the angels' also had their place in it (*E & I*, pp. 28–52) *circle*: in *A*, p. 375 Yeats described the Tree of Life as a geometrical figure made up of ten circles or spheres called Sephiroth joined by straight lines *the demons*: they may be demons of abstract thought seeking to hold up the soul on its way to truth   *a fatal image*: the Tree of Knowledge as opposed to that of Life

P. 236   'The Magi'   *unsatisfied ones*: the Magi, the three wise men from the East who came to see the Christ child have not been satisfied by Christ's death on the cross at Calvary outside Jerusalem (l. 7).   *hoping to find once more . . . the mystery*: they are made to express Yeats's belief that the Christian revelation was not final, that history occurs in alternate movements. (See, for instance, 'The Second Coming' and 'The Gyres'.) They are again searching for an incarnation which, because it will change the world, is uncontrollable   *turbulence*: Yeats thought the Christian era overthrew preceding eras. The birth of the child, Jesus Christ, was a sign of an antithetical revelation   *the bestial floor*: the stable in which Christ was born

P. 236   'Ego Dominus Tuus'   The title comes from the Italian writer Dante Alighieri (1265–1321), *Vita Nuova* (?1292–3) which Yeats read in a translation published in 1861 by Dante Gabriel Rossetti (1818–82) and in that by C. L. Shadwell (1892 and 1915). Dante sees a 'Lord of terrible aspect' who says to him 'ego dominus tuus' (*Latin*, I am your master). The poem takes the form of a dialogue between *Hic* and *Ille*, Latin pronouns meaning this and that, or the former and the latter (or the latter and the former) or the one, the other. *Hic* defends objective views, *Ille* subjective; the poem embodies Yeats's theories of the anti-self, developed in the prose of *Per Amica Silentia Lunae* (*Latin*, through the friendly silences of the Moon) and in *A Vision*   *wind-beaten tower*: Yeats's tower, Thoor Ballylee, which was often buffeted by westerly winds coming in off the Atlantic   *Michael Robartes*: an invented character, who appears in Yeats's story 'Rosa Alchemica' and in *AV* (1925)   *Magical shapes*: in *AV* (1925) Robartes traced on Arabian sands diagrams – those of *AV* – 'whose gyres and circles grew out of one another . . . there was a large diagram . . . where lunar phases and zodiacal symbols were mixed with various unintelligible symbols'   *I call to my own opposite*: see *A*, p. 503, where Yeats wrote that 'all happiness depends on the energy to assume the mask of some other self . . . We put on a grotesque or solemn painted face to hide us from the terrors of judgement, invent an imaginative Saturnalia where one forgets reality, a game like that of a child, where one loses the infinite pain of self-realisation'. This phrase in the poem cannot be fully understoood until it is expanded in Ille's final speech 'I call to the mysterious one . . .' answered by Hic's query which, in effect, asks why pursue unreality?   *gentle sensitive mind . . . the old nonchalance*: modern work, Ille replies, lacks inspiration; modern culture is passive, self-analytical, but men of the middle ages and the Renaissance 'made themselves overmastering creative persons by turning from the mirror to meditation on a mask' (*M*, p. 333)   *that hollow face . . . the hunger that made it hollow*: Yeats saw Dante not only moved by the purity of Beatrice and Divine Justice, her death and his own banishment from Florence, but also because he had to struggle in his own heart with his unjust anger and his lust. (See *NC*, pp. 168–77 and *M*, pp. 329–31.)   *Lapo and Guido*: probably Lapo Gianni (*c*. 1270–*c*. 1330) and Guido Calvalcante (*c*. 1230–1300), Italian poets, friends of Dante   *Bedouin's horse-hair roof*: some Bedouins (tent-dwellers in Arabic) are still nomadic, inhabiting the deserts of Arabia   *doored and windowed cliff*: probably suggested by Petra, in south-west Jordan

P. 239   'The Phases of the Moon'   This poem presents one of the central ideas later expressed in *AV* in a similar manner to that of 'Ego Dominus Tuus' ('To some extent', Yeats remarked in his note in *CP*, he wrote the poems 'as a text for exposition'); here Michael Robartes and Owen Aherne are speaking, Aherne being another invented character; they appear in three of his stories   *a bridge*: the bridge crossing the river which flowed past one of the tower's walls   *Connemara cloth*: see note on 'The Fisherman', p. 315   *he is reading*: Yeats   *Mere images*: Milton's Platonist derives from John Milton's (1608–74) *Il Penseroso* (1632):

> Or let my lamp, at midnight hour,
> Be seen in some high lonely tower,
> Where I may oft outwatch the *Bear*,
> With thrice great *Hermes*, or unsphere
> The spirit of *Plato*, to unfold
> What worlds, or what vast regions hold
> The immortal mind that hath forsook
> Her mansion in the fleshly nook; . . .

This lamp is 'the lonely light' in an illustration entitled 'The Lonely Tower' by the artist Samuel Palmer (1805–81) in *The Shorter Poems of John Milton* (1889). Percy Bysshe Shelley's (1792–1822) visionary prince is the title character of *Prince Athanase* (1817), whose soul sat apart from men 'as in a lonely tower' which has affinities with Milton's poem, in the lamp in Laian's turret.

> The Balearic fisher, driven from shore,
> Hanging upon the peaked wave afar,
> Then saw their lamp from Laian's turret gleam,
> Piercing the stormy darkness, like a star, . . .

Other parallels are drawn in *NC*, pp. 205–6   *extravagant style* . . . *Pater*: Walter Pater (1839–94), the academic critic whose involuted style affected Yeats's prose in the 1890s, particularly in the stories of *The Secret Rose* (1897)   *Said I was dead*: in the story 'Rose Alchemica' *M*, pp. 267–92; his death is also mentioned in 'The Tables of the Law' *M*, pp. 290–293   *Twenty and eight*: see the diagram from *AV*, p. 418; the phrases are linked to the relevant parts of *AV* in *NC*, pp. 175–8   *Athena*: see notes on 'Michael Robartes and the Dancer', p. 326   *Achilles . . . dust*: in Greek mythology, the son of Peleus and Thetis; he killed Hector, eldest son of Priam, king of Troy, and his queen, Hecuba; this is described in Homer's *Iliad* I, 197 and XXII, 30   *Nietzsche*: Friederick Nietzsche (1844–1900), the German philosopher, whom Yeats began reading in 1902   *Sinai's top*: Mount Sinai, where Moses received the Ten Commandments (see the Bible, Exodus XIX and XX); it is on the Sinai peninsula, between the Mediterranean and the Red Sea   *the man within*: Yeats

P. 244   'The Double Vision of Michael Robartes'   *rock of Cashel*: the Rock of Cashel, Co. Tipperary, has several ecclesiastical ruins on it, including the chapel Cormac MacCarthy had constructed in the twelfth century, mentioned in the last stanza   *the cold spirits*: they come from the later phases of the moon in *AV*   *Constrained*: in the last gyre, in *AV*, decadence is predicted; it may 'suggest bubbles in a frozen pond – mathematical Babylonian starlight'. The new era will bring 'its stream of irrational force'. The eight lines beginning 'Constrained' were quoted in Yeats's essay 'A People's Theatre' (*E*, pp. 258–9) to conclude a passage distinguishing between the arts and 'visible history, the discoveries of science, the discussions of politics'   *A Sphinx*: the 'introspective knowledge of the mind's self-begotten unity'; in Greek mythology a sphinx usually has the head and bust of a woman, the body of a lion, and wings. It was originally a monster, later a messenger of the gods   *A Buddha*: 'the outward-looking mind'. Both Buddha and Sphinx guard the mystery of the fifteenth phase of *AV*. Gautama Buddha (*c.* 563–*c.* 483 BC) was the Indian founder of Buddhism   *between these two a girl*: the girl represents art; she dances between the intellect (the Sphinx) and the heart, the emotions (the Buddha), art being a balance between, a combination of intellect and emotion   *Homer's paragon*: Helen of Troy, a symbol usually suggesting Maud Gonne

P. 246 'The Second Coming' This poem deals with Christ's prediction of the second coming in Matthew XXIV and St John's description of the beast of the Apocalypse in Revelations. Yeats is, however, predicting the arrival of a rough beast in Christ's birthplace, Bethlehem near Jerusalem (see 1.22) traditionally associated with gentle innocence of infancy and human maternal love *the widening gyre*: see note on 'Demon and Beast', p. 333 *the falcon . . . the falconer*: the falcon presumably represents modern civilisation, becoming out of touch with Christ, the falconer *Mere anarchy*: Yeats was disturbed by the effects of the Russian Revolution. He regarded Marxism as 'the spear-head of materialism and leading to inevitable murder'. He was also worried by a breakdown in respect for the law in Ireland after the Civil War *some revelation*: Christ's birth had been the revelation of the Christian era *the Second Coming*: the new era seemed to be likely to be one of irrational force. See notes on 'The Double Vision of Michael Robartes', p. 365 *Spiritus Mundi*: in a note of 1921 Yeats glossed this as 'a general storehouse of images which have ceased to be a property of any personality or spirit' A *shape with lion body*: in a note to his play *The Resurrection* Yeats wrote of imagining 'a brazen winged beast' that he associated with 'laughing ecstatic destruction'

P. 247 'Leda and the Swan' Yeats was asked for a poem for the *Irish Statesman* by the editor, his friend George Russell, and thought that 'after the individualist, demagogic movement, founded by Hobbes [Thomas Hobbes (1588–1679), the English philosopher] and popularised by the Encyclopaedists' [the authors of the French *Encyclopédie* (1751–72) which helped to bring about the French Revolution in 1789]:

> . . . we have a soil so exhausted that it cannot grow that crop again for centuries'. Then I thought 'Nothing is now possible but some movement, or birth from above, preceded by some violent annunciation'. My fancy began to play with Leda and the Swan for metaphor and I began this poem; but as I wrote, bird and lady took such possession of the scene that all politics went out of it, and my friend tells me that 'his conservative readers would misunderstand the poem'.

The Greek myth recounts how Leda, wife of Tyndareus, king of Sparta, was seen bathing in the river Eurotas by Zeus who coupled with her in the form of a swan; of this union Castor and Pollux were born, and Helen. (See notes on 'Among School Children', for the 'Ledean body' of Maud Gonne.) Yeats had a copy of Michelangelo's painting of 'Leda and the Swan' at Venice and there was a copy of a statuette of the union of Zeus and Leda at the Coopers' house, Markree Castle, at Collooney in Co. Sligo. It is likely that poems on the subject by Yeats's friend Oliver St John Gogarty (1878–1957) may also have had an effect on this poem which also echoes the language – the swan's 'rush' – of Spenser's *Faerie Queene* III, xi, 32 *The broken wall . . . burning roof . . . Agamemnon dead*: Leda's daughter Helen, who married Menelaus the king of Sparta, ran away with Paris, son of King Priam, to Troy. The Greeks assembled an army to get her back led by Agamemnon, brother of Menelaus. On his return from the successful destruction of Troy ('the broken wall') he was murdered by Clytaemnestra (a daughter of Leda by her husband Tyndareus) and her lover Aegisthus *his knowledge*: Zeus's divine knowledge. Yeats saw the union of Leda and Zeus, the human and divine, as the annunciation of Greek civilisation

P. 248 'Her Vision in the Wood' *a wounded man*: probably the Adonis legend (see notes on 'Vacillation' II, p. 339) is suggested here, though T. R. Henn, *The Lonely Tower* (1950), p. 246, suggested it might be Diarmid, the Irish hero killed by a boar on Ben Bulben, a Sligo mountain *the beast*: in Greek mythology a wild boar killed Adonis, a beautiful young man beloved by Aphrodite; the anemone flower was said to have sprung from his blood. Persephone restored him to life on condition he spent six months of the year with her, and six with

Aphrodite (this implied a summer-winter symbol); his death and revival were celebrated in several festivals *Quattrocento*: Italian word meaning the fifteenth century, also used in 'Among School Children' *Mantegna*: Andrea Mantegna (1431–1506) born near Vicenza, Italy; he left Padua *c.* 1459, having painted 'The Agony in the Garden' there; he moved to Mantua, where he painted the 'Madonna della Vittoria'

P. 249 'Sailing to Byzantium' In a BBC radio talk of 8 September 1921, Yeats said

> Now I am trying to write about the state of my soul, for it is right for an old man to make his soul, and some of my thoughts upon that subject I have put into a poem called 'Sailing to Byzantium'. When Irishmen were illuminating the Books of Kells [in the eighth century] and making the jewelled croziers in the National Museum, Byzantium was the centre of European civilisation and the source of its spiritual philosophy, so I symbolise the search for the spiritual life by a journey to that city.

That: Ireland *salmon-falls, the mackerel-crowded seas*: Yeats took a delight in salmon going upstream to spawn, particularly at the Salmon Leap at Leixlip, Co. Dublin and at the salmon-weir at Galway; the Irish hero Cuchulain was famous for his 'salmon-leap'. Shoals of mackerel 'come in', in great profusion, to Irish shores. Both images reinforce the vigorous 'sensual music' of l.7 *Byzantium*: the Roman emperor Constantine (?287–337), a convert to Christianity in 312, chose Byzantium as his capital, inaugurating it under the name Constantinople in 330. Yeats wrote of it thus in *AV* (1925), pp. 190–2, and (1937), pp. 279–81:

> I think if I could be given a month of Antiquity and leave to spend it where I chose, I would spend it in Byzantium, a little before Justinian opened St. Sophia and closed the Academy of Plato. I think I could find in some little wine-shop some philosophical worker in mosaic who could answer all my questions, the supernatural descending nearer to him than to Plotinus even, for the pride of his delicate skill would make what was an instrument of power to princes and clerics, a murderous madness in the mob, show as a lovely flexible presence like that of a perfect human body.
>
> I think that in early Byzantium, maybe never before or since in recorded history, religious, aesthetic and practical life were one, that architect and artificers – though not, it may be, poets, for language had been the instrument of controversy and must have grown abstract – spoke to the multitude and the few alike. The painter, the mosaic worker, the worker in gold and silver, the illuminator of sacred books, were almost impersonal, almost perhaps without the consciousness of individual design, absorbed in their subject-matter and that the vision of a whole people. They could copy out of old gospel books those pictures that seemed as sacred as the text, and yet weave all into a vast design, the work of many that seemed the work of one, that made building, picture, pattern, metal work of rail and lamp, seem but a single image; and this vision, this proclamation of their invisible master, had the Greek nobility, Satan always the still half-divine Serpent, never the horned scarecrow of the didactic Middle Ages.
>
> The ascetic, called in Alexandria 'God's Athlete', has taken the place of those Greek athletes whose statues have been melted or broken up or stand deserted in the midst of cornfields, but all about him is an incredible splendour like that which we see pass under our closed eyelids as we lie between sleep and waking, no representation of a living world but the dream of a somnambulist. Even the drilled pupil of the eye, when the drill is in the hand of some Byzantine worker in ivory, undergoes a somnambulistic change, for its deep shadow

among the faint lines of the tablet, its mechanical circle, where all else is rhythmical and flowing, give to Saint or Angel a look of some great bird staring at a miracle. Could any visionary of those days, passing through the Church named with so un-theological a grace 'The Holy Wisdom', can even a visionary of today wandering among the mosaics at Ravenne or in Sicily, fail to recognise some one image seen under his closed eyelids? To me it seems that He, who among the first Christian communities was little but a ghostly exorcist, had in His assent to a full Divinity made possible this sinking-in upon a supernatural splendour, these walls with their little glimmering cubes of blue and green and gold.

sages . . . Gold's holy fire . . . gold mosaic: the martyrs in the frieze at S. Apollinare Nuova at Ravenna which Yeats saw in 1907. His memories of that visit may have been aroused by a visit he made to Sicily in 1924 where he saw Byzantine mosaics *perne in a gyre*: see notes on 'Demon and Beast', p. 333   *such a form*: Yeats's note states that he had read 'somewhere' that in the Emperor's palace at Byzantium was 'a tree made of gold and silver, and artificial birds that sing'. He probably remembered being read Hans Andersen's tale 'The Emperor's Nightingale' as a child, possibly from the edition which had for cover an illustration of the Emperor and his court listening to the artificial bird. Other sources, however, have been suggested; see *NC*, p. 257

P. 250   'Two Songs from a Play'   These are two songs sung by the chorus of musicians in Yeats's play *The Resurrection* (1931), the theme of which is Christ's first appearance to the Apostles after the Crucifixion; the play puts Yeats's view that Christianity terminated a 2000-year period of history, and ushered in the beginning of another era with radical violence. See Yeats's Introduction to the play in *W & B*. (See also *E*, pp. 392–8, quoted *NC*, pp. 285–9.) This poem can be linked with 'The Second Coming'   *a staring virgin . . . play*: this stanza draws a parallel between the myth of Dionysus, born of a mortal, Peresephone, and Zeus. He was torn in pieces by the Titans, but Athena, the 'staring virgin' goddess, snatched his heart from his body and brought it to Zeus, who swallowed it, killed the Titans, and begat Dionysus again upon another mortal, Semele   *Magnus Annus but a play*: see notes on the Great Year or the Platonic Year in 'Nineteen Hundred and Nineteen', p. 344. The Muses sing of it as a play because they regarded the ritual death and rebirth of the god as recurring, part of the cycles of history. Yeats wrote in *W & B* of the myth; 'Ptolemy thought the precession of the equinoxes moved at the rate of a degree every hundred years, and that somewhere about the time of Christ and Caesar the equinoctial sun had returned to its original place in the constellations, completing and recommencing the thirty-six thousand years, of three hundred and sixty incarnations of a year apiece, of Plato's man of Ur. Hitherto almost every philosopher had some different measure for the Greatest Year, but this Platonic Year, as it was called, soon displaced all others. (*E & I*, p. 395)   *Another Troy*: Yeats is thinking of the Roman poet Virgil's (70–19BC) *Eclogue* IV (40BC) which tells how Astraea, daughter of Jupiter and Themis, is the last to leave Earth at the end of the Golden Age and becomes the constellation Virgo, but will return again bringing back the golden age:

Yet shall some few traces of olden sin lurk behind, to call men to essay the sea in ships, to gird towns with walls, and to cleave the earth with furrows. A second Tiphys shall then arise, and a second Argo to carry chosen heroes; a second warfare, too, shall there be, and again shall a great Achilles be sent to Troy.

This prophecy of Virgil's was later taken by Christians to foretell the coming of the Virgin Mary (equated with Astraea in Virgo) and Christ, the Star of Bethlehem (equated with Spica, the main star in the constellation Virgo) *Another Argo's painted prow* . . . *flashier bauble*: a further echo of Virgil; Jason with his Argonauts stole the golden fleece (the 'flashy bauble') from Colchis with the aid of Medea, daughter of the king of Colchis. The prow of the ship Argo was made of oak from Dodona (the seat of a famous oracle) and could prophesy (see William Morris (1834–96) *The Life and Death of Jason*, Bk IV) *Roman Empire . . . appalled . . . called*: because the empire would be destroyed by Christianity. There is a parallel drawn here between Astraea and Spica, Athene and Dionysus, Mary and Christ *fabulous darkness*: Yeats wrote in *AV* of ' "that fabulous formless darkness" as it seemed to a philosopher of the fourth century', a description of Christianity taken either from Proclus (a fourth-century philosopher whom Yeats read in Thomas Taylor's transaltion of 1816) or from Eunapius (*c*. 347–420), paraphrased by E. R. Dodds, *Select Passages Illustrating Neo Platonism* (1923), p. 8, as describing the church as 'a fabulous and formless darkness mastering the loveliness of the world' *that room*: presumably, as in *The Resurrection*, where the last supper was eaten *Galilean turbulence*: Jesus Christ's ministry was chiefly in Galilee, in Palestine *Babylonian starlight*: this is referred to in *AV* (1925), pp. 181 and 213. Yeats thought the development of astrology (which he associated with science) in Babylon reduced man's status *Platonic . . . Doric*: Plato's philosophy and the Doric style of architecture symbolise the classical world replaced by Christianity *The painter's brush . . . dreams*: Yeats wrote in 'The Tragic Generation' (*A*, pp. 315) that no school of painting outlasts its founders, 'every strike of the brush exhausts the impulse, Pre-Raphaelitism had some twenty years; Impressionism thirty perhaps'

P. 252 'Wisdom' *sawdust . . . carpenter*: probably founded upon pre-Raphaelite paintings, such as 'Christ in the house of his parents' by John Everett Millais (1829–96) *working-carpenter*: Joseph *Chryselephantine*: a Greek term used for statues overlaid with gold and ivory *His . . . Mother*: the Virgin Mary, the mother of Jesus Christ *Babylon*: see note on 'Babylonian Starlight' in 'Two Songs from a Play', p. 368 *Noah's freshet*: the flood, described in Genesis VI, 5–7, 19, as covering the whole world *King Abundance . . . Innocence*: allegorical account of God's creation of Christ through the Virgin Mary

P. 252 'Byzantium' The prose draft is in Yeats's 1930 Diary:

> Subject for a poem. Death of a friend . . . Describe Byzantium as it is in the system towards the end of the first Christian millennium. A walking mummy. Flames at the street corners where the soul is purified, birds of hammered gold singing in the golden trees, in the harbour [dolphins] offering their backs to the wailing dead that they may carry them to Paradise.

In the MS of 'Modern Ireland', *Massachusetts Review*, Winter 1964, Yeats wrote that in his later poems he called it Byzantium ['it' being 'an example of magnificence: and style, whether in literature or life, comes, I think, from excess, from that something over and above utility, which wrings the heart'], that city where the Saints showed their wasted forms upon a background of gold mosaic, and an artificial bird sang upon a tree of gold in the presence of the Emperor; and in one poem I have pictured the ghosts swimming, mounted upon dolphins, through the sensual seas, that they may dance upon its pavements.' *cathedral song*: the great *semantron*, a board suspended in the porch of churches, beaten by mallets *dome*: of Santa Sophia *image, man or shade*: Yeats wrote in a note on his play *The Dreaming of the Bones*, included in *Four Plays for Dancers* (1921), pp. 77–8, of

> the world wide belief that the dead dream back for a certain time, through the more personal thoughts and deeds of life. The wicked, according to Cornelius Agrippa, dream themselves

to be consumed by flames and persecuted by demons. . . . The Shade is said to fade out at last, but the Spiritual Being does not fade, passing on to other states of existence after it has attained a spiritual state, of which the surroundings and aptitudes of early life are a correspondence.

Hades' bobbin: probably taken from the spindle in Plato's mythology of the myth of Er (*The Republic*, 820) Hades, son of Kronos, was a lord of the lower world in Greek mythology   *Emperor's pavement*: an open space, an extension of the Forum of Constantinople, called the pavement from its finished marble floor. Yeats got this from W. G. Holmes, *The Age of Justinian and Theodora* (2nd ed. 1912) I, p. 69   *blood-begotten spirits*: Richard Ellmann, *The Identity of Yeats* (1953), p. 221, quoted notes Yeats made two years before writing 'Byzantium':

At first we are subject to Destiny . . . but the point in the Zodiac where the whirl becomes a sphere once reached, we may escape from the constraint of our nature and from that of external things, entering upon a state where all fuel has become flame, where there is nothing but the state itself, nothing to constrain it or end it. We attain it always in the creation or enjoyment of a work of art, but that moment though eternal in the Daimon passes from us because it is not an attainment of our whole being . . .

complexities . . . leave: after purgation   *dolphins' mire and blood*: dolphins carried dead men or their souls in transit to the Isles of the Blest. Yeats's information came from Mrs A. Strong's *Apothesis and After Life* (1915), pp. 153, 195, 215, 266   *Marbles . . . floor*: see note on 'pavement' above   *The . . . smithies*: also derived from W. G. Holmes, *The Age of Justinian and Theodora*, p. 69

P. 254   'There'   This poem was numbered 4 in the series *Supernatural Songs* in *FMIM* (1935)   *There*: perfection, the sphere in the thirteenth core of *A Vision* (see *AV* (1937), p. 240)

P. 254   'Ribh considers Christian Love insufficient'   This poem was numbered 3 in the series *Supernatural Songs* in *KGCT* (1934), V in the same series in *FMIM* (1935). It has been suggested by Richard Ellmann, *The Identity of Yeats*, p. 283, that this poem may have developed out of Mrs Yeats's automatic writing. See notes on 'Owen Aherne and his Dancers', p. 335. Yeats put in a journal the ideas of a 'communicator' which Mrs Yeats was writing down in automatic script:

He insisted on being questioned. I asked about further multiple influx. He said 'hate God', we must hate all ideas concerning God that we possess, that if we did not absorption in God would be impossible . . . always he repeated 'hatred, hatred' or 'hatred of God' . . . said, 'I think about hatred'. That seems to me the growing hatred among men [which] has long been a problem with me.

Ellmann adds that the soul has to enter some significant relationship with God even if this be one of hatred.

P. 255   'What magic drum?'   This poem was numbered VII in the series *Supernatural Songs* in *FMIM* (1935)

P. 255   'Lapis Lazuli'   Yeats was given by Henry [Harry] Clifton a lapis lazuli carving as a seventieth-birthday present on 4 July 1935   *nothing drastic . . . Aeroplane and Zeppelin*: a reflection of the mounting political tension in the 1930s. The Italians had invaded Abyssinia in 1935; the Germans reoccupied the Rhineland in 1936; and there was a general fear of war and air raids. German Zeppelins, rigid-frame airships named after their designer Graf Von

Zeppelin (1838–1917), had raided London in the 1914–18 war, in which aeroplanes were first used for military purposes   *King Billy*: King William III (William of Orange), an echo of a ballad 'The Battle of the Boyne':

> King James he pitched his tents between
> The lines for to retire;
> But King William threw his bomb-balls in
> And set them all on fire

Hamlet . . . Lear . . . Cordelia . . . Ophelia . . . Do not break up their lines: The characters of Shakespearean tragedy (Cordelia and Ophelia are implicitly contrasted with the contemporary 'hysterical women') convey, Yeats wrote in 'A General Introduction for my Work' (see *E & I*, pp. 522–3), through their looks, or through the metaphorical patterns of their speech, 'the sudden enlargement of their vision, their ecstasy at the approach of death'   *Gaiety . . . transfiguring . . . dread*: the 'General Introduction' continues 'There may be in this or that detail painful tragedy, but in the whole work none. I have heard Lady Gregory say, rejecting some play in the modern manner "Tragedy must be a joy to the man who dies" '   *Callimachus*: a Greek sculptor of the late fifth century BC who invented the running drill but was thought to have ruined his art by over-elaboration. He made a golden lamp (in the shape of a palm tree with a long bronze chimney) for the Erechtheum at Athens, included in the *Description of Greece*, I, 26, 6–7, by Pausanias (*fl* c.150)   *Two Chinamen . . . instrument*: these lines describe the lapis lazuli carved, as Yeats described it in a letter of 6 July 1935 to Lady Dorothy Wellesley, 'into the semblance of a mountain with temple, trees, paths and an ascetic and pupil about to climb the mountain. Ascetic, pupil, hard stone, eternal theme of the sensual east. But no, I am wrong, the east has its solutions always and therefore knows nothing of tragedy. It is we, not the east that must raise the heroic cry.'

P. 257   'The Gyres'   *The gyres*: see notes on 'Demon and Beast', p. 333, and see 'The Second Coming'   *Old Rocky Face*: some seer, possibly akin to Shelley's Ahasuerus, the cavern-dwelling Jew, 'master of human knowledge' in *Hellas* (MSS versions of 'The Gyres' refer to the 'old cavern man')   *Empedocles*: Empedocles (c. 490–430BC), a Greek philosopher, who thought all things were composed of earth, air, fire and water, mingled by love or separated by strife   *Hector . . . Troy*: see notes on 'The Phases of the Moon', p. 364   *tragic joy*: this attitude to decay and death was strongly held by Yeats. It is well put in 'J. M. Synge and the Ireland of his Time' (*E & I*, p. 322):

> There is in the creative joy of acceptance of what life brings, because we have understood the beauty of what it brings, or a hatred of death for what it takes away, which arouses within us, through some sympathy perhaps with all other men, an energy so noble, so powerful that we laugh aloud and mock, in the terror or the sweetness of our exaltation, at death and oblivion.

P. 257   'The Great Day'   the MS of this poem included a line: 'Many violent leading articles: the cannons shoot'

P. 258   'Long-legged Fly'   *Caesar*: presumably Gaius Julius Caesar (100/102–44BC) the Roman general, orator, author and statesman, who transformed the Roman republic into a government under a single ruler   *the topless towers . . . that face . . . She*: an echo of Christopher Marlowe's (1564–93) *The Tragical History of Dr Faustus* (1604) V, 1, 94–5: 'Was this the face that launched a thousand ships/And burnt the topless towers of Ilium?' The face is that of Helen of Troy; the thought moves via Helen of Troy to Maud Gonne whose feet 'practise a

tinker shuffle'   *the first Adam* . . . *Pope's chapel* . . . *Michael Angelo*: the stanza describes the
painting of Adam about to be wakened into life by God by Michelangelo (see notes on 'Michael
Robartes and the Dancer', p. 326) in the Sistine Chapel, Rome

P. 259   'The Statues'   A passage in Yeats's posthumous *On the Boiler* (1939) clarifies some of the
meaning of the poem:

> There are moments when I am certain that arts must once again accept those Greek
> proportions which carry into plastic art the Pythagorean numbers, those faces which are
> divine because all there is empty and measured. Europe was not born when Greek galleys
> defeated the Persian hordes at Salamis; but when the Doric studios sent out those
> broad-backed marble statues against the multiform, vague, expressive Asiatic sea, they gave
> to the sexual instinct of Europe its goal, its fixed type. (*E*, p. 451)

Pythagoras . . . *numbers*: Pythagoras (*c*. 582–507 BC) developed a theory of numbers and this
paved the way for the art of Greek sculptors who carved their statues by exact proportions and
measurements ('plummet-measured' of 1.8)   *Salamis*: in the naval battle of Salamis 480 BC the
Greeks defeated the Persians. Yeats is saying that Greek intellect was the real force that
defeated the Persians   *All Asiatic vague immensities* . . . *Phidias*: cf. *AV* (1925), p. 182 and *AV*
(1937), p. 270:

> Side by side with Ionic elegance there comes after the Persian wars a Doric vigour, and the
> light-limbed dandy of the potters, the Parisian-looking young woman of the sculptors, her
> hair elaborately curled, give place to the athlete. One suspects a deliberate turning away
> from all that is Eastern, or a moral propaganda like that which turned the poets out of Plato's
> Republic, and yet it may be that the preparation for the final systematisation had for its
> apparent cause the destruction, let us say, of Ionic studios by the Persian invaders, and that
> all came from the resistance of the *Body of Fate* to the growing solitude of the soul. Then in
> Phidias Ionic and Doric influence unite – one remembers Titian – and all is transformed by
> the full moon, and all abounds and flows.

For Phidias the Athenian sculptor, see notes on 'Nineteen Hundred and Nineteen', p. 344; see
also 'Under Ben Bulben' IV   *One image* . . . *dreamer of the Middle Ages*: Yeats wrote to Edith
Shackleton Heald on 28 June 1938:

> In reading the third stanza remember the influence on modern sculpture and on the great
> seated Buddha of the sculptors who followed Alexander. Cuchulain is in the last stanza
> because Pearse and some of his followers had a cult of him. The Government has put a statue
> of Cuchulain in the rebuilt post office to commemorate this. (*L*, p. 911) [See next stanza of
> the poem]

No Hamlet . . . *flies*: cf. Yeats's 'Four Years 1887–1891', *A*, pp. 141–2, for the 'dreamer of the
Middle Ages' as 'a mind that has no need of the intellect to remain sane, though it gives itself to
every fantasy . . . It is

> "the fool of Faery . . . wide and wild as a hill", the resolute European image that yet half
> remembers Buddha's motionless meditation, and has no trait in common with the
> wavering, lean image of hungry speculation, that cannot but because of certain famous
> Hamlets of our stage fill the mind's eye. Shakespeare himself foreshadowed a symbolic

change, that is, a change in the whole temperament of the world, for though he called his Hamlet 'fat' and even 'scant of breath', he thrust between his fingers agile rapier and dagger.

Empty eye-balls: cf. *AV* (1937), pp. 275–7 where Yeats discusses the decay of Roman civilisation at about AD 1 to AD 250:

. . . Roman sculpture – sculpture made under Roman influence whatever the sculptor's blood – did not, for instance, reach its full vigour, if we consider what it had for Roman as distinct from Greek, until the Christian Era. It even made a discovery which affected all sculpture to come. The Greeks painted the eyes of marble statues and made out of enamel or glass or precious stones those of their bronze statues, but the Roman was the first to drill a round hole to represent the pupil, and because, as I think, of a preoccupation with the glance characteristic of a civilisation in its final phase. The colours must have already faded from the marbles of the great period, and a shadow and a spot of light, especially where there is much sunlight, are more vivid than paint, enamel, coloured glass or precious stone. They could now express in stone a perfect composure. The administrative mind, alert attention had driven out rhythm, exaltation of the body, uncommitted energy. May it not have been precisely a talent for this alert attention that had enabled Rome and not Greece to express those final *primary* phases? One sees on the pediments troops of marble Senators, officials serene and watchful as befits men who know that all the power of the world moves before their eyes, and needs, that it may not dash itself to pieces, their unhurried, unanxious, never-ceasing care. Those riders upon the Parthenon had all the world's power in their moving bodies, and in a movement that seemed, so were the hearts of man and beast set upon it, that of a dance; but presently all would change and measurement succeed to pleasure, the dancing-master outlive the dance. What need had those young lads for careful eyes? But in Rome of the first and second centuries, where the dancing-master himself has died, the delineation of character as shown in face and head, as with us of recent years, is all in all, the sculptors, seeking the custom of occupied officials, stock in their workshops toga'd marble bodies upon which can be screwed with the least possible delay heads modelled from the sitters with the most scrupulous realism. When I think of Rome I see always these heads with their world-considering eyes, and those bodies as conventional as the metaphors in a leading article, and compare in my imagination vague Grecian eyes gazing at nothing, Byzantine eyes of drilled ivory staring upon a vision, and those eyelids of China and of India, those veiled or half-veiled eyes weary of world and vision alike.

Grimalkin: a name for a cat. The description of Hamlet thin with eating flies may have suggested the introduction of Grimalkin, as cats are often supposed to grow thin by eating flies *When Pearse summoned Cuchulain . . . Post Office*: Pearse is envisioned as calling intellectual and aesthetic forces into being (by an appeal to the Irish heroic past) as well as skills of measuring and numbering so that the Irish can return to their Pythagorean proportions, their 'Greek' proportions. Pearse (see notes below on 'Easter 1916', p. 384) fought in the General Post Office, Dublin, in 1916; he had 'a cult' of Cuchulain. For Cuchulain see notes on 'To the Rose upon the Rood of Time', p. 313 and entry for Cuchulain in Glossary

P. 260 'News for the Delphic Oracle' *the golden codgers*: the immortals, viewed ironically. See notes below on 'The Delphic Oracle on Plotinus', p. 377 *silver dew*: F. A. C. Wilson, *Yeats and Tradition* (1958), p. 219, suggests this relates to the nectar described in the oracle *Man-picker . . . Oisin*: Yeats is blending Irish mythology with Greek, Niamh, daughter of Aengus and Edain, chose Oisin to accompany her to the magic islands, described in 'The Wanderings of Oisin' *Pythagoras . . . Plotinus*: see notes on 'The Delphic Oracle upon Plotinus', p. 377, and on 'Among School Children', p. 338 and, for Plotinus, notes on 'The Tower', p. 345 *a dolphin's back*: see notes on 'Byzantium', p. 369. This poem is referring to pictures in Rome (School of Raphael in the Papal Apartments at Castel S. Angelo) which include nymphs, satyrs and dolphins *Those Innocents*: possibly the Holy Innocents (male children under two whom Herod had killed, in an attempt to eliminate Jesus Christ. See Matthew II 16–18). Yeats knew Raphael Santi's (1483–1520) statue of the Dolphin carrying one of the Holy Innocents to Heaven *the choir of love*: see notes on 'The Delphic Oracle upon Plotinus', p. 377 *Peleus on Thetis stares*: Yeats is referring to Nicolas Poussin's (1594–1665) 'The Marriage of Peleus and Thetis' (now entitled 'Acis and Galatea'), a Lane bequest picture in the National Gallery of Ireland. In Greek mythology the marriage of Peleus, son of Aeacus and Endeis, to Thetis, a Nereid, daughter of Nereus and Doris, was celebrated on Mount Pelion. Their surviving son was the hero Achilles *Pan's cavern*: Pan was a fertility god in classical mythology, usually represented with small horns in his human head, with the legs, thighs and tail of a goat. He was thought to have invented the flute, and was reputed to delight in caverns

P. 261 'The Black Tower' *Those banners*: political propaganda *the dead upright*: a reference to the custom of the Irish of occasionally burying the bodies of kings and chieftains upright in armour facing the territories of their enemies *great king's horn*: W. J. Keith has suggested, in 'Yeats's Arthurian Black Tower', *MLN*, lxxv, February 1960, that this image derives from the Arthurian legend that Arthur, Guinevere, all his court and a pack of hounds sleep in a vault beneath the Castle of Sewingshields in Northumberland. The king waits till someone blows the horn which lies on a table and cuts a garter laid beside it with a sword of stone. A farmer found the vault, cut the garter and Arthur woke, only to fall asleep again as the sword was sheathed with these words:

> O woe betide that evil day
> On which the witless wight was born
> Who drew the sword – the garter cut
> But never blew the bugle horn.

Section 16: ADAPTATIONS AND TRANSLATIONS

P. 265 'Down by the Salley Gardens' Yeats described the poem as an attempt 'to reconstruct an old song from three lines imperfectly remembered by an old peasant woman in the village of Ballysodare, Sligo'. The poem closely resembles the first two stanzas of the following folk poem with the same title (text in the National Library of Ireland, Dublin):

> Down by the Sally Gardens my own true love and I did meet
> She passed the Sally Gardens, a tripping with her snow white feet.
> She bid me take life easy just as leaves fall from each tree;
> But I being young and foolish with my true love would not agree.
>
> In a field by the river my lovely girl and I did stand.
> And leaning on her shoulder I pressed her burning hand.
> She bid me take life easy, just as the stream flows o'er the weirs
> But I being young and foolish I parted her that day in tears.

I wish I was in Banagher and my fine girl upon my knee.
And I with money plenty to keep her in good company.
I'd call for liquor of the best with flowing bowls on every side.
Kind fortune ne'er shall daunt me, I am young and the world's wide.

salley gardens: gardens of willow used for thatching roofs

P. 265 'When You Are Old' This poem, written to Maud Gonne, is founded upon Pierre de Ronsard's (1524–85) 'Quand Vous Serez Bien Vieille', *Sonnets pour Hélène* II (1578)

P. 266 'Seven paters seven times' A poem from Yeats's story 'The Adoration of the Magi', *M*, pp. 308–15. In this story, first published privately in *The Tables of the Law and The Adoration of the Magi* (1897), he included the text in Irish of the first eight lines of a poem by Domnall O'Fotharta, included in *Siamsa an Gheimhridh* (1892). See *M*, p. 315 and *NC*, p. 464 for Irish original *Mary . . . Son*: the Virgin Mary; Jesus Christ her son *Bridget*: Saint Brigid (*c.*453–*c.*523), who founded a famous double monastery in Co. Kildare

P. 266 'A Thought from Propertius' *Propertius*: the Roman poet Sextus Propertius (*c.*50–*c.*16BC) who wrote many poems to 'Cynthia'. This poem is based on the second poem of Book II *She*: Maud Gonne *Pallas Athene*: Yeats compared Maud Gonne to the Greek goddess Pallas Athene (he spelled the name Athene and Athena) elsewhere; she was the Greek goddess of wisdom, and patroness of the arts of peace; cf. 'Beautiful Lofty Things', p. 61

P. 266 'Make way for Oedipus. All People Said' The final chorus in *Sophocles' King Oedipus*, Yeats's translation of the tragedy by the Greek playwright Sophocles (496–406BC). He began work on the play about 1904, using a translation by R. C. Jebb, *Sophocles, The Plays and Fragments* I, 2nd ed. (1887) and a schoolboys' crib. His friend Oliver St John Gogarty prepared a translation for him in 1904. Yeats intended to produce his first version in the Abbey Theatre Dublin early in 1910, but this idea was abandoned, though he was again working on the translation in 1911–12, with the aid of Dr Rynd, of Norwich, then visiting Dublin. Later in the 1920s, with his wife's encouragement he began work again, using, with her aid, Paul Masqueray's translation of the play into French, *Sophocle*, I (1900). And he got Gogarty to chant passages to him in Greek as he was completing the translation. (See Ulick O'Connor, *Oliver St John Gogarty: A Poet and his Times* (1965), p. 45.) Lady Gregory then assisted him in the final revision. The play was first staged at the Abbey Theatre on 7 December 1926 *Oedipus . . . fortunate . . . storms*: in Greek legend, Oedipus was the son of Laius, King of Thebes and his wife Jocasta. An oracle foretold Laius would be killed by his son, and the king ordered the child to be destroyed. Oedipus was exposed, but rescued by a shepherd; later he killed his father in ignorance of their relationship, went to Thebes which was then plagued by the Sphinx, and solved the Sphinx's riddle. As a reward for ridding the country of the pest he was given the kingdom by Creon (the regent and brother of Jocasta) and Jocasta's hand in marriage. He had two sons, Polyneices and Eteocles, and two daughters, Ismene and Antigone, by his mother. In horror at discovering what he had done (he had murdered his father and committed incest by marrying his mother) be blinded himself and Jocasta hanged herself. Oedipus, led by Antigone, retired to Colonus in Attica where he died

P. 267 'From "Oedipus at Colonus" ' This translation was made at the same time as *Sophocles' King Oedipus* (see note on 'Make way for Oedipus', p. 375) but Yeats thought work on that play made his approach 'less literal and more idiomatic and modern' in *Sophocles' Oedipus at Colonus*. It was first staged at the Abbey Theatre, Dublin, on 12 September 1927.

This chorus comes at the point of the play where Polyneices, the son of Oedipus, asks permission to speak to Oedipus (in order to ask his help in his attack on Thebes, made because his brother Eteocles had refused to give up the throne at the appointed time, both brothers

having agreed to reign in alternate years). Antigone intercedes to ask Oedipus to listen to
Polyneices

P. 267   'I call upon Persephone, queen of the dead'   A chorus from Yeats's translation of *Sophocles'*
Oedipus at Colonus; see notes on 'From "Oedipus at Colonus" ' above. *Persephone*: a daughter (*Latin*
Proserpine) of Zeus and Demeter, who was carried off by Pluto (Hades) and made queen of the
lower world. Her mother Demeter sought her; she was eventually allowed by Zeus to spend six
months on earth, six with Pluto   *Hades*: or Pluto, a son of Kronos, lord of the lower world,
and Rhea. He was a brother of Zeus and Poseidon   *the Furies*: the Erinyes   *Stygian hall*: the
Styx was the main river in Hades, the lower world   *hundred-headed dog*: Cerberus, a monstrous
dog who guarded the entrance to the lower world; he is variously described as having three,
fifty or a hundred heads   *the daughter of Earth and Tartarus*: Richard Jebb's translation gives
'the son'; Paul Masqueray's 'Fille'. (Yeats, who did not know Greek, knew both translations
well, mainly using Masqueray's French version when preparing his own translation of this
play. See note on 'Make way for Oedipus', p. 375.) The son of Typhoeus, the daughter
Echidna; Echidna, half-woman, half-serpent, was the mother of other monsters including
Cerberus, Orthrus the dog of Geryon, the Chimaera, the Sphinx and the Hydra. Tartarus was
one of the regions of Hades where the most impious of mankind were punished

P. 268   'I am of Ireland'   Yeats's note describes the poem as 'developed from three or four lines of
an Irish fourteenth century dance song somebody repeated to me a few years ago'. Frank
O'Connor (Michael O'Donovan, 1903–66) read Yeats this version from J. E. Wells, *Manual of
Middle English Writing*, p. 492:

> Icham of Irlande
> Aut of the holy lande of Irlande
> Gode sir pray ich ye
> For of saynte charite
> Come and daunce wyt me,
> In Irlaunde

Mrs W. B. Yeats thought the source was St John D. Seymour, *Anglo-Irish Literature,
1200–1582* (1929) who described the lines as 'placed in the mouth of an Irish girl, and so
presumably . . . composed by an Anglo-Irish minstrel'

P. 269   'Swift's Epitaph'   This is a translation of the Latin epitaph in St Patrick's Cathedral,
Dublin, where Jonathan Swift, Dean of the Cathedral, is buried. Yeats's addition to the
epitaph is the epithet 'World-besotted'. The Latin reads:

> *Hic* depositum est Corpus
> JONATHAN SWIFT S.T.D.
> Hujus Ecclesiæ Cathedralis
> Decani,
> *Ubi* saeva indignatio
> Ulterius
> Cor lacerare nequit.
> Abi Viator
> Et imitare, si poteris,
> Strenuum pro virili
> Libertatis Vindicatorem
> Obiit 19° Die Mensis Octobris
> A.D. 1745 Anno Aetatis 78.

P. 269   'The Dancer at Cruachan and Cro-Patrick'   *Cruachan*: Yeats's note states that Cruachan
was 'pronounced Crockhan in modern Gaelic'. Cruachan, fabled capital of Connaught, in Co.
Roscommon, was called after Queen Maeve's mother Cruacha   *Cro-Patrick*: or Croagh Patrick
(Patrick's Heap) a mountain near Westport, Co. Mayo, to which an annual pilgrimage (called
'Climbing the Reek') is made on the last Sunday in July. St Patrick is reputed to have fasted on
its summit and, when there, to have banished snakes from Ireland. See notes on 'The
Wanderings of Oisin', p. 341 and cf. 'The Pilgrim' *I*: Cellach MacAodh, Archbishop of
Armagh (1105–29), St Celsus, of whom Yeats read in Standish O'Grady, 'Life of S. Cellach of
Killala', *Silva Gadelica* (1892).

P. 269   'The Delphic Oracle upon Plotinus'   The oracle at Delphi (in a rocky cleft on the
southwest slopes of Mount Parnassus) was the chief of Greek oracles, its greatest point of
influence being between the eighth and fifth centuries BC   *Plotinus*: see note on 'The Tower',
p. 345. The poem is based upon the oracle given to Amelius who consulted Delphi to find out
where the soul of Plotinus had gone after his death. This is in Porphry's *Life of Plotinus* which
Yeats read in Thomas Taylor's translation, and in Stephen MacKenna's translation of 1917:

> . . . the bonds of human necessity are loosed for you and, strong of heart, you beat your
> eager way from out the roaring tumult of the fleshy life to the shores of that wave-washed
> coast free from the thronging of the guilty, thence to take the grateful path of the sinless
> soul: /where glows the splendour of God, where Right is throned in the stainless place, far
> from the wrong that mocks at law. /Oft-times as you strove to rise above the bitter waves of
> this blood-drenched life, above the sickening whirl, toiling in the mid-most of the rushing
> flood and the unimaginable turmoil, oft-times, from the Ever-Blessed, there was shown to
> you the Term still close at hand: /Oft-times, when your mind thrust out awry and was like to
> be rapt down unsanctioned paths, the Immortals themselves prevented, guiding you on the
> straightgoing way to the celestial spheres, pouring down before you a dense shaft of light
> that your eyes might see from amid the mournful gloom. /Sleep never closed those eyes:
> high above the heavy murk of the mist you held them; tossed in the welter, you still had
> vision; still you saw sights many and fair not granted to all that labour in wisdom's quest.
> /But now that you have cast the screen aside, quitted the tomb that held your lofty soul, you
> enter at once the heavenly consort; /where fragrant breezes play, where all is unison and
> winning tenderness and guileless joy and the place is lavish of the nectar streams the
> unfailing Gods bestow, with the blandishments of the Loves, and delicious airs, and
> tranquil sky:/where Minos and Rhadamanthus dwell, great brethren of the golden race of
> mighty Zeus; where dwells the just Aeacus, and Plato, consecrated power, and stately
> Pythagoras and all else that form the choir of Immortal Love, there where the heart is ever
> lifted in joyous festival.
> O Blessed One, you have fought your many fights; now crowned with unfading life, your
> days are with the Ever-Holy./
> Rejoicing Muses, let us stay our song and the subtle windings of our dance; thus much I
> could but tell, to my golden lyre, of Plotinus, the hallowed soul. (S. MacKenna, *Plotinus*,
> 'Porphry's Life of Plotinus', pp. 22–4; revd. ed. (1946) p. 16.)

Rhadamanthus: in Greek mythology, a son of Zeus and Europa who was a judge of souls in the
underworld, in Elysium, the place to which favoured heroes exempt from death were sent by
the gods   *Golden Race*: either the immortals, or more likely, from MacKenna's translation,
'the great brethren of the golden race of Zeus', that is, Rhadamathus and Minos (see 1.8).
Porphry also adds Aeacus as the third enthroned judge of souls   *dim*: they looked dim to

Plotinus but poured down a dense shaft of light so that he could see 'amid the mournful gloom'   *salt blood*: Plotinus was struggling to free himself, to rise above 'the bitter waves of this blood-drenched life'   *Plato . . . Minos . . . choir of Love*: this is very close to MacKenna's translation, one of Yeats's favourite quotations. See quotations from it above, beginning with the passage 'Where Minos' down to 'joyous festival'

P. 270   'Imitated from the Japanese'   Yeats wrote to Dorothy Wellesley in December 1936 saying he had made his poem 'out of prose translation of a Japanese Hokku in praise of spring'. The likely source for this poem is Gekko's (1745–1824) 'My Longing after Departed Spring':

> My longing after the departed spring
> Is not the same every year

A hokku (or haiku) has seventeen syllables, divided into three lines of, respectively, five, seven and five syllables.

Section 17: AGE AND AFTER

P. 273   'The poet, Owen Hanrahan, under a bush of may'   This poem was included in Yeats's story, 'The Curse of Hanrahan the Red', first published in 1894. See *The Secret Rose* (1897). The names of the characters are fictitious   *Hanrahan*: Yeats probably had in mind the Irish poet Owen O'Sullivan the Red (1748–84) whose name, as 'O'Sullivan Rua', is given to a poet-hero in early versions of Yeats's stories; he became 'Red Hanrahan' in *Stories of Red Hanrahan* (1904); cf. 'The Tower': 'And I myself created Hanrahan'   *may*: hawthorn   *Ballygawley Hill*: five miles south of the town of Sligo. Ballydawley (*Irish* Baile Dhalaigh, O'Daly's townland) is the correct version of the name   *Steep Place of the Strangers*: see note on 'The Man who dreamed of Faeryland', p. 357   *Gap of the Wind*: possibly a gap in the townland of Carrickhenry, opposite Carraroe Church, Co. Sligo   *Castle Dargan*: near Ballygawley. See note above   *Well of Bride*: Brigid's Well (*Irish* Tober Bride), near Coloney, Co. Sligo, dedicated to St Bridget   *Peter Hart . . . Michael Gill . . . Shemus Cullinan*: imagined characters   *the Green Lands*: an unfenced portion of land, at Rosses Point, Co. Sligo   *Paddy Doe*: another imagined character

P. 274   'The Three Hermits'   This poem, probably written under the influence of Ezra Pound (who was acting as Yeats's secretary at the time and urging him to toughen up his verse) and probably also influenced by Synge's plays with their country characters, discusses different theories about reincarnation

P. 275   'A Song'   *dumb-bell and foil*: Ezra Pound taught Yeats fencing in the winter of 1912–13; he had also been doing Sandow exercises with dumb-bells to keep fit

P. 276   'Men improve with the Years'   *A . . . marble triton*: one of a race of sea deities in Greek legend, usually represented in semi-human form, as a bearded man with the hindquarters of a fish, usually holding a trident or a shell   *this lady's beauty*: probably Iseult Gonne, Maud Gonne's daughter, who finally rejected Yeats's proposal of marriage in 1917

P. 276   'Death'   This poem was written about the assassination of Kevin O'Higgins (1892–1927), Minister of Justice in the Irish Free State. He was convinced that the Irish civil war could only be ended by the execution of anyone captured carrying arms; it was thought that he was shot on 10 July 1927 on his way to mass at Booterstown, Dublin, as an act of revenge   *knows death*: Yeats wrote to Mrs Shakespear, in April 1933, that he remembered a saying of O'Higgins to his wife, 'Nobody can expect to live who has done what I have'

P. 277   'At Algeciras – A Meditation upon Death'   *Algeciras*: in southern Spain, where Yeats was staying at the Hotel Reina Christina in November 1928; he had been seriously ill with congestion of the lungs in October, and was sent south from Ireland to Spain in search of sunshine   *Morocco*: on the African side of the straits of Gibraltar   *Newton's metaphor*: Newton's words were

> I do not know how I may appear to the world; but to myself I seem to have been only like a boy, playing on the seashore, and divering myself, in now and then finding another pebble or prettier shell than ordinary, while the great ocean of truth lay all undiscovered before me.

Rosses' level shore: At Rosses Point near Sligo   *Great Questioner*: God

P. 277   'A Prayer for Old Age'   After Lady Gregory died in 1932, Yeats said that he had nothing in his head, 'and there used to be more than I could write'. He decided to force himself to write, and visited Ezra Pound (1885–1972) saying 'I am in my sixty-ninth year, probably I should stop writing verse, I want your opinion upon some verse I have written lately'. Pound eventually took the manuscript, denouncing Dublin 'as a reactionary hole' because Yeats had told him that he himself was rereading Shakespeare, would go to Chaucer, and found all that he wanted of modern life 'in detection and the wild west'. Next day Pound's judgement came, 'and that in a single word "Putrid".' This poem is in reply to Pound and expresses Yeats's dislike of 'intellectual' poetry. He had earlier written in 'The Cutting of an Agate', *E & I*, p. 235, of having belief only in those thoughts that have been conceived not in the brain but in the whole body'

P. 278   'The Four Ages of Man'   This poem was numbered 5 in the series *Supernatural Songs*, in *KGCT* (1934), but numbered IX in that series in *FMIM* (1935). Yeats wrote to Mrs Shakespear in a letter of 7 August 1934 that these are the four ages of individual man but 'also the four ages of civilisation'. In an earlier letter of 24 July 1934 he had written to her:

The Earth   =Every early nature-dominated civilisation
The Water=An armed sexual age, chivalry, Froissart's chronicles
The Air   =From the Renaissance to the end of the 19th Century
The Fire   =The purging away of our civilisation by our hatred

P. 279   'Why should not old men be mad?'   *a drunken journalist*: probably R. M. Smyllie (1894–1954), editor of the *Irish Times*, whose father edited the *Sligo Times*   *a girl . . . Dante*: Iseult Gonne. See notes on 'To a Child dancing in the Wind', p. 324 and 'To a Young Beauty', p. 326   *a dunce*: Francis Stuart (*b*. 1902), Irish novelist and poet   *Helen*: probably Maud Gonne. For Helen see notes on 'No Second Troy', p. 354 and 'When Helen Lived', p. 354

P. 279   'What Then?'   *comrades at school*: at the High School, then situated in Harcourt Street, Dublin, an Erasmus Smith foundation. This poem first appeared in *The Erasmian*, the school magazine. Yeats's comrades included the critic John Eglinton (W. K. Magee, 1868–1961) and Charles Johnson (see *A*, pp. 89–92), who shared Yeats's interest in eastern religion and theosophy, marrying the niece of Madame Blavatsky (1831–91), the Russian founder of the Theosophical Society in New York in 1875   *small old house*: see notes on 'An Acre of Grass', below

P. 280   'An Acre of Grass'   *acre of green grass . . . old house*: Riversdale, Rathfarnham, Co. Dublin, 'a little creeper-covered farmhouse', which Yeats leased in 1932 for thirteen years; he described it in a letter to Mrs Shakespear in that summer as having 'apple trees, cherry trees, roses, smooth lawns, and no long climb upstairs . . . I shall have a big old fruit garden all to myself –

the study opens into it and it is shut off from the flower garden and the croquet and tennis lawns and from the bowling green' *Timon*: known as the Misanthrope, he was a contemporary of Socrates (*d.* 399BC) at Athens; he was attacked by the comic writers for his disgust with mankind (caused by the ingratitude of his early friends). Shakespeare's *Timon of Athens* follows the story told in William Painter's *Palace of Pleasure* (1566–1567) *Michael Angelo*: see notes on 'Michael Robartes and the Dancer', p. 326 *eagle mind*: Yeats was rereading the German philosopher Friederich Wilhelm Nietzsche in 1936–7, and this idea may come from his *The Dawn of Day*, p. 347, where minds of men of genius are described as 'but loosely linked to their character and temperament, like winged beings which easily separate themselves from them, and then rise far above them'

P. 281   'In Tara's Halls'   *Tara's Halls*: the Hill of Tara, Co. Meath, reputedly the seat of the High Kings of Ireland

P. 282   'Man and the Echo'   *Alt*: a steep rocky glen at Knocknarea, a mountain in Sligo   *play of mine . . . shot: Cathleen ni Houlihan* (1902) in which Maud Gonne performed the title role, first produced in Dublin, 2 April 1902. Stephen Gwynn (1864–1950), the Irish author, remarked in his *Irish Literature and Drama in the English Language* (1936), p. 158:

> The effect of Cathleen ni Houlihan on me was that I went home asking myself if such plays should be produced unless one was prepared for people to go out to shoot and be shot. Yeats was not alone responsible; no doubt but Lady Gregory had helped him to get the peasant speech so perfect; but above all Miss Gonne's impersonation had stirred the audience as I have never seen another audience stirred.

Certain men: presumably he is thinking here of the leaders of the 1916 rising. See notes on 'Easter 1916', p. 384   *reeling brain*: Margot Collis or Ruddock, an English poetress whom Yeats befriended. She temporarily became insane in Barcelona and Yeats paid her return fare to England. He wrote an account of this happening to Mrs Shakespear on 22 May 1936; see his *Letters*, p. 856; *Ah, Sweet Dancer* (1970) is a volume of the correspondence between Yeats and Margot Ruddock   *house lay wrecked*: probably Coole Park, see notes on 'Coole and Ballylee, 1931', p. 316   *bodkin*: symbol of suicide. Cf. *Hamlet* III, 1, 'When he himself might his quietus make/With a bare bodkin'   *rocky voice*: cf. notes on 'Old Rocky Face' of 'The Gyres', p. 371

P. 284   'Under Ben Bulben'   *Ben Bulben*: see note on 'The Tower', p. 345 and note below   *Mareotic Lake . . . Witch of Atlas*: see notes on 'Demon and Beast', p. 333. Shelley's 'Witch of Atlas' passed along the Nile 'by Moeris and the Mareotid Lakes'   *those horsemen . . . women/Complexion and form*: possibly the visionary beings described to Yeats by Mary Battle, his uncle George Pollexfen's servant, as coming from Knocknarea:

> 'Some of them have their hair down, but they look quite different [from Queen Maeve?], more like the sleepy-looking ladies one sees in the papers. Those with their hair up are like this one ['the finest woman you ever saw' described earlier]. The others have long white dresses, but those with their hair up have short dresses, so that you can see their legs right up to the calf.' And when I questioned her, I found that they wore what might well be some kind of buskin. 'They are fine and dashing-looking, like the men one sees riding their horses in twos and threes on the slopes of the mountains with their swords swinging. There is no such race living now, none so finely proportioned' (*A*, p. 266)

Ben Bulben . . . the scene: probably because some events in the Fenian cycle of tales take place there, notably the death of Diarmid (see notes on 'Her Vision in the Wood', p. 366) *Mitchel's prayer*: John Mitchel (1815–75), the Irish nationalist, parodied the prayer 'Give us peace in our time, O Lord' in his entry for 19 November 1953, *Jail Journal* (1854) with 'Give us war in our time, O Lord'   *Phidias*: See note on 'The Statues', p. 372   *Michael Angelo . . . Sistine Chapel . . . Adam*: see notes on 'Michael Robartes and the Dancer', p. 326 and on 'Long Legged Fly', p. 371   *Quattrocento*: see notes on 'Among School Children', p. 338   *Gyres*: see notes on 'Demon and Beast', p. 333   *Calvert*: Edward Calvert (1799–1883), English visionary artist   *Wilson*: Richard Wilson (1714–82) landscaper painter   *Blake*: William Blake (1757–1827) poet and engraver   *Claude*: Claude Lorrain (1600–82) French landscape painter   *Palmer's phrase*: for earlier mention of Samuel Palmer see notes on 'The Phases of the Moon', p. 365. He described Blake's illustrations to Thornton's *Virgil* as 'the drawing aside of the fleshy curtain, and the glimpse which all the most holy, studious saints and sages have enjoyed, of that rest which remaineth to the people of God' in *The Life and Letters of Samuel Palmer* (1892), pp. 15–16   *the lords and ladies gay*: a phrase from Frank O'Connor's translation of the Irish poem, *Kilcash*, 'the earls, the lady, the people beaten into the clay'; cf. notes on 'The Curse of Cromwell', p. 349   *An ancestor*: Rev. John Yeats; see notes on 'Introductory Rhymes', p. 331   *Cast a cold eye . . .*: Yeats's tombstone has this epitaph cut on it; his body was brought from France and reinterred in Drumcliff Churchyard on 17 September 1948

Section 18: POLITICS AND POLEMICS

P. 291   'An Appointment'   *government*: Yeats regarded the Viceroy, Lord Aberdeen (1847–1934; Viceroy in 1886 and 1905–15) and Augustine Birrell (1850–1933), Chief Secretary for Ireland (1907–16), as reprehensible for appointing Count Plunkett, whom Yeats regarded as a timid nonentity, to the position of Curator of the National Museum in Dublin, and disregarding the claims of Sir Hugh Lane, whom he regarded as 'the man of genius', the best man for the post. (Lane was later appointed Director of the National Gallery of Ireland in 1914.) See *NC*, p. 125

P. 291   'On Those that hated "The Playboy of the Western World", 1907'   The production, at the Abbey Theatre, Dublin, of *The Playboy of the Western World* by John Millington Synge was greeted by riots in the theatre. Arthur Griffith (1872–1922) who founded and edited the *United Irishman* and *Sinn Fein* had attacked Synge's plays in these journals, arguing that literature should be subordinate to politics. Yeats was comparing 'Griffith and his like' to the Eunuchs in Charles Rickett's (1866–1931) paintings of eunuchs watching Don Juan riding through hell. Ricketts, an artist, stage and book designer, sculptor and critic, was a friend of Yeats. Yeats thought that Irish nationalist journalists and politicians suffered from a cultivation of hatred which made them regard creative work such as that of Synge with the jealousy of eunuchs; he thought the sterility of much Irish writing was due to sexual abstinence   *Don Juan*: a legendary Spanish libertine, delivered to devils by the statue of the father of a girl he attempted to ravish

P. 292   'Upon a House Shaken by the Land Agitation'   The prose draft of this poem read as follows:

Subject for a Poem. A Shaken House. How should the world gain if this house failed, even though a hundred little houses were the better for it, for here power has gone forth, or lingered giving energy, precision; it gives to a far people beneficent rule; and still under its roof loving intellect is sweetened by old memories of its descents from far off; how should the world be better if the wren's nest flourish and the eagle's house is scattered.

Yeats's explanation of the poem read:

I wrote this poem on hearing the result of reduction of rent made by the courts. One feels that when all must make their living they will live not for life's sake but the work's and all be the poorer. My work is very near to life itself and my father's very near to life itself but I am always feeling a lack of life's own values behind my thought. They should have been there before the stream began, before it became necessary to let the work create its values. This house has enriched my soul out of measure because here life moves within restraint through gracious forms. Here there has been no compelled labour, no poverty-thwarted impulse.

this house: Coole Park, Lady Gregory's house in Co. Galway   *lidless eye* a reference to a belief that only an eagle can stare into the sun without blinking   *Mean roof-trees*: the cottages or farmhouses, whose inhabitants would pay less for renting estate land, or farm more of it   *gifts that govern men*: Lady Gregory's husband, Sir William Gregory (1817–92), had been governor of Ceylon   *a written speech*: a reference to Lady Gregory's plays and her books, notably those translating Irish legends, *Cuchulain of Muirthemne* (1902) and *Gods and Fighting Men* (1904)

P. 292   'To a Wealthy Man who promised a second subscription to the Dublin Municipal Gallery if it were proved the People wanted Pictures'   Sir Hugh Lane (1874–1915), Lady Gregory's nephew, offered his collection of French paintings to Dublin provided they would be properly housed. He himself liked a design by Sir Edward Lutyens for a bridge gallery over the river Liffey. (This and another design by Lutyens for a site in Stephen's Green are reproduced in Lady Gregory, *Hugh Lane* (1973), plates 27–29 between pp. 162–3.) Disgusted by Dublin Corporation's reaction to his proposed gift, he placed the pictures in the National Gallery, London, leaving them to London in his will; but he added a pencilled codicil to this will (which was not properly witnessed) leaving them to Dublin. He then went to America on the *Lusitania* and died when the liner was torpedoed by a German submarine. The pictures were retained in the Tate Gallery in London until a compromise agreement was reached by the British and Irish governments in 1959 through which the pictures are shared between London and Dublin. For Yeats's notes see *NC*, pp. 105–7   *You*: Lord Ardilaun   *Paudeen's . . . Biddy's*: Paudeen, a diminutive for Patrick; the names are used contemptuously, for common people   *blind and ignorant*: in the controversy over Lane's pictures Yeats particularly disliked the philistine attacks on Lane made in the *Irish Independent*. This poem was itself, as Yeats put it in a letter to Lane, part of the controversy, being published in the *Irish Times*, to counter political (anti-Home Rule) objections to supporting the gallery and still more to meet the 'argument of people like Ardilaun that they should not give unless there is a public demand'   *Duke Ercole*: Ercole de l'Este (1431–1505), Duke of Ferrara, a generous, discriminating patron of the arts   *his Plautus*: the Duke had five plays by Plautus (*c.* 254–184BC), the Latin comic dramatist, performed at his son Alphonso's wedding in 1502   *Guidobaldo*: Guidobaldo di Montefeltro (1472–1508) Duke of Urbino   *That grammar school*: the Duke's court was cultivated, elegant and refined. Yeats read about it in the Italian humanist Baldassare Castiglione's (1478–1529) *Il Cortegiano* [*The Courtier*] (1528) in the translations by Sir Thomas Hoby (1561) and L. E. Opdycke (1902). He also visited Urbino in 1907; it is finely situated on the slopes of the Apennines   *Cosimo*: Cosimo de Medici (1389–1464) member of a Florentine family who began its glorious epoch, encouraging art, literature and providing splendid buildings at Florence; he was exiled for a year in Venice (1433–34)   *Michelozzo*: Michelozzo de Bartolommeo Michelozzi (1396–1472), Italian sculptor and court architect to Cosimo de Medici, responsible for the San Marco Library in Florence among other fine buildings (notably the Ricardi Palace)   *Greece*: presumably because of the influence of classical Greek culture upon the Italian Renaissance   *the sun's eye*: cf. notes on 'Upon a House Shaken by the Land Agitation', p. 381, the eagle symbolises nobility, activity, objectivity, and greatness

P. 294   '**September 1913**'   *you*: the people of Ireland   *greasy till*: an image reflecting Yeats's dislike of contemporary Ireland's materialism; 'a little greasy huxtering nation' if 'the present intellectual movement failed'   *O'Leary*: John O'Leary (1830–1907), influenced by the Young Ireland movement, became identified with the Fenian movement which succeeded it. Arrested in 1865, he was condemned to twenty years' penal servitude but released after four years on condition that he kept out of Ireland for fifteen years. He lived in Paris and returned to Dublin in 1885; he lent Yeats books by Irish authors and translations of Irish literature and influenced his moving from his father's Home Rule views to more nationalist attitudes. Yeats saw him as belonging to the traditions of an older Irish nationalism, that of Henry Grattan (1746–1820), based on the reading of Homer and Virgil, and that of Thomas Davis, influenced by the idealism of the Italian idealist and patriot Giuseppe Mazzini (1805–72)   *the wild geese*: Irishmen who served in the armies of France (which had an Irish Brigade up to the Revolution), Spain and Austria, being excluded from holding commissions in the British Army as a result of the Penal laws passed after 1691   *Edward Fitzgerald*: Lord Edward Fitzgerald (1763–98), a romantic figure who served in America, became an MP for Kildare in the Irish Parliament (which sat in Dublin), then joined the United Irishmen in 1796, was president of its military committee and died of wounds received when he resisted arrest   *Emmet*: Robert Emmet (1778–1803) led an abortive revolt in 1803, was tried for high treason and publicly hanged in Dublin   *Tone*: Theobald Wolfe Tone (1763–98) was called to the Irish bar in 1789; he founded the United Irish Club, and he and his friends turned to France for help. He left Ireland for America, then was appointed adjutant-general in the French army, sailed with the French fleet in an abortive expedition to Ireland in 1796; in 1798 he was captured when a small French fleet was defeated at Lough Swilly. He was sentenced by a court martial in Dublin to be hanged but committed suicide in prison   *delirium*: Yeats is contrasting the 'delirium' of his past heroes with the uncultured excitement of his own time, probably using the word deliberately as a counter to Swinburne's use of it, attacking Yeats indirectly in *William Blake* (1966). See *NC*, p. 111   *You'd cry*: the modern middle classes of Ireland cannot understand the love these past heroes had for their country   *some woman's . . . hair*: 'We Irish', Yeats thought, 'had never served any abstract cause except that of Ireland', and that 'we personified by a woman'. The woman was Cathleen ni Houlihan; Yeats's own patriotic love for Ireland, linked with Maud Gonne through this image, is thus associated with that of the patriots of the past

P. 295   '**To a Shade**'   *the town*: Dublin   *thin Shade*: the ghost of Charles Stewart Parnell, leader of the Irish parliamentary party, repudiated by the English Prime Minister Gladstone and by many of the Irish party because of the disclosure of his affair with Mrs O'Shea. See notes on 'Come Gather Round Me, Parnellites', p. 385   *monument*: the Parnell monument at the northern end of O'Connell Street, Dublin   *gaunt houses*: of Dublin   *a man*: Sir Hugh Lane   *what*: the gift of French impressionist paintings he offered to Dublin (see note on 'To a Wealthy Man . . . Pictures', p. 382)   *an old foul mouth*: William Martin Murphy who had replied to Yeats's poem 'To a Wealthy Man . . . Pictures' from 'Paudeen's point of view'   *set the pack*: a reference to the influence of Murphy's two popular papers (the *Irish Independent* and the *Evening Herald*) and probably an echo of Goethe's description of the Irish as 'like a pack of hounds, always dragging down some noble stag' quoted by Yeats in *A*, p. 316   *Glasnevin* *coverlet*: Parnell was buried in Glasnevin cemetry, in north Co. Dublin, on 11 October 1891. See notes on 'Parnell's Funeral', p. 348

P. 296 'Easter, 1916' This poem records Yeats's reactions (he was staying with Maud Gonne MacBride at her house, Les Mouettes, at Colleville, Calvados, Normandy) to the Easter rising of 1916. The centre of Dublin was occupied on 24 April by about 700 republicans (members of the Irish Volunteers and the Irish Citizen Army) who held out until 29 April against British troops. After a series of courts martial from 3–12 May fifteen of the leaders were executed. From 1. 17 onwards Yeats is naming some of the leaders *them*: the revolutionaries *eighteen-century houses*: Dublin has many houses built of granite from the hills, others of limestone from the plains *the club*: probably the Arts Club, founded in Dublin in 1907 *That woman's days*: Countess Constance Markievicz, born a Gore-Booth of Lissadell, Co. Sligo, cf. 'In Memory of Eva Gore-Booth and Con Markievicz'. When they were both art students in Paris she married Casimir Dunin-Markievicz, a Polish landowner; she became an Irish nationalist in 1908, founded the Fianna, a nationalist boys' organisation, joined the Citizen Army, was a staff officer in the Rising and was sentenced to death. Her sentence commuted to life imprisonment, she was released in an amnesty in 1917. Imprisoned again in 1918, she became the first woman to be elected to the Westminster Parliament; she did not take her seat, but became shadow minister of Labour in Dail Eireann in 1919; she served gaol sentences in 1919, 1920 and 1923, having opposed the Treaty. She joined the Fianna Fail party and was elected to the Dail in 1927 *rode to harriers*: cf. 'On a Political Prisoner' *This man*: Patrick Pearse (1879–1916). He founded St Enda's School, was a member of the Irish Bar, an orator, who published poetry and prose in Irish and English. A leader of the IRB Section in the Irish Volunteers, he was in charge of the General Post Office in the Easter Rising in 1916. See notes on 'The Rose Tree', below *This other*: Thomas MacDonagh (1878–1916), a poet, dramatist, and critic who taught English literature at University College, Dublin *This other man*: Major John MacBride (1865–1916) who had fought against England in the Boer War; he married Maud Gonne in 1903 *most bitter wrong*: a reference to his behaviour after his marriage to Maud Gonne *near my heart*: Maud Gonne and Iseult *a stone*: a symbol for those who devote themselves to some cause without thought of life or love. The 'stone of the heart' (1.58) refers to Maud Gonne's devoting herself to revolutionary ideals *needless death*: there was initially little welcome for the Rising in Ireland, but the execution of the leaders altered this *may keep faith*: the Bill creating Home Rule for Ireland had been passed by Westminster in 1913, but suspended on the outbreak of the war in 1914; it was promised that it would be introduced after the war was over *their dream*: of an independent Ireland *Connolly*: James Connolly (1870–1916), a trade union organiser who founded the *Irish Worker*, organised the Citizen Army, and was Commandant General of the insurgent forces (the Citizen Army and Irish Volunteers combined as the Irish Republican Army) in Dublin in the 1916 Rising. He was wounded in the fighting and brought to his execution in a wheel-chair

P. 298 'The Rose Tree' *Pearse to Connolly*: see notes on 'Easter, 1916' above *our Rose Tree*: Ireland *our own red blood*: Pearse believed in the 'blood sacrifice', thought that 'the blood of the sons of Ireland' was needed for Ireland's redemption. This poem may have been influenced by a ballad 'Ireland's Liberty Tree' (the symbol derives from the 'arbres de la liberté' planted in France in 1790 to celebrate Revolution and Liberty) about the tree 'watered with tears of the brave' which also celebrates the martyr cult:

> The pure blood of Ireland's Martyrs
> gave it strength and it [the tree] shall never die

Another possible source is Aubrey De Vere's poem 'The Little Black Rose shall be red at last'

P. 299   'The Leaders of the Crowd'   *to keep their certainty*: 'In Poetry and Tradition', *E & I*, pp. 249–50, Yeats wrote that the political movement with which Maud Gonne was associated, finding it hard to build up any fine lasting thing, 'became content to attack little persons and little things'. He thought all movements were held together more by what they hate than by what they love   *gutter . . . Helicon*: this line contrasts gutter-press journalism and poetry. Yeats particularly disliked *Sinn Fein*, edited by Arthur Griffith; see notes on 'On those that hated "The Playboy of the Western World" 1907', p. 381. Helicon, a mountain in Boeotia in Greece, was sacred to the Muses. On it was Hippocrene, the fountain which rose from the ground when struck by a hoof of the winged horse Pegasus. ('Our colt' in 'The Fascination of What's Difficult'; the 'high horse' of 'Coole and Ballylee, 1931')   *the student's lamp . . . no solitude*: the lamp is the image in 'Ego Dominus Tuus', and 'The Phases of the Moon' of 'mysterious wisdom won by toil'. See also 'Meditations in Time of Civil War' II with the 'candle and written page'; 'that lamp' may link the Miltonic, Shelleyan and Yeatsian images of solitary study with the 'everlasting taper' in 'The Mountain Tomb'. The 'crowd' necessarily has none of the solitude necessary for achieving wisdom

P. 300   'On a Political Prisoner'   *She*: Countess Markievicz, then imprisoned in Holloway Gaol (for a second time, from May 1918 to March 1919) for being a Sinn Fein leader, having been making 'seditious speeches'   *Ben Bulben*: see note on 'Under Ben Bulben', p. 380. Cf. 'Easter, 1916'

P. 301   'Reprisals'   This poem was written for *The Nation* in 1921, but was withheld (see Jeffares, *M & P*, p. 328, fn 50); it was first published in *Rann. An Ulster Quarterly of Poetry*, Autumn 1948, and is not included in *CP*, nor in *PNE*, though it is in the *Variorum Edition of the Poems of W. B. Yeats* (1957). It is written about Major Robert Gregory. See notes on 'In Memory of Major Robert Gregory', p. 325 and 'An Irish Airman foresees his death', p. 344   *German planes*: Gregory was a pilot in the British Royal Flying Corps   *Italian tomb*: he was shot down in error on 23 January 1918 by an Italian pilot over Italy   *Kiltartan cross*: near Coole, Co. Galway   *the cause*: of the allies against the Germans   *a fine affair*: as a defence of small nations, the invasion of Belgium leading to the war   *half-drunk: . . . soldiery*: references to atrocities in Co. Galway in the 1920s

P. 301   'Should H. G. Wells afflict you'   Included in Yeats's 'Introduction to *Fighting the Waves*', *Dublin Magazine* April–June 1932, later in *Wheels and Butterflies* (1934)   *H. G. Wells*: H. G. Wells (1866–1946) the novelist, cast some of his work in the form of science fiction   *Science – opium of the suburbs*: a parody of Karl Marx's (1818–83) dictum that 'religion is the opium of the people'

P. 302   'Church and State'   this poem was entitled 'A Vain Hope' when first published; its imagery is based upon the Christian symbolism of the bread and wine deriving from the Last Supper, when 'as they were eating, Jesus took bread, and blessed and broke it; and he gave it to the disciples and said, take, eat; this is my body. And he took the cup, and gave thanks, and gave it to them, saying, Drink ye all of it; for this is my blood of the new testament, which is shed for many for the remission of sins'. (St Matthew XXVI, 26–28)

P. 302   'Come Gather Round Me, Parnellites'   *Parnellites*: followers of Charles Stewart Parnell; see notes on 'To a Shade', p. 383   *underground*: see notes on 'Parnell's Funeral', p. 348   *the might of England . . . a farmer's got*: a reference to Parnell's achievements as leader of the Irish party in the House of Commons and to his having been the first president of the Land League; the land war of 1879–1882 led to the eventual creation of a system of peasant proprietorship of the land. Parnell was imprisoned in 1881, released in 1882; the election of 1885 was a triumph for him and persuaded Gladstone that he should support Home Rule for Ireland   *loved a lass*:

after a special commission found letters accusing him of complicity in murder and outrage in the land war were forgeries, Parnell reached the summit of his career, but in 1890 he was named co-respondent by Captain Henry O'Shea in a divorce action against his wife Kathleen   *the Bishops and the party . . . sold . . . betrayed*: Parnell was repudiated by Gladstone and the Irish hierarchy. Yeats, influenced by Henry Harrison, *Parnell Vindicated: The Lifting of the Veil* (1931), published his views in 'Parnell', *Essays 1931–1936* (1937), p. 2: 'Captain O'Shea knew of their liaison from the first . . . he sold his wife for money . . . for £20,000 could Parnell have raised that sum, he was ready to let the divorce proceedings go, not against Parnell, but himself'

P. 304   'The Ghost of Roger Casement'   Sir Roger Casement (1864–1916), knighted for public services, retired from the colonial service in 1912, and joined the Irish National Volunteers in 1913. He went to Germany in 1914, tried unsuccessfully to enlist Irish prisoners of war to fight against the Allies, landed from a German submarine in Tralee, was arrested, tried for treason and hanged in Pentonville Gaol in 1916. His remains were reinterred in Glasnevin cemetry, Dublin, in 1965. This poem is complementary to 'Roger Casement', which was provoked by Yeats's reading William J. Maloney, *The Forged Casement Diaries* (1936). This book claimed that diaries written by Casement showing him to be a homosexual, which were circulated during his trial and subsequent appeals against his sentence, were forgeries. For background to that poem see *NC*, pp. 464–69. Casement's biographers Rene MacColl and Brian Inglis think that the diaries were probably authentic   *John Bull . . . India*: John Bull, popular name for the English nation. Dominion status for India (declared part of the British Empire when, in one of Disraeli's periods as Prime Minister, Victoria became Queen Empress in 1877) was not agreed until 1947   *a village church . . . family tomb*: an echo of Thomas Gray's (1716–71) 'Elegy written in a country churchyard'; the MSS versions of the poem echoed the Hampden and Milton (though not the Cromwell!) of Gray's poem. Casement had told his cousin, Gertrude Bannister, on her last visit to him in gaol that he wanted to be buried at Murlough Bay

P. 305   'Parnell'   see notes on 'To a Shade', p. 383 and on 'Come Gather Round me, Parnellites', p. 385

P. 305   'The O'Rahilly   *a 'the'*: 'the' is a hereditary title in Ireland, denoting the head of a clan   *Pearse and Connolly*: see notes on 'Easter, 1916', p. 384   *to great expense . . . Kerry men*: he was head of the O'Rahilly clan in Kerry; he had tried to stop the plans for the 1916 Rising by arguing vainly with Pearse and then by persuading Professor Eoin MacNeill (1867–1945), who had been elected chairman of the Council forming the Irish Volunteers in 1913, and was later chief of staff, to countermand the orders for the Rising. (These were given initially without MacNeill's knowledge to the Irish Volunteers, by the secret IRB membership of the movement, and with the support of Connolly and his Citizen Army.) The Rising, after Casement had been made captive and a German ship, the *Aud*, bringing arms had been scuttled off the Irish coast, seemed doomed to fail   *that he might be there*: the O'Rahilly took part in the fighting in Dublin in 1916; he was in the Post Office in Sackville (now O'Connell) Street and was killed in Henry Street, a street running at right angles to O'Connell Street

P. 307   'Politics'   The quotation from Thomas Mann (1875–1955), the German author, Yeats got from an article by the American poet Archibald MacLeish (1892–1982), 'Public Speech and Private Speech in Poetry', *Yale Review*, 27, 3 March 1938. Yeats liked the article because it commended his language as 'public'

APPENDIX I   YEATS'S TECHNIQUE AS A POET

I said 'A line will take us hours maybe;
Yet if it does not seem a moment's thought
our stitching and unstitching has been naught'

'Adam's Curse'

Yeats put a great deal of hard work into writing his poetry. He usually made prose drafts first, then verse drafts which he revised extensively. The manuscripts which survive provide clear evidence of the process of composition, and studies such as those listed in Section III of the Bibliography (see p. 420) indicate the complex process of selection, repetition, rejection or alteration that went to the making of a poem.* Yeats used to murmur or chant his verses aloud when composing them: Maud Gonne talked of him 'booming and buzzing like a bumble bee' when making a poem; and F. R. Higgins recorded Yeats telling him that most of his poems were composed to some vague tune, which Higgins described as a 'halting lilt'.

The poems were sometimes written in manuscript books, sometimes in loose-leaf notebooks and sometimes on scraps of paper. Yeats's handwriting can be virtually indecipherable; his sight, never good, became increasingly myopic, and towards the end of his life he often could not himself read what he had written. After he had completed his work on the verse drafts a poem could, he wrote to Dorothy Wellesley, 'come right with a click like a closing box,' but the process of finding how to close the box was usually a long one. Even when he had reached the apparently final stage of having a fair copy made he frequently altered the typewritten versions made by Mrs Yeats or a professional typist. And he was often not satisfied with poems when he saw them in print (they usually appeared for the first time in magazines). He had chanted the poems aloud as he wrote them and Mrs Yeats described how he subsequently 'sang his proofs and often forgot to consider whether song and printed word corresponded'. He continued to alter the texts of many of his poems in successive printings. The numerous revisions he made to the printed versions of the poems are recorded in *The Variorum Edition of the Poems of W. B. Yeats* (1957).

To discuss fully the variety of techniques to be found in the five hundred and seven poems included in *The Poems: A New Edition* – and Yeats wrote more poems than those included in this edition – would not be possible here, but the range of Yeats's poetic skills should be recognised. He used many verse forms: he was at home in the couplet, the quatrain, the ballad, the sonnet; he employed blank verse in some of his longer poems and in his plays; six, seven, eight, ten or twelve-line stanzas or longer single units were all at his command. By 1908 he could write in 'Words':

. . . I have come into my strength
And words obey my call.

---

* See also A. Norman Jeffares, 'Yeats and his Methods of Writing Verse', reprinted from *The Nineteenth Century and After*, March 1946 in *The Permanence* of Yeats, ed. James Hall and Martin Steinmann, New York, 1950; 1961, pp. 270–6.

The prose draft of this poem which states that Maud Gonne never understood his plans or nature or ideas ended with the remark: 'if she understood I should lack a reason for writing, and one can never have too many reasons for doing what is so laborious'.

The care Yeats took with technique can be seen in his use of rhyme. In the differing forms of his verse he employed a variety of rhyme schemes; while often using couplets or alternating rhyming lines in four-line stanzas, he developed more complex patterns of rhyme in longer stanzas. Throughout his career – he was writing verse for about fifty-eight years – and despite the changes in his style, he continued to practise his craft of rhyming. In his early poetry he was more regular. In the ballads, for instance, such as 'The Ballad of Moll Magee' he used the *abcb* scheme (it reappears naturally enough in the late poem 'Roger Casement' and in other late poems that deal with public themes in a manner reminiscent of street songs or broadsheets). In poems with four-line stanzas, such as 'When You are Old' he used an *abba* scheme. Early poems with eight-line stanzas such as 'The Pity of Love' have an *ababcbcb* scheme. There are variations in the schemes to be found in his twelve-line stanzas, such as the *ababcdcdefef* of 'A Dream of Death' and *abbacddceffe* of 'The Man who Dreamed of Fairyland', used a little later in 'The Unappeasable Host'. The two twenty-line stanzas of 'The Two Trees' have a subtle linkage created by the repetition of the rhyme of lines 13 and 15 of the first stanza in the corresponding lines of the second stanza. In the two stanzas the rhyme of the first four lines is repeated in the final four lines although in the second stanza, admittedly, the final four lines rhyme only if the rhyming vowel sound of 'wind' and 'unkind' is allowed to chime with 'guile' and 'while'. (Incidentally, Yeats nearly always rhymed 'wind' as if the vowel sound corresponded to that in 'find'.) Of the early poems only 'Fergus and the Druid' lacks a clear rhyme scheme.

More subtlety can be found, as might be expected, in some of the poems of *The Wind Among the Reeds*. For instance, 'The Everlasting Voices' uses an *abacbaca* scheme, while 'The Song of Wandering Aengus' has an *abcbdefe* scheme in its first stanza, and an *ababcdec* in its second. Simple rhyming schemes are used, however, in poems with complex symbolism, such as 'The Secret Rose'.

After the turn of the century there is a greater use of half-rhymes or off-rhymes. *The Green Helmet* has several examples of these, for instance, 'young' and 'wrong', 'ago' and 'do', 'gone' and 'bone'. And some poems in this volume depart from a strict pattern of rhyming. Irregular rhyming is used in the 'Introductory Rhymes' of *Responsibilities*, though Yeats does retain alternate rhymes in many of the poems in this volume. The presence of an unrhymed line, however, in some of the poems can be very effective, as in 'When Helen Lived', or 'A Coat' (where the emphasis is thus thrown on the word 'naked'). And the regularity of the three rhymes in each of the other four-line stanzas of 'Beggar to Beggar Cried' is relaxed in the outspoken second stanza, while 'Running to Paradise', which rhymes the fourth, fifth and sixth lines strictly in its first stanza, uses strict rhyme in only two of these three lines in the second, third and fourth stanzas.

By the time of writing the title poem of *The Wild Swans of Coole* Yeats carried a looser treatment of rhyme further. Here the third line in each of the five stanzas is not rhyming, though the final word of this line is in some cases repeated or rhymed internally in a succeeding line. (The first stanza repeats 'water' in its fifth line; the third stanza echoes 'twilight' with 'lighter' in its sixth line; the fourth stanza rhymes 'air' with the 'where' of its fifth line.)

In the six-line stanzas of 'Under the Round Tower' the first and third lines are unrhymed. There is an increase in half-rhymes, for instance in 'The Scholars', 'Lines written in Dejection' and 'Memory'. 'The Dawn' uses irregular rhyming as does 'Broken Dreams', while 'The People', 'Ego Dominus Tuus', 'A Prayer on going into my House' and 'The Phases of the Moon' avoid rhyme. But *The Wild Swans at Coole* contains a notable development, Yeats's elaborate use of the eight-line stanza in 'In Memory of Major Robert Gregory' with its rhyme scheme running *aabbcddc*, a scheme used earlier by the seventeenth-century poet Abraham Cowley in his 'Ode on the Death of Mr William Harvey'

(Yeats was patently considering past achievements in the genre of the elegy – and particularly elegies written by poets on poets). Milton's *Lycidas* was in his mind, obviously, and 'Shepherd and Goatherd', another of his poems of this period, a pastoral mourning the loss of Robert Gregory, was inspired by Spenser's *Astrophel*, a lament for Sir Philip Sydney, and to a lesser degree, by Virgil's Fifth Eclogue, itself probably founded on the 'Elegy on Daphnis' by Theocritus.

Many of the major poems of Yeats's maturity were written in eight-line stanzas in which the rhyme scheme differs from poem to poem. 'A Prayer for my Daughter', in *Michael Robartes and the Dancer*, uses the *aabbcddc* pattern first deployed in 'In Memory of Major Robert Gregory', as do 'The Tower. II' and 'Colonus' 'Praise' in *The Tower*. 'Sailing to Byzantium', however, has the classic pattern of *ottava rima*, an *abababcc* rhyme scheme, as have Sections I and IV of 'Meditations in Time of Civil War', 'Nineteen Hundred and Nineteen. I' and 'Among School Children'. 'Meditations in Time of Civil War. VII' uses the *ababcdcd* scheme; 'A Prayer for my Son' the *ababcddc*, while 'Two Songs for a Play' employs another symmetrical pattern with its *abbacddc* scheme.

The eight-line stanzas of *The Winding Stair* show similar variations. 'A Dialogue of Self and Soul' has an *abbacddc* scheme, 'Byzantium' the *aabbcddc* scheme of 'In Memory of Major Robert Gregory' while 'Coole Park 1929', 'Coole and Ballylee, 1931' and 'Vacillation. I and II', employ *ottava rima*, the *abababcc* scheme.

In his later verse Yeats also used *ottava rima* most successfully (often with half-rhymes) in his more serious poems such as 'The Gyres', 'The Municipal Gallery Revisited', 'The Statues' and 'The Circus Animals' Desertion'. There are other poems with loosely rhymed eight-line stanzas. Readers will notice variations of rhyme in poems with six, seven, nine, ten or twelve-line stanzas as well, while apart from those poems with consecutively or alternately rhyming lines, many not arranged in stanza form have a large diversity of rhyme schemes. There are also poems with irregular rhyming, though in general Yeats seems to have been happier with rhyme – his free verse was probably written under Ezra Pound's influence and as he was emerging from the period of writing his heroic verse plays for the Abbey Theatre.

Yeats's use of refrains occurs at intervals throughout his career. An early example can be found in 'The Madness of King Goll', *'They will not hush, the leaves a-flutter round me, the beech leaves old'*. The four italicised lines repeated at the end of each of the first three stanzas of 'The Stolen Child' serve in the fourth, when *'Come away, O human child!'* is altered to *'For he comes, the human child'*, as an apt conclusion to the fairies' appeal to the child. The effect of the last two italicised lines of each stanza in 'The Withering of the Boughs' – *'No boughs have withered because of the wintry wind/The boughs have withered because I have told them my dreams'* – is atmospheric, chorus-like and rather similar to the italicised stanzas repeated in 'The Happy Townland'. The last line of a stanza is repeated in several poems with a shift in emphasis in the final case, as in 'September 1913' where 'It's with O'Leary in the grave' finally alters, weightily, in the poem's last line to 'They're with O'Leary in the grave'. Poems probably written under the influence of Synge's plays, such as 'Beggar to Beggar Cried', and 'Running to Paradise', use the regularly repeated refrain as a motif, whereas in 'Easter 1916' the line 'A terrible beauty is born', used three times, builds up a cumulative effect, since each time it is used the meaning of the phrase is extended. The refrains in *Words for Music Perhaps* are repeated, perhaps to give the effect of musical accompaniment, for example, see 'Crazy Jane and the Bishop', 'Crazy Jane Reproved', 'Crazy Jane on the Day of Judgement', 'Crazy Jane on God', and 'Crazy Jane Grown Old looks at the Dancers'. The repeated line *Mad as the mist and snow* is, however, an integral part of the poem 'Mad as the Mist and Snow', as in a poem of the 1890s, 'Red Hanrahan's song about Ireland', where the last line of each stanza belongs to the preceding lines but is also an intensification, a concentration upon 'Cathleen, the daughter of Houlihan'. Several of the later poems were intended as songs, 'Three Marching Songs', 'Three Songs to the Same Tune', for instance. Yeats's use of the refrain increased in his latter years. Sometimes it was used ironically as counter-pointing to the stanzas preceding it, as in 'What Then?' (where the last line shifts emphatically) or to emphasise the poem's mood as in 'The Curse of Cromwell' with its stubborn stoicism:

> O what of that, O what of that,
> What is there left to say?

The refrain can be used ironically, as in 'The Statesman's Holiday' with its 'Tall dames go walking in grass green Avalon', or to give an air of authority, as in 'The Old Stone Cross', or to carry the main weight of the poem, as in 'The Ghost of Roger Casement'. Again, it appears in the style of a chorus in which an audience can join, as in 'The Pilgrim' with its fol de rol de rolly O preceded variously in the five stanzas by 'Is', 'But', 'Was', 'But', and 'Is' – the symmetry, as ever, is deliberately maintained.

Yeats sometimes rounded off his early poems by repeating the opening line of a poem at its conclusion, as in 'The Secret Rose', sometimes with a minor variation, as in 'The White Birds', 'The Lover tells of the Rose in his Heart, 'Peace' and 'Why should not Old Men be Mad?'. He also repeated the last lines of stanzas, as in 'The Ragged Wood', 'O Do Not Love too Long', 'The Mountain Tomb', 'Meditations in Time of Civil War. VI' (with its repeated 'Come build in the empty house of the stare'), and 'For Anne Gregory'.

More remarkable, however, is his use of the repetition of single words. A good example of this is to be found in the intensifying repetitions of 'Byzantium'. In the first stanza the definite article is repeated twice (lines 1 and 2) as is the indefinite article (line 5); 'All' is repeated (lines 6 and 7) and the definite article repeated again (line 8). This repetition creates a pattern within the stanza but the second stanza develops a further complex pattern through the repetition of nouns and 'more' in its first and second lines: 'an image, man or shade/Shade more than man, more image than a shade'. The repetition continues in the 'no' of line 5, and then is given a paradoxical enrichment in line 8 with 'death-in-life and life-in-death'. The third stanza carries on the process with its 'Miracle, bird or golden handiwork,/More miracle than bird or handiwork'; the golden bird and bough are contrasted with 'Common bird or petal' while the eighth line's 'complexities of mire and blood' echo the eighth line of the first stanza, 'The fury and the mire of human veins'. The paradox continues in the fourth stanza linked with alliteration and the repetition of 'flames' and the negative 'no . . . nor . . . Nor': 'Flames that no faggot feeds, nor steel has lit,/Nor storm disturbs, flames begotten of flame'.

The echoes and repetition continue: the spirits are 'blood begotten'; the 'all complexities' and the 'complexities of mire and blood' of the third stanza recur in the fourth, while 'An agony' is repeated in lines seven and eight, linked the second time to 'flame'. The image of the 'mire and blood' of the fifth stanza echoes the earlier imagery of the first and third stanzas. The repetition and alliteration of 'Spirit after Spirit' are echoed in the alliterative repetition of the 'smithies', the second instance echoing the 'golden' of the third stanza; the complexities are now 'bitter furies of complexities'; and continuity is established by the 'images' which 'Fresh images beget'. The final line with its repetition of 'That' catches up the dolphins of the beginning of the stanza and links the 'gong-tormented sea' with the earlier image of the 'great cathedral gong' which had set the opening tone of the poem. Yeats has linked the whole poem together most skilfully, enriched it in complexity, endowed it with an authoritative strength, and made excitingly vivid its memorable qualities, enhanced by the cumulative effect of repeated words and images that are held together by the poem's firm structure of rhythm and rhyme.

While his early poetry tended to be dominated by adjectives ('dreamy, dim, gentle, pale, bitter, murmuring, defeated, grey', etc.), in his middle period Yeats used articles, copulas and relative pronouns freely, and this gave his poetry much of its liveliness and its distinctive character. His early poetry used symbolism which probably relied too much on suggestion and was not initially explicit enough. Thus precise meanings of, say, the Rose, or the Boar without bristles, or the Shadowy Horses, would not have been clear to many readers at the time they were published because, in the words of 'To Ireland in the Coming Times', his

> . . . rhymes more than their rhyming tell
> Of things discovered in the deep . . .

The subject matter of Irish legends and mythology and of local west of Ireland folklore and belief in the supernatural were new enough to many of Yeats's readers, Irish as well as English, in the 1890s; the images which derived from his interest in magic and the occult were even less obvious. In one of his essays, however, 'The Philosophy of Shelley's Poetry' of 1900, he stressed the need for 'the poet of essence and pure ideas' (a description that might well have been applied to his own symbolism in the lyrical poetry of *The Rose* and *The Wind Among the Reeds*) to seek in 'the half lights that glimmer from symbol to symbol as if to the ends of the earth, all that the epic and dramatic poet finds of mystery and shadow in the accidental circumstance of life'. But while he realised not only the effect of Shelley's continually repeated symbols (some of which appear in his own poetry – the sea, the river, the fountain, the shells, the Mareotic lakes, the cave, the tower . . .) he considered the Morning and Evening Star to be 'the most important, the most precise of all Shelley's symbols, the one he uses with the fullest knowledge of its meaning'. This emphasis on Shelley's precision (which may not always be as clear to modern readers as it was to Yeats) reflects, perhaps, his own shifting away from the glimmering half-lights of the symbolism of his Celtic twilight poetry into the barer, more concrete symbolism he was to use so successfully in the poems written after his marriage, which first emerge in their full strength in *The Wild Swans at Coole* (1919). His own new symbolism, centring upon the tower, and upon the thought of *A Vision* with its images of the gyres and the phases of the moon, can carry more precision. This appears in personal poems, the antithesis between the claims of the soul and the body – the ageing body; in the continuing challenge, the philosophical problems presented by love – and hate; and in the wider contrasts between man's creative and destructive powers, the seemingly inevitable building up and knocking down of civilisations. This precision is achieved through repetition but Yeats has learned how to use symbolism so that its repetition has become a means rather than a mysterious essence, an end in itself.

The process begun in the public poems of *Responsibilities*, some of them published in the daily press, became polished by use: this was now a personal and highly effective rhetoric. The praise of the American poet Archibald MacLeish greatly pleased Yeats in his last years for it praised his poetry as 'public speech'.

What personal characteristics mark this kind of rhetoric in Yeats's middle and later poetry? Apart from the subtle use of rhyme and rhythm, the very deliberately chosen different kinds of repetition of words and phrases,* Yeats made two other features perhaps particularly his own. He uses the query with great effect and in many different ways – look, for instance, at 'The Wild Swans at Coole', 'The Scholars', 'Among School Children', 'What Then?'. The final question in a poem is sometimes partially a statement, or an ironic twist, or a heartfelt cry, or a confession of ignorance. He can employ questions most effectively to set the scene, or point a succeeding comment, or pose a philosophical problem. Consider, for example, the queries in 'Upon a House Shaken by the Land Agitation' (with its resumptive question in the last sentence), 'The People', 'Michael Robartes and the Dancer' (where the position of the question put by the man is significant), and 'Meditations in Time of Civil War. IV'. There is the haunting query of 'Nineteen Hundred and Nineteen. I':

---

* The scope of Yeats's repetition can be realised by an examination of *A Concordance to the Poems of Yeats*, ed. Stephen Maxfield Parrish (1963).

> But is there any comfort to be found?
> Man is in love and loves what vanishes,
> What more is there to say?

There is the challenge of 'The Tower II':

> Does the imagination dwell the most
> Upon a woman won or woman lost?

And there is the piercing, desperate, virtually final query of 'Man and the Echo'

> O Rocky Voice,
> Shall we in that great might rejoice?

    Another characteristic of Yeats's poetry is his mastery of the syntax that enabled him to place a complete sentence within a stanza and to weld these sentence-stanzas into the expression of a mood, a thought, an argument. The balance of the stanza within a poem is well-judged; the reader is left with a sense of satisfaction, a recognition of the aesthetic, architectonic integrity of the whole, the ordering that came from so much careful construction, the 'stitching and unstitching' that took so many hours of concentrated work.

    Yeats knew when to cut, in the interests of the taut structure and flow of a poem. If we look, for instance, at some of the complex variety of language and syntax in 'Sailing to Byzantium', we find that this poem uses treble movements. The human young, the birds, the salmon and mackerel are summed up as 'fish, flesh, or fowl'; the nature of life is 'Whatever is begotten, born, and dies', a phrase to be caught up in the final line's 'What is past, or passing, or to come'. The imperative verbs in the third stanza follow: 'Come . . . perne . . . and be'. These treble movements are balanced by dualism − the contrast of the old and young in the first stanza is followed by the balance of salmon-falls and mackerel-crowded seas; the second stanza uses apposition to give us the image of the aged man intensified by the image of a scarecrow; the verb 'sing' is intensified by repetition, while the repeated linkage of 'and' gives deliberation to the decision to move to Byzantium. The repetitions continue in the 'holy fire' of the third stanza; apposition is used to show that the living human heart is part of a dying animal: the fourth stanza carefully balances dual elements against the underlying threefold view of nature from which the poet seems to escape through the image of the artificial bird, and so 'form' is repeated, as is the 'gold' from the third stanza in the hammered gold and the gold enamelling, echoed in the golden bough, while the lords and ladies, the male and female elements of life, emphasise the flow of time 'past, or passing, or to come' − to experience which is the lot of 'whatever is begotten, born, and dies'. The *MSS* of the drafts of the poem include some material which Yeats rejected, and though a stanza such as the following (it was to be the second stanza) had great potential, its omission can be understood when we examine the closely compressed texture which gives the completed poem its intensity:

> I therefore travel towards Byzantium
> Among these sun brown pleasant mariners
> Another dozen days and we shall come
> Under the jetty and the marble stair

This version was altered in detail, and then read:

> But now these pleasant dark skinned mariners
> Carry me towards that great Byzantium
> Where all is ancient, singing at the oars
> That I may look in the great churches dome
> On gold-embedded saints and emperors
> After the mirroring waters and the foam
> Where the great drowsy fins a movement rise
> Of fish that carry souls to Paradise

Various alterations moved the poem in a new direction as Yeats worked on it, away from Byzantium to the struggle between the intellect or soul and the ageing body.

There are so many more aspects of Yeats's style to notice: his use of proper names, both separately and conjointly, as in the Anglo-Irish writers grouped in 'Blood and the Moon'; his creation of characters to suit particular subjects, for example, Hanrahan, Crazy Jane or Tom O'Roughley, Malachi Stilt-Jack; the emphasis conferred by his use of the emphatic 'That', as in 'That is no country for old men' in 'Sailing to Byzantium'; his selection of a particular moment or gesture, as in the 'Sound of a stick upon the floor' in 'Coole and Ballylee, 1931', or in the tale of the hysterical women in 'Lapis Lazuli'; his memories encapsulated in evocative, economical imagery, setting a scene for contemplation, as in the opening lines of 'In Memory of Eva Gore-Booth and Con Markciewicz'; the reversal of the earlier romantic imagery, as when the fairy Niamh' of the early 'The Wanderings of Oisin' becomes 'Man-picker Niamh' in 'News for the Delphic Oracle'; the elevation of his friends into larger than life stature as in 'Beautiful Lofty Things': 'All the Olympians; a thing never known again'.

The style itself has become elevated, lofty, though still rooted in the vigour of direct speech, still using the interrogatives, the imperatives, and the great affirmations which mark the art of the rhetoric, which remains Yeats's supreme human attribute, the communication of his highly idiosyncratic thoughts and ideas, his moods of joy and despair.

APPENDIX II GLOSSARY OF IRISH PEOPLE AND PLACES IN THE POEMS

This glossary has frequently drawn on an admirable reference work by James P. McGarry, *Place Names in the Writings of W. B. Yeats* (1976) for information on the original Irish names of places mentioned in the poems. The names of Irish persons mentioned are also included. Other names and places are explained in the Notes.

Aedh [Aodh]	Irish form of Hugh; but also the Irish for fire. Aedh was a personage in Yeats's *The Secret Rose* (1897)
Aengus	Yeats's spelling of Aonghus (modern Oengus), the 'Master of Love', also known as Angus Og. He was Niamh's father, the lover of Caer, and lived at Brugh-na-Boinne
Ailell	husband of Maeve, queen of Connacht
Aillinn	legendary lover of Baile; they were turned into swans by Aengus
Almhuin	Sid Almhain, the Hill of Allen, Co. Kildare, site of Finn MacCool's palace; one of the three residences of the kings of Leinster
Alt	a glen on Knocknarea, mountain in Co. Sligo
Aodh	Aodh, Hugh
Aoife	(i) a Scottish warrior-queen, mother of Cuchulain's son, whom he killed not knowing who he was (ii) 'Rock nurtured' Aoife, a woman of the sidhe, a 'malignant phantom', probably Aoibhell of Craigh Liath, the Grey Rock, Killaloe, Co. Clare
Aoibhill/Aoibhell	see Aoife
Ardan	(i) brother of King Eochaid (Ailell Anguba in the original tale) (ii) brother of Naoise, one of the sons of Usna/Usnach
Armstrong, an	Yeats's grandfather, the Rev. William Butler Yeats, married Jane Grace Corbet in 1835: she was the daughter of William Corbet and Grace Armstrong; both Corbet and Armstrong families had military traditions
Artisson, Robert	Robert, son of Art, an evil spirit in Kilkenny, who was the incubus of Dame Alice Kyteler in the fourteenth century
Aslauga Shee	an sluagh sidhe, the fairy host of the mound
Baile	(i) Baile, son of Buan and Aillin, the daughter and heir of Lugaidh (Lugaidh was the son of Curoi MacDaire, a King of Munster), the lover of Aillinn (ii) Traigh mbaile, Baile's Strand, near Dundalk, Co. Louth, near Cuchulain's fort
Ballygawley Hill	Baile Dhalaigh, Ballydawley, O'Daly's townland, about five miles from Sligo
Ballylee	Baile an Liagh, Baile ui Laoi, the townland of Ballylee, Co.

	Galway, about three miles from Gort, Co. Galway. Yeats's tower, Thoor, is situated in it
Balor	a Fomorian king who led the hosts of darkness at the battle of Moytura (Magh Tuiridh, the plain of the pillars, or Magh Turach, the towered plain) near Sligo. The battle marked the final overthrow of the Firbolgs by the Tuatha de Danaan
Barach	a Red Branch warrior who, at Conchubar's instigation, asked Fergus to a feast when he was in charge of Deirdre, Naoise and his brothers. The absence of Fergus, the safe conduct, led to the murder of the men
bawn	a fortified enclosure
bell-branch	a legendary branch, the shaking of which 'cast all men into a gentle sleep'
Ben Bulben	Beann Ghulben, Binn Gulbain, Gulban's peak, mountain in Co. Sligo
Bera of Ships	Beare Island, Bantry Bay, Co. Cork
Berkeley	George Berkeley (1685–1753), Bishop of Cloyne and distinguished philosopher
Biddy	pet form of Bridget, sometimes used contemptuously
Billy, King	William of Orange, William III (1650–1702)
Blanid	a daughter of the Lord of Manainn, she was claimed as a prize by Curaoi Mac Daire who helped Cuchulain in the sacking of Manainn. She was killed by Curaoi's harper Feircheirtne in revenge for conspiring with Cuchulain to kill Curaoi
boreen	boirin, a lane
Boyne	An Bhoinn, the river Boyne, which enters the sea near Drogheda, Co. Louth. The river's goddess Boann and her husband Dagda lived at Bruigh na Boinne, New Grange. The battle of the Boyne, at which James II was defeated, took place in 1690
Bran	one of Finn's cousins; his aunt Uirne was transformed when pregnant; Finn's other hound cousin was Sceolan, their third whelp was Lomair
Bride's well	Tober Bride/Tubberbride, a townland in Collooney, Co. Sligo, named after a holy well dedicated to Saint Brigid
Bridget	newly married bride of O'Driscoll, character in 'The Host of the Air', founded on a ballad
Bruen, Paddy	imagined character
Bual	Probably Ethal (or Etal) Anbuail (or Anbual), father of Caer
Bual's hill	Anbual's hill, probably the residence of Anbuail, Sid Uamain, the fairy mount of Uaman in Connacht
Bull, brown and bull, white-horned	the brown bull of Cooley, coveted by Maeve to replace her own white-horned bull which went to her husband's herds. *The Tain bo Cuailgne* arose from the seizure of this bull
Burke	Edmund Burke (1729–97), Irish statesman, author and orator
Butler	see Ormondes
Byrne, Billy	William Byrne (?–1798) a member of the Leinster Directorate of the United Irishmen.

Byrnes	a Wicklow family
Caoilte	Caoilte MacRonain (Ronan), Finn's favourite warrior and a friend of Finn's son Oisin. He drove the gods out of their liss or fort at Ossory (or Asseroe) and he appears as a 'flaming man' in 'The Hosting of the Sidhe'
Casement	Sir Roger Casement (1864–1916) retired from the British Colonial Service in 1912, joined the Irish National Volunteers in 1913, tried to enlist Irish prisoners in Germany for an Irish rising, landed in Ireland from German submarine, was arrested and hanged in 1916
Cashel/the Rock of Cashel	Caiseal, Cashel of the Kings, Cashel of the Steps, Co. Tipperary, at one time capital of Munster, an imposing rock site with a round tower, Cormac's chapel and a ruined cathedral on it
Castle Dargan	Caiseal Locha Deargain, the stone fort of Loch Dargain, near Ballygawley, Co. Sligo
Cathleen-ni-Houlihan	a female figure who traditionally symbolises Ireland
Clare	an clar, the stone (corner) of contention, name of Irish county taken from small village, now Clarecastle
Clare-Galway	Baile an Chlair, the townland of the Plain, Co. Galway
Cloone, bog of	near Gort, Co. Galway, where one of the country beauty Mary Hynes's admirers accidentally drowned himself on his way to see her
Clooth na Bare	Cailleach Beare, the old woman Bare. The Cailleach Beare's house is an ancient monument on Ballygawley Mountain, Co. Sligo. Yeats describes her seeking a lake deep enough to drown her fairy life and finding it in Lough Ia (Lough Dagea, the lake of the two geese) on Sliabh da-En, Slieve Daene, the mountain of the two birds, Co. Sligo
Cloyne	Cluain-uamha (or Cluain more), the meadow of the cave, Co. Cork, name of diocese of which George Berkeley was bishop
Comedian, the Great	Yeats's term for Daniel O'Connell (1775–1847), Irish political leader who won Catholic emancipation in 1829
Conall Carnach	One of Conchubar's twelve chief heroes, known as the Victorious
Conan	Conon Maol, Conan the baldheaded, a braggart Fenian warrior, described by Yeats as the Thersites of the Red Branch cycle of tales
Conchubar	Conor MacNessa, King of Ulster in the Red Branch cycle of tales
Connacht	Coicid Connacht, fifth of Connacht, one of the fifths, into which the legendary Firbolgs divided Ireland. The name may derive from the descendants of Conn the Hundred Fighter who settled there, or from a tribe called Ulnegmacht who were aboriginal dwellers there
Connemara	Conmaicne Mara, an area in Co. Galway named after the descendants of Conmac, one of the sons of Maeve and Fergus

	MacRoy. He was known as Conmaicne, and a branch of his family as Conmaicne Mara, the Hounds of the Sea
Connolly, James	(i) James Connolly (1868–1916), socialist leader, organiser of the Citizen Army, executed by firing squad for his part in the 1916 rising (ii) 'the player Connolly', an abbey actor, shot in the fighting on Easter Monday 1916
Coole/Coole Park	an cuil, the corner, near Gort, Co. Galway. The Gregory estate of Coole Park was purchased in 1768; the house was pulled down in 1941
Cormac	Cormac MacCarthy, King of Desmond or South Munster, who had a chapel constructed in the twelfth century on the Rock of Cashel
Cormac's ruined house	the twelfth-century chapel on the Rock of Cashel, Co. Tipperary
County of the Young	see Tir-na-nOg
Crazy Jane	invented character, based on a real person, 'Cracked Mary' who lived near Gort, Co. Galway
Crevroe	Craobh Ruadh, a building at Emain Macha, in which the Red Branch heroes lived
Cromlech	a neolithic construction of stones, usually with one large horizontal stone resting upon three or four smaller vertical stones
Cro-Patrick	Croagh Patrick, Patrick's Heap, a mountain near Westport, Co. Mayo, site of an annual pilgrimage. St Patrick is reputed to have fasted on its summit and when there to have banished snakes from Ireland
Cruachan	Cruacha, Uaimh Cruacha, near Tulsk, Co. Roscommon, named after Cruatha, mother of Maeve. It was the capital of Connacht, a royal site and the burial ground associated with the *Tain bo Cuailgne*
Cuchulain	Cu Culann, the hound of Culain, a name given to the Red Branch hero, also called the Hound of Ulster. He was the son of Sualtim and Dechtire (Conor Macnessa's (Conchubar's) sister); at the age of seven he made his way to Conchubar's palace at Emain Macha and later in self-defence killed the hound of Culain the Smith. In compensation the boy offered to protect Culain's possessions and his herds and was consequently called Cuchulain by Cathbad the druid
Cullinan, Shemus	imagined character
Cummen/Cummen Strand	Cuimin, the little common, between Strandhill and Sligo Town, Co. Sligo
Danaan	of the Tuatha de Danaan, see Sidhe and Tuatha de Danaan
Dargan, Castle	see Castle Dargan
Davis	Thomas Davis (1814–45), Irish poet and nationalist, founded *The Nation* newspaper in 1842 and led the Young Ireland Party

Dean, the	*see* Swift
Derg, Lough	a small lake on the borders of Co. Donegal and Co. Fermanagh; an island is known as St Patrick's Purgatory. (He was alleged to have fasted there and had a vision in a cave of the next world.) It is the site of a famous annual pilgrimage
de Valéra	Eamon de Valéra (1882–1975), revolutionary, scholar, politician, and President of Ireland
Doe, Paddy	invented character
Dooney/Dooney Rock	Dun Aodh, Aodh's (Hugh's) Fort, on the shore of Lough Gill, Co. Sligo, a place where, in Yeats's youth, James Howley, a blind fiddler, played the music for outdoor dancing
Down, County	Irish county; the poet's grandfather, Rev. William Butler Yeats, was curate at Moira and Rector at Tullylish in that county
Druid	wiseman, magician, soothsayer
Drumahair/Dromohair/Dromahair	Drom-dha-eithiar, the ridge of the two demons, Co. Leitrim, at the Leitrim end of Lough Gill, the site of O'Rorke's Castle and banqueting hall
Drumcliff/Drumcliffe	Druim Chliabh, the ridge of the hazels, Co. Sligo, at the foot of Ben Bulben near the mouth of the Glencar Valley. It was the site of a monastery founded by Saint Columkille in 575. There remain part of a round tower, a high cross and the shaft of an older cross in the churchyard where Yeats is buried along with his grandfather, Rev. John Yeats (1774–1846) who was rector of the parish
Dublin merchant	Yeats's paternal great-great grandfather Benjamin Yeats (1750–95) who married Mary Butler (1751–1834)
Dun	a fort
Echtge	Sliabh [Sleev] Echte (Aughty), a mountain range running from Loughrea, Co. Galway, to near Lough Derg, Co. Clare; it was named after Echte of the Tuatha de Danaan, whose marriage dowry it was
Edain	Edain (Etain) Echraide whom Midhir (already married to Fuamnach) took to wife. She was driven out of Bri Leith by a druid's spells at Fuamnach's request, and Aengus (Angus Og) looked after her; Fuamnach turned her into a fly. Aengus struck off Fuamnach's head and searched for Etain who was blown about for seven years before being drunk in wine by Etar's wife who bore her as a daughter nine months later. She was again called Etain, and married Eochaid Fiedlech (later Airem) the High King. Midhir, king of the Sidhe, appeared to her when Eochaid's brother Ailell was ill, and appealed to her to return to him. He played chess with Eochaid, won a kiss from Etain in the third game, and took her away. Eventually she was brought back to Tara after Eochaid had besieged and dug into Midhir's mound at Bri Leith (called after Leith, son of Celtchar of Cualir, a young man of the Sidhe)

Eire	Irish for Ireland. It was originally the name of a queen of the Tuatha de Danaan
Emain Macha	Emain Macha, Macha's Height, the capital of Uladh (Ulster) near modern Armagh, founded by Macha of the Golden Hair, queen of Cimbaeth, King of Ulster. For more than six hundred years it continued to be the residence of the Ulster Kings
Emer	Cuchulain's wife, daughter of Forgall Manach
Emmet	Robert Emmet (1778–1803), United Irishman, who was publicly hanged after the failure of the rebellion he led in 1803
Emmet's friend	Rev. John Yeats (1774–1896), Yeats's great grandfather, rector of Drumcliff, Co. Sligo
Enniscrone	Inis Crabhann, the promontory of Crone, a seacoast village in Co. Sligo where Yeats's sister Susan Mary 'Lily' (1866–1949) was born
Eochaid, King	Eochaid Airem, a High King of Ireland (Yeats's note gives the pronunciation of his name as 'Yohee'). He was called Airem ('of the plough') because he taught his people to yoke their oxen by the neck and shoulder as the Sidhe did. *See also* Edain
Esserkelly plain	Esirtkelly/Dysert Cheallagh/Disert Ceallagh, Ceallagh's hermitage near Ardrahan, Co. Galway, named after St Ceallagh, eldest son of Eoghan Bel (see Knocknarea)
Fand	Fand was the daughter of Aedh Abratane, wife of Mannannan MacLir, god of the sea. She was loved for a time by Cuchulain after she had enchanted him. She returned to Mannannan and the druids made Cuchulain and his wife Emer forget the affair
father, my	John Butler Yeats (1839–1922), barrister, artist and conversationalist
Fenians, the	Yeats explained them as 'the great military order of which Finn was chief'. Their deeds are collected in the Fenian or Ossianic cycle of tales
Fergus	Fergus MacRoigh (MacRoy), king of Ulster, married to Ness/Nessa, renounced his kingdom for a year in favour of his stepson Conor MacNessa (Conchubar) but did not regain it. He became Maeve's lover later
Ferguson	Sir Samuel Ferguson (1810–1886) Irish poet, translator, antiquarian
findrinny	findruine, an alloy (white bronze)
Finn	Finn MacCumhail (MacCool) leader of the Fenians, killed on the Boyne 283AD
Firbolgs	legendary invaders of Ireland (Fir, man; Builg, god of lightning) who partitioned Ireland into five provinces ruled by the five sons of Dela who led them to Ireland from the Mediterranean. They were at the peak of their power *c.* 300BC, and were defeated at the Battle of Moytura
Fitzgerald	Lord Edward Fitzgerald (1763–98), soldier in British army, served in US and Canada, joined United Irishmen, headed a

military Committee planning 1798 rising, died of wounds incurred when resisting arrest

French   Mrs French (*née* O'Brien) lived at Peterswell, Co. Galway in the eighteenth century

Gabhra   site of battle, near Garristown, north Co. Dublin, in which the Fenians were heavily defeated

Gallery, the   the National Gallery of Ireland, Merrion Square, Dublin

Galway   Cathair na Gaillimh [Gol-yiv], Galway the city of the Tribes, west coast city and seaport

Gap of the Wind   *see* Windy Gap

Gill, Michael   invented character

Glasnevin coverlet   Glas-Naeidhen, Naeidhe's little stream, Glasnevin, Co. Dublin, site of Dublin's main cemetry, where Parnell was buried

Glencar/Glen-çar/   An Chairthe, Gleann-an Chairthe, the Glen of the standing
Glencar Lough   Stone, Co. Sligo

Glendalough   Glendalocha, the Glen or valley of the two lakes, Co. Wicklow; site of St Kevin's hermitage, with ruined churches, crosses and a round tower

Goban   Goibniu/Goibhniu, the god of the Smiths, who made and repaired weapons for the Tuatha de Danaan before the battle of Moytura

Goban's mountain top   Sliagh Anieran, the iron mountain, Co. Leitrim

Goldsmith   Oliver Goldsmith (1728–74) Irish author

Gonne   Maud Gonne (1866–1953) revolutionary, met Yeats in 1889, had two children by Lucien Millevoye, married John Mac-Bride 1903; their son Sean was born 1904; she separated from MacBridge 1905; arrested 1918, in Holloway gaol six months, later lived in Dublin

Gore-Booth   the Gore-Booth family owned Lissadell, Co. Sligo, from early in the eighteenth century. In 1894–5 Yeats visited the Gore-Booth sisters, Constance (1868–1927) who married Casimir de Markievicz, and Eva (1870–1926)

Gort   Gort-Innse-Guaire: the island field of Guaire (*see* Guaire), a market town in Co. Galway, two miles south of Coole Park

Grania   she fled with Diarmid (Dermot) to escape the love of Finn, then aged; in Standish O'Grady's version of the tale she returns to Finn after Diarmid was killed in Sligo

Grattan   Henry Grattan (1746–1820), Irish parliamentarian and orator, after whom 'Grattan's Parliament' was named

Great Plain, the   the great plain of the other world, the Land of the Dead and Happy

Green Lands   the Greenlands, unfenced part of Rosses Point, Co. Sligo, sandhills stretching inland from Deadman's Point

Gregory   Anne Gregory (*b.* 1911) daughter of Robert and granddaughter of Lady Gregory. Lady Isabella Augusta (1852–1932), Irish authoress and friend of Yeats, co-Director of the Abbey Theatre with Yeats and Synge. Robert Gregory (1881–1918),

RFC pilot, only child of Lady Gregory, killed in action over Italy

Grey Rock, the — Craig Liath, the grey stone, near Killaloe, Co. Clare, the house of Aoibheal (whom Yeats called Aoife in 'The Grey Rock') of the Sidhe

Griffith — Arthur Griffith (1871–1922) Irish political leader and journalist, led plenipotentiaries to negotiations which resulted in the Anglo-Irish Treaty of December 1921

Guaire — a sixth-century king of Connacht, who lived at Gort, Co. Galway

Hanrahan — Red Hanrahan, an invented character in Yeats's *Stories of Red Hanrahan*, a poet probably founded on Eoghan Ruadh O'Suilleabhain (1748–84), a lyric and satiric Irish poet

Hart Lake — originally Loch Minnaun, called Hart Lake after the family living near it, in the Ox Mountains, Co. Sligo

Hart, Peter — imagined character

Heber — one of the sons of Miled: he gained the two provinces of Munster, his brother Leinster and Connacht, Ulster being given to Eimher, the Son of Ir, another son of Miled

Henry Street — Dublin street running at right angles to Sackville (now O'Connell) Street

Houlihan — father of Cathleen (see Cathleen ni Houlihan)

House, an old/A small old — Riversdale, Rathfarnham, Co. Dublin

Howth — the name (pronounced Hoth) is derived from Danish Hovud, the Irish name being Ben Eadair, Eadar's peak. Howth is a peninsula forming the northern arm of Dublin bay

Hyde — Douglas Hyde (1860–1949) poet, translator, founder of the Gaelic League and first president of Ireland

Innisfree — Inisfraoich/Inisfree, the heathery island, in Lough Gill, Co. Sligo

Invar Amargin — The mouth of the river Avoca, Co. Wicklow; landing place of the druid Amergin who came to Ireland with the Milesians

Ith — Magh Itha the valley of the Lagan river, Co. Donegal; named after Ith, a Milesian, the 'first of the Gael to get his death in Ireland'

Kerry — Ciarraighe, Kerry, Irish county, named after the Lady Ceasair, an invader, who landed at Dunmore, Co. Kerry

Kiltartan/Kiltartan Cross — townland near Gort, Co. Galway, after some of which Lady Gregory's books (and her prose style) are named

Kilvarnet — Cill Bhearnais, the Church in the gap, a townland near Ballinacarrow, Co. Sligo, which contains the ruins of a church

Kinsale — Cionntsaile, the head of the sea, seaport in Co. Cork

Knockfefin — Sliabh na mban Feimhinn, the mountain of the women of the Feimhenn (Femen), Co. Tipperary, a fairy place called Sid ar Femen, the home of Bodb Derg, son of Dagda where the Sidhe enchanted Finn MacCool. It is now known as Slievenamahon. The women, Te and Men, were wives of two bards of the Tuatha de Danaan

Knocknarea	Cnoc na Riaghadh, Cnoc na Riogh, the hill of the king (or, less likely, the hill of the execution). A mountain in Co. Sligo. A cairn on its summit is reputedly the burial place of Queen Maeve, but more likely to have been that of Eoghan Bel, the last pagan king of Connacht, whose body was later buried by his enemies face down near Sligo. Maeve is more likely to have been buried at Cruachan, at Reilig na Riogh, the royal burial place
Kyteler Lady	Lady Alice Kyteler, member of an Anglo-Norman family in Kilkenny, four times married, and accused of sorcery, and of having relations with an incubus, Robin, son of Art
Laban	a sister of Fand, the wife of Mannannan MacLir; she was changed into an otter by her magic well when she neglected it
Land of the Tower	possibly the tower or house of glass belonging to Aengus. It may be Toraigh, Tory island, a place of Towers, Co. Donegal
Lane-under-wave	Tir-fa-thon, an enchanted underworld beneath the sea
Lane	Sir Hugh Lane (1875–1915) art collector and critic who offered his collection of modern paintings to Dublin
Liss	a fort
Lissadell	lis-a-doill, the fort of the blind man, Co. Sligo; the house owned by the Gore-Booth family was built there in 1832
Lomair	one of Oisin's hounds, named in 'The Wanderings of Oisin' with Bran and Sceolan, one of their three whelps. Bran and Sceolan were Finn's cousins
Lough Derg	see Derg, Lough
Loughlann waters	Lochlann, norse/scandinavian waters, the North Sea
Lugnagall	Lug na nGall, the hollow of the strangers (not, as Yeats translates it, the 'steep place' of the strangers) a townland in Glencar Valley, Co. Sligo, at the foot of Cope's mountain
Lavery	Lady Hazel Lavery (d. 1935) an American painter, 2nd wife of Sir John Lavery; her portrait appeared on Irish banknotes from 1923. Sir John Lavery (1856–1941), successful painter, famous for his conversation pieces
MacBride	John MacBride (1865–1916) fought in Boer War against the British, married Maud Gonne in 1903, executed for taking part in 1916 Rising
MacBride	Maud Gonne MacBride, see Maud Gonne
MacDonagh	Thomas MacDonagh (1878–1916) a poet and critic; executed in 1916 for taking part in the Rising
MacNessa	Conor MacNessa (Conchubar) King of Ulster, leader of the Red Branch knights
Maeve	Queen of Connacht, married to Ailill; had love affair with Fergus. Her wish to outdo Ailill led her to want the Brown Bull of Cooley and this led to the war celebrated in the *Tain bo Cuailgne*
Magh Ai	Machaire Connacht, the great plain dominated by Cruachan in Co. Roscommon
Magee, Moll	invented character

Maines	Maeve's son, married to Ferbe, killed by Conchubar
Maines, the children of the	usually considered the children of Maeve and Ailill, but they could be the children of Maeve's son Maines and Ferbe
Malachi (Stilt Jack)	biblical name; Malachi was a fifth-century Hebrew prophet. Yeats uses the name for a circus clown
Mangan	James Clarence Mangan (1803–49), Irish poet
Mannannan	Mannannan MacLir, god of the sea, husband of Fand
Mayo	Mayo, the plain of the Yew trees, a western Irish county which derives its name from a village where St Colman founded a monastery in the seventh century
Middleton, the smuggler	William Middleton (?1770–1832), Yeats's maternal great grandfather
Midhir/Midir	a king of the Sidhe who was in love with Edain, King Eochaid's wife
Midhir's wife	(i) Fuamnach, killed by Aengus for her treatment of Etaine/Edain (ii) see Edain
Mitchel	John Mitchel (1815–75) wrote for The Nation, founded the United Irishman, arrested in 1848, sentenced to fourteen years' transportation, escaped from Van Dieman's Land (Tasmania)
Mocharabuiee	Machaire Bui, Magheraboy, the yellow plain, south west of Sligo town
Mooneen	Moneen, moinin, the little bog, near Esserkelly, by Ardrahan, Co. Galway
Mourteen	Irish name
Moytura	Magh Tuireadh, the plain of the pillars (or Magh Turach, the towered plain) Co. Sligo, site of defeat of Firbolgs by Tuatha de Danaan
Municipal Gallery, the	situated in the former Charlemont House, Parnell Square, Dublin
Murrough	Murrough (Murchad) son of King Brian Boru, who killed Earl Sigurd in the Battle of Clontarf (1014) but was himself mortally wounded by Anrad the Dane
Naoise	Naoise, the son of Usna, ran away with Deidre whom Conor intended to marry: accompanied by his brothers Ainnle and Ardan they went to Scotland; returned under Fergus's safe conduct. The sons of Usna were killed treacherously by Conchubar
Nessa	Ness/Nessa; mother of Conchubar/Conor, she cheated Fergus her husband into giving up the kingdom to his step-son Conor
Niam	Niam/Niamh, the fairy princess who brought Oisin to the underworld where he stayed three hundred years. She was the daughter of Aengus
O'Byrnes	a Co. Wicklow family
O'Driscoll	an invented character, in 'The Host of the Air', a poem founded on an old ballad; he lost his wife Bridget to the fairies

O'Duffy	Eoin O'Duffy (1892–1944), first commissioner of the Garda Siochana 1922–33; he led an Irish Brigade to fight for France in the Spanish Civil War
Ogham	an ancient alphabet of twenty characters
O'Grady	Standish James O'Grady (1846–1928), historian and novelist, whose writings awakened a sense of the epic past of Ireland
O'Higgins	Kevin O'Higgins (1892–1927) Minister of Justice in the Irish Free State, took a strong line against the Republicans in the Civil War and was assassinated in 1927
Oisin	son of Finn, leader of the Fenians, and Saeve of the Sidhe. Yeats described him as the poet of the Fenian cycle. In 'The Wanderings of Oisin' he spent three hundred years visiting the other world with Niamh, a fairy princess
old queen	Macha, who measured the circumference of Emain Macha, the town she was founding, with the pin of her brooch, enclosing eighteen acres of land
O'Leary	John O'Leary (1830–1907), a Fenian, sentenced to twenty years' imprisonment, who was released after serving four on condition he did not return to Ireland, spent his exile in Paris, returned to Dublin in 1885
ollave	ollamh, ollave, a learned person; the equivalent of the holder of a doctorate; there were ollaves of the different professions; their courses lasted twelve years
O'Rahilly	the O'Rahilly (1875–1910), head of a Co. Kerry clan, was shot in the fighting during the 1916 Rising
Orchil	a Fomorian sorceress
Ormondes	members of the ducal family of the Butlers, descended from Theobald Walter ('Le Botiller', butler to Prince John), who was the first of the family to settle in Ireland
O'Roughley, Tom	invented character
Oscar	son of Oisin; he was killed at the Battle of Gabhra near Garristown, Co. Dublin, in 824
Oscar	Oscar Wilde (1854–1900) Irish dramatist, poet, critic and wit
Pairc-na-lee	Pairc na laoi/laoigh the park or field of the calves
Parnell	Charles Stewart Parnell (1846–1891) Protestant Irish landowner and statesman who led the Irish party at Westminster most successfully; it split when he was named co-respondent in the O'Shea divorce case of 1890, and married Mrs O'Shea in 1891
Parnellites	followers of Charles Stewart Parnell
Patrick	Saint Patrick (d?490), a native of Roman Britain, captured by Irish raiders, who escaped from slavery in Antrim and subsequently returned to begin the conversion of Ireland to Christianity. 17 March is annually celebrated as his and the national festival
Paudeen	diminutive of Padhraig, Patrick; a contemptuous name
Pearse	Patrick (Padraig) Henry Pearse (1879–1916) educationalist,

	writer and revolutionary, condemned to death by court martial and executed for leading the Easter 1916 Rising
Place of the Strangers, the	*see* Steep Place . . . Strangers
Steep Plain	
Plain, the Great	*see* Great Plain, the
Pollexfen	George Pollexfen (1839–1910) Yeats's maternal uncle, a hypochondriac who lived in Sligo, interested in horses and occultism. 'An old cross Pollexfen' probably William Pollexfen (1811–1892) the 'silent and fierce old man' of 'Introductory Rhymes', Yeats's maternal grandfather, a sea captain and merchant, who lived in Sligo
Post Office, the	the General Post Office, Sackville (now O'Connell) Street, Dublin, seized by insurgents and ruined in the fighting of Easter 1916
Rachlin	Reachlainn/Rechru, Rathlin Island, off the coast of Co. Antrim
Raftery, 'dark'	Antoine/Anthony Raftery (*c.*1784–1835) a blind (hence 'dark') folk poet born in Co. Mayo who lived mostly in Co. Galway in the Gort and Loughrea areas
Raftery's cellar	an soilear, a swallow hole; the river that runs by Yeats's tower forms a deep pool and runs underground not far from the tower, the local limestone being porous
rann	Irish, a verse of a poem
Red Branch, the	the knights/heroes of the Red Branch were a kind of militia for the defence of the throne of Ulster, notably under Conor MacNessa (Conchubar) who lived in Emain Macha. The Red Branch cycle of tales deals with them, the best known being the *Tain bo Cuailgne*
Ribh	Irish name: it occurs in Lady Gregory's 'Angus Og', *Gods and Fighting Men* (1904; 1970)
Rosses/Rosses Point	Ros Ceite, Co. Sligo, a seaside village about five miles from Sligo, where the Yeats family spent summer holidays with relatives
Roxborough	Craig-a-Roiste, Roche's Rock, Co. Galway; the name was changed to Roxborough in 1707. It was the Persse estate, on which Lady Gregory (*née* Persse) grew up
Salley Gardens	willow gardens, probably those on the bank of the Ballisodare river, Co. Sligo, near the mills at Ballisodare
Sandymount Corbets	Sandymount Castle, Sandymount Green in south Dublin, was owned by Robert Corbet, great-uncle of Yeats, who lived there with his mother and an aunt. Yeats's paternal grandfather, the Rev. William Butler Yeats, had a small house near it after he retired from Tullylish parish
Scanavin	tober sceanmhan, the well of Scanavin, the well of fine shingle; a small village a mile from Collooney, Co. Sligo
Sceolan	one of Oisin's hounds, a cousin of his, Uirne his aunt having been transformed when pregnant
Sennachies	story tellers

seven woods, the	the seven woods of Coole. Yeats listed them in 'In the Seven Woods' as Shan walla (either Sean balla, old wall, or sean bealach, old road); Kyle-dortha (Coill dorracha, the dark wood); Kyle-na-No (Coill na gno, the wood of the nuts); Pairc-na-Lee (Pairc na Laoigh, the field of the calves); Pairc na-Carraig (Pairc na Carraig, the field of the rock, but known locally as the Fox Rock); Pairc-na-Tarav (Pairc na tara, the bull field or park); and Inchy wood (Incha wood)
Shawe-Taylor	John Shawe-Taylor (1866–1911), a landowner, nephew of Lady Gregory, who called a crucial conference to settle the land question
Sidhe	the gods of ancient Ireland, the Tuatha de Danaan or tribes of the goddess Dann or the Sidhe, from Aes Sidhe or Sluagh Sidhe, the people of the faery hills. Sidhe also means whirling winds as well as the people of Faery
Sleuth Wood	from Sliu, a slope. The wood, known usually as Slish Wood, from Slios, inclined or sloped, is situated on the Killery mountains at the edge of Lough Gill, Co. Sligo
Slievenamahon	Slievenamon, slieve-na-man, sliabh na mban Feimhenn, the mountain of the two women (Fe and Men, wives of two Tuatha de Danaan poets), Co. Tipperary
Sligo	Sligeach, the shelly river (or the place of shells), a reference to the Garavogue River which drains Lough Gill, Co. Sligo, and reaches the sea at Sligo
Steep Place of the Strangers, the	Lug na nGall, the hollow of the strangers, Co. Sligo; it is situated in a townland in Glencar Valley at the foot of Cope's mountain
Swift	Jonathan Swift (1667–1745) author and Dean of St Patrick's Cathedral, Dublin
Synge	John Millington Synge (1871–1909), Irish author; the name is pronounced sing
Tara	Temair/Temhair, a place with a view, near Navan, Co. Meath, the seat of the High King of Ireland. The kings were inaugurated there on the Lia Fail, the Stone of Destiny
thraneen	Irish word meaning a dry stalk of grass or straw
Tir-nan-Oge	Tir-na-nOg, the country of the young, the Gaelic other world
Thoor Ballylee	see Ballylee
Three Rock	mountain in Co. Dublin, one part of which is the Three Rock Mountain, the other the Two Rock Mountain
Tom the Lunatic	invented character
Tone	Theobald Wolfe Tone (1764–98), one of the founders of the United Irishmen; left Ireland for US, went to Paris, sailed as French adjutant-general in abortive expedition of 1796; then was in expedition of 1798 to Lough Swilly; captured and sentenced to be hanged, he committed suicide in prison
Tower of Glass	created by Aengus to hold Edain after Fuamnach had turned her into a purple fly (see Edain)
Tower, the	Thoor Ballylee, Yeats's tower in Co. Galway, see Ballylee

town, the	Dublin
Tuatha de Danaan	*see* Sidhe
Uladh	Ulster, the northern province of Ireland. Ster is a northern addition to the name Ulaid. Yeats means the territory ruled from Emain Macha, which was destroyed in 450AD
Usna/Usnach	Uisnech, a place of fawns, Co. Westmeath. The hill of Uisneach was regarded as the centre of Ireland, the meeting place of the original five provinces. Naoise and his brothers Ainnle and Ardan were the sons of Usna/Usnach
Wadding	Luke Wadding (1588–1657) an Irish Franciscan, founder of the college of St Isodore at Rome; his picture by José Ribera is in the National Gallery, Dublin
Well of Bride	*see* Bride's Well
Windy Gap	Bearna na Gaoithe, possibly the Windy Gap in the townland of Carrickhenny, Co. Sligo, opposite Carraroe Church
Wood of Wonders	a place described in the tale of the *Adventures of the King of Norway*
Wood-woman	a woman who tells Cod in the Wood of Wonders that the daughter of the king of Greece had turned her lover into a blue-eyed hawk
Yeats	a 'red-haired Yeats', probably Yeats's paternal grandfather, Rev. William Butler Yeats (1806–1862) curate of Moira, Co. Down, later Rector of Tullylish, Co. Down
Yeats	William Butler Yeats (1865–1939), the poet, buried in Drumcliff Churchyard, Co. Sligo

APPENDIX III PRONUNCIATION OF IRISH NAMES

Modern Irish has three main dialects and three acceptable pronunciations of most items. Dr Loreto Todd has kindly provided the most widely accepted pronunciation of each of the words in Yeats, but where common variants occur, these are given.

She has also provided simple phonetic equivalents of all names and an approximate pronunciation using the orthographic conventions of Standard English. The pronunciations given in square brackets are those of Lady Gregory, which would have been known to Yeats. The phonetic system used is as follows:

VOWELS ( ) Sounds in parentheses are optionally pronounced, cf. the 't' in 'often'.

Short Vowels
i	the sound of the vowel in	'bit'
e		'get'
a		'hat'
o		'got'
u		'put'
ʌ		'but'
ə		unstressed first vowel in 'ago'

Long Vowels
i:	the sound of the vowel in	'bee'
e:		French 'the'
a:		the BBC pronunciation of 'path'
ɔ:		'saw'
o:		French 'peau'
u:		'who'
ə:		the BBC pronunciation of 'church'

Diphthongs
ei	the sound of the vowel in the BBC pronunciation of	'day'
ou		'go'
au		'house'
ai		'high'
oi		'boy'

CONSONANTS

Consonants have their normal Standard English values but the following should be noted:
x	is used to represent the final sound of the Scottish pronunciation of 'Loch'
k	is always used for the initial sound in words like 'cat'
t	is pronounced like the initial sound in French 'tant'
d	'dans'
θ	'thought'

ð   is pronounced like the initial sound in 'then'
j   is always used for the initial sound in words like 'June'
ly   is one sound, roughly the equivalent of a rapid pronunciation of 'will + you'
ny   is one sound, roughly the equivalent of the British pronunciation of 'n' in 'news'
ˈ   prefixes the syllable with the strongest stress

Name in Yeats	Phonetic Equivalent	English Approximation
Aedh/Aodh	eː	'Ay' as in 'day' [Ae, rhyming to 'day']
Aengus	ˈengis	'Engus' like Genghis
Ailell	ˈɔlyil/ailyil	All + yill/Aisle + yill
Aillinn	ˈɔlyin	All + yin
Almhuin	ˈɔluin/lwin	All + oo + in/All + win [All-oon or Alvin]
Alt	olt	Ollt
Aoibhell	ˈiːvəl	Eevel [Evill]
Aoife	ˈiːfə	Eefa [Eefa]
Ardan	ˈaːrdaːn/aːrdan	Arrdawn/Arrdan
Aslauga Shee	a(n)ˈsluaˈshiː	A(n) sloo + a Shee
Baile	ˈbolyə	Boll + ye
Ballygawley Hill	baliˈg ːliː hil	Ballygawlee Hill
Ballylee	baliˈliː	Ballylee
Balor	ˈbaːlor/beːlor	Barlor/Baylor
Barach	ˈbarax	Barach
bawn	bɔːn	bawn
bell-branch	ˈbel braːnsh	bell-branch
Ben Bulben	ben bʌlbin	Ben Bulben
Bera of Ships	bera av ships	Bera of Ships
Biddy	biddi	Biddy
Blanid	ˈblanid/blanij	Blan + id/Blan + idj
boreen	boəriːn	bore + een
Boyne	boin	
Bran	bran	
Bride's well	ˈbraidz wel	
Bual	ˈbuəl	Boo + el
Bual's hill	buəlz hil	
Bull (brown)	bul (braun)	
white-horned	wait hɔrnd	
Byrne, Billy	bəːrn, bili	
Byrnes	bəːrnz	
Caoilte	ˈkiːltshə	Keel + chih [Cweeltia]
Cashel/the Rock of Cashel	ˈkashəl/ðə rok əv ˈkashəl	
Castle Dargan	kasəl daːrgon	

Cathleen-ni-Houlihan	'kotshli:n ni: 'hu:ləhan	Cotchleen nee Hool+i+hawn
Clare	'kle:ər on klɔ:r	
Clare-Galway	'kle:r-'gɔ:lwei bolye on hlɔ:r	
Cloone, bog of	klu:n, bog əv	
Clooth na Bare	klu:(x) nə ba:r	
Cloyne	kloin kluən ua	
Conall Cearnach	'konəl 'kyarnax	Conal Cyarnach
Conan	'konan	
Conchubar	'konər	Conor [Conachoor]
Connacht	'konət	
Connemara	konə'mara	
Coole/Coole Park	ku:l/ku:l pa:rk	
Cormac	'kormak	
Cormac's ruined house	'kormaks ruind haus	
Crevroe	'krivro/'kriəv'ruə	Kree+iv roo+a
Cromlech	'kromlex	
Cro-Patrick	kro(x)'patrik	
Cruachan	'kruəxən	
Cuchulain	ku'hʌlən	Koo+hullin [Cuhoolin, or Cu-hullin]
Cullinan, Shemus	'kʌlənən, she:mis	Shame+us
Danaan	da'neən	Da:nayan
Derg, Lough	lox'də:rg	
Doe, Paddy	do: padi	
Dooney/Dooney Rock	'duni/'duni rok	
Down, County	daun, kaunti	
Dromahair	dɹʌma'heər	Drumahairr
Druid	'druəd	
Drumcliff	dɹʌm'klif	
Dun	ɖu:n	Dhoon [Doon]
Echte	'extgyə	Echt+gyeh [Acht-ga]
Edain	'e:di:n	Aydheen
Eire	'e:ərə	Ayera
Emain	'e:wən	Aywin [Avvin]
Emain Macha	'e:wan moxə	Aywin Moh+ha
Emer	'e:mər/e:vər	Aymir/Ayvir
Enniscrone	inish'kro:n	Innishcrone
Eochaid	'yɔ:xi:/'ɔ:xi	Yawhee/Awe+hee [Eohee]
Esserkelly Plain	'esərkeli 'plein	
Fand	fan(d)	Fan(dh)
Fenians, the	'fi:nyinz	Feen+yans
Fergus	'fə:rgəs	
Ferguson	'fə:rg sən	

findrinny	fin'drini:	
Finn	fin	
Firbolgs	fir'bologz	Firr bollogs
Gabhra	'gaura/gauvra	Gowra/Gow+vra
Galway	gɔ:lwei	
Gap of the Wind	'gap əv ðə 'wind	
Glasnevin coverlet	glas'nevin 'kʌvərlət	
Glencar	glen'ka:r	
Glencar Lough	'glenka:r 'lox	
Glendalough	'glendalox	
Goban	'gauwan/'gʌbən	Gowan/Gubbin
Goban's mountain top	gauwanz mauntin top	
Goldsmith	'go:l(d)smiθ	
Gort	gʌrt	Guh+rt
Grania	grɔ:ny/gra:ny	Grawnya
Green Lands	'gri:n landz	
Gregory	'gregəri	
Grey Rock	'gre: rok	
Guaire	'guairə/guərə	Gwai+ra/Goo+ir+eh
Hanrahan	'hanrəhan	
Hart Lake	'hart 'leik	
Hart, Peter	'hart 'pi:tər	
Heber	'(h)e:vər	(H)ayver
Houlihan	'hu:ləhan	
Howth	ho:θ	Hoe+th
Innisfree	'inish'fri:	Innishfree
Invar Amargin	'invər 'amərgin	
Ith	i:x	Eech/Ech
Kiltartan Cross	kil:tartən	
Kerry	'keri	
Kilvarnet	kil'varnət	
Kinsale	kin'seil	
Knockfefin	nok'fefin	Knock feffin
Knocknarea	'noknar'i/noknare:	Knock+na+ree
Laban	'lavan/'laban	Lavan/Laban
Land of the Tower	'land əv ðə 'tauər	
Land-under-Wave	'land ʌndər 'weiv	
Liss	lis	
Lomair	'lʌmər	Lummer
Loughlann waters	'loxlən 'wɔtərz	
Lugnagall	'lʌgnə'gɔ:l	
MacDonagh	mak'dʌna	
MacNessa	mak'nesa	
Maeve	me:v	May+iv
Magee, Moll	mə'gi:, mol	
Magh Ai	mox'ai/mai ai	Moch Aye/My+eye

Maines	'mainis/mwi:nis	Minus/Mween + us
Malachi (Stilt Jack)	'maləkai	
Mannannan	'mananən	Man + an + an [Mănănuan]
Mayo	'me:o:	May + o [Muigheo]
Midhir	'mid̪ər/mi:r	Meedher/Meer
Midhir's wife	'mi:d̪ərz waif/ mi:rz waif	
Mocharabuiee	'moxəra 'bwi:	Moh + her + abwee
Mooneen	'muəni:n	Moo + ineen
Mourteen	'mu:rti:n	Moor + teen
Moytura	'moiturə/moichu:rə	[Moytirra]
Murrough	'murxu:	Moor + uh + oo
Naoise	'ni:shə	Neesha
Niam	'ni:əv	Nee + iv [Nee-av]
Nessa	'nesa	
O'Byrnes	o:'bə:rnz	
O'Duffy	o:'dʌfi:	
Ogham	'ogom	Oh + gomm
Oisin	'oshi:n	Osheen
ollave	'olu:/oləv	olloo/ollave
O'Rahilly	o:'rahili	
O'Roughley	o:'roxli:	O + Roch + lee
Orchil	'orxil	Orh + hill
Oscar	'oskər	
Pairc-na-lee	'poərk nə́li:	Paw + erk nalee
Patrick	'patrik	
Paudeen	'po:di:n/po:ji:n	Paw + jean
Place of the Strangers	'pleis əv ðə 'streinjarz	
Rachlin	'raθlin	Rath + linn
Raftery, 'dark'	'raftəri, 'da:rk	
Raftery's cellar	'raftəriz 'selər	
rann	ran̪	rannnn
Ribh	ri:v	Reeve
Rosses/Point	'rosiz/point	
Roxborough	roksbʌrə	
Sandymount Corbets	'sandimaunt 'ko:rbəts	
Scanavin	'skanavin	
Sceolan	sko'lo:n	Sco + lawn [Skolaun]
Sennachies	'shanaxi:z	Shanaheez
Seven Woods	'sev(e)n 'wudz	
Sidhe	shi:	Shee [Shee]
Sleuth Wood	'slux wud	Slooh
Slievenamon	'sli:vnə'mo:n/ 'shli:vnə'maən	
Sligo	'slaigo:	

Tara	'tyauər/tara	T + yower
		[T'yower or Tavvir]
Thoor Ballylee	'ʈuːr bali'liː	Thoor Ballylee
Thraneen	'trɔːnyiːn	Thraw + nyeen
Tir-nan-Oge	'ʈiːr nə 'noːg	Theer na nogue
Tone	toːn	
Tuatha de Danaan	'tuəxə'dədə'neən	Thoo aha da danayan
		[Too-ă-hă-dae Donnan]
Uladh	'ʌlə	Ulla
Usna	'ushna	Ooshna
Windy Gap	'windi 'gap	

APPENDIX IV   MAPS

0   50
kilometres

ULSTER

Ballyshannon

BELFAST

CO. DOWN

Innismurray

Killala Bay

Ben Bulben
Glencar L.
SLIGO
L. Gill
Dromahair
Knocknarea

ARMAGH

Enniscrone

Ox Mountains

Ballisodare

Boyle
French Park
L. Key
Cruachan

CO. MAYO

CONNAUGHT

Westport

Cro-Patrick

Elphin

Moore Hall

R. Boyne

Drogheda

L. Corrib

Lissoy

ATHLONE

Hill of Tara

DUBLIN

Howth
Sandymount
Rathfarnham

GALWAY

Tulira

Loughrea

LEINSTER

R. Liffey

Two Rock
Mountain

Aran
Islands

Durras
House
Coole Park
Gort

Ballylee

L. Derg

Glendalough

WICKLOW

CO. CLARE

LIMERICK

Kilkenny

MUNSTER

Cashel

Tipperary

WEXFORD

CORK

Ballylee (*W. B. Yeats*)
Sandymount (*Yeats's birthplace*)
Rathfarnham (*Yeats's last Irish residence*)
Aran Islands (*J. M. Synge*)
Coole Park (*Lady Gregory*)
French Park (*Douglas Hyde*)

Tulira (*Edward Martyn*)
Lissoy (? *The Deserted Village*)
Moore Hall (*George Moore*)
Elphin (*Oliver Goldsmith*)
Cloyne (*Bishop Berkeley*)
Ballyshannon (*Wm. Allingham*)

YEATS'S IRELAND

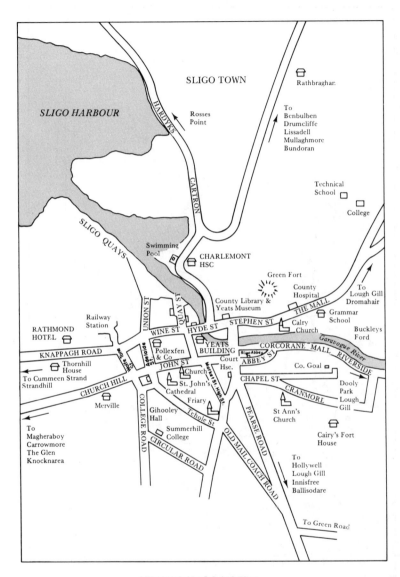

YEATS'S SLIGO TOWN

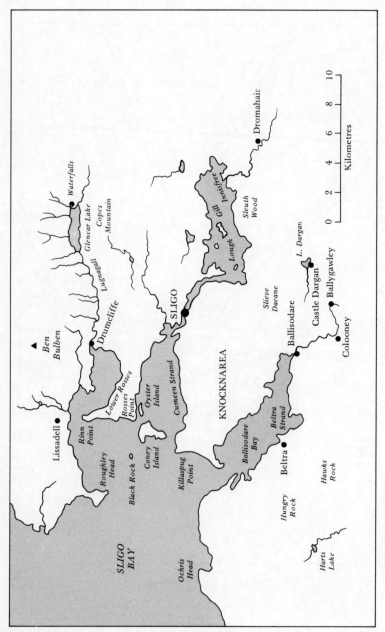

YEAT'S CO. SLIGO

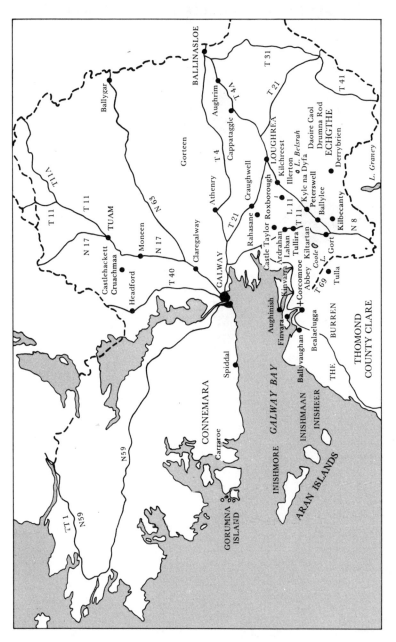

YEATS'S CO. GALWAY

APPENDIX V   DIAGRAM FROM 'A VISION'

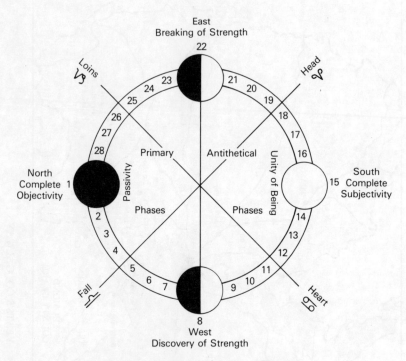

The Great Wheel of the Lunar Phases

BIBLIOGRAPHY

I. SELECT BIBLIOGRAPHY OF WRITING ON YEATS'S POETRY

Ellmann, Richard, *The Identity of Yeats* (London, Faber & Faber, 1954).

Henn, T. R., *The Lonely Tower* (London, Methuen, 1950).

Jeffares, A. Norman, *The Poetry of W. B. Yeats* (London, Edward Arnold, 1961).

—, *W. B. Yeats*, Profiles in Literature Series (London, Routledge & Kegan Paul, 1971).

—, *A New Commentary on the Poems of W. B. Yeats* (London, Macmillan, 1984).

Melchiori, Giorgio, *The Whole Mystery of Art: Pattern into Poetry in the Work of W. B. Yeats* (London, Routledge & Kegan Paul, 1960).

Stock, A. G., *W. B. Yeats. His Poetry and Thoughts* (Cambridge, Cambridge University Press, 1961).

Unterecker, John, *A Reader's Guide to W. B. Yeats* (London, Thames and Hudson, 1959).

Ure, Peter, *Towards a Mythology: Studies in the Poetry of W. B. Yeats* (Liverpool, Liverpool University Press, 1946).

II. SELECT BIBLIOGRAPHY OF OTHER WORKS ON YEATS

Cosgrave, Patrick, 'Yeats, Fascism and Conor O'Brien', *London Magazine*, 7, No. 4 (July 1967), 22–41.

Cullingford, Elizabeth, *Yeats and Politics* (London, Macmillan, 1980).

Donoghue, Denis, *Yeats*, Fontana Modern Masters (London, Collins, 1971).

Ellmann, Richard, *Yeats: The Man and the Masks* (London, Faber & Faber, 1948).

Flannery, Mary Catherine, *Yeats and Magic: the Earlier Works* (Gerrards Cross, Colin Smythe, 1977).

Harper, George Mills (ed.), *Yeats and the Occult* (Toronto, Macmillan of Canada; Maclean-Hunter Press, 1975).

Hone, Joseph, *W. B. Yeats 1865–1939* (London, Macmillan, 1942).

Jeffares, A. Norman, *Yeats: man and poet* (London, Routledge & Kegan Paul, 1949; 1962).

—, *The Circus Animals. Essays on W. B. Yeats* (London, Macmillan, 1970).

McGarry, James, *Place Names in the Writings of William Butler Yeats* (Gerrards Cross, Colin Smythe, 1976).

MacLiammóir, Mícheál, and Boland, Eavan, *W. B. Yeats and His World* (London, Thames and Hudson, 1971).

Malins, Edward, *A Preface to Yeats* (New York, Charles Scribner's Sons, 1974).

Rajan, B., *W. B. Yeats. A Critical Introduction* (London, Hutchison, 1965).

Ronsley, Joseph, *Yeats's Autobiography: Life as symbolic pattern* (London, Oxford University Press, 1968).

Saul, George Brandon, *Prolegomena to the Study of Yeats's Poems* (Oxford, Oxford University Press, 1957).

Torchiana, Donald T., *Yeats and Georgian Ireland* (Evanston, Northwestern Press, 1966).

Tuohy, Frank, *Yeats* (London, Macmillan, 1976).

Ure, Peter, *Yeats* (Edinburgh and London, Oliver and Boyd, 1963).

Wilson, F. A. C., *W. B. Yeats and Tradition* (London, Gollancz, 1958).

—, *Yeats's Iconography* (London, Gollancz, 1960).

III. SELECT BIBLIOGRAPHY OF WORKS ON YEATS'S METHODS OF WORK

Bradford, Curtis, *Yeats at Work* (Illinois, Southern Illinois University Press, 1965).
Clark, David R., *Yeats At Songs and Choruses* (Gerrard's Cross, Colin Smythe, 1983).
Stallworthy, Jon, *Between the Lines. Yeats's Poetry in the Making* (Oxford, Clarendon Press, 1963).
—, *Vision and Revision in Yeats's Last Poems* (Oxford, Clarendon Press, 1963).

IV. COLLECTIONS OF CRITICAL COMMENT

Donoghue, Denis and Mulryne, J. R. (eds), *An Honoured Guest. New Essays on W. B. Yeats* (London, Edward Arnold, 1965).
Hall, James, and Steinmann, Martin (eds), *The Permanence of Yeats* (New York, Macmillan, 1950; New York, Collier Books, 1961).
Jeffares, A. Norman (ed.), *W. B. Yeats: the critical heritage* (London, Henley and Boston, Routledge & Kegan Paul, 1977).
Jeffares, A. Norman and Cross, K. G. W. (eds), *In Excited Reverie. A Centenary Tribute to W. B. Yeats 1865–1939* (London, Macmillan; New York, St. Martin's Press, 1965).
Maxwell, D. E. S. and Bushrui, S. B. (eds), *W. B. Yeats 1865–1965. Centenary Essays* (Ibadan, Ibadan University Press, 1965).
Pritchard, William H. (ed.), *W. B. Yeats. A Critical Anthology* (Harmondsworth, Penguin Books, 1972).
Unterecker, John (ed.), *Yeats: a collection of critical essays* (Englewood Cliffs, New Jersey, Prentice-Hall, 1963).

INDEX TO POEM-TITLES

INDEX TO FIRST LINES